Pets
Welcome™

New England
SECOND EDITION

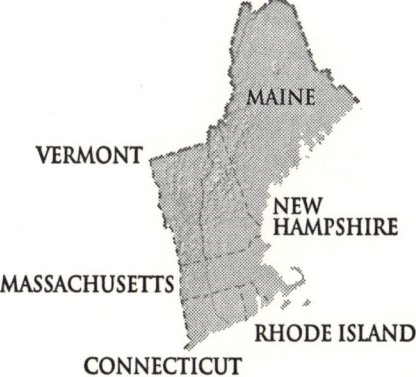

MAINE

VERMONT

NEW
HAMPSHIRE

MASSACHUSETTS

RHODE ISLAND

CONNECTICUT

By Hugo N. Gerstl
Editor-in-Chief: Colleen M. Flores

Contributors: Herb Chelner, Tracy Corchine, Jeff Gerstl, Lorraine Gerstl, Nadine Guarrera, River Gurtin, Eric Jepson, Elaine MacDonald, Erle T. MacDonald, Greg Migdale, Karen Migdale, Roslyn Migdale, Kristi Padley

FOUR
PAWS
PRESS

All rights reserved. No portion of this book may be reproduced or transmitted in any form or by any means, electronic or mechanical, including photocopying or conversion to computer reading or internet software, without permission in writing from the publisher, except for brief quotations in a review.

Library of Congress Cataloguing-in-Publication Data

Pets Welcome™ New England Second Edition:
The Best and Most Informative Guide to Hotels, Motels, Inns & Resorts That Welcome You and Your Pet

Gerstl, Hugo N. (1941 -)
ISBN 0-971008-92

$16.95 Soft Cover
Includes Index
1) Pet Travel; 2) Pet Travel, New England; 3) Travel, U.S. Regional;
4) Travel, Pets

Cover by Full Steam Marketing & Design, a division of Smith Bowen Communications, Inc., Salinas, CA, www.smithbowen.com

Interior by Cimarron Design, Boulder, CO, www.cimarrondesign.com

Copyright ©2002 by Hugo N. Gerstl

Published by Four Paws Press, LLC
2600 Garden Road, Suite 224
Monterey, CA 93940
www.fourpawspress.com

Although the authors, editors and publisher have tried to make the information as accurate as possible, they accept no responsibility for any loss, injury or inconvenience sustained by any person using this book.

Printed in the United States of America by Banta Book Group

Published May 2002

20 18 16 14 12 10 9 8 7 6 5 4 3 2 1

Contents

Abbreviations Used in This Book 4
Introduction 5
What Is Meant by "Types of Lodging" in This
    Pets Welcome™ Guide 9
Pets Welcome™ Hints for Traveling With Your Pet 11
Pets Welcome™ Hints for Two-legged Travelers 19
Map of the New England States 23

CONNECTICUT 25
    Recreation Areas For You and Your Pet 26

MAINE 60
    Recreation Areas For You and Your Pet 61

MASSACHUSETTS 115
    Recreation Areas For You and Your Pet 116

NEW HAMPSHIRE 170
    Recreation Areas For You and Your Pet 171

RHODE ISLAND 212
    Recreation Areas For You and Your Pet 213

VERMONT 221
    Recreation Areas For You and Your Pet 222

Index 271
About the People Who Put This Book Together 277

Abbreviations Used in this Book

AAA   American Automobile Association
ABA   American Breeders Association
AKC   American Kennel Club
AARP American Association of Retired Persons

Introduction

FROM THE PUBLISHER

Welcome to the Second Edition of *Pets Welcome™: New England 2002-2003 Edition.* We've received your letters, suggestions, phone calls, e-mails, plaudits, and brickbats—and we've listened to your concerns. You said:

- **Give us less artist drawings, more places, and more hard information.** We've responded. There are more than twice as many lodgings as in any other *Pets Welcome™* regional edition—over 450 lodgings that will make you and your pet feel at home, wherever you travel in the New England area—Connecticut, Maine, Massachusetts, New Hampshire, Rhode Island, or Vermont. Artist renditions are pretty, but they really don't give you the information you need. You'll find this edition packed with useful information, parks, historical tidbits, and facts about the area as well as the lodging.

- **Give us a book that's easy to carry on the trip—and make it inexpensive enough that we can self-destruct it without feeling guilty.** No problem. If you keep this book a year, it costs less than 5¢ a day! At that price, you can simply tear out those pages you think you'll need on this trip, stuff them in your purse, glove compartment, or even your back pocket, and add only a few ounces to your baggage. And if you want to take the whole book along, it's in a very portable 5" × 8" format. While we've expanded from 224 to 288 pages, it's still lighter than our first series of books because we've used lighter-weight, fully opaque paper.

We dedicate this edition to you and to that wonderful pet or yours—dog, cat, bird, horse, even more unusual pets—without whom there'd be no need for this book.

About the Pets Welcome™ Series

This is the third *Pets Welcome™* book published by Four Paws Press, but it's actually the eleventh *Pets Welcome™* book to be published. Our story began in 1996, when our predecessor, a small cookbook-guidebook publisher was looking for a new series of interesting books. As we were brainstorming one morning, we came upon a common denominator: All of us had pets or had grown up with pets. All of us felt we were betraying a member of the family when we had to leave a beloved pet at home. We felt—erroneously, as it turns out—that those places that accepted pets were…well… *doggy*. The few guides that were around were dog specific, or they were little more than lists culled from another book or from the Internet. Hints about traveling with your pet were minimal, guesswork or nonexistent.

We started with one book, *Pets Welcome™: California*. While the entries were good, and while we provided a rating system (3 Paws, 4 Paws or 5 Paws), the book wasn't really *complete*. That often happens first time out. But as our predecessor expanded, we learned from our mistakes. Each book was better than the last.

Today, *Pets Welcome™* covers the 48 contiguous United States, with entries for Alaska as well. Because of rather stringent quarantine requirements in Hawaii, we've not yet done a Hawaii-specific book, but we hope that will come some day. Our goal remains the same as it was at the beginning: to make it possible for you to travel with your pet **and** to provide a meaningful, happy experience for each of you.

Updates

Four Paws Press thoroughly updates each guidebook as often as possible. Between editions, we urge you to contact us at our website, **www.fourpawspress.com.** You may rest assured of one thing: *we will respond to you.*

Research and Ratings

Our researchers try to gather sufficient practical information to enable you to make informed choices and to ensure that you and your pet have the happiest travel experience possible. They also research areas of interest to your pet in different regions of our great country. They don't stay in every hotel, motel, B&B or lodge recommended in this book. However, our editorial staff consists of seasoned travelers who are able to cut through the promotional materials, photographs and word descriptions and get a "feel" for a given lodging. Once a candidate for listing has been pre-screened, we seek information, including the names of pet-friendly references. In some instances, we will telephone and speak with employees of the establishment under consideration. On occasion, we may visit and spot check accommodations to check standards and prices, but the most important feedback comes from *you*, our readers. Sometimes members of our staff work under cover. Other times they're quite open. But one thing has been—and always will be—a constant:

> *No one at Four Paws Press ever accepts freebies, gifts, money, discounts, or anything else in exchange for a positive write-up. And none of our Pets Welcome™ guidebooks contain any advertising for any accommodation listed in this or any of our Pets Welcome™ books.*

What the Ratings Mean

At the heart of this book are our ratings for each listed establishment. Any rating system is highly subjective and is a "snapshot" or a series of snapshots of a given lodging at a given time. Sometimes you may not agree with our ratings, or you will find that a lodging has changed since you were last there. A Holiday Inn® may metamorphose into a Comfort Inn® as management contracts change or properties are exchanged. Prices may be higher or lower than we show in this guide, although we do the best we can to obtain accurate prices as close to the time this book is printed as possible. Our ratings are based on a number of factors, including appearance of the accommodations, cleanliness, amenities for humans and pets, price, pet friendly attitude, and nearby attractions designed to give your pet as wonderful a holiday as you. As in our earlier editions, we use the "paw" system. Lodgings are rated 2, 3, 4, or 5 paws.

2 Paws   Clean, comfortable establishment with better than average amenities for humans and pets.

3 Paws   Significant first-class amenities and accommodations, definitely upscale with large, very comfortable rooms and "extras."

4 Paws   Luxury class accommodations, extra touches, fine furnishings, elegant public areas and/or landscaping, gracious extra services.

5 Paws   Top of the heap. Truly one-of-a-kind, world-class lodging that is often a vacation destination in and of itself.

What Is Meant by "Types of Lodging" in this Pets Welcome™ Guide

Hotel:
Low- or high-rise establishment with a full range of services, as well as on-premises food or beverage outlets or restaurants, shops, conference facilities, and recreation facilities. May have a concierge service to help you make reservations for restaurants, entertainments, sightseeing trips, etc.

Motel:
Less formal than a hotel. Usually low-rise (1-4 stories), with fewer services than a hotel. May or may not have restaurants (usually adjacent), limited public areas, and limited recreational facilities.

Resort:
A full-service establishment, which may be a self-contained vacation destination. Usually on quite ample grounds with substantial recreational facilities (tennis, golf, swimming, etc.), food and beverage outlets, ranging from informal to formal, an extensive range of recreational and entertainment facilities, concierge services, and programs for the whole family.

Bed & Breakfast (B&B):
Long on charm, but generally quite limited service. Usually a smaller, owner-operated establishment that emphasizes the "personal touch." May be historical, quirky, or eclectic. Don't count on absolute privacy. A Continental or full, hot breakfast is included in the room rate.

Condominium or Apartment:
Apartment-style units with limited services, including limited house-keeping services, but more room for your money. May include kitchen facilities, dishes in suite, and a homey feel.

Motor Inn or Motor Lodge:
More services than a motel, but less services than a hotel. Usually a single or multi-story place that offers on-premises food and/or beverage service, meeting and banquet facilities, and some recreational facilities.

Cottage or Cabin:
Limited service. Individual housing units that offer one or more separate sleeping areas, a living room, and cooking facilities. May be quite rustic. Generally very informal.

Suites:
May be in a hotel, motel, motor inn, etc. One or more bedrooms and a living room/sitting area, closed off by a wall. May or may not have a partition bedroom door.

A Word About Prices

The prices quoted in this book do _not_ include state, county, city, or other taxes, which might add a substantial amount to the price of the lodging. Also, if you see the word "fee" in parentheses, that means there is an extra charge for this service.

Pets Welcome™ Hints for Traveling With Your Pet

If you are planning a trip and you share your life with a pet, you have a few decisions to make before you set off. The following are some tips to help you plan a safer and smoother trip for both you and your pet.

Should You Take Your Pet?

Some pets are not suited for travel because of temperament, illness, or physical impairment. If you have any doubts about whether it is appropriate for your pet to travel, talk to your veterinarian. If you decide your pet should not travel with you, consider the alternatives: have a responsible friend or relative look after your pet, board your pet at a kennel, or hire a sitter to visit, feed, and exercise your pet.

If a friend or relative is going to take care of your pet, ask if that person can take your pet into his or her home. Animals can get lonely when left at home alone. Be sure your pet is comfortable with his or her temporary caretaker and any pets that person has.

If you choose to board your pet, get references and inspect the kennel thoroughly. Your veterinarian or local shelter can help you select a facility. If you are hiring a sitter, interview the candidates, check their references, and introduce your pet to the prospective sitter to see first hand how they get along together. A pet sitter may be preferable if your pet is timid or elderly and needs the comfort of familiar surroundings during your absence.

Whatever option you choose, remember that your pet should be up to date on all vaccinations and in sound health. Whoever is caring for your pet should know the telephone numbers at which you can be reached, the name and telephone number of your veterinarian, and your pet's medical or dietary needs. Be sure your pet is comfortable with the person you have chosen to take care of him or her.

Bringing Your Pet

1 Bring your pet's own food, dishes, grooming supplies, bedding, waste removal supplies, leash, collar with I.D. tags, a first-aid kit, a bottle of water from home, and a favorite blanket and/or toy. These will make your pet more comfortable, decrease the chances of an upset stomach from a strange brand of food, and help prepare you for emergencies. Maintain your pet's normal feeding and walking schedules as much as possible. Be sure to bring old bath towels or paper towels in case of an accident, and plastic bags in which to dispose of your pet's waste. It's a good idea to bring a color picture of your pet for identification purposes in case you and your pet become separated. Creative Pet Products' "Pet Passport" is a most worthwhile document to take with you.

2 Bring your pet's vaccination records with you when you travel within the state, and a health certificate when traveling out of state. If you plan on boarding your pet at any time during your vacation, call the kennel to reserve his or her space, to see what they require you to bring, and to find out if they require a health certificate.

Although pets may travel freely throughout the United States as long as they have proper documentation, Hawaii requires a 120-day quarantine for all dogs and cats. Hawaii's quarantine regulations vary by species, so check prior to travel.

If you and your pet are traveling from the United States to Canada, you must carry a certificate issued by a veterinarian that clearly identifies the animals and certifies that the dog or cat has been vaccinated against rabies during the preceding 36-month period. Different Canadian provinces may have different requirements. Be sure to contact the government of the province you plan to visit.

If you and your pet are traveling to Mexico, you must carry a health certificate prepared by your veterinarian within two weeks of the day you cross the border. The certificate must include a description of your pet, the lot number of the rabies vaccine used, indication of distemper vaccination, and a veterinarian's statement that the animal is free from infectious or contagious disease. The certificate must be stamped by an office of the U.S. Department of Agriculture (USDA). At the time of publication, the fee for the stamp was $4.00.

3 **Tape the address of where you are staying on the back of your pet's I.D. tag,** or add a laminated card or new I.D. tag to your pet's collar, or add a second collar with a friend's or family member's phone number. It is always a good idea to have a second contact person on your pet's collar in case of a natural disaster so that someone out of your area can be contacted if you and your pet become separated.

4 **Do not leave your pets unattended in the hotel/motel room at any time.** The surroundings are new and unfamiliar to your animal, which may cause him or her to become upset and destroy property he or she normally would not, or to bark excessively and disturb your neighbors. You also run the risk of your pet escaping. If a maid should open the door to clean your room, your pet may see that as a chance to escape to find you, or he or she may attack the maid out of fear.

5 **Train your pet to accept being in a carrier.** This will come in handy if you ever need to travel by plane. Make sure the carrier has enough room for your pet to stand up comfortably and to turn around inside. Be sure to trim your pet's nails so they don't get caught in the carrier's door or ventilation holes. It is wise to acclimate your pet to the carrier in the months or weeks preceding your trip. Permit your pet to explore the carrier. Place your pet's food dish and a favorite toy or blanket inside the carrier and confine him or her to the carrier for brief periods.

Pet carriers may be purchased from pet-supply stores or bought directly from domestic airlines. Select a carrier that has enough room to permit your animal to sit and lie down, but is not large enough to allow your pet to be tossed around during travel. You can make the carrier more comfortable by lining the interior with shredded newspaper, a towel, or, even better, a blanket or towel your pet has gotten used to, one that bears your smell.

To introduce your pet to car travel in the carrier, confine him or her in the carrier and take short drives around the neighborhood. If properly introduced to car travel, most dogs and cats will quickly adjust to and even enjoy car trips.

Carriers come in handy in hotel/motel rooms, too. If your pet is already used to being in a carrier, he or she will not object if you leave him/her in one long enough to go out to breakfast.

Never take your pet with you if you will have to leave him/her in the car. If it is 85° F outside, within minutes the inside of the car can reach 160° F, even with the windows cracked, causing heat stroke and possibly death. According to The Humane Society of the United States®, the signs of heat stress are: heavy panting, glazed eyes, a rapid pulse, unsteadiness, a staggering gait, vomiting, or a deep red or purple tongue. If heat stroke does occur, the pet must be cooled by dousing it with water and applying ice packs to its head and neck. He/she should then be taken to a veterinarian immediately.

6 **When your pet is confined to a crate or carrier, the best way to provide water** is to freeze it in the cup that hooks onto the door of the crate or carrier. That way your pet will get needed moisture without splashing all over the crate. Freezing water in your pet's regular water bowl also works well for car trips.

7 **Be sure to put your pet's favorite toys and bedding in the crate or carrier.** Label the crate with "LIVE ANIMAL" and "THIS END UP," plus the address and telephone number of your destination, as well as your home address and telephone number and the number of someone to contact in case of an emergency.

8 **Do not feed your pet before traveling.** Small amounts of water can be given before the trip. If possible, put ice cubes in the water tray attached to the inside of your pet's carrier (See Travel Tip #6). This reduces the risk of an upset stomach or an accident in the pet's crate or in your car.

9 **Stop frequently for "rests."** When traveling by car, remember that your pet needs rest stops as often as you do. It's a good idea for everyone to stretch his or her legs from time to time. Stop frequently to allow your pet to exercise and eliminate. *Never* permit your pet to leave the car without a collar, I.D. tag, and leash.

10 *Gradually* get your pet used to car trips. If your pet is unfamiliar with car travel, get him/her accustomed to the car gradually. Start a few weeks before your trip with short trips around town. Extend the trips a little each time. Then he/she will become accustomed to the car before your trip and it will be more pleasant for all involved.

11 Before any trip, have your veterinarian examine your pet to insure that he or she is in good health. A veterinary examination is a requisite to obtaining the legal documents required for many forms of travel. In addition to the examination, your veterinarian should provide necessary vaccinations, such as rabies, distemper, infectious hepatitis and leptospirosis. If your pet is already up to date on these, obtain written proof. Do not give your pet any drug not prescribed or given to you by your veterinarian.

12 Ask your veterinarian for names of veterinarians in the area where you'll be traveling. Perhaps you might also ask for a letter of introduction.

13 Dogs who enjoy car travel need not be confined to a carrier if your car has a restraining harness (available at pet supply stores) or if you are accompanied by a passenger who can restrain the dog. Because most cats are not as comfortable traveling in cars, for their own safety, as well as yours, it is best to keep them in a carrier.

Dogs and cats should always be kept safely inside the car. Pets who are allowed to stick their heads out the window can be injured by particles of debris or become ill from having cold air forced into their lungs. *Never* transport a pet in the back of an open pickup truck. *Never leave your pet unattended in a parked car!* (See Travel Tip #5). Furthermore, an animal left alone in a car is an open invitation to pet thieves!

14 IF YOUR PET IS LOST: Whenever you travel with your pet, there is a chance that you and your pet will become separated. It takes only a moment for an animal to stray and become lost. If your pet is missing, immediately canvass the area. Should your pet not be located within a few hours, take the following actions:

- If you have subscribed to 1-800 HELP 4 PETS, call them as soon as you notice your pet missing and follow the instructions they give you to help them locate your pet.

- Contact the animal control departments, humane societies, and SPCAs within a sixty-mile radius of where your pet strayed. Check with them each day.

- Post signs at intersections and in storefronts—particularly supermarkets, large drugstores, warehouse clubs, etc.—throughout the area.

- Provide a description and a photograph of your missing pet to the police, letter carriers, or delivery people.

Traveling by Air

Since September 11, 2001, the airline industry has been undergoing a critical reappraisal of all aspects of air travel, including the imposition of certain restrictions on traveling with your pet. We advise you to check very carefully with your airline to determine how these changes may affect you and your pet.

15 When traveling by plane, **be sure to book the most direct flights possible.** The less your pet has to be transferred from plane to plane, the less chance of you being separated. This is also very important when traveling in hot or cold weather. You don't want your pet to have to wait in the cargo hold of a plane or be exposed to bad weather any longer than necessary. Check with the airlines for the type of crate or carrier they require and any additional requirements. They are very strict about the size and type of crate or carrier you may carry on board.

16 If your pet is a cat or small dog, try to take him or her on board with you. Be sure to contact the airlines to find out the specific requirements for this option. Generally, you have two choices: airlines will accept either hard-sided carriers or soft-sided carriers, which may be more comfortable for your pet. Only certain brands of soft-sided carriers are acceptable to certain airlines, so call your airline to find out what carrier to use.

 **17** If your pet must travel in the cargo hold, you can increase your chances for a safe and secure flight for your pet by following these tips:

- **Use direct flights.** You will avoid the mistakes that occur during airlines transfers and possible delays in getting your pet off the plane.

- **Always travel on the same flight as your pet.** Ask the airline if you can watch your pet being loaded into and unloaded from the cargo hold.

- **Do not ship pug-nosed dogs and cats (such as Chow Chows, Pekingese, and Persians) in the cargo hold.** These breeds have short nasal passages that leave them vulnerable to oxygen deprivation and heat stroke in cargo holds.

- **If traveling during the summer or winter months, choose flights that will accommodate the temperature extremes:** early morning or late evening flights are better in the summer; afternoon flights are better in the winter.

- **Fit your pet with two pieces of identification**—a permanent I.D. tag with your name, home address, and telephone number, and a temporary travel I.D. with the address and telephone number where you or a contact person can be reached, or, better yet, a **1-800-HELP 4 PETS I.D.**

- **Affix a travel label to the carrier,** stating your name, permanent address, telephone number, and your final destination. The label should clearly state where you or a contact person can be reached as soon as the flight arrives.

- **Do not give your pet tranquilizers unless they are prescribed by your veterinarian.** Make sure your veterinarian understands that this prescription is for air travel.

- **Do not feed your pet for four to six hours prior to air travel.**

- **Put a favorite blanket, perhaps one with your or his/her smell, and a favorite pet toy in the carrier or crate.**

- **Try not to fly with your pet during busy travel times, such as holidays and summer.** Your pet is more likely to undergo rough handling and possible loss during hectic travel periods.

- **Carry a current photo of your pet, or, better yet, a CREATIVE PET PRODUCTS "Pet Passport" with you.** If your pet is lost during the trip, a photograph will make it easier for airline employees to search effectively.

18 When you arrive at your destination, open the carrier or crate as soon as you are in a safe place and examine your pet. If anything seems wrong, take your pet to a veterinarian immediately. Get the results of the examination in writing, including the date and time. *Do not hesitate to complain if you witness the mishandling of an animal—either yours or someone else's—at any airport.*

Traveling By Train

Amtrak currently does not accept pets for transport unless they are assistance dogs. Many trains in European countries allow pets. Generally, it is the passengers' responsibility to feed and exercise their pets at station stops.

Traveling By Ship

With the exception of assistance dogs, only a few cruise lines accept pets—normally only on ocean crossings and frequently confined to kennels. Some lines permit pets in private cabins. Contact cruise lines in advance to find out their policies and which of their ships have kennel facilities. If you must use the ship's kennel, make sure it is protected from the elements. Follow the general guidelines suggested for other modes of travel when planning a ship voyage.

Do Your Part to Make Your Pet a Welcome Guest

Many hotels, motels, restaurants, and individuals will give your pet special considerations during your travels. It is important for you to do your part to ensure that dogs and cats will continue to be welcomed as traveling companions. Obey local animal control ordinances, keep your animal under restraint, be thoughtful and courteous to other travelers, and **have a wonderful trip!**

Pets Welcome™ Hints for *Two-legged* Travelers

Although we realize that this book is primarily for the benefit of traveling pets, we feel it would be remiss if we did not include what we feel are important travel hints for those *two-legged* travelers who accompany their four-legged friends.

Packing

- Always carry important travel documents, medications, jewelry, currency, passports, and anything else of substantial value in your carry-on luggage or on your person.

- Always make sure you carry proof of medical insurance, driver's license, motorists' insurance identity card, portable alarm clock, and AARP, AAA, or other membership cards needed to get you the best deals.

- Pack light!!! A good hint is to pack *half* of what you think you'll need, *then cut that amount in half!* Bring only what you think you will need, pack tightly to maximize your space. If possible, two carry-ons should be plenty, no matter how long you'll be away—even if you travel overseas. Pack drip-dry, easy maintenance clothing, and *don't worry about making an impression by wearing a new outfit every day. For the most part, you'll only stay a day or two at most places you visit, and you most likely won't see the same people.*

- Pack toiletries in plastic bottles and store them in a separate plastic bag in case of leakage.

- Check seasonal weather conditions for the area you'll be visiting. Include necessities like a *small* folding umbrella, jacket, etc.

- If you'll be traveling overseas, pack an electric adapter kit for small appliances. Make sure you have the proper adapter for the countries you'll be visiting.

- Make certain you label each piece of your luggage with your name and address. Consider purchasing baggage and contents insurance and short-term medical insurance as well as trip cancellation insurance.

Airline Travel

- Proper identification—with a photo of yourself—is a must.

- Book as far in advance as possible and stay over a Saturday if you can, to get the lowest cost fares. Check with your travel agent, services such as www.Priceline.com, www.Orbitz.com, www.Travelocity.com, or the airlines themselves to determine the lowest possible fares you can get. *Don't forget that the lowest possible fares are **very** restrictive—there are steep cancellation charges, change-of-flight charges, etc.—but you really can save a bundle if you shop around.* On a recent cross-country flight, fares varied from $198 round trip to $1,800 for the same round trip! **Planning in advance is essential.**

- Check in at least one hour prior to domestic flights and two hours prior to international flights (may be much longer after Sept. 11). This is particularly important when traveling with your pet.

- When checking luggage, give yourself extra time for processing. Most airlines have limitations on the number or size of bags that can be checked or taken on board as carry-on baggage.

- On longer flights, pack reading material, special medication or dietary needs, and a warm jacket or sweater to make yourself more comfortable.

- As soon as you are seated in the plane, set your watch forward or back to the time zone at your intended place of arrival.

- Get terminal, flight, and gate information when meeting family or friends at the airport.

- Advise the airline of any special dietary needs well in advance of your flight—preferably when booking your flight.

Car Rental Tips

- Have your current driver's license and insurance card ready to present before renting any vehicle.

- Call or book on-line in advance for rental reservations, a list of additional locations where the car can be returned at no, or very little, extra charge, and hours of operation for all rental locations where you might be.

- Find out in advance if you qualify for special discount rates. AAA, AARP, corporate, military, and some insurance company discounts can save you money. Compare each rate. Some are better than others.

- Check weekly rates, weekend rates, anything that will get you the lowest cost. Don't hesitate to compare rates of different rental companies to make sure you get the absolute lowest rate available for the size or type of vehicle you want. Remember, the smaller the car, the better the gas mileage.

- Find out if your credit card covers such things as insurance, collision damage waiver, etc. The most expensive insurance you can buy are the policies or collision damage waiver coverage sold by the car rental agency.

- If there is any damage to the vehicle, take photographs for your own records *before* you drive the car out of the car rental lot. If there is any damage to the vehicle caused when it is in your possession, take photographs for your own records *before* you turn the car back in.

- Always return your car with a tank full of gas. Car rental agencies often charge up to *three times the going rate per gallon* for the fuel they have to put into your rental car to top it off.

- When returning your vehicle, allow adequate time for an inspection and resolution of any extra billing charges, discrepancies, questions, or disputes.

Hotels, Motels, and Other Accommodations

- When you make reservations, find out what special rates are available for such memberships as AAA, AARP, corporate, military, affinity groups, etc. Compare each rate—some are better than others. Check weekly rates, weekend rates, anything that will get you the lowest cost.

- Hotels may offer seasonal discounts or promotional rates. Contact the hotel concerned or your travel agent to find out about any special discounts for which you might qualify.

- When making reservations, be sure to indicate your room preferences, such as non-smoking, double bed, etc., and *let the lodgings know you'll be coming with your pet.*

- If you are not satisfied with your room on check-in, contact the front desk immediately to request a room change or extra amenities to make your stay more comfortable.

- Try to check in as early as possible on the day you arrive. Often, you have the better choice of rooms before the lodgings fill up for the night.

- Ask the front desk for sightseeing trips, dining reservations, special promotional discount events, or help in getting tickets to special events.

- Ask about shuttle service to and from major airports. On a recent trip, we were able to rent a car one day later than usual and return it one day earlier than usual, thus saving *two days* worth of needless car rental expense—money that went into *our* pockets, *not* the car rental agency's.

- Make sure that people at home will know the key points along your route, when you'll be there, and how to contact you in emergency. And HAVE A WONDERFUL TRIP!

Map of the New England States

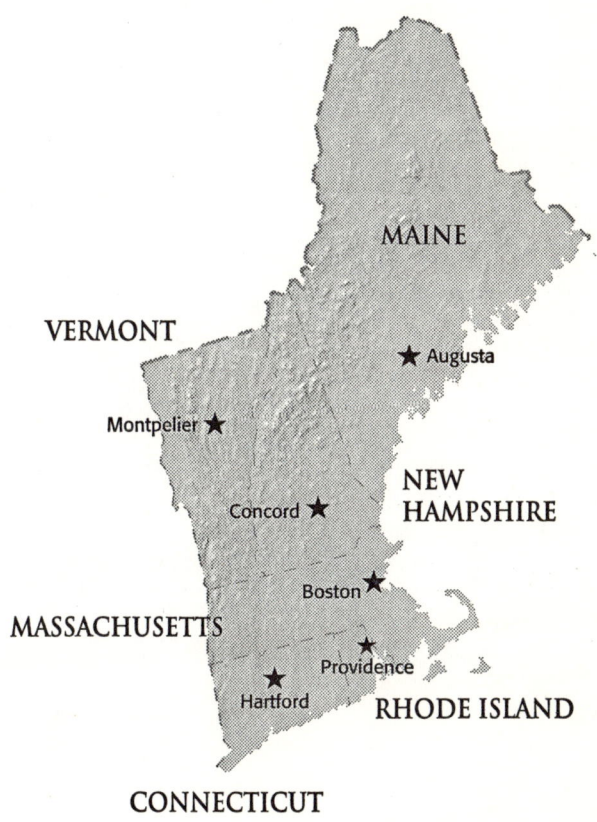

MAINE

VERMONT

★ Augusta

Montpelier ★

NEW
HAMPSHIRE

Concord ★

Boston ★

MASSACHUSETTS

★ Providence

★
Hartford

RHODE ISLAND

CONNECTICUT

CONNECTICUT

Nickname: Constitution State; Nutmeg State
Population: 3,405,565 (29th)
Area: 5,543 sq. miles (48th)
Climate: Moderate; winters: slightly below freezing; warm, humid summers.
Capital: Hartford
Entered Union: January 19, 1788 (5th)
Motto: *Qui transtulit Sustinet* (He who, transplanted, still sustains).
Song: Yankee Doodle

Flower: Mountain laurel
Tree: White oak
Bird: American robin
Famous Nutmeggers: Ethan Allen, P.T. Barnum, Samuel Colt, Jonathan Edwards, Richard D. Gorman, Nathan Hale, Katherine Hepburn, Isaac Hull, Robert Mitchum, J. P. Morgan, Eugene O'Neil, Israel Putnam, Wallace Stevens, Harriet Beecher Stowe, Mark Twain, Noah Webster, Eli Whitney.

History: The Algonquin peoples—among them the Mohegans and Pequot—lived in the area at the time of first European contact. Dutch explorer Adriaen Block was the first European visitor (1614). By 1634, settlers from Plymouth Bay (Massachusetts) had started colonies. By 1662, England gave the Connecticut colony its charter. Connecticut soldiers and privateers were engaged in most major campaigns of the Revolutionary War. The oldest American newspaper in the U.S., the Hartford Courant, commenced publication in 1764. The State's fabled whaling industry reached its peak in the 1840's and 1850's. The nation's first atomic submarine, the *Nautilus,* was launched from Groton in 1954, and twenty years later Ella Grasso became the state's first female governor. In 1810, the Hartford Fire Insurance Company, the country's first such business, led to the insurance industry, the key to Connecticut's economy.

Geography: Highest Point: 2,380 ft., Mount Frissell. Lowest Point: Sea level, Long Island Sound. Time Zone: Eastern. Capital: Hartford. Major cities: Hartford (145,000), Bridgeport (145,000), New Haven (135,000), Waterbury (109,000). Connecticut's landscape is quite varied for such a small state. The highest elevations are in the Berkshires in the northwest. A hilly eastern upland is drained by rivers. The center of the state is a narrow lowland. The southwest corner is convenient to New York City. The Northeast affords a true Colonial feel.

Tourist Information: 1-800-CTBOUND. Website: www.ctbound.org.

Recreation Areas
For You and Your Pet

All of these areas permit pets on a leash.

State Recreation Areas

American Legion State Park: 782 acres, 1 mile north of Pleasant Valley on West River Road. Camping, picnicking, hiking trails, fishing, winter sports.

Burr Pond State Park: 438 acres, 5 miles north of Torrington off State Route 8. Camping, picnicking, hiking trails, boating, boat ramp, boat rentals, fishing, swimming, winter sports, food service.

Cockaponset State Park: 15,652 acres, 3 miles west of Chester on State Route 148. Snowmobiling, picnicking, hiking trails, fishing, swimming, winter sports.

Day Pond State Park: 180 acres, ½ mile north of Westchester on State Route 149. Horse trails, picnicking, hiking trails, fishing, swimming.

Gay City State Park: 1,569 acres 8 miles southeast of Manchester on State Route 85. Ice skating, horse trails, picnicking, hiking trails, fishing, swimming, winter sports.

Hurd State Park: 884 acres west of Haddam Neck off State Rout 151. Picnicking, hiking trails, fishing, winter sports.

Mansfield Hollow State Park: 2,328 acres 1 mile east of Mansfield Center off State Route 89. Picnicking, hiking trails, boating, boat ramp, fishing, winter sports.

Mount Tom State Park: 232 acres, 3½ miles west of Bantam off US 202. Ice skating, scuba diving, picnicking, hiking trails, boating, fishing, swimming, winter sports, food service.

Natchaug State Park: 12,935 acres, 4 miles south of Phoenixville on State Route 198. Historic, snowmobiling, camping, picnicking, hiking trails, fishing, swimming, winter sports, food service.

Osbornedale State Park: 350 acres, 1 mile northwest of Derby off US 34. Ice skating, picnicking, hiking trails, fishing, winter sports.

Pachaug State Park: 23,938 acres, 1 mile north of Voluntown. Camping, picnicking, hiking trails, boating, boat ramp, boat rentals, fishing, winter sports, visitor center.

Penwood State Park: 787 acres, 4 miles west of Bloomfield on State Route 185. Picnicking, hiking trails, winter sports.

Peoples State Park: 2,942 acres, 1 mile north of Pleasant Valley on East River Road. Snowmobiling, picnicking, hiking trails, fishing, winter sports.

Putnam Memorial State Park: 183 acres north of Redding at State Routes 107 and 58. Horse trails. Picnicking, hiking trails, fishing, winter sports.

Quaddick State Park: 116 acres, 7 miles northeast of Putnam off State Route 44. Ice skating, picnicking, hiking trails, boating, boat ramp, fishing, swimming, winter sports, food service.

Sleeping Giant State Park: 1,439 acres, 3 miles north of Hamden off State Route 10. Picnicking, hiking trails, fishing.

Southford Falls State Park: 120 acres, 4 miles southwest of Southbury on State Route 188. Picnicking, hiking trails, fishing, winter sports.

Stratton Brook State Park: 148 acres, 2 miles west of Simsbury on State Route 309. Picnicking, hiking trails, fishing, swimming, bicycle trails, winter sports, food service.

Wadsworth Falls State Park: 285 acres, 3 miles southwest of Middlefield on State Route 157. Picnicking, hiking trails, fishing, swimming, winter sports.

Wharton Brook State Park: 96 acres, 2 miles south of Wallingford on US 5. Picnicking, fishing, swimming, food service.

Other Notable Recreation Areas

Stanley Quarter Park: 225 acres in New Britain, north of Central Park on Stanley Street. Skateboarding, picnicking, hiking trails, fishing, swimming, bicycle trails, winter sports.

Penwood Bed & Breakfast

c/o Nutmeg Bed & Breakfast Agency
P.O. Box 1117 West
West Hartford, CT 06127-1117
800-727-7592 • 860-236-6698

Type of Lodging: Bed & Breakfast

Room Rates: $75–$100, including full breakfast.

Pet Charges and Deposits: None.

Pet Policy: All Pets Welcome

Amenities: 2 stories, interior corridors.

Rated: 2 Paws — 2 rooms with fireplace and deck, 1 suite.

Penwood Bed & Breakfast is situated in a park-like setting, surrounded by golden daffodils in the springtime. Enjoy a full breakfast featuring home-baked goods and piping hot beverages. The second floor is reserved for guests and features a large master bedroom with king-sized bed, private bath, fireplace, outside deck, and a huge wall of picture windows to enjoy the wonderful view. Another large guest room has twin beds and also features a private bath. A small twin-bedded room shares a hall with a bath and another bedroom with a ½ bed and connecting playroom. This is an ideal arrangement for a family, as your host will not book these rooms separately. The Penwood is located across the street from Penwood State Forest, offering a full range of year-round recreation for walkers, joggers, and cross-country skiers. Bloomfield is just a few miles northwest of Hartford.

Motel 6

320 E. Main Street
Branford, CT 06405
203-483-5828

Type of Lodging: Motel

Room Rates: $43–$66. AARP discounts.

Pet Charges and Deposits: None.

Pet Policy: Small pets only.

Amenities: Extended cable TV, movies, restaurant adjacent, data port/modem telephones, 2 stories, interior corridors.

Rated: 2 Paws — 100 rooms.

Motel 6—the "We'll leave the light on for you™" folks—can always be depended on to provide you with clean, simple, comfortable accommodations, and the Branford unit is certainly no exception. Do not miss having at least one meal at the *USS Chowder Pot III*, a local favorite for years—great seafood, attentive service, catch the buffet if you can. Established in 1644, the coastal town of Branford became a popular vacation spot early in the 20th century. Harrison House (1724) has period furnishings, local historical items, and an herb garden and barn with colonial farm implements. The nearby Thimble Islands are tiny, but scenic, and Thimble Island Cruises offer 45 minute narrated trips through the 25 islands. Bittersweet Farms is intriguing: artists and artisans work in restored farm buildings creating hand-blown glass, stained glass, metal sculptures, and other such objets d'art.

Holiday Inn

1070 Main Street
Bridgeport, CT 06604
203-334-1234

Type of Lodging: Hotel

Room Rates: $139–$179. AAA and AARP discounts.

Pet Charges and Deposits: None.

Pet Policy: Small pets only.

Amenities: Cable TV, movies, dual phone lines, voice mail, irons, hair dryers, heated pool, whirlpool, exercise room, area transportation, gift shop, valet laundry, conference facilities, administrative services, fax, restaurant, cocktails, radios, coffee makers, data port/modem telephones, some refrigerators, free newspaper, 9 stories, interior corridors.

Rated: 3 Paws — 234 rooms.

High-rise Holiday Inn, one of the tallest buildings in Bridgeport, is also one of the classiest. It boasts a large, modern lobby with sunken lounge area, and probably the most posh rooms in the city. Bridgeport is not the most touristed city in America. That having been said, Bridgeport was the home of the legendary P.T. Barnum, as well as his "mitiest" attraction, Charles Thurwood Stratton, who ultimately reached a height of 40 inches, and who achieved fame under the name "General" Tom Thumb. The three story Barnum Museum, at 820 Main Street, chronicles the life and times of the world's greatest showman. The Discovery Museum contains art displays and interactive art and science exhibits, including the *Challenger* Learning Center and Planetarium. Beardsley Zoo, situated in 35 acres, displays 120 species of animals.

Twin Tree Inn

1030 Federal Road
Brookfield, CT 06804
203-775-0220

Type of Lodging: Motel

Room Rates: $75–$95. AAA and AARP discounts.

Pet Charges and Deposits: $10 per day per pet.

Pet Policy: All Pets Welcome.

Amenities: Extended cable TV, restaurant adjacent, data port/modem telephones, some refrigerators, 1-2 stories, interior and exterior corridors.

Rated: 2 Paws — 47 rooms.

Twin Tree in is a Colonial structure, and rooms keep the theme intact, with comfortable and attractive décor. The Twin Tree sits at the foot of a small mountain (or a large hill, if you prefer), and the establishment boasts attractive and well-tended grounds. Nearby Candle Wood Lake is one of Connecticut's larger inland bodies of water. Brookfield is a suburb of Danbury, in the southwestern quadrant of the state. The Brookfield Craft Center houses a craft school known for its innovative workshops and classes in some wonderful "ancient" arts, such as woodworking, blacksmithing, and pottery making.

Inn at Chester

318 West Main Street
Chester, CT 06412
800-949-STAY • 860-526-9541
www.innatchester.com

Type of Lodging: Inn

Room Rates: $115–$225, including Continental breakfast.

Pet Charges and Deposits: None.

Pet Policy: All Pets Welcome.

Amenities: Exercise room, library, pool table, 1-2 stories, interior corridors.

Rated: 3 Paws — 40 rooms and 2 suites.

The Inn at Chester is the perfect getaway for an escape from the ordinary. Serenity abounds in this country inn located on 12 luscious acres in the Connecticut River Valley. An 18th century farmhouse was the inspiration for this 42-unit full-service inn. Each room is individually appointed with Eldred Wheeler reproduction antiques to complement to Colonial décor. Rooms are quiet, comfortable, and unpretentious. Guest amenities include a well-equipped exercise room and the Carriage Parlor, which hosts a library and pool table. Enjoy elegant but comfortable dining in the Post & Beam dining room, which serves award-winning cuisine. Dunk's Landing tavern serves libations and offers lighter, but equally delicious, fare. You can enjoy year-round activities at the inn, including tennis, hiking, bocce, croquet, cycling, or simply relaxing in the hammock next to a peaceful pond. The surrounding countryside near the Connecticut River, in the extreme south-central portion of the state, offers many adventures.

Cornwall Inn

c/o Nutmeg Bed & Breakfast
* Agency*
P.O. Box 1117
West Hartford, CT 06127-1117
800-727-7592 • 860-236-6698

Type of Lodging: Inn

Room Rates: $99–$125, including Continental breakfast.

Pet Charges and Deposits: None.

Pet Policy: All Pets Welcome.

Amenities: Cable TV, outdoor pool, restaurant, pub, 2 stories, interior corridors.

Rated: 3 Paws — 13 rooms.

Recently renovated Cornwall Inn consists of a charming main house with a contemporary addition. The Inn has five guest rooms on the second floor, three with private bath. The remaining two guest rooms are booked together for families or couples traveling together. The additional guest rooms feature queen- or king-sized beds, private bath, and TV. All accommodations are comfortably furnished and tastefully decorated. A restaurant on the premises serves lunch and dinner. The Cornwalls, comprising Cornwall, Cornwall Bridge, Cornwall Center, Cornwall Hollow, and West Cornwall, are in series of upland bowls among steep, forested hills in the far western part of Connecticut. The charming scenery of the Cornwalls has attracted many artists, and one of the few remaining covered bridges remaining in Connecticut crosses the Housatonic River at West Cornwall.

Holiday Inn

*80 Newtown Road
Danbury, CT 06810
203-792-4000*

Type of Lodging: Motor Inn

Room Rates: $139–$149. AAA and AARP discounts.

Pet Charges and Deposits: None.

Pet Policy: All Pets Welcome.

Amenities: Cable TV, movies (fee), video games, voice mail, irons, hair dryers, heated pool, health club adjacent, area transportation, valet laundry, meeting rooms, fax (fee), free newspaper, restaurant, cocktails, radios, coffee makers, data port/modem telephones, some refrigerators, some microwaves, 4 stories, interior corridors.

Rated: 3 Paws — 114 rooms.

Although it's one of the smaller Holiday Inn venues, the Danbury version of the chain does not short you on quality, comfort, or service. Situated in a retail area, Holiday Inn-Danbury features luxuriously furnished, spacious rooms, and a pet-friendly atmosphere. Danbury is a good-sized city, right on the New York border. For nearly two centuries, Danbury was the hat capital of the world, but when hats went out of fashion, the city remanufactured itself and today has a solid industrial base related to high technology products and pharmaceuticals. Musical presentations take place in summer at Charles Ives Concert Park, located near the home of Pulitzer Prize-winning composer Charles Ives, a Danbury native.

Ramada Inn

*116 Newtown Road
Danbury, CT 06810
203-792-3800*

Type of Lodging: Motel

Room Rates: $69–$149. AAA and AARP discounts.

Pet Charges and Deposits: None.

Pet Policy: All Pets Welcome

Amenities: Extended cable TV, movies (fee), voice mail, irons, heated pool, health club adjacent, coin laundry, meeting rooms, fax (fee), free newspaper, radios, coffee makers, data port/modem telephones, some refrigerators, some microwaves, 2-5 stories, interior corridors.

Rated: 2 Paws — 181 rooms.

Ramada Inn offers reasonably-priced, value conscious accommodations in a commercial area at the I-84, Exit 8, in the northeast corner of Danbury. Rooms are comfortable and quiet here. Danbury was founded by eight families in 1684 and served as a supply depot during the Revolutionary War. In 1777, General William Tryon's British troops destroyed the stores and burned many of the town's buildings. Danbury is at the southwestern end of Connecticut and sits squarely on the New York border. Wooster Mountain State Park is just adjacent to the southwest corner of Danbury. The Danbury Museum and Historical Society, which consists of the John and Mary Rider House (1785), the Dodd Hat Shop (1790), a one-room schoolhouse, the Charles Ives Birthplace, and the Danbury Fair Mural.

Residence Inn by Marriott

22 Segar Street
Danbury, CT 06810
203-797-1256

Type of Lodging: Apartment Hotel
Room Rates: $175–$209, some whirlpool units.
Pet Charges and Deposits: $25 per stay.
Pet Policy: All Pets Welcome.
Amenities: Extended cable TV, movies (fee), video game, voice mail, irons, hair dryers, heated pool, whirlpool, exercise room, complimentary evening beverages (Monday through Thursday), area transportation, coin laundry, meeting rooms, fax (fee), restaurant adjacent, radios, coffee makers, data port/modem telephones, refrigerators, microwaves, 4 stories, interior corridors.
Rated: 3 Paws — 78 suites, some whirlpool suites.

Marriott's Residence Inn Group provides you with ideal accommodations for more than one person—you get a small, luxurious apartment for little more than you'd pay for a hotel room. This property is particularly charming, and the Monday through Thursday evening beverage two hours is a particularly elegant and welcome touch. The Military Museum of Southern New England displays armored vehicles and artillery pieces from World War II, the Korean conflict, and the Vietnam war. The Danbury Railway Museum is situated in Danbury's restored 1903 station. The museum features the history of railroading in the northeast, and includes period equipment, photos, scale models, and a guided tour through the rail yard.

Holiday Inn Express

16 Tracey Road
Dayville, CT 06241
860-779-3200

Type of Lodging: Motel
Room Rates: $79–$139. AAA and AARP discounts.
Pet Charges and Deposits: $30 refundable deposit.
Pet Policy: Small pets only.
Amenities: Extended cable TV, movies, dual phone lines, voice mail, irons, hair dryers, heated pool, exercise room, coin laundry, meeting rooms, restaurant adjacent, radios, coffee makers, data port/modem telephones, some refrigerators, some microwaves, 3 stories, interior corridors.
Rated: 3 Paws — 78 rooms.

Holiday Inn Express is the largest, most comfortable place to stay in the small New England town of Danville. Clean, friendly, and quiet—three adjectives that describe this lodging to a tee. Dayville is in the northeast corner of Connecticut, less than 5 miles to the Rhode Island border. If you're in a hurry to go north or south, I-395 is rapid, but we strongly recommend State Highway 169 as a particularly scenic alternative. Mashamoquet Brook State Park, and the Wolf Den and Natchaug State Forests are great places for your pet to roam—they're not huge, you can enjoy them, then turn east and get to Providence, R.I. in less than an hour. If you go straight north, you're about 40 minutes from Massachusetts.

Clarion Inn

156 Kings Highway
Groton, CT 06340
860-446-0660

Type of Lodging: Hotel

Room Rates: $75–$175, some whirlpool units, $150–$220. AAA and AARP discounts.

Pet Charges and Deposits: None.

Pet Policy: All Pets Welcome

Amenities: Extended cable TV, movies, heated pool, whirlpool, sauna, exercise room, game room, coin laundry, meeting rooms, free newspaper, restaurant, coffee makers, data port/modem telephones, some refrigerators, some microwaves, 3 stories, interior corridors.

Rated: 3 Paws — 69 rooms.

Heed the Clarion call, and stay in richly-furnished, spacious rooms at the Clarion Inn in Groton. Public areas are particularly welcoming and attractive in this very manageable-sized lodging house. Groton is General; Dynamics' electric boat division headquarters. The *USS Nautilus*, America's first atomic-powered submarine, was produced and launched from Groton in 1954, and is now on permanent display. The names of 3,600 American submariners who died in the line of duty during World War II are displayed on the black granite, 60-foot long Wall of Honor at Bridge and Thames streets. The Museum at the opposite end of the *USS Nautilus* pier uses models, films, and equipment to trace the history and development of the American submarine force. Highlights include a model of Captain Nemo's *Nautilus* from Jules Verne's "Twenty Thousand Leagues Under the Sea."

Morgan Inn & Suites

135 Gold Star Highway
Groton, CT 06340
860-448-3000

Type of Lodging: Suite Motel

Room Rates: $69–$150, some suites, $99–$195, some whirlpool units, $129–$165. AAA and AARP discounts.

Pet Charges and Deposits: None.

Pet Policy: Designated rooms only.

Amenities: Cable TV, movies, irons, hair dryers, outdoor heated pool, health club adjacent, coin laundry, meeting rooms, radios, coffee makers, data port/modem telephones, some VCRs, some refrigerators, some microwaves, 3 stories, interior corridors.

Rated: 3 Paws — 56 units, including rooms and suites.

Morgan Inn & Suites—clean, restful, and spacious—is located close to the Naval base. The suites are particularly suited to families, and there are lots of welcome amenities. Project Oceanology and The Lighthouse Program departs from the University of Connecticut at Avery Point, You'll take a 2½ hour hands-on education cruise aboard the Projects research vessel *EnviroLab*. You'll learn how to identify fish, measure lobsters, and test sea water. The Lighthouse Program cruises include a boat tour of New London Harbor and a tour of the 1909 New London Ledge Lighthouse. These trips are educational, entertaining, and environmentally sensitive. Fort Griswold State Park was the scene of a massacre in 1781 when British forces led by Benedict Arnold took the fort and burned New London and Groton. The wounded were taken to the nearby Ebenezer Avery House (1850), still furnished with numerous period pieces.

Bed & Breakfast at B

c/o Nutmeg Bed & Breakfast
 Agency
P.O. Box 1117
West Hartford, CT 06127-1117
800-727-7592 • 860-236-6698

Type of Lodging: Bed & Breakfast

Room Rates: $109, including full breakfast.

Pet Charges and Deposits: None.

Pet Policy: All Pets Welcome.

Amenities: 2 stories, interior corridors.

Pet Amenities: Fenced back yard.

Rated: 2 Paws — 2 rooms.

This lovely contemporary home is situated on spacious grounds with a one-acre fenced back yard for pets to roam. The upper level is reserved for guests and features one guest room with either twin or king-sized bed, each with private bath. There is also a single room available if there is a third person in the party. The common areas include a sitting room for reading or television and a spacious screened deck with a heated pool. The house is air conditioned for summer comfort. Breakfast is served in the private dining room or outside on the deck during warmer months. This home is conveniently located within walking distance to Guilford town green, churches and shops. Beach passes are available for nearby Jacobs' Beach and the lake. The Henry Whitfield State Museum is housed in the oldest stone house in New England (1639). It and the Hyland House, an example of early saltbox construction (1660) contain period furnishings and décor.

THE GREATER

Hartford

AREA

Including

Avon

Cromwell

East Hartford

East Windsor

Enfield

Farmington

Manchester

Windsor

Windsor Locks

Crowne Plaza Hartford Downtown

50 Morgan Street
Hartford, CT 06120
860-549-2400

Type of Lodging: Hotel
Room Rates: $195–$215. AAA and AARP discounts.
Pet Charges and Deposits: $25 per day per pet, plus $50 refundable deposit.
Pet Policy: Small pets only.
Amenities: Cable TV, movies (fee), voice mail, irons, some hair dryers, exercise room, gift shop, area transportation, coin laundry, conference facilities, restaurant, cocktails, radios, coffee makers, data port/modem telephones, some refrigerators, some microwaves, 18 stories, interior corridors.
Rated: 4 Paws — 350 rooms.

Crowne Plaza is an elegant, luxury choice in Connecticut's largest city, with all the comforts and amenities you'd expect of a first class establishment. Although the first thing that comes to mind when you think of Hartford is insurance, the city has a long, colorful history. It started life as a Dutch trading post in 1633. The English established the first actual settlement there in 1636. The name of the city is derived from Hertford, where co-founded Samuel Stone was born. In 1687, Hartford became the site of the first effort to resist English rule. The English governor demanded that its citizens relinquish a 25-year-old charter that had given the city its independence. The colonists hid the charter in the trunk of what has become known as the charter oak for three days. That famous oak remained standing until 1856.

Goodwin Hotel

1 Haynes Street
Hartford, CT 06103
860-246-7500

Type of Lodging: Hotel (Historic)
Room Rates: $199–$289, some whirlpool units. AAA and AARP discounts.
Pet Charges and Deposits: $200 refundable deposit.
Pet Policy: Small pets only.
Amenities: Cable TV, movies (fee), voice mail, irons, hair dryers, exercise room, game room, valet laundry, meeting rooms, fax, restaurant, radios, data port/modem telephones, some refrigerators, some VCRs, 5-6 stories, interior corridors.
Rated: 4 Paws — 124 rooms.

Goodwin Hotel is a wonderful find—a European-style hotel centrally located in downtown Hartford, directly across from the Civic Center. This classic accommodation has a rather steep deposit for pets, but, if they behave and your room stays reasonably clean, it's refundable. Harriet Beecher Stowe Center, a 17-room house built in 1871, was the noted author and abolitionist's home from 1873 until her death in 1896. The author's paintings and memorabilia are an attractive slice of nineteenth century Americana. The Elizabeth Park Rose Gardens contain 15,000 plants—750 different varieties of roses. You can play at lawn bowling in summer and go ice skating in winter in the area of the Gardens. The Roman Catholic Cathedral of St. Joseph is a striking structure that contains 26 huge stained glass windows.

Hilton Hartford

315 Trumbull Street
Hartford, CT 06103
860-728-5151 • 800-HILTONS

Type of Lodging: Hotel
Room Rates: $89–$229. AAA and AARP discounts.
Pet Charges and Deposits: None.
Pet Policy: All Pets Welcome
Amenities: Cable TV, movies (fee), voice mail, irons, hair dryers, heated pool, whirlpool, sauna, health club adjacent, valet laundry, conference facilities, administrative services, fax, restaurant, cocktails, radios, data port/modem telephones, coffee makers, some refrigerators, some VCRs, connected by sky bridge to shopping mall, 22 stories, interior corridors.
Rated: 4 Paws – 388 rooms.

Hilton Hartford bills itself—and accurately—as "Your Hospitality Headquarters in Downtown Hartford." It's a huge high-rise, very well-priced for this city, within walking distance to numerous restaurants, museums, theaters, and other attractions. It's connected to the Hartford Civic Center Mall and the Coliseum—as centrally located as you can get—yet it's only 15 minutes from Bradley International Airport. Rooms are decidedly upscale, fully and luxuriously equipped. There's a full workout facility and two fine restaurants, The Stage Grille and Conrad's Lounge and Restaurant. You could hardly ask for finer accommodations in Connecticut's largest city. See Mark Twain's chest—and his bed and his billiard table—and a tremendous amount of Twainorabilia at the Mark Twain House, where he lived for 17 years. This unusual orange and black brick mansion has turrets and arches and large porches, and the first floor was decorated by Tiffany.

Red Roof Inn

100 Weston Street
Hartford, CT 06120
860-724-0222

Type of Lodging: Motel
Room Rates: $59–$75. AAA discounts.
Pet Charges and Deposits: None.
Pet Policy: Small pets only.
Amenities: Cable TV, movies (fee), voice mail, meeting rooms, free local telephones, free newspaper, radios, data port/modem telephones, 2 stories, exterior corridors.
Rated: 2 Paws – 115 rooms.

If you're budget conscious in Hartford, you can't do much better than the dependable Red Roof Inn, just west of the city center off the I-91, Exit 33. The clean, comfortable, restful accommodations are housed in a Hacienda-style structure, giving them a relaxed feeling. The Menczer Museum of Medicine and Dentistry demonstrates medical and dental technology and displays devices from the Revolutionary War to the mid-Twentieth century. The Wadsworth Athenaeum, founded in 1842, is the nation's oldest continuously operated public art museum, and houses some 50,000 works, including a large collection of the Hudson River School landscape paintings, 16th and 17th century European paintings, Impressionist art, and two galleries of African-American art and artifacts.

Residence Inn by Marriott / Downtown

942 Main Street
Hartford, CT 06103
860-524-5550

Type of Lodging: Apartment Hotel

Room Rates: $99–$299. AAA and AARP discounts.

Pet Charges and Deposits: $25 per day per pet.

Pet Policy: All Pets Welcome.

Amenities: Extended cable TV, movies, dual phone lines, voice mail, irons, hair dryers, exercise room, valet and coin laundry, meeting rooms, restaurant adjacent, radios, data port/modem telephones, coffee makers, refrigerators, microwaves, 8 stories, interior corridors.

Rated: 3 Paws — 100 units (small apartments).

Residence Inn is more than an apartment hotel—it's a part of Hartford's history. Designed by the renowned architect H.H. Richardson and considered one of the first "mall structures" integrating multi-use businesses under one roof, it was built in the 1870's. Of course, the accommodations are spiffed up and as modern as today, and as comfortable as a well-furnished, modern apartment can be. The standout Old State House, at 800 Main Street, was designed by Charles Bullfinch and built in 1796. It was the site of the first *Amistad* trial. One of the nation's oldest state houses, it served as Connecticut's seat of government for eighty-two years. The present State Capitol, built in 1878, is constructed of white Connecticut marble and adorned with Gothic spires, a gold leaf dome, statues, medallions, and historic relics.

Super 8 Motel

57 West Service Road
Hartford, CT 06120
860-246-8888

Type of Lodging: Motel

Room Rates: $55–$70. AAA and AARP discounts.

Pet Charges and Deposits: None.

Pet Policy: All Pets Welcome.

Amenities: Cable TV, movies (fee), coffee makers, data port/modem telephones, some refrigerators (fee), 2 stories, interior corridors.

Rated: 2 Paws — 100 rooms.

Comfortable, pet-welcoming, with clean, simple, spacious rooms and most reasonable prices, Super 8—Hartford is an excellent budget choice a mile southeast of the Hartford city center, off I-91 exit 33. In the 1870's, Hartford had the highest per capital income in the country, and world literary figures made their homes here. Mark Twain and Harriet Beecher Stowe were neighbors in the posh Nook Farm area. Richard D. Gorman, noted attorney and artist, was born and grew up in adjacent West Hartford. When the Hartford Fire Insurance Company was founded in the city in 1810 it started the industry, which is synonymous with the city even today. Hartford's rejuvenated riverfront district is a choice venue for river walks, picnics, and recreational pursuits.

Avon Old Farms Hotel

279 Avon Mountain Road
Avon, CT 06001
860-677-1651

Type of Lodging: Hotel

Room Rates: $149–$199, some suites. AAA and AARP discounts.

Pet Charges and Deposits: $50 deposit.

Pet Policy: Small pets only. Designated rooms only.

Amenities: Winter plug-ins, extended cable TV, movies, voice mail, irons, hair dryers, outdoor pool, sauna, exercise room, valet laundry, meeting rooms, restaurant, cocktails, radios, data port/modem telephones, some refrigerators (fee), 2-3 stories, interior/exterior corridors.

Rated: 3 Paws — 160 rooms, including some suites.

Avon Old Farms Hotel, a lodging with a variety of room sizes, and such relaxing activities as a sauna and exercise room, afford very attractive, comfortable accommodations in Avon, just northwest of Hartford. Talcott Mountain State Park is close by. Nearby Avon Old Farms Inn, a traditional Colonial inn, which has been doing business here since 1757, offers delicious classic fare of prime rib, sea bass with citrus sauce, banana mashed sweet potatoes, filet mignon, and other delectables. You can dine or enjoy your favorite cocktail in the wonderful old forge room. Old Avon Village offers 50 shops and eateries, while Riverdale Farms Shopping Center is situated on a restored and landscaped 19th century dairy farm.

Comfort Inn

111 Berlin Road
Cromwell, CT 06416
860-635-4100

Type of Lodging: Motel

Room Rates: $68–$105, including Continental breakfast. AAA and AARP discounts.

Pet Charges and Deposits: $15 per day per pet.

Pet Policy: All Pets Welcome.

Amenities: Extended cable TV, irons, hair dryers, health club adjacent, valet laundry, meeting rooms, restaurant adjacent, free newspapers, radios, coffee makers, data port/modem telephones, some refrigerators (fee), 4 stories, interior corridors.

Rated: 3 Paws — 77 rooms.

Spacious, well-furnished and well-equipped rooms, complete with business desk, await you at Cromwell's Comfort Inn. Cromwell is more of an exurb than part of Hartford—it's some fifteen miles south of the big city on State Route 9, adjoining the wide Connecticut River. The past comes alive at Hartford's Butler-McCook Homestead—four generations' worth of 18th and 19th century furnishings, original to the 1772 house. Behind the house, you'll find a restored Victorian Garden. Close by, the Travelers Tower (527 feet high) is one of the tallest structures in New England. Trinity College has wonderful "collegiate gothic" architecture set on a 96-acre campus, while the University of Connecticut School of Law is on 20 picturesque acres near Elizabeth Park.

Super 8 Motel

1 Industrial Park Road
Cromwell, CT 06416
860-632-8888

Type of Lodging: Motel
Room Rates: $59–$74. AAA and AARP discounts.
Pet Charges and Deposits: None.
Pet Policy: All Pets Welcome.
Amenities: Extended cable TV, movies (fee), valet laundry, restaurant adjacent, coffee makers, data port/modem telephones, 3 stories, interior corridors.
Rated: 2 Paws — 116 rooms.

Super 8—as always pet friendly and budget friendly—contains simple, comfortable units in a Tudor style building, south of Hartford on the Connecticut River. In nearby East Granby, you'll find the Old New-Gate Prison and Copper Mine. The Colonial copper mine served as a Revolutionary War prison and, in 1776, became the first state prison in the nation. It was abandoned in 1827, but you can visit the old prison buildings and underground caves today. Roaring Brook Nature Center in Canton boasts six miles of self-guiding trails through 115 acres of woodland—perfect for you and your pet to take "time off" for a roam or a romp. The oldest continuously operating amusement park in the nation, Lake Compounce Theme Park, is located in Bristol, an exurb of Hartford.

Holiday Inn

363 Roberts Street
East Hartford, CT 06108
860-528-9611

Type of Lodging: Hotel
Room Rates: $139. AAA and AARP discounts.
Pet Charges and Deposits: None.
Pet Policy: All Pets Welcome.
Amenities: Cable TV, movies (fee), voice mail, irons, hair dryers, heated pool, exercise room, area transportation, coin laundry, meeting rooms, restaurant, cocktails, data port/modem telephones, some refrigerators, some microwaves, 5 stories, interior corridors.
Rated: 3 Paws — 130 rooms.

Holiday Inn rooms are always clean, inviting, attractive, and beautifully furnished, and the East Hartford venue is no exception. You'll find lots to do here besides sleep—a fully-exercise room, restaurant, cocktail lounge, and a large number of amenities. In Bristol, several miles to the southwest, you'll find the American Clock and Watch Museum—more than 3,000 clocks and watches dating from the 1590's—grandfather clocks, shelf clocks, novelty clocks, even church-tower clocks can be found here. North of East Hartford, you'll find Windsor Locks. Penwood State Park is northwest of the town, and if you continue a little farther west, you'll come to a delightful cross-country ski area.

Wellesley Inn & Suites

333 Roberts Street
East Hartford, CT 06108
860-289-4950

Type of Lodging: Motor Inn
Room Rates: $69–$110, including Continental breakfast. AAA and AARP discounts.
Pet Charges and Deposits: $5 per day per pet.
Pet Policy: All Pets Welcome.
Amenities: Cable TV, movies (fee), voice mail, valet laundry, health club adjacent, radios, free local telephone calls, data port/modem telephones, coffee makers, some refrigerators, some microwaves, 4 stories, interior corridors.
Rated: 3 Paws — 103 rooms and suites.

You'll find very well-equipped small-to-medium-sized units in East Hartford's Wellesley Inn & Suites—and extraordinary inn at an affordable price. Experience the value and comfort of a fine bed & breakfast wrapped in the luxury of an extraordinary inn. Guest rooms are beautifully appointed, and there are fine amenities here. In the occasionally cockeyed way geography sometimes works in New England, East Hartford is actually Hartford's *northern* suburb. Among outdoor recreation areas in or about Hartford, you'll find Bolton Notch State Park, Meshomasic State Forest, the ski area of Farmington, and Penwood State Park—all fine areas to explore with your pet.

Best Western Colonial Inn

161 Bridge Street
East Windsor, CT 06088
860-623-9411

Type of Lodging: Motor Inn
Room Rates: $69–$200, some whirlpool units, including Continental breakfast. AAA and AARP discounts.
Pet Charges and Deposits: $25 deposit.
Pet Policy: Designated rooms only.
Amenities: Cable TV, movies, exercise room, valet laundry, meeting rooms, restaurant, cocktails, radios, coffee makers, free local telephone calls, data port/modem telephones, 2 stories, interior corridors.
Rated: 3 Paws — 120 rooms.

Best Western Colonial Inn affords you all the comforts—and the same welcoming philosophy—as you'll find throughout the world's largest chain of independently owned motor inns and motels. This lodging is conveniently located well north of Hartford, across the Connecticut River from Windsor Locks, and very convenient to Bradley International Airport. East Windsor was founded in 1636 by William Pynchon as a storage facility. Today, it's the northernmost of the four Windsors. The Connecticut Fire Museum houses a collection of antique fire equipment from 1894 through the mid-twentieth century. Spend a delightful hour or two at the Connecticut Trolley Museum (same address as the Fire Museum—58 North Road) where you'll find displays of operating trolleys and rail cars dating from 1894-1947. While there, take the 3½ mile antique trolley car ride.

Red Roof Inn

5 Hazard Avenue
Enfield, CT 06082
860-741-2571

Type of Lodging: Motel
Room Rates: $51–$111. AAA discounts.
Pet Charges and Deposits: None.
Pet Policy: Small pets only.
Amenities: Cable TV, movies (fee), voice mail, free local telephone calls, free newspapers, radios, data port/modem telephones, some refrigerators (fee), some microwaves (fee), 2 stories, exterior corridors.
Rated: 2 Paws — 108 rooms.

One of two superlative budget choices in Enfield, Red Roof Inn features all the room comforts and amenities you need for a good night's rest. You even get a free newspaper in the morning. Enfield is in the extreme northern part of Connecticut, located halfway between Hartford and Springfield, Massachusetts. Enfield is a far north exurb of Hartford, actually closer to Springfield, Massachusetts than to Connecticut's insurance capital. You can find great cross-country skiing at nearby Thompsonville. You're minutes away from Bradley International Airport, Windsor Locks, and Shenipsit State Forest. In nearby Springfield, Mass., the Basketball Hall of Fame is a state of the art museum where, in the midst of gawking at basketball memorabilia and interactive videotape monitors, you can shoot baskets and test your jumping skills.

Super 8 Motel

1543 King Street
Enfield, CT 06082
860-741-3636

Type of Lodging: Motel
Room Rates: $47–$109, including Continental breakfast. AAA and AARP discounts.
Pet Charges and Deposits: $10 per day per pet.
Pet Policy: All Pets Welcome.
Amenities: Extended cable TV, movies, coin laundry, meeting rooms, restaurant adjacent, data port/modem telephones, some refrigerators, some microwaves, 1-2 stories, exterior corridors.
Rated: 2 Paws — 65 rooms.

Super 8 is clean, comfy, roomy—and you get a free continental breakfast. A great budget pick in Enfield. This northern Connecticut exurb of Hartford is convenient to Bradley International Airport, Springfield, Mass., and Hartford. Enfield is "halfway to everywhere." It's halfway between Hartford and Springfield, Massachusetts. Although it's in the far northern part of the state, it's practically in the very center between east and west. While you're located on the Connecticut River, you're also in a woodland paradise. Head south to State Route 20, then take a particularly scenic road from East Granby to Tunxis State Forest and Bark Farmstead Reservoir for an ingratiating "out of the cities" look at northern Connecticut.

Centennial Inn

c/o Nutmeg Bed & Breakfast Agency
P.O. Box 1117
West Hartford, CT 06127-1117
800-727-7592 • 860-236-6698

Type of Lodging: Inn
Room Rates: $125–$169, including Continental breakfast.
Pet Charges and Deposits: None.
Pet Policy: Manager's prior approval required.
Amenities: Extended cable TV, movies, heated pool, whirlpool, exercise room, fireplaces, data port/modem telephones, some refrigerators, some microwaves, 2 stories, interior corridors.
Rated: 3 Paws — 150 suites

The Centennial Inn is located in the aristocratic old town of Farmington, laden with historical treasures, cultural richness, a ski area, and only about a dozen miles from Hartford. This contemporary inn offers one- and two-bedroom suites with comfortable queen-sized beds, sleeper couches, kitchens, private baths, and inviting fireplaces. In the morning, you awaken to the aroma of freshly-brewed coffee and enjoy a deluxe continental breakfast. The Farmington area, despite its proximity to Connecticut's largest city, offers unspoiled scenic grandeur, where historic homes and museums sit cheek-by-jowl with antique shops and charming restaurants. You may enjoy a visit to Jackie O's alma mater, Miss Porter's School, or shop 'til you drop at West Farms, one of Connecticut's largest and finest shopping malls.

Farmington Inn

827 Farmington Ave.
Farmington, CT 06032
800-648-9804 • 860-677-2821

Type of Lodging: Inn
Room Rates: $129–$169, including Continental breakfast, afternoon beverages and tea. AAA, AARP, AKC, ABA, and *inquire about Pets Welcome*™ discounts.
Pet Charges and Deposits: None.
Pet Policy: Manager's prior approval required.
Amenities: Cable TV, award-winning restaurant, offsite health membership included, 2 stories, interior/exterior corridors.
Rated: 3 Paws — 59 rooms and 13 suites.

The Farmington Inn is nestled in the heart of one of Connecticut's oldest towns, where stately white homes built by bankers and merchants in post-Revolutionary days still line the main street. Antique buffs will enjoy treasure hunting through the region's many antique shops. Close by are historic homes, museums, and West Farms Mall, one of Connecticut's largest shopping areas. The Inn welcomes guests in a warm and comfortable lobby decorated with fresh flowers, antiques, and original works of art. Guest rooms are beautifully appointed, featuring white Italian Carrera marble bathrooms, matching Nightingale pattern drapes and bedspreads, and numerous travelers' amenities. The elegant suites offer terry cloth bathrobes and handsome armoires.

Residence Inn Manchester

201 Hale Road
Manchester, CT 06040
860-432-4242

Type of Lodging: Extended Stay Motel

Room Rates: $85–$184. AAA discounts.

Pet Charges and Deposits: $75 deposit, $8 per day.

Pet Policy: All Pets Welcome.

Amenities: Cable TV, movies, dual phone lines, voice mail, irons, hair dryers, heated pool, whirlpool, exercise room, sports court, coin laundry, meeting rooms, restaurant adjacent, radios, data port/modem telephones, coffee makers, refrigerators, microwaves, 3 stories, interior corridors.

Rated: 3 Paws — 96 suites.

Residence Inn—Manchester affords you comfortable mini-suites at a price *you* can afford. As with all Marriott-owned properties, this lodging caters to those who desire upscale, comfortable accommodations on well-tended grounds, with sparkling public areas. Manchester, fifteen miles east of Hartford, is a substantial city in its own right and one of Connecticut's major manufacturing centers. The town produced gunpowder that was used during the Revolutionary War. 215 acres Wickham Park houses Oriental and lotus gardens, an aviary, and a log cabin. You'll find everything from walking and fitness trails to children's play areas, as well as tennis and volleyball courts, picnic areas, and softball fields. See firefighting equipment and memorabilia, including leather fire buckets used by Colonial settlers, at Manchester's Fire Museum, 220 Pine Street, in a restored 1901 fire house.

Residence Inn by Marriott

100 Dunfey Lane
Windsor, CT 06095
860-688-7474

Type of Lodging: Apartment Hotel

Room Rates: $169–$175. AAA discounts.

Pet Charges and Deposits: $100–$200 per stay.

Pet Policy: All Pets Welcome.

Amenities: Cable TV, movies, voice mail, irons, hair dryers, heated pool, whirlpool, sports court, complimentary evening beverages (Monday through Thursday coin laundry, meeting rooms, health club adjacent, radios, data port/modem telephones, coffee makers, refrigerators, microwaves, 2 stories, exterior corridors.

Rated: 3 Paws — 96 suites.

No surprises here—just highly attractive, well-furnished accommodations, lots of amenities, a Monday-through-Thursday happy hour, and everything you'd expect from the extraordinary Marriott chain. Like so many New England cities and towns, Windsor is four, interrelated towns. Windsor is just northwest of South Windsor, but significantly south of Windsor Locks and East Windsor. It's convenient to the big city (Hartford) as well as to Bradley International Airport. See the huge Queen of the Skies and more than 80 other historic aircraft at Bradley Airport's New England Air Museum, the largest aviation museum in the northeast. Wethersfield, to the south, claims, along with Windsor, to be the oldest permanent English settlement in Connecticut. The Webb-Deane-Stevens Museum contains three restored 18th century houses and furnished to depict the typical colonial home.

Baymont Inn & Suites Hartford Airport

64 Ella T. Grasso Turnpike
Windsor Locks, CT 06096
860-623-3336

Type of Lodging: Motel
Room Rates: $89, including Continental breakfast. AAA and AARP discounts.
Pet Charges and Deposits: None.
Pet Policy: Small pets only.
Amenities: Cable TV, movies (fee), voice mail, irons, hair dryers, coin laundry, meeting rooms, area transportation, restaurant adjacent, cocktails, radios, coffee makers, data port/modem telephones, some refrigerators, some microwaves, 4 stories, interior corridors.
Rated: 3 Paws — 102 rooms and suites.

Baymont Inn & Suites is located on a commercial strip on State Route 75 just north of State Route 20, north of Hartford on the Connecticut River. Units are very well-priced—you get a lot of space, convenience, and luxury for the money. The First Church in Windsor is now housed in its "new" building (1794). The adjoining cemetery contains tombstones dating from the 1600's. Palisado Green occupies part of the site of the old stockade, built during the 1637 Pequot War. Nearby Wethersfield's Buttolph-Williams House (built 1710-1720) has a medieval appearance and period furnishings, while Cove Warehouse, at the north end of Main Street in Cove Park, Wethersfield, was built in the 1600's and is the only one that was left standing after a major flood in 1692. The warehouse displays maritime exhibits that hark to the area's seafaring past.

Homewood Suites by Hilton

65 Ella T. Grasso Turnpike
Windsor Locks, CT 06096
860-627-8463

Type of Lodging: Extended Stay Hotel
Room Rates: $169–$209. AAA and AARP discounts.
Pet Charges and Deposits: $150 per stay.
Pet Policy: All Pets Welcome. Seven night minimum stay.
Amenities: Extended cable TV, movies, voice mail, irons, hair dryers, whirlpool, exercise room, sports court, area transportation, gift shop, coin laundry, meeting rooms, administrative services, PC, VCRs, radios, coffee makers, data port/modem telephones, refrigerators, microwaves, 3 stories, interior/exterior corridors.
Rated: 3 Paws — 132 suites.

Homewood Suites is more than a hotel. Here you'll enjoy all the comfort, convenience, and privacy of an apartment for the price of a hotel room. The apartment-style suites are comfortably furnished with all the features and amenities you'd expect from luxury accommodations. Suites include wood-burning fireplaces, two remote-controlled color TVs, VCRs, ceiling fans, electronic voice mail system, computer jacks, and fully equipped kitchens. Homewood Suites' center of activity is the Lodge, where you can relax and socialize. The grounds offer pet exercise areas, and Northwest Park is nearby. The Homewood Suites provides 24-hour transportation to Bradley International Airport. And, of course, all the attractions of Hartford are less than 15 miles away.

Sheraton Hotel–Airport

1 Bradley International Airport (in the terminal)
Windsor Locks, CT 06096
860-627-5311

Type of Lodging: Hotel
Room Rates: $99–$225. AAA and AARP discounts.
Pet Charges and Deposits: None.
Pet Policy: Small pets only.
Amenities: Cable TV, movies (fee), dual phone lines, voice mail, irons, hair dryers, heated pool, sauna, exercise room, valet laundry, conference facilities, restaurant, cocktails, radios, data port/modem telephones, coffee makers, some refrigerators, 8 stories, interior corridors.
Rated: 3 Paws — 237 rooms.

Sheraton Hotel affords you great convenience to Bradley International Airport. More than that, it gives you finely furnished, luxurious rooms of traditional Sheraton quality, and lots of activities and amenities right within the hotel itself. West Hartford is surprisingly close to Windsor Locks, and there you'll find three worthwhile attractions, the Museum of American Political Life, the Noah Webster House/Museum, and the Science Center of Connecticut. The first of these attractions, located on the University of Hartford campus, has all kinds of intriguing, sometimes kitzschy, political memorabilia. The Webster House/Museum was the 1758 birthplace of Noah Webster, author of the first American dictionary. The Science Center of Connecticut is a hands-on science, technology, and nature museum that features a 30-foot walk-in kaleidoscope.

Inn at Iron Masters

229 Main Street
Lakeville, CT 06039
860-435-9844

Type of Lodging: Inn
Room Rates: $85–$155, including Continental breakfast. AAA discounts.
Pet Charges and Deposits: None.
Pet Policy: Designated rooms only. Signed pet agreement required.
Amenities: Extended cable TV, voice mail, hair dryers, outdoor pool, whirlpool, gift shop, restaurant adjacent, radios, coffee makers, data port/modem telephones, some refrigerators, some microwaves, 1 story, exterior corridors.
Rated: 3 Paws — 28 rooms.

Known as the "Southern Berkshires best-kept secret," the Inn at Iron Masters offers elegant accommodations in the scenic village of Lakeville, situated in the heart of the Litchfield Hills. The grounds are dotted with authentic Victorian gazebos surrounded by charming English country gardens. Each guest room is individually decorated, graced with a spacious sitting area and private bath. You can relax by the outdoor swimming pool or warm yourself by the large fieldstone fireplace in the Hearth Room. Discover hundreds of things to do and sights to see, including water sports, mountain climbing, biking, horseback riding, or hiking through numerous nature preserves and gardens. Golf in the splendor of the Berkshires, soar above it all in a hot air balloon, or explore the caves of the Berkshire Mountains with experienced spelunkers.

Interlaken Inn Resort & Conference Center

74 Interlaken Road
Lakeville, CT 06039
860-435-9878

Type of Lodging: Resort Complex

Room Rates: $139-319, some suites, $299, some whirlpool units, $319.

Pet Charges and Deposits: $10 per day per pet.

Pet Policy: All Pets Welcome.

Amenities: Extended cable TV, some hair dryers, heated pool, whirlpool, saunas, beach, swimming, boating, canoeing, paddleboats, boat dock, fishing, two tennis courts, hiking trails, bicycles (fee), health club adjacent, gift shop, valet laundry, massage (fee), meeting rooms, restaurant, cocktails, VCRs, radios, some coffee makers, data port/modem telephones, some refrigerators (fee), some microwaves (fee), 2 stories, interior/exterior corridors.

Rated: 4 Paws — 82 units, including rooms and suites.

Interlaken Inn Resort & Conference Center rates a sterling four paw rating from Pets Welcome™. It's set on beautifully tended and landscaped grounds in a peaceful setting in the southern Berkshires. You have a very wide variety of choice accommodations here. Spacious townhouses, with modern rooms and warm country décor are available, as are Bed & Breakfast style rooms in either a graceful Tudor-style house or a luxurious Victorian period structure. There's a wonderful "country inn" feel to these outstanding lodgings. Leisure activities include swimming, boating, lake beaches, canoeing, saunas, and a heated pool. You're in the northwestern corner of the state, less than 5 miles from the New York border.

The Mare's Inn Bed & Breakfast

333 Colonel Ledyard Highway
Ledyard, CT 06372
860-572-7556

Type of Lodging: Bed & Breakfast

Room Rates: $100–$165, including full breakfast. AAA, AARP, AKC, ABA, and *ask about Pets Welcome™* discounts.

Pet Charges and Deposits: None unless damage sustained.

Pet Policy: Small pets only. Manager's prior approval required.

Amenities: Extended cable TV, whirlpool, VCRs, radios, some coffee makers, data port/modem telephones, some refrigerators, some microwaves, smoke free premises, 2 stories, interior corridors.

Rated: 3 Paws — 4 rooms and 1 suite.

Nestled in the rolling foothills near historic Mystic and the extraordinary Foxwoods Casino-Resort (developed by the same Sol Kurzner who built Sun City in South Africa and Atlantis in the Bahamas), the Mare's Inn invites you to experience gracious New England hospitality. The grounds beckon exploration with a walking trail through the woods, and benches along the way for resting or reading. Inside the high hedges, the lawn has plenty of room for sunbathing, picnicking, or thinking deep thoughts. Guest accommodations are comfortable and cozy and feature a private bath. After a good night's rest, wake up to the delightful aroma of homemade bread and freshly ground coffee. A wall of glass in the dining room lets you appreciate the beauty of the grounds while you feast in steak and eggs, blueberry pancakes, or French toast stuffed with raspberry cream cheese.

Tollgate Hill Inn

Route 202 and Tollgate Road
Litchfield, CT 06759
800-445-3903 • 860-567-4545

Type of Lodging: Inn

Room Rates: $119–$185, including Continental breakfast.

Pet Charges and Deposits: $10 per day per pet.

Pet Policy: All Pets Welcome

Amenities: 2 stories, interior corridors, award-winning restaurant and pub.

Rated: 4 Paws — 16 rooms and 5 suites with wood-burning fireplaces.

Tollgate Hill Inn, situated on ten wooded acres, is designed to live up to its centuries-old heritage of providing memorable hospitality. Listed in the National Register of Historic Places and built in 1745, the main house became a popular way station for travelers during Colonial times. The 18th century paneling, floorboards, and fireplaces have been carefully restored to near-original condition. The guest rooms and suites have been renovated with meticulous respect for detail, featuring canopied beds and working fireplaces. Litchfield is located in the heart of Connecticut's antique country, where auction-going is a major local sport. Local attractions include the White Memorial Foundation, the state's largest nature center, consisting of 4,000 acres with 35 miles of trails for hiking, horseback riding, fishing, cross-country skiing, and camping, as well as ten acres of display gardens featuring nationally known English tuberous begonias.

Residence Inn by Marriott

390 Bee Street
Meriden, CT 06450
203-634-7770

Type of Lodging: Suite Hotel

Room Rates: $93–$185. AAA discounts.

Pet Charges and Deposits: $200 deposit per stay.

Pet Policy: All Pets Welcome.

Amenities: Cable TV, movies (fee), voice mail, irons, hair dryers, heated pool, whirlpool, exercise room, sports court, complimentary evening beverages (Monday through Thursday), meeting rooms, radios, coffee makers, data port/modem telephones, refrigerators, microwaves, 3 stories, interior/exterior corridors.

Rated: 3 Paws — 106 suites.

Despite the steep $200 pet deposit, which is refundable, the Residence Inn by Marriott is certainly the pick of the crop in Meriden. Spacious, comfortable, hospitable, and extraordinarily well-priced for such upscale accommodations, this is truly a fine lodging in this medium-sized city. Meriden was one of the more famous silverware centers in the country from the 19th century through the 1970's. Asa Rogers invented electroplating here in 1847. Beautiful 900-acre Hubbard Park is situated two miles west of the city in the Hanging Hills. Castle Craig, at an elevation of 1,007 feet, contains a stone observation tower. The Merimere Reservoir is wonderfully scenic. You'll find nature trails, drives, paths, tennis courts, and all manner of recreational facilities in this surprisingly lovely area.

Amerisuites

224 Greenmanville Ave.
Mystic, CT 06355
850-536-9997

Type of Lodging: Suite motel

Room Rates: $69–$269, including Continental breakfast. AAA and AARP discounts.

Pet Charges and Deposits: None.

Pet Policy: Small pets only.

Amenities: Extended cable TV, movies (fee), voice mail, irons, hair dryers, outdoor pool, exercise room, coin laundry, meeting rooms, administrative services, free newspaper, VCRs, radios, data port/modem telephones, coffee makers, refrigerators, microwaves, 3 stories, interior corridors.

Rated: 3 Paws — 80 suites.

Amerisuites Mystic / I-95 & Seaport, is a decidedly upscale, luxurious place, with large, very spacious units, fine furnishings, and a bountiful breakfast buffet. Well-equipped business units are available within the complex. By the middle of the 19th century, the fastest clipper ships in America were being produced in Mystic. In 1861, the first ironclad vessel, the *Galena* was built in the Mystic shipyards. Mystic was the prototypical maritime town, and today it's still a fascinating stop. Mystic Seaport, on the Mystic River, displays 17 acres of historic houses, shops, and trade buildings. The last of the wooden whaling ships, the *Charles W. Morgan,* the 1882 training ship *Joseph Conrad,* and the 1908 steamboat *Sabino* are among the ships you can board there. Mystic Whaler Cruises offers everything from a lobster dinner cruise to multi-day excursions aboard an 83-foot schooner.

Harbour Inne & Cottage

15 Edgemont Street
Mystic, CT 06355
860-572-9253

Type of Lodging: Inn

Room Rates: $85–$265, including kitchen privileges.

Pet Charges and Deposits: $10 per day per pet, $50 refundable deposit.

Pet Policy: All Pets Welcome

Amenities: Cable TV, common area with fireplace and antique piano. 1-2 stories, interior/exterior corridors.

Rated: 2 Paws — 4 rooms and 1 cottage with hot tub spa on deck.

Located in the heart of historic Mystic, the Harbour Inne invited you to relax and enjoy the beautiful views of the Mystic River from its waterfront gazebo. The Inn is an easy walk from all the shops, restaurants, and sights of downtown Mystic, including Seaport Museum and the Mystic Marine Life Aquarium. Each of the four bedrooms has a private bath, kitchen privileges, and cable TV. The separate cedar cottage features a bedroom with fireplace, a kitchen, and a private deck with hot tub. The Harbour Inne and Cottage is the perfect place to stay while you explore all the attractions of southeastern Connecticut. The Mystic Aquarium displays more than 3,500 living sea creatures. Its Challenge of the Deep exhibit explores the world of deep-sea wrecks and artifacts. There are areas where you can see African black-footed penguins, both above and below the water, as well as a landscape similar to the Pribilof Islands where you can watch cavorting northern fur seals and sea lions.

Fairfield Inn–New Haven

400 Sargent Drive
New Haven, CT 06511
203-562-1111

Type of Lodging: Motel

Room Rates: $85–$105.

Pet Charges and Deposits: $25 deposit.

Pet Policy: Small pets only.

Amenities: Extended cable TV, movies, voice mail, irons, hair dryers, exercise room, area transportation, coin laundry, data port/modem telephones, some VCRs, 8 stories, interior corridor.

Rated: 3 Paws — 152 rooms.

Fairfield Inn, a member of the Marriott chain, afford you modern, contemporary guest room décor with warm, restful, earth tone colors, in a high-rise, centrally located building off the I-95, exit 46. There are lots of welcome amenities in this fine lodging. New Haven gave birth to the steamboat, the corkscrew, the steel fishhook, and the lollipop. It's also known as the "Birthplace of America's Hits," since many of the world's most popular actors, musicians, and dancers debuted at the Shubert College Street. Oh, yes, there's a university in New Haven named Yale, which started *its* life in Branford in 1701 and moved to New Haven 15 years later. Connecticut Hall (1752) is the oldest of Yale's ivy-covered buildings still in use. The Yale University Art Gallery is the oldest university art museum in the Western Hemisphere.

Residence Inn by Marriott

3 Long Wharf Drive
New Haven, CT 06511
203-777-5337

Type of Lodging: Apartment hotel

Room Rates: $139–$199. AAA and AARP discounts.

Pet Charges and Deposits: $10 per day per pet.

Pet Policy: All Pets Welcome.

Amenities: Extended cable TV, movies, voice mail, irons, hair dryers, outdoor pool, whirlpool, sports court, complimentary evening beverages (Monday through Thursday), area transportation, coin laundry, meeting rooms, health club adjacent, radios, coffee makers, data port/modem telephones, refrigerators, microwaves, 2 stories, exterior corridors.

Rated: 3 Paws — 112 suites.

Studio- and one-bedroom apartments at the Residence Inn are luxurious and highly satisfying. Accommodations are housed in cluster buildings, giving the feel of a townhouse community rather that transient facilities. There are fireplaces and kitchens in each of the 112 suites. From 1703 to 1875, Connecticut was the only Colony, and thereafter the only state in the union, to have *two* capitals, Hartford and New Haven. New Haven was laid out by Puritans in 1638, in nine equal squares; the central square, the Green, was reserved for the public. Today, these 16 acres remain as plotted by the original settlers. Three churches on Temple Street, the First Church of Christ (1687, then renovated), Trinity Church (Episcopal), built in 1812-1814, and the United Church on the Green, from which the Reverend Henry Ward Beecher preached his anti-slavery sermons in the 1850's. West Rock Ridge State Park encompasses more than 1,500 acres offering fishing, hiking, mountain biking, and scenic views.

Red Roof Inn

707 Colman Street
New London, CT 06320
860-444-0001

Type of Lodging: Motel
Room Rates: $45–$91. AAA discounts.
Pet Charges and Deposits: None.
Pet Policy: All Pets Welcome.
Amenities: Extended cable TV, movies (fee), voice mail, data port/modem telephones, radios, 2 stories, exterior corridors.
Rated: 2 Paws — 108 rooms.

A great budget choice, Red Roof Inn affords small to medium units, simply furnished, clean, comfortable, and inviting, at I-95 exit 82-83, just north of the city center. For a relatively small city, New London has a substantial assortment of attractions. Among the most noteworthy are the Connecticut College Arboretum (20 acre native plant collection), the Hempstead Houses (1678 and 1758), the Lyman Allan Art Museum, the Monte Cristo Cottage, boyhood home of Nobel prize winner Eugene O'Neill, Ocean Beach Park, the Science Center of Eastern Connecticut, and the U.S. Coast Guard Academy.

Blackberry River Inn

536 Greenwoods Road
Norfolk, CT 06058
860-542-5100

Type of Lodging: Historic Bed & Breakfast
Room Rates: $75–$135, some suites, $175–$215, some whirlpool units, $125–$195, including full breakfast.
Pet Charges and Deposits: None.
Pet Policy: Pets in cottage only.
Amenities: Extended cable TV, irons, hair dryers, smoke-free premises, outdoor pool, radios, data port/modem telephones, some refrigerators, some VCRs, meeting rooms, 2 stories, interior corridors.
Rated: 3 Paws — 17 rooms, suites, and cottage.

Blackberry River Inn is an independently owned, thoroughly charming Colonial Inn situated in a rural area. Rooms vary in size; a few of them have fireplaces. If you're coming with your pet, you're limited to accommodations in the adjacent cottage, but you still get all the benefits this lovely lodging has to offer. Norfolk is in the northwest corner of the state, on scenic U.S. Highway 44, in an area surrounded by mountains, lakes, and forests. Haystack Mountain State Park is less than two miles away, Housatonic State Forest is eight miles distant, and there are no less than ten lakes and reservoirs in the immediate vicinity. This is one of the few places in Connecticut that's not heavily peopled, and that means you're close to the great—and beautiful—New England outdoors.

Holiday Inn

201 Washington Avenue
North Haven, CT 06473
203-239-4225

Type of Lodging: Hotel

Room Rates: $79–$129. AAA and AARP discounts.

Pet Charges and Deposits: None.

Pet Policy: All Pets Welcome.

Amenities: Extended cable TV, movies, voice mail, irons, hair dryers, heated pool, sauna, exercise room, area transportation (fee), valet laundry, conference facilities, restaurant, cocktails, radios, coffee makers, data port/modem telephones, some VCRs (fee)some refrigerators (fee), some microwaves (fee), 2 stories, interior corridors.

Rated: 3 Paws — 140 rooms.

Holiday Inn is North Haven's largest lodging. Here you'll find both nicely renovated units and some with early vintage accoutrements and appointments. It's a fine, comfortable place with a pet-friendly philosophy and amenities galore. North Haven is only six miles from the center of its magnet town, New Haven and about fifteen miles south of Meriden. It's surrounded by Qunnipiac River State Park, Wharton Brook State Park, Sleeping Giant State Park, Tri-Mountain State Park, East Rock Park, West Rock Park, and Lakes Saltonstall, Gaillard, and Bethany—all convenient, manageable-sized recreation venues to give you an outdoor flavor, while allowing you to conveniently see and attend the numerous cultural venues of New Haven, and the northern shores of Long Island Sound.

High Acres

c/o Nutmeg Bed & Breakfast Agency
P.O. Box 1117
West Hartford, CT 06127-1117
800-727-7592 • 860-236-6698

Type of Lodging: Historic Bed & Breakfast

Room Rates: $159, including full breakfast.

Pet Charges and Deposits: None.

Pet Policy: Manager's prior approval required.

Amenities: Common sitting area with fireplace and color TV. 2 stories, interior corridors.

Rated: 3 Paws — 4 rooms and on 150-acre horse farm.

This classic circa 1742 New England farmhouse is situated on 150 scenic acres. Currently a working equestrian farm, High Acres offers king- and queen-sized beds with private baths in delightfully furnished guest rooms. Guests enjoy relaxing on the spacious glassed-on porch overlooking grassy fields dotted with beautiful horses. A common sitting area is equipped with an inviting fire and color TV. Awake to a delicious full breakfast served in the formal dining room, featuring home-baked goods, steaming beverages, and fresh juice. High Acres is said to provide the best views in Connecticut. What better way to enjoy this lovely setting than on horseback during an organized trail ride, or, if you prefer, get out your hiking boots and explore this beautiful section of southeastern Connecticut.

Homestead Guest Studios

400 Main Avenue
Norwalk, CT 06851
203-847-6888

Type of Lodging: Extended stay motel

Room Rates: $139–$144.

Pet Charges and Deposits: $100 per stay.

Pet Policy: Small pets only.

Amenities: Cable TV, movies, voice mail, irons, exercise room (fee), coin laundry, radios, data port/modem telephones, coffee makers, refrigerators, microwaves, some VCRs (fee), 3 stories, interior corridors.

Rated: 2 Paws — 140 suites.

Homestead Guest Studios feature comfortable, roomy mini-suites with kitchenettes, off the Merritt Parkway (U.S. 15) at exit 40B, just north of the center of the city. It's convenient to New York City as well as New Haven. Today a suburb of New York, Norwalk was an agricultural town before the Revolution. Seized and burned by the British in 1779, a kiln was built a year later, and Norwalk Stoneware Pottery soon became a name of national renown. The partially restored 60-room Lockwood-Mathews Mansion, built by Civil War financier LeGrand Lockwood, is a chateau in the French style that contains stenciled walls, inlaid woodwork, and a skylit rotunda. The Maritime Aquarium at Norwalk is situated in a 5-acre restored 19th Century factory. Highlights include an aquarium with more than 1,000 animals native to the Long Island Sound, a touch tank, and an IMAX theater.

Old Lyme Inn

85 Lynne Street
Old Lyme, CT 06371
860-434-2600

Type of Lodging: Historic Country Inn

Room Rates: $99–$175, including Continental breakfast. AAA discounts.

Pet Charges and Deposits: None.

Pet Policy: All Pets Welcome.

Amenities: Extended cable TV, hair dryers, meeting rooms, free local telephone calls, restaurant, radios, data port/modem telephones, some refrigerators, 2 stories, interior corridors.

Rated: 3 Paws — 13 rooms.

Old Lyme Inn is a wonderfully restored circa 1850 home that affords you a surprising array of modern-yet-homey touches, and surrounds you with an aura of romantic charm. Once upon a time every house in Old Lyme was occupied by a sea captain. Those old salts, who were in constant contact with foreign ports, returned home with their treasures. Today, Old Lyme is home to an art community which was the nucleus of American Impressionism in the early 1900's. The Florence Griswold Museum houses many of the finest American Impressionist and Barbizon paintings, as does nearby Lyme Academy of Fine Arts and the Lyme Art Association Gallery, reportedly the nation's oldest art group to have held continuous exhibitions in its own gallery. Old Lyme is just across the Connecticut River from Old Saybrook, where the first one-man battle submarine, the *Turtle* was invented and built in 1776. The *Turtle* actually served briefly during the American Revolution.

Old Riverton Inn

436 East River Road
Riverton, CT 06065
860-379-8678

Type of Lodging: Historic Country Inn
Room Rates: $55–$210, including Continental breakfast.
Pet Charges and Deposits: None.
Pet Policy: Designated rooms only. Manager's prior approval required.
Amenities: Extended cable TV, meeting rooms, restaurant, radios, data port/modem telephones, some refrigerators, 3 stories (no elevator), interior corridors. A forest for exercising your pet nearby.
Rated: 3 Paws — 12 rooms.

Old Riverton Inn was originally opened in 1796 by Jesse Ives and was known as Ives Tavern. Today, the Inn has twelve comfortable guest rooms, all of which have private baths and cable TV. Canopy beds, fireplaces, and antique décor complete the quaint and comfortable accommodations. The restaurant serves bountiful cuisine with fresh seafood fare. Guests may choose from two separate dining rooms and enjoy libations and good times at the Hobby Horse Bar. Peoples State Forest and American Legion Forest nearby offer outstanding recreation. The village invites strolling the several antique and specialty shops, as well as a visit to the Hitchcock Chair Company and Museum. Riverton, in the northwestern corner of Connecticut, is surrounded by hills and is situated on the Farmington River. Even today, it maintains its early 1800's appearance.

White Hart

15 Undermountain Road
Salisbury, CT 06068
800-832-0041 • 860-435-0030

Type of Lodging: Country Inn
Room Rates: $85–$200.
Pet Charges and Deposits: $10 per day per pet.
Pet Policy: Manager's prior approval required.
Amenities: Tennis, fitness center, babysitting services, laundry and dry cleaning services, three restaurants, two taverns, 3 stories, interior corridors.
Rated: 3 Paws — 23 rooms and 3 suites

White Hart is situated in the extreme northwest corner of Connecticut, in the foothills of the Berkshires. The White Hart draws its name from its counterpart in England. Enjoying a long and illustrious career as a country inn, the White Hart was, at one time, owned by Edsel Ford. The Ford Room is located within the original part of the building and features a canopy bed and a view of the village green. Each of the 26 guest quarters vary in accommodations, but all include private bath and furnishings of either Thomasville Mahogany or Lane Country Pine, with Waverly wall coverings and fabrics. You have three restaurants to choose from at White Hart—the Tap Room, the Garden Room, or the American Grill. The White Hart's location enables guests to enjoy the recreational activities of both the Litchfield Hills and the Berkshires.

Amerisuites

695 Bridgeport Avenue
Shelton, CT 06484
203-925-5900

Type of Lodging: Suite Motel

Room Rates: $155–$175, including Continental breakfast. AAA and AARP discounts.

Pet Charges and Deposits: None.

Pet Policy: Cats only.

Amenities: Cable TV, movies (fee), dual phone lines, voice mail, irons, hair dryers, heated pool, exercise room, area transportation, coin laundry, meeting rooms, administrative services, restaurant adjacent, free newspaper, radios, coffee makers, data port/modem telephones, refrigerators, microwaves, 4 stories, interior corridors.

Rated: 3 Paws — 128 suites.

Amerisuites Shelton provides you with high-end, *tout confort* lodgings throughout the year. There are lots of amenities, both for the business and for the casual traveler, and you'll get a feeling of caring hospitality anywhere on the premises. Note that "pets" in this place means cats, so you need not worry about any noise within the confines of the lodging. Shelton is situated on a bend of the Housatonic River in southwestern Connecticut, northeast of Bridgeport and northwest of New Haven. Naugatuck State Forest, large by Connecticut standards, is less than 15 miles north of Shelton. Nearby Stratford was noted for its shipbuilding and oystering industries, both of which still exist. Judson House and Museum in Stratford is a fine example of the clapboard-sheathed post-and-beam construction that was typical of 18th century New England. It was built in 1750 and furnished in period décor.

Homestead Guest Studios

945 Bridgeport Avenue
Shelton, CT 06484
203-926-6868

Type of Lodging: Suite motel

Room Rates: $79. AARP discounts.

Pet Charges and Deposits: $85 per stay.

Pet Policy: All Pets Welcome.

Amenities: Cable TV, voice mail, irons, coin laundry, restaurant adjacent, radios, coffee makers, data port/modem telephones, refrigerators, microwaves, some VCRs (fee), 3 stories, interior corridors.

Rated: 3 Paws — 140 suites.

At Homestead Guest Studios, you get unsurpassed value for the money, with many of the creature comforts of home. It's conveniently located near an area of business parks, which gives you lots of green space. Accommodations are very inviting, and you get a fresh, clean feeling throughout the units. Boothe Memorial Park and Museum in nearby Stratford is the 32-acre former homestead of the Boothe family, which resided here from 1663-1949. Ten of the twenty historic buildings have been restored. The carriage house contains antique buggies and an award-winning rose garden.

Ramada Plaza Hotel

780 Bridgeport Avenue
Shelton, CT 06484
203-929-1500

Type of Lodging: Hotel
Room Rates: $69–$194. AAA and AARP discounts.

Pet Charges and Deposits: None.

Pet Policy: Small pets only.

Amenities: Extended cable TV, movies (fee), video games, voice mail, irons, hair dryers, heated pool, sauna, exercise room, coin laundry, conference facilities, administrative services, free newspaper, restaurant, cocktails, radios, coffee makers, data port/modem telephones, some refrigerators, some microwaves, 7 stories, interior corridors.

Rated: 3 Paws — 155 rooms.

Ramada Plaza Hotel is a wonderful, slightly quirky place, with art-deco lobby décor, lots of amenities, and fine, spacious rooms. This is certainly one of the nicer Ramada units we've seen in New England. In Bridgeport, make sure you see the Barnum Museum, which celebrates the life and times of the 19th century's greatest showman. The three story museum has three themes—Barnum the Man, Barnum's Bridgeport, and Showman to the World. Bridgeport's Discovery Museum contains art displays and interactive art and science exhibits. Bridgeport was a New England whaling town that gave way to industry when the railroad came to the area.

Residence Inn by Marriott

1001 Bridgeport Avenue
Shelton, CT 06484
203-926-9000

Type of Lodging: Suite hotel
Room Rates: $189–$299. AAA and AARP discounts.

Pet Charges and Deposits: $350 per stay.

Pet Policy: All Pets Welcome.

Amenities: Extended cable TV, movies, voice mail, safes (fee), irons, hair dryers, outdoor pool, whirlpool, sports court, coin laundry, meeting rooms, health club adjacent, radios, coffee makers, data port/modem telephones, refrigerators, microwaves, 2 stories, exterior corridors.

Rated: 3 Paws — 96 suites.

Residence Inn has done it with style—again. The apartment units in this wonderful establishment are very large, and some have lofts. All of the suites come with kitchen, 24 of them are two-bedroom units, and they're all up to the high standards you've come to expect when the name Marriott is on the marquis. New Haven, not far from Shelton, is home to Yale University and its plethora of libraries, art galleries, and ivy-covered buildings. Shelton's smaller twin city, Derby, is home to the Osborne Homestead Museum, encompassing the estate of turn-of-the-20th-century industrialist Francis Osborne Kellogg. The Colonial Revival residence contains American and European period pieces, formal gardens, a rock garden, and ornamental shrubs. The Kellogg Environmental Center features exhibits, naturalist programs, and nature trails.

Hilton Southbury

1284 Strongtown Road
Southbury, CT 06488
203-598-7600

Type of Lodging: Hotel
Room Rates: $104–$130. AAA and AARP discounts.
Pet Charges and Deposits: $100 deposit.
Pet Policy: First floor rooms only. Small pets only.
Amenities: Cable TV, movies (fee), dual phone lines, voice mail, irons, hair dryers, heated pool, whirlpool, sauna, exercise room, area transportation, valet laundry, conference facilities, restaurant, cocktails, radios, coffee makers, data port/modem telephones, some VCRs (fee), some refrigerators (fee), some microwaves (fee), 3 stories, interior corridors.
Rated: 3 Paws — 198 units, including rooms and some suites.

Hilton Southbury, a low-rise place for a Hilton, has wonderfully decorated public areas, and spacious, clean, first-rate rooms. There's a stunning proliferation of welcome amenities, and the prices ensure that you receive good value. Southbury, between Danbury and Waterbury in western Connecticut, is at the south end of the Litchfield Hills, an area of beautiful foothills, forests, and inland waterways. Paugussett State Forest and Kettletown State Park are in the immediate vicinity; Southford Falls State Park and Naugatuck State Forest are less than twenty miles away. You'll find cross-country and even some alpine skiing just north of the Woodbury area, and, since everything is manageably small in Connecticut, you'll find Bridgeport and New Haven less than an hour-and-a-half away.

Fairfield Inn–Stamford

135 Harvard Avenue
Stamford, CT 06902
203-357-7100

Type of Lodging: Motel
Room Rates: $75–$115.
Pet Charges and Deposits: None.
Pet Policy: Small pets only.
Amenities: Extended cable TV, voice mail, irons, hair dryers, heated pool, exercise room, game room, coin laundry, meeting rooms, data port/modem telephones, radios, some refrigerators (fee), some microwaves (fee), 8 stories, interior corridors.
Rated: 3 Paws — 158 rooms. Newly renovated, December, 2000.

Brand-new-out-of-the-box renovated Fairfield Inn is a wonderful, affordable, crisp, fresh choice when you're in Stamford. Rooms are capacious and inviting, spotlessly clean, and comfortable. The Bartlett Arboretum contains 63 acres of ecology trails, a swamp walk, display greenhouses, and collections of azaleas, rhododendrons, dwarf conifers, and wildflowers. The Whitney Museum of American Art—Fairfield County, a branch of the Whitney Museum of American Art in New York City, sponsors five major exhibitions a year. Stamford is less than an hour's easy drive from New York City, much less to White Plains.

Holiday Inn Select

700 Main Street
Stamford, CT 06901
203-358-8400

Type of Lodging: Motor Inn

Room Rates: $215, some suites, $350–$400. AAA and AARP discounts.

Pet Charges and Deposits: $75 per day, $75 deposit.

Pet Policy: All Pets Welcome.

Amenities: Cable TV, movies (fee), voice mail, irons, hair dryers, heated pool, exercise room, gift shop, coin laundry, conference facilities, administrative services, PC, fax, restaurant, cocktails, radios, coffee makers, data port/modem telephones, some refrigerators (fee), 10 stories, interior corridors.

Rated: 3 Paws — 383 units, including rooms and suites.

Holiday Inn Select is an impressive choice of lodgings in Stamford, the closest Connecticut city to the Big Apple. As you enter, you come into a spacious atrium multi-level lobby. The restaurant and pool areas face onto a flat level water screen. Rooms are capacious and beautifully furnished, and a plethora of amenities make your stay even more pleasurable. The Stamford Museum and Nature Center—118 acres—includes nature trails, a boardwalk, a pond exhibit, and a working farm. Kids can climb, slide, and crawl on equipment designed to imitate animals' habitats at Nature's Playground. There's a museum, a planetarium, art and nature galleries, and a lake with waterfowl and picnic areas. The magnificent First Presbyterian Church contains abstract colored-glass windows and a walk of more than 100 stones depicting the history of religion from the time of Abraham and Moses.

Days Inn

395 Winsted Road
Torrington, CT 06790
860-496-8808

Type of Lodging: Motel

Room Rates: $69–$99, some whirlpool units, $125–$145, including Continental breakfast. AAA and AARP discounts.

Pet Charges and Deposits: $15 per day per pet.

Pet Policy: All Pets Welcome.

Amenities: Extended cable TV, movies, hair dryers, free newspaper, outdoor pool, restaurant adjacent, radios, data port/modem telephones, some refrigerators, some microwaves, 2 stories, exterior corridors.

Rated: 2 Paws — 70 rooms.

Days Inn-Torrington is a fine budget-range property with significant upscale amenities, clean, well-appointed rooms, and a pet-friendly philosophy. After Israel Coe started making brass kettles in 1835, Torrington became an international producer and exporter of brass products. One of the state's largest commercial centers, Torrington still ranks high in the manufacture of ball bearings, machinery, roller skates, and woolens. The Hotchkiss-Fyler House is a Victorian mansion, which contains glassware, porcelain, Oriental carpets, and paintings by Connecticut artists. Torrington lies in the scenic and outdoors-enjoyable Litchfield Hills.

House on the Hill

92 Woodlawn Terrace
Waterbury, CT 06710
203-757-9901

Type of Lodging: Historic Bed & Breakfast

Room Rates: $110–$185, including full breakfast.

Pet Charges and Deposits: None.

Pet Policy: Small pets only.

Amenities: Radios, coffee makers, data port/modem telephones, smoke free premises, some refrigerators, some microwaves, 3 stories, interior corridors.

Rated: 3 Paws — 4 rooms.

The House on the Hill is a charming 1888 Victorian perched, as the name says, on a hill half a mile northeast of the city center. The owner-operator has traveled the world, and the house is filled with eclectic collections from his world travels. It's situated in a quiet residential neighborhood, and everyone involve does their very best to insure that your stay is memorable. In 1686, two scouts reported that the Waterbury townsite was so poor it could accommodate no more than 30 families. Wrong. Waterbury became one of the world's greatest brass centers, and it's somewhat larger than 30 families today. Waterbury is just east of the Litchfield Hills, and is surrounded by lakes, reservoirs, ponds, and forest. Mountains Unlimited offers white water rafting trips. The Green on West Main Street contains several war memorials, 18×16-foot "mansion houses" of the original settlers, and castle-like St. John's Episcopal Church. And the Italian-Renaissance style Church of the Immaculate Conception surrounds the Green.

Sheraton Waterbury Hotel

3580 East Main Street
Waterbury, CT 06705
203-573-1000

Type of Lodging: Hotel

Room Rates: $125–$205. AAA discounts.

Pet Charges and Deposits: None.

Pet Policy: All Pets Welcome.

Amenities: Cable TV, movies (fee), voice mail, irons, hair dryers, heated pool, whirlpool, sauna, exercise room, racquetball court, gift shop, coin laundry, conference facilities, fax (fee), restaurant, cocktails, radios, data port/modem telephones, coffee makers, some refrigerators (fee), some microwaves (fee), 4 stories, interior corridors.

Rated: 3 Paws — 279 rooms.

Sheraton Waterbury is a premier property in the chain. When you enter, you walk into a tropical atrium with a lounge, many flowering plants, and a waterfall. Rooms run from medium to quite large, and they are invariably beautifully furnished and well-equipped. Waterbury's Mattatuck Museum, facing the Green, displays decorative arts and 18th and 19th century landscape and portrait paintings, as well as sculpture by American artists. One of the oddest and most interesting pieces of "furniture" is Charles Goodyear's rubber desk. Waterbury, in west central Connecticut, is equidistant from Danbury, Bridgeport, New Haven, Meriden, and Hartford, each of which is less than an hour away.

Maples Motel

1935 Boston Post Road
Westbrook, CT 06498
860-399-9345

Type of Lodging: Motel

Room Rates: $40–$85. AAA and AARP discounts.

Pet Charges and Deposits: None.

Pet Policy: All Pets Welcome.

Amenities: Extended cable TV, heated pool, data port/modem telephones, some coffee makers, some refrigerators, some microwaves, 1 story, exterior corridors.

Rated: 2 Paws — 18 rooms.

Maples Motel, a traditional, small, independently owned and run motel, is a charming property located amidst many trees. Cottage units are bright and modern. The motel units, somewhat older, have wonderfully nostalgic features. Rooms are large and furnishings are certainly adequate to afford you a comfortable stay. Westbrook was founded in 1648 and was the birthplace of David Bushnell, a Revolutionary War patriot who is credited with inventing the submarine. The Military Historians Museum contains one of the largest collections of military uniforms in the United States. Here you'll find medals, swords, women's uniforms, band uniforms, and military vehicles.

Sleep Inn

327 Ruby Road
Willington, CT 06279
860-684-1400

Type of Lodging: Motel

Room Rates: $75–$115, including Continental breakfast. AAA and AARP discounts.

Pet Charges and Deposits: $20 deposit.

Pet Policy: All Pets Welcome.

Amenities: Cable TV, movies (fee), exercise room, meeting rooms, free local telephone calls, restaurant adjacent, radios, data port/modem telephones, some refrigerators, 3 stories, interior corridors.

Rated: 2 Paws — 62 rooms.

Sleep Inn, adjacent to a travel park rest area, is a well-priced, convenient, and comfortable rest stop between Hartford and Worcester, Massachusetts. Since it's part of the Choice Hotels International chain, you can rest assured that you will be 100% satisfied. Willington is in the northeast quadrant of the state, about halfway between Hartford and Worcester, Massachusetts. It's one of a trio of communities of the same name—East Willington, West Willington, and plain old Willington. Nearby, you'll find several state parks and forests for pet walking, including Nye Holman and Natchaug State Forests and Bolton Notch and Mansfield Hollow State Parks.

MAINE

Nickname: Pine Tree State
Population: 1,274,923 (40th)
Area: 35,385 sq. miles (39th)
Climate: Southern interior and coastal influenced by air masses from south and west; harsh in north climate; over 100 inches of snow in winter
Capital: Augusta
Entered Union: March 15, 1820 (23rd)
Motto: *Dirigo* (I direct)
Song: State of Maine Song

Flower: White pine cone and tassel
Tree: Eastern white pine
Bird: Chickadee
Famous "Down Easters": L.L. Bean, James G. Blaine, Cyrus H. K. Curtis, Claire Keenan Gorman, Hannibal Hamlin, Stephen King, Henry Wadsworth Longfellow, Edna St. Vincent Millay, George Mitchell, Edmund Muskie, Edward Arlington Robinson, Joan Benoit Samuelson, Kate Douglas Wiggin, Ben Ames Williams

History: Historians believe that John and Sebastian Cabot explored Maine's coast in 1498-1499. Algonquian peoples already inhabited the area. French settlers arrived at the St. Croix River in 1604, followed three years later by the English, who settled on the Kennebec River. Both settlements failed. Maine was made part of the Massachusetts Colony in 1691. It broke away from Massachusetts and became a separate state in 1820. Maine has always been emblematic of small town New England, indeed, "A'yuh!" is the state cliché. The always quiet corner of our northeast seems to have become a trifle more sinister with the tales from Stephen King.

Geography: Highest Point: 5,268 ft., Mount Katahdin. Lowest Point: Sea level, Atlantic Ocean. Time Zone: Eastern. Capital: Augusta. Major cities: Portland (65,000), Lewiston (40,000), Bangor (33,000), Augusta (25,000). The Appalachian Mountains extend through the "Down East" state (the most northeasterly state in the Continental U.S.). The western borders exhibit a rugged terrain. There are long sand beaches on the southern coast, while the northern coast is mostly rocky, with incredibly dramatic promontories, peninsulas, and fjords.

Tourist Information: 1-888-MAINE45. Website: www.visitmaine.com.

Recreation Areas
For You and Your Pet

All of these areas permit pets on a leash.

National Park

Acadia National Park: 41,409 acres. Camping, picnicking, hiking trails, boating, boat ramp, fishing, swimming, bicycle trails, winter sports, visitor center, food service.

State Recreation Areas

Allagash Wilderness Waterway: River and lakes in northwestern Maine. Camping, boating, boat ramp, boat rentals, fishing, swimming, winter sports.

Aroostook State Park: 577 acres, 4 miles south of Presque Isle on U.S. 1, then west and south via park road. Scenic, cross-country skiing, snowmobiling, camping, picnicking, hiking trails, boating, boat ramp, boat rentals, fishing, swimming, winter sports.

Bradbury Mountain State Park: 272 acres west of Freeport off U.S. 95 on State Route 136, then north on State Route 9. Camping, picnicking, hiking trails, winter sports.

Camden Hills State Park: 5,474 acres 2 miles north of Camden on U.S. 1. Scenic, Camping, picnicking, hiking trails, swimming, winter sports.

Cobscook Bay State Park: 868 acres 2 miles southeast of Dennysville off U.S. 1. Camping, picnicking, hiking trails, boating, boat ramp, fishing, winter sports.

Damariscotta Lake: 17 acres in Jefferson off State Route 32. Picnicking, fishing, swimming.

Ferry Beach: 117 acres in Saco on State Route 9. Nature trails, picnicking, hiking trails, swimming.

Grafton Notch: 3,112 acres 14 miles north of Bethel on State Route 26 between Upton and Newry. Picnicking, hiking trails, fishing.

Lake St. George: 360 acres 2 miles west of Liberty on State Route 3. Camping, picnicking, boating, boat ramp, boat rentals, fishing, swimming, winter sports.

Lamoine Beach: 55 acres 61/2 miles southeast of Ellsworth on State Route 184. Camping, picnicking, boating, boat ramp, fishing.

Lily Bay State Park: 924 acres 8 miles northeast of Greenville on Lily Bay Road. Camping, picnicking, boating, boat ramp, fishing, swimming, winter sports.

Mount Blue State Park: 1,273 acres (two areas) north of Weld on a gravel road. Camping, picnicking, hiking trails, boating, fishing, swimming, winter sports.

Peaks-Kenny State Park: 839 acres 6 miles north of Dover-Foxcroft on State Route 153. Camping, picnicking, hiking trails, boating, boat ramp, boat rentals, fishing, swimming.

Popham Beach State Park: 529 acres west of Popham Beach via State Route 209. Windsurfing, picnicking, fishing, swimming.

Rangeley Lake State Park: 691 acres southwest of Rangeley via State Route 17 on the south shore of Rangeley Lake. Camping, picnicking, boating, boat ramp, fishing, swimming, winter sports.

Range Ponds State Park: 750 acres in Poland off State Route 122. Picnicking, boating, boat ramp, fishing, swimming, winter sports.

Reid State Park: 768 acres 2 miles east of Georgetown on State Route 127. Picnicking, fishing, swimming, food service.

Roque Bluffs State Park: 275 acres 7 miles south of Machias off U.S. 1 on Roque Bluffs Road. Picnicking, fishing, swimming.

Swan Lake: 67 acres north of Swanville off State Route 141. Picnicking, fishing, swimming.

Warren Island State Park: 70 acres in Penobscot Bay. Camping, picnicking, fishing.

Other Notable Recreation Areas

Bigelow Preserve: 29,000 acres north of New Portland off State Route 27. Camping, picnicking, hiking trails, boating, fishing, swimming, winter sports.

Gero Island: 3,000 acres northwest of Millinocket off State Route 11. Ice fishing, Camping, picnicking, boating, boat ramp, fishing, swimming, winter sports.

Scraggly Lake: 10,000 acres off Grand Lake Road northwest of Mount Chase. Camping, picnicking, hiking trails, boating, boat ramp, fishing, swimming, visitor center.

Auburn Inn

1777 Washington Street
Auburn, ME 04210
207-777-1777

Type of Lodging: Motor Inn

Room Rates: $70–$150, including Continental breakfast. AAA and AARP discounts.

Pet Charges and Deposits: None.

Pet Policy: All Pets Welcome.

Amenities: Cable TV, hair dryers, irons, some honor bars, seasonal outdoor swimming pool, valet and coin laundry, meeting rooms, restaurant, radios, coffee makers, data port/modem telephones, some refrigerators (fee), some VCRs (fee), 2 stories, exterior corridors.

Rated: 2 Paws — 114 units including rooms and some suites.

You'll find newly renovated, inviting guest rooms and a 24-hour convenience gas station next door at friendly Auburn Inn. It's close to Bates College and golf courses, Shaker Village is 15 miles away, as is Oxford Speedway. Auburn was a famous shoe manufacturing center between 1830 and 1870. Auburn is on the Androscoggin River, thirty miles inland from its mouth. It adjoins the larger city of Lewiston, both of which offer fine outdoor activities. Great fishing can be found at Lake Auburn, three miles north of town.

Best Western Senator Inn & Spa

284 Western Avenue
Augusta, ME 04330
207-622-5804
www.senatorinn.com

Type of Lodging: Motor Inn

Room Rates: $82–$152, some suites, $152–$252, including full, cooked-to-order breakfast. AAA discounts.

Pet Charges and Deposits: $50 refundable deposit.

Pet Policy: All Pets Welcome.

Amenities: Extended cable TV, movies, voice mail, some hair dryers, heated pool, whirlpool, sauna, exercise room, massage (fee), nature trails, valet and coin laundry, meeting rooms, restaurant, radios, coffee makers, data port/modem telephones, some refrigerators, some microwaves (fee), 2 stories, interior/exterior corridors.

Rated: 3 Paws — 100 units, including rooms and suites.

Family-owned and operated Best Western Senator Inn & Spa features rooms ranging from standard to luxurious, some with working fireplace. Heated indoor and outdoor pool and a pet-friendly ambience complete the picture. It's conveniently located at I-95 and Western Avenue. Augusta, Maine's capital since 1827, differs from most Maine towns in that, although it straddles both sides of the Kennebec River, it is a single city, not twin cities. The 1829 State House contains interpretive wall plaques, battle flags, and portraits of Maine's most famous and honored personages—and it's free.

Motel 6

18 Edison Drive
August, ME 04330
207-622-0000

Type of Lodging: Motel
Room Rates: $40–$60. AARP discounts.
Pet Charges and Deposits: None.
Pet Policy: Small pets only.
Amenities: Cable TV, movies, restaurant adjacent, data port/modem telephones, some refrigerators, some microwaves, coin laundry, 2 stories, interior corridors.
Rated: 2 Paws — 69 units, including rooms and some suites

Accor's Augusta Motel 6 property is conveniently situated off I-95 Exit 30 in Augusta's commercial district. Rooms are comfortable and, as always, a very good bargain. The Maine State Museum, in the State House complex, exhibits Maine's prehistory, it's social history, and a salute to its industry. The museum's "Made in Maine" exhibit features a water-powered woodworking mill, a two-story textile factory, and more than 1,500 Maine-made objects. You'll find one of America's oldest locomotives, as well as Native American basketry. At the Children's Museum, children get to play many different roles at a simulated diner, grocery store, post office, film studio, and live stage. It's great fun!

Travelodge Hotel

390 Western Avenue
Augusta, ME 04330
207-622-6371

Type of Lodging: Motor Inn
Room Rates: $59–$169, suites $150–$230, including Continental breakfast. AAA and AARP discounts.
Pet Charges and Deposits: None.
Pet Policy: All Pets Welcome.
Amenities: Cable TV, movies, outdoor pool, coin laundry, restaurant, cocktails, free appetizers in Margarita's Restaurant & Lounge, free admission to "Fort Western," free local calls, children under 18 stay free in parents' room, radios, coffee makers, data port/modem telephones, some refrigerators, some microwaves, 2 stories, exterior corridors.
Rated: 2 Paws — 128 units, including rooms and some suites.

Off I-95's Exit 30B, Travelodge is a convenient, comfortable lodging when you're visiting Maine's capital. The Plymouth Colony founded a trading post in August in 1628. Among its founders were John Alden and Captain Miles Standish, immortalized by Henry Wadsworth Longfellow. In 1754, Fort Western—the oldest surviving wooden fort in New England, was established on the east bank of the Kennebec River. Costumed interpreters help guide and entertain you, with depictions of the fort's military activity, it's early life, its stores, and even its residential areas.

Best Western White House Inn

155 Littlefield Avenue
Bangor, ME 04401
207-862-3737

Type of Lodging: Motel

Room Rates: $60–$110, including Continental breakfast. AAA and AARP discounts.

Pet Charges and Deposits: None.

Pet Policy: All Pets Welcome.

Amenities: Extended cable TV, irons, hair dryers, outdoor heated pool, sauna, coin laundry, restaurant & cocktails adjacent, radios, coffee makers, data port/modem telephones, refrigerators, some VCRs (fee), 3 stories, exterior/interior corridors.

Rated: 3 Paws — 65 rooms.

Best Western White House Inn is situated in a rural location—Exit 44 off the I-95—bordering a truck stop diner—a slice of an earlier age of Americana. There are 30 acres of fields behind the motel—plenty of room to roam for you and your pet. It's only five miles to downtown Bangor, 46 miles to Acadia National Park, and near Route 2 to Vermont. The fall foliage is nothing short of stunning. One of our nation's most popular National Parks, Acadia National Park, situated on Mount Desert Island, occupies more than 50 square miles of fabulous ocean and mountain scenery. This is the penultimate example of New England's "stern and rockbound coast." Some 500 species of wildflowers grow in the park, and most of the areas 15 peaks are bare at their summit, due to countless centuries of erosion.

Country Inn At The Mall

936 Stillwater Avenue
Bangor, ME 04401
207-941-0200

Type of Lodging: Motel

Room Rates: $45–$80. AAA and AARP discounts.

Pet Charges and Deposits: None.

Pet Policy: Small pets only.

Amenities: Cable TV, movies, valet laundry, meeting rooms, restaurant adjacent, data port/modem telephones, some VCRs (fee), 2 stories, interior corridors.

Rated: 2 Paws — 96 rooms.

Located at Exit 49 to the I-95, Country Inn is set back from the highway in a quiet area, yet very close to a nearby mall. Bangor's standout attraction is the Cole Land Transportation Museum, which contains more than 200 vehicles from wagons, to automobiles, to 18-wheeler trucks. Here you'll find antique RV's, motorcycles, snowplows, logging trucks, fire trucks, a locomotive, and a railroad station, even a 72-foot covered bridge from the 1840's. The Maine State Memorial is nearby.

Holiday Inn–Bangor

404 Odlin Road
Bangor, ME 04401
207-947-0101

Type of Lodging: Hotel

Room Rates: $90–$95. AAA and AARP discounts.

Pet Charges and Deposits: None.

Pet Policy: All Pets Welcome.

Amenities: Extended cable TV, movies (fee), irons, hair dryers, two pools (one heated, one indoor), whirlpool, sauna, health club adjacent, coin laundry, conference facilities, restaurant, cocktails, radios, coffee makers, data port/modem telephones, some refrigerators (fee), some microwaves (fee), 3 stories, interior corridors.

Rated: 3 Paws — 207 rooms.

The Holiday Inn-Bangor, at exit 45B off the I-95, at the junction of I-395 and Odlin Road, features restful courtyard and pool areas, with luxurious guest units and public areas. There are some smaller guest units, but most are of substantial size. As expected in any Holiday Inn, the décor is modern, comfortable, and inviting. The Maine State Memorial, adjacent to the outstanding Cole Land Transportation Museum, features hundred of military artifacts, from the Civil War to World War II. A full-size bronze statute of a jeep and driver sits on the front lawn. You'll also find more than 2,000 early Maine photographs here.

Ramada Inn

357 Odlin Road
Bangor, Maine
207-947-6961

Type of Lodging: Motor Inn

Room Rates: $59–$114. AAA and AARP discounts.

Pet Charges and Deposits: None.

Pet Policy: All Pets Welcome.

Amenities: Extended cable TV, movies (fee), hair dryers, heated pool, exercise room, valet laundry, meeting rooms, administrative services, restaurant, cocktails, radios, data port/modem telephones, some refrigerators, some microwaves, 2 stories, interior corridors.

Rated: 2 Paws — 115 rooms.

Ramada Inn boasts, "We'll do our personal best to exceed your expectations." The Bangor venue of this chain, located at the junction of I-395 and Odlin Road, is a comfortable lodging with friendly, personable staff to look after your needs. Bangor, on the Penobscot River, is the principal retail, cultural, and business center for eastern and northern Maine. During the mid-to-late 19th century, Bangor became the leading lumber port of the world, and its harbor area became notorious as the Devil's Half-Acre because of uncontrolled drinking and gambling. There are changing exhibits of the city's past at the Bangor Historical Society Museum, an 1836 Greek Revival house at 159 Union Street.

❖ ❖ ❖ ❖ ❖

Balance Rock Inn 1903

21 Albert Meadow
Bar Harbor, ME 04609
207-288-2610
barhrbrinns@aol.com

Type of Lodging: Historic Bed & Breakfast

Room Rates: $125–$575, some suites, $195–$575, some whirlpool units, $125–$575, including full breakfast. AAA discounts.

Pet Charges and Deposits: None.

Pet Policy: All Pets Welcome.

Amenities: Extended cable TV, movies, irons, hair dryers, heated pool, steam baths, exercise room, afternoon tea, valet laundry, libations, VCRs, radios, data port / modem telephones, some refrigerators, some microwaves, 3-story turn-of-the-century mansion with interior and exterior corridors.

Rated: 5 Paws — 16 units, including rooms and suites.

The stellar 5-paw Balance Rock Inn is housed in a restored oceanfront mansion, replete with spectacular Bar Harbor views. Each unique room or suite pampers you with amenities like fireplaces, steam baths, and porches. There are sweeping ocean vistas from most rooms. The Balance Rock Inn is one of the historic Shore Path mansions down a quiet cul-de-sac near the heart of downtown Bar Harbor. Bar Harbor's location is unmatched anywhere in Maine. It's at the entrance to Acadia National Park on Mount Desert Island and, by the turn of the 20th century, had become the summer playground of the likes of J.P. Morgan, Joseph Pulitzer, and John D. Rockefeller, who owned "cottages" here.

Bar Harbor Inn

Newport Drive, Box 7
Bar Harbor, ME 04609
800-248-3351 • 207-288-3351

Type of Lodging: Resort
Room Rates: $95–$145, including Continental breakfast.
Pet Charges and Deposits: $15 per day per pet.
Pet Policy: Manager's prior approval required.
Amenities: Extended cable TV, movies, heated pool, whirlpool, valet laundry, conference facilities, fax, restaurant, cocktails, data port/modem telephones, some refrigerators, some microwaves, 2-3 stories, interior corridors.
Rated: 4 Paws — 153 rooms.

The Bar Harbor Inn, at the head of picturesque Frenchman Bay, is a full service oceanfront resort. Noted for exceptional accommodations, service that attends to every need, and elegant dining, the Bar Harbor Inn has long been the destination of choice for discriminating visitors to Bar Harbor, Mount Desert Island, and Acadia National Park. Three separate and distinctively different resort accommodations are available: The Oceanfront Lodge and the Newport Motel are contemporary in design and offer comfortable queen- and king-sized beds and ocean views. The Newport Building houses 38 comfortable guest rooms, all with private patios or balconies. Stroll or relax on the spacious grounds where flower gardens explode with color. Sail on Frenchman Bay aboard the Natalie Todd, docked at the private pier, or visit shops, galleries, or museums.

Best Western Inn

State Route 3 (P.O. Box 1127)
Bar Harbor, ME 04609
207-288-5823

Type of Lodging: Motel
Room Rates: $74–$110, including Continental breakfast. AAA and AARP discounts.
Pet Charges and Deposits: None.
Pet Policy: Small pets only.
Amenities: Cable TV, movies, heated pool, coin laundry, free local telephone calls, data port/modem telephones, some refrigerators, 1 story, exterior corridors, at-door parking.
Rated: 2 Paws — 70 rooms.

Situated in a quiet rural area on State Route 3, Best Western Inn affords a convenient, reasonably priced alternative to the luxurious "other part" of Bar Harbor, that part of the town which fell upon hard times in the early-to-mid 20th century. Income taxes, World War I, and the Great Depression decimated the leisure class by the 1930's, and in 1947, a great fire destroyed 237 homes, mostly estates, and nearly 17,200 acres. Today, the town has made a comeback, in part due to its proximity to Acadia National Park. Whale-watching cruises, sailing charters, and working lobster boat excursions compete with bus ferries offering high-speed catamaran car and passenger service from Bar Harbor to Yarmouth, Nova Scotia, between May and October.

The Ledgelawn Inn

66 Mount Desert Street
Bar Harbor, ME 04609
207-288-4596
barhbrinns@aol.com

Type of Lodging: Historic Bed & Breakfast

Room Rates: $75–$295, some suites, $195–$295, some whirlpool units, $75–$295, including full breakfast. AAA and AARP discounts.

Pet Charges and Deposits: Extra charge per day (inquire).

Pet Policy: All Pets Welcome.

Amenities: Extended cable TV, movies, voice mail, irons, heated pool, libations, radios, data port/modem telephones, 3 stories (no elevator), interior/exterior corridors, the inn consists of a 1904 mansion and carriage house.

Rated: 4 Paws — 33 units, including rooms and some suites.

The Ledgelawn Inn is another of those wonderfully restored turn-of-the-20th century mansions in the center of elegant Bar Harbor. One of the town's last remaining "grand ladies of yesteryear," the newly renovated Inn and Carriage House feature beautifully decorated and furnished rooms. Each of these sumptuous rooms has a private bath, TV and telephone. Some have working fireplaces, sauna baths, and porches. Luxury, pampering, and comfort surround you.

Primrose Inn

73 Mount Desert Street
Bar Harbor, ME 04609
207-288-4031

Type of Lodging: Historic Bed & Breakfast

Room Rates: $75–$175, including full breakfast.

Pet Charges and Deposits: None.

Pet Policy: Dogs only, sorry, no cats. Designated rooms only.

Amenities: Extended cable TV, radios, some coffee makers, data port/modem telephones, some VCRs, some refrigerators, some microwaves, 2 stories, interior corridors, smoke free premises.

Rated: 3 Paws — 15 units, including rooms and some suites

Yet another prize property, this striking 1878 Victorian mansion is tastefully decorated and furnished with period antiques or reproductions. There are some units with whirlpool bath, to increase your comfort. While the first place you'll want to visit is Acadia National Park, the Bar Harbor Oceanarium is a unique aquarium combining the Maine Lobster Museum and a working lobster hatchery. You'll see demonstrations on how lobster traps are made, and you'll get to board a working lobster boat. Bar Harbor's Museum of Natural History displays dioramas of mounted mammals and birds, and a hands-on whale skeleton that you can assemble and disassemble. There are numerous whale watching trips leaving the harbor daily.

Holiday Inn Bath / Brunswick

139 Richardson Street
Bath, ME 04530
207-443-9741

Type of Lodging: Motor Inn

Room Rates: $65–$145. AAA and AARP discounts.

Pet Charges and Deposits: None.

Pet Policy: All Pets Welcome.

Amenities: Extended cable TV, movies (fee), dual phone lines, voice mail, irons, hair dryers, heated pool, whirlpool, sauna, exercise room, valet laundry, meeting rooms, restaurant, radios, coffee makers, data port/modem telephones, refrigerators, microwaves, 4 stories, interior corridors.

Rated: 3 Paws — 141 rooms.

Holiday Inn Bath / Brunswick, recently renovated, caters to both business travelers and tourists. Bath's main (Maine?) attraction is its Maritime Museum, a 10-acre site located on a Nineteenth century shipyard where large wooden sailing ships were built. The shipyard is home to a Boat Shop. Visitors can watch the building process and visit five of the original shipyard buildings. You can board seagoing vessels when they dock at the site. Bath, on the west bank of the Kennebec River, has been an active shipbuilding center since the early 1600's. Nuclear naval vessels and large merchant ships are still being built at the Bath Iron Works.

Belfast Bay Meadows Inn

192 Northport Avenue (U.S. 1)
Belfast, ME 04915
207-338-5715
bbmi@baymeadowsinn.com

Type of Lodging: Country Inn

Room Rates: $80–$190, including full breakfast. AAA discounts.

Pet Charges and Deposits: $15 per day per pet.

Pet Policy: All Pets Welcome.

Amenities: Playground, radios, some refrigerators, data port/modem telephones, 2 stories, interior and exterior corridors, Victorian and contemporary rooms, smoke free premises.

Rated: 3 Paws — 20 rooms.

The grounds of Belfast Bay Meadows Inn extend out to Penobscot Bay—lots of room for you and your pet to roam. The complimentary breakfast here includes lobster omelet and strawberry pancakes—yummy! Belfast, formerly a wealthy shipbuilding center, features a multitude of restored Federal and early Victorian homes built by former sea merchants. Fall foliage is resplendent, and Belfast has, of late, become quite an artists', artisans', and writers' colony. The Belfast Maskers theater group gives year-round productions.

Belfast Harbor Inn

½ mile from Junction of U.S. 1 and State
 Route 3 (RR5, Box 5230)
Belfast, ME 04915
207-338-2740
stay@belfastharborinn.com

Type of Lodging:

Room Rates: $45–$124, including
Continental breakfast. AAA and AARP
discounts.

Pet Charges and Deposits: $10 per day
per pet.

Pet Policy: All Pets Welcome.

Amenities: Cable TV, free local calls, data
port/modem telephones, outdoor pool,
meeting and banquet facilities, restaurant
adjacent, 2 stories, interior/exterior corridors.

Rated: 2 Paws — 61 rooms.

Its advertisement proclaims, "Escape to the
Heart of Coastal Maine," and the ad is accurate. Gorgeous ground—more than
ample for the friskiest pet—lead down to
Penobscot Bay. All rooms are either ocean
view or poolside, and there are greenswards
everywhere. Belfast is a town where you'd
want to stroll—and walking tour brochures
are available from the Chamber of Com-
merce at #1 Main Street. The Belfast &
Moosehead Lake Railroad was chartered in
1867. At Unity Station (in nearby Unity),
an original Armstrong turntable demonstrates the history of locomotives. A 1913
Swedish steam locomotive takes passengers
on a two-hour scenic and historic tour of the
area.

The Briar Lea Inn & Restaurant

150 Mayville Road
Bethel, ME 04217
207-824-4717

Type of Lodging: Historic Country Inn

Room Rates: $54–$114.

Pet Charges and Deposits: None.

Pet Policy: All Pets Welcome. Advance
reservations required.

Amenities: Extended cable TV, cross-
country skiing, data port/modem telephones, restaurant, smoke-free premises,
3 stories (no elevator), interior corridors.

Rated: 3 Paws — 6 rooms.

The Briar Lea is located in a renovated
1855 farmhouse, decorated with country-
themed antiques. Guest rooms still have the
original hardwood floors. Cross-country
skiing is nearby. Bethel, settled in 1774 as
Sudbury-Canada, is one of the oldest villages in northwestern Maine. It did not de-
velop rapidly. By 1781, it had only ten
families. Ski Mount Abram, a noted winter
sports area, is 5 miles south of the town on
U.S. 2. Bethel is less than 15 miles from the
New Hampshire border. You'll truly enjoy
strolling through the Broad Street Historic
District and Bethel Hill Village.

The Inn at Rostay

186 Mayville Road
Bethel, ME 04217
207-824-3111

Type of Lodging: Motel

Room Rates: $40–$115.

Pet Charges and Deposits: $10 per day per pet.

Pet Policy: All Pets Welcome.

Amenities: Extended cable TV, coin laundry, restaurant, data port/modem telephones, some VCRs, some refrigerators, some microwaves, 1 story, exterior corridors.

Rated: 2 Paws — 18 rooms.

The Inn at Rostay is situated in Bethel's ski country, near Mount Abram and the Sunday River. There are two buildings: the older building features cozy, individually decorated rooms, while the newer building houses standard motel units. Bethel lies along a stretch of the Androscoggin River, near the Mahoosuc and White Mountains. Swimming, camping, bicycling, boating, fishing, and rock hounding are among summer activities you'll find here. White Mountain National Forest in New Hampshire is an easy drive.

L'Auberge Country Inn

22 Mill Hill Road
Bethel, ME 04w217
207-824-2774

Type of Lodging: Historic Country Inn

Room Rates: $80–$135, some suites, $120–$135. AAA discounts.

Pet Charges and Deposits: None.

Pet Policy: All Pets Welcome. Advance reservations required.

Amenities: No TVs, smoke-free premises, radios, 2 stories, interior corridors.

Rated: 3 Paws — 6 rooms.

L'Auberge is a very attractive country inn dating from the mid-Nineteenth century. Spacious rooms, mountain views, and a five acre parcel of property where you and your pet can roam to your hearts' content, completes a restful, bucolic picture. One of the guest rooms was a movie theater in the silent movie era. The Bethel Historical Society's Dr. Moses Mason House Museum and Regional History Center is a nine-room house built in 1813, which was the home of the U.S. Congressman from Maine, 1833-1837. Numerous murals depict seascapes and foliage, and there are changing exhibits about northern New England history and culture.

Hillside Acres Cabins & Motel

Adams Pond Road (P.O. Box 300)
Boothbay, ME 04537
207-633-3411

Type of Lodging: Cabins and Motel

Room Rates: $45–$80.

Pet Charges and Deposits: None.

Pet Policy: All Pets Welcome. Pets in cabins only.

Amenities: Cable TV, outdoor pool, some data port/modem telephones, some coffee makers, some refrigerators (fee), some microwaves, 1-2 stories, interior/exterior corridors.

Rated: 2 Paws — 14 units, including rooms and efficiencies.

Individual rustic cabins and standard motel units are a feature of Hillside Acres. Boothbay and its adjacent Boothbay Harbor retain the atmosphere of a typical old New England fishing village. Fishing boats are moored alongside wharves that follow quiet, winding village streets. Boothbay Railway Village is a turn-of-the Twentieth century Maine village containing railroad artifacts, a general store, little red schoolhouse, circa 1847 Town Hall, and a ride on a narrow gauge, coal-fired steam engine.

Kenniston Hill Inn

P.O. Box 125 (10 miles south on State
* Route 27)*
Boothbay, ME 04537
207-633-2159

Type of Lodging: Historic Bed & Breakfast

Room Rates: $75–$135, including breakfast. AAA discounts.

Pet Charges and Deposits: None.

Pet Policy: All Pets Welcome (resident pet on premises).

Amenities: No TVs, no phones, smoke-free premises, radios, 2 stories, interior/exterior corridors.

Rated: 3 Paws — Ten rooms (five with fireplace).

Kenniston Hill Inn was built as an inn in 1786 and is the oldest lodging in Boothbay. It features attractive landscaped grounds. Five of the units have fireplaces for added ambience and comfort. Artists and yachtsmen started vacationing in Boothbay Harbor in the early 1900's and the area transitioned from shipping center to resort area. Nationally known attorney Richard D. Gorman spent his teen summers working the tourist centers here, as did numerous other young men and women, who went on to successful careers throughout the country, always longing to return for summers in Boothbay Harbor. River cruises, ocean cruises, whale watches, and deep sea fishing trips leave local piers each day.

White Anchor Motel

RR 1, Box 438
(7½ miles south on State Route 27)
Boothbay, ME 04537
207-633-3788

Type of Lodging: Motel

Room Rates: $40–$80, including Continental breakfast. AAA discounts.

Pet Charges and Deposits: Credit card refundable deposit.

Pet Policy: All Pets Welcome.

Amenities: Extended cable TV, free local telephone calls, some data port/modem telephones, 2 stories, interior/exterior corridors.

Rated: 2 Paws — 29 rooms.

You'll find an assortment of unit styles at White Anchor Motel, ranging from quite small, cozy rooms, to quieter rooms in the rear portion of the property. Boothbay Harbor's waterfront affords you a look at the Maine coast's seafaring history and nautical activities. Cap'n Fish's Whale Watching and Scenic Nature Cruises offer a variety of sightseeing trips along the Maine Coast.

The Pines Motel

30 Sunset Road
Boothbay Harbor, ME 04538
207-633-4555

Type of Lodging: Motel

Room Rates: $55–$95, including Continental breakfast. AAA discounts.

Pet Charges and Deposits: None.

Pet Policy: All Pets Welcome. Advance reservations required.

Amenities: Extended cable TV, heated pool, tennis court, playground, free local telephone calls, data port/modem telephones, refrigerators, 1 story, exterior corridors.

Rated: 2 Paws — 30 rooms.

The Pines Motel is located on spacious grounds on the east side of Boothbay Harbor. Its location is quiet and restful. Boothbay Harbor's Hendricks Hill Museum contains a restored early 19th century house, a woodworking building, early fishing boats, and tools from the ice harvesting industry. The Kenneth E. Stoddard Shell Museum boasts several thousands of shells in wood-and-glass cases. Its uniqueness is underlined by the fact that it is housed in a building inside a covered bridge.

Viking Motor Inn

287 Bath Road
Brunswick, ME 04011
207-729-6661

Type of Lodging: Motel

Room Rates: $46–$96. AAA and AARP discounts.

Pet Charges and Deposits: $5 per day per pet.

Pet Policy: All Pets Welcome.

Amenities: Extended cable TV, above-ground pool with deck, free local telephone calls, radios, data port/modem telephones, some refrigerators, some microwaves, 1 story, interior/exterior corridors.

Rated: 2 Paws — 28 rooms.

The Viking Inn as a small motel with units of varying sizes. It's centrally located, near outlet shopping (L.L. Bean), beaches, museums, antiques, Bowdoin College, and the Naval Air Station. Brunswick is the chief city of eastern Casco Bay. Its industry began in the 1620's. Harriet Beecher Stowe's inspiration for *Uncle Tom's Cabin* came from a sermon delivered at Brunswick's First Parish Church. 110-acre Bowdoin College, home of the Maine State Music Theater, was established in 1794. Maine Street, 198 feet wide, is one of the broadest streets in New England. The Peary-MacMillan Arctic Museum has displays related to the two Arctic explorers as well as displays of life in the Arctic region.

Best Western Jed Prouty Motor Inn

State Route 15 (P.O. Box 826)
Bucksport, ME 04416
207-469-3113

Type of Lodging: Motel

Room Rates: $69–$124. AARP discounts.

Pet Charges and Deposits: None.

Pet Policy: Small pets only.

Amenities: Extended cable TV, restaurant adjacent, radios, data port/modem telephones, 4 stories, interior corridors.

Rated: 2 Paws — 41 rooms.

The Best Western property borders the Penobscot River. Many of the large, comfortable guest units have wonderful views of historic Fort Knox and the Bucksport Harbor. L'Ermitage is an historical French restaurant housed in a modest 19th century home with a Colonial atmosphere. The Northeast Historic Film Museum, housed in a renovated 1916 movie theater, displays the history of movie going in northern New England. You'll find an outstanding collection of historic films, as well as projectors, ticket machines, and popcorn machines,

Calais Motor Inn

293 Main Street
Calais, ME 04619
207-454-7111

Type of Lodging: Motor Inn
Room Rates: $59–$84. AAA discounts.
Pet Charges and Deposits: None.
Pet Policy: All Pets Welcome.
Amenities: Extended cable TV, heated pool, whirlpool, sauna, exercise room, game room, free local telephone calls, restaurant, cocktails, radios, data port/modem telephones, some refrigerators, some microwaves, 2 stories, interior/exterior corridors.
Rated: 2 Paws — 70 rooms.

Calais Motor Inn has a main building and two annex sections. Rooms are comfortable, and some have at-door parking. The pool area is particularly attractive. Calais, about as far east as you can go in the "Down East" state, is on the west bank of Passamaquoddy Bay, at the mouth of the St. Croix River. It is right on the Canadian border, and the International Bridge between Calais and St. Stephen, New Brunswick, makes Calais a truly international (albeit small) city. The Holmes Cottage Museum, a two-story Cape Cod-style structure built in 1804, housed the practices of several country doctors. Displays of medical and dental equipment abound.

International Motel

276 Main Street
Calais, ME 04619
207-454-7515

Type of Lodging: Motel
Room Rates: $49–$79, some suites and whirlpool units, $79–$124. AAA and AARP discounts.
Pet Charges and Deposits: None.
Pet Policy: Small pets only.
Amenities: Cable TV, some hair dryers, free local telephone calls, restaurant adjacent, data port/modem telephones, coffee makers, some refrigerators, 2 stories, exterior corridors.
Rated: 2 Paws — 61 units, including rooms and some suites.

The International Motel has older units, which are quite comfortable, and newer units, which are quite modern, and which overlook the St. Croix River. Calais was first settled nearly 400 years ago, in 1604, and became an important lumbering and ship-building center. The section of US Highway 1 between Calais and Bar Harbor is especially scenic: look out for nesting eagles. Moosehorn National Wildlife Refuge is a 24,500 acre migratory bird refuge. There are nature and hiking trails in summer, and cross-country skiing and snowshoeing in winter.

Camden Harbour Inn

83 Bayview Street
Camden, ME 04843
207-236-4200

Type of Lodging: Historic Bed & Breakfast

Room Rates: $90–$260 including full breakfast.

Pet Charges and Deposits: $20 per day per pet.

Pet Policy: Dogs only, sorry, no cats.

Amenities: Hair dryers, libations, radios, data port/modem telephones, some refrigerators, 3 stories (no elevator), interior corridors.

Rated: 3 Paws — 22 rooms.

Camden Harbour Inn has been doing business at the same location since 1874. Some of its rooms have working fireplaces, and all are furnished and decorated in a most attractive period fashion. There are views of the surrounding hills or of Penobscot Bay. Camden, the jewel of the Maine coast, is a year-round seaside resort town, whose beauty has attracted many writers, artists, and artisans, including Edna St. Vincent Millay. The toboggan run at Camden Snow Bowl is open to the public. Summer highlights include schooner races, art shows, folk festivals, lobster festivals, concerts, and antique shows. The Mary Meeker Cramer Museum, in the Old Conway House, exhibits ship models, quilts, costumes, and other Maine memorabilia.

Inn by the Sea

40 Bowery Beach Road
Cape Elizabeth, ME 04107
207-799-3134

Type of Lodging: Suite Motor Inn

Room Rates: $149–$549. AAA and AARP discounts.

Pet Charges and Deposits: None.

Pet Policy: Management requires advance notification at time of reservations.

Amenities: Extended cable TV, dual phone lines, voice mail, irons, hair dryers, some CD players, VCRs, heated pool, beach, swimming, lighted tennis courts, jogging, shuffleboard, volleyball, valet laundry, meeting rooms, restaurant, radios, coffee makers, data port/modem telephones, refrigerators, microwaves, smoke free premises, 2 stories, interior/exterior corridors, condominium suites, cottages.

Rated: 4 Paws — 43 units, consisting of rooms, cottages, and suites.

The Inn by the Sea overlooks the ocean and is set on meticulously landscaped grounds, with lush gardens throughout. The inn offers condominium-style units in the main house, or beach cottages. There are 43 units with kitchen, 18 two-bedroom units, and some suites. Captain John Smith named Cape Elizabeth in 1615 for Charles I's sister, Princess Elizabeth. The Cape has become a residential center for the greater Portland area. Portland Head Light, in Fort Williams Park, was first operated in 1791 under the authorization of President George Washington. It is one of the oldest continuously operated lighthouses in the country.

Caribou Inn & Convention Center

19 Maine Street
Caribou, ME 04736
207-498-3733

Type of Lodging: Motor Inn

Room Rates: $59–$94, some whirlpool units, $99–$124. AAA and AARP discounts.

Pet Charges and Deposits: None.

Pet Policy: All Pets Welcome.

Amenities: Extended cable TV, movies, voice mail, irons, hair dryers, heated pool, whirlpool, sauna, exercise room, gift shop, coin laundry, meeting rooms, free local telephone calls, restaurant, cocktails, radios, data port/modem telephones, refrigerators, 2 stories, interior corridors.

Rated: 3 Paws — 73 rooms, some with kitchen.

The Caribou Inn highlights a large, pleasant atrium pool area, and some units overlook the pool. Caribou Inn has a excellent exercise room, and its Greenhouse Restaurant is the premier restaurant in Caribou. The city is in the center of one of the largest potato-shipping areas in the world and is the source of 90% of Maine's potato crop. The Nylander Museum contains a very extensive collection of rocks, minerals, fossils, shells, marine specimens, and Native American artifacts, as well as an herb garden, wildflowers, butterflies, and mounted birds.

Pentagoet Inn

Main Street (P.O. Box 4)
Castine, ME 04421
207-326-8616

Type of Lodging: Historic Country Inn

Room Rates: $72–$152.

Pet Charges and Deposits: None.

Pet Policy: Designated rooms only. Management's advance approval required.

Amenities: No TVs, no telephones, restaurant, cocktails, 3 stories (no elevator), interior corridors, smoke free premises

Rated: 3 Paws — 16 rooms.

This wonderful, expressive property is located in the center of a small New England town. The main building is an 1894 Victorian Inn, and there are additional accommodations in the adjoining 200-year-old colonial home. Castine, strategically located, was, for two centuries, disputed by Native Americans, French, British, Dutch, and Americans. The training vessel *T/V State of Maine,* formerly the *USNS Tanner,* is a 500-foot long ship used by the Maine Maritime Academy. The Wilson Museum contains prehistoric items from around the world, as well as the Jon Perkins House, a pre-Revolutionary War structure.

Midway Motel

South Hiram Road (RR 1, Box 22)
Cornish, ME 04020
207-625-8835

Type of Lodging: Motel

Room Rates: $41–$72, some whirlpool units, $81–$94.

Pet Charges and Deposits: Extra charge (inquire).

Pet Policy: By reservation only.

Amenities: Extended cable TV, some hair dryers, restaurant adjacent, radios, coffee makers, data port/modem telephones, some VCRs (fee), some refrigerators (fee), some microwaves (fee), 2 stories, interior/exterior corridors.

Rated: 3 Paws — 12 rooms.

One of the friendliest places we've found, the tiny, charming Midway Motel is less than one mile from the center of the village, on State Route 25 near its junction with Hiram Road. Units are spotless and nicely decorated. Need a break from ooh'ing and ahh'ing from the incredible fall colors? Stop at the home-style Stone Ridge Restaurant nearby. Cornish is one of those tiny New England villages where you simply lose yourself in the days of long ago, renewing and recharging your spirit.

Overlook Motel

North Main Street (P.O. Box 347)
Eagle Lake, ME 04739
207-444-4535

Type of Lodging: Motel

Room Rates: $49–$129, some whirlpool units, $84–$96.

Pet Charges and Deposits: None.

Pet Policy: Small pets only.

Amenities: Cable TV, winter plug-ins, meeting rooms, radios, data port/modem telephones, refrigerators, microwaves, some VCRs, 2 stories, interior/exterior corridors.

Rated: 2 Paws — 14 units, including rooms, suites, and cottages.

The Overlook Motel commands a beautiful location overlooking Eagle Lake. Guest units are large, comfortable, and very well-appointed. Each room offers a view, and some of them have balconies. Two cottages border the lake. This small motel is a perfect getaway in one of the loveliest areas in the "down east" state.

Smuggler's Cove Motor Inn

State Route 96 (HC 65, Box 837)
East Boothbay, ME 04544
207-633-2800 • 800-633-3008
www.smugglerscovemotel.com

Type of Lodging:
Room Rates: $72–$172. AAA discounts.

Pet Charges and Deposits: $10 per day per pet plus $50 refundable deposit.

Pet Policy: All Pets Welcome.

Amenities: Extended cable TV, heated pool, private sandy beach, each room has balcony, charter sailing and fishing from motel's pier, rowboats, free local telephone calls, data port/modem telephones, some coffee makers, some refrigerators, some microwaves, 2 stories, exterior corridors.

Rated: 2 Paws — 60 rooms.

Stay at Smuggler's Cove and you're just minutes from Boothbay Harbor. The spectacular ocean and sunset views overlooking the bay from your private balcony are breathtaking. Charter sailing and fishing trips depart from the Smuggler's pier. The Motor Inn has been doing business successfully for more than thirty years. East Boothbay, adjacent to Boothbay Harbor, affords you all the pleasures of the area—Boothbay Railway Village, a turn-of-the-20th century village; the Stoddard Shell Museum; and Hendricks Hill Museum on Southport Island. This is a perfect vacation venue.

Todd House Bed & Breakfast

1 Capen Avenue—Todd's Head
Eastport, ME 04631
207-853-2328

Type of Lodging: Historic Bed & Breakfast

Room Rates: $65–$95, including expanded Continental breakfast.

Pet Charges and Deposits: None.

Pet Policy: All pets welcome.

Amenities: Cable TV, data port/modem telephones, 2 stories, interior/exterior corridors.

Rated: 3 Paws — 6 rooms.

Built on Todd's Head during the Revolutionary War, the Todd House is a classic New England full cape structure with massive center chimney and unique "good morning" staircase. Guest rooms are furnished with period antiques, enhanced by a collection of local historic artifacts. Owned by a local historian and educator, the Todd House has a library filled with volumes of local history. Breakfast is served in the common room before a huge fireplace and bake oven, in surroundings reminiscent of the Revolutionary era. Wild Maine blueberry muffins are a specialty of the house. The spacious yard hosts barbecues and affords an ever-changing view of the bay and its islands. Glorious sunrises and sunsets enhance the natural beauty of the area.

Sheepscot River Inn

306 Eddy Road
Edgecomb, ME 04556
207-882-6343

Type of Lodging: Motor Inn

Room Rates: $65–$130, some suites, $91–$130. Inquire for AAA discounts.

Pet Charges and Deposits: None.

Pet Policy: By reservation only.

Amenities: Extended cable TV, tennis court, cross-country skiing, nature program, shuffleboard, coin laundry, meeting room, restaurant, radios, data port/modem telephones, some refrigerators, some coffee makers, 2 stories, interior/exterior corridors.

Rated: 2 Paws — 40 units, including rooms, suites, and cottages.

Sheepscot River Inn is located in a wooded setting overlooking the harbor, on the east side of Davies Bridge, one mile east of Wiscasset. There are a variety of styles here, so make sure you indicate what kind you want. There are some older, more modest cottages, as well as newer, motel-style units. Fort Edgecomb State Historic Site, three acres at the south end of Davis Island, contains an 1809 wooden blockhouse used in the War of 1812. There are remains of earthworks in the vicinity. It's a great place to enjoy a picnic.

Colonial Travelodge

321 High Street
Ellsworth, ME 04605
207-667-5548

Type of Lodging: Motor Inn

Room Rates: $59–$124, some suites, $102–$159. AAA and AARP discounts.

Pet Charges and Deposits: None.

Pet Policy: All Pets Welcome.

Amenities: Cable TV, heated pool, whirlpool, restaurant, radios, coffee makers, data port/modem telephones, some refrigerators, 2 stories, interior corridors.

Rated: 2 Paws — 68 units, including rooms and some suites.

The Colonial Travelodge has a two story main building with one story annex. Rooms are varied in style, size, and age, and some rooms have at-door parking. Guest rooms in the back are quieter. At Ellsworth Marina Waterfront Park, off Water Street, you can see eagles, ospreys, harbor seals, and other wildlife. Stanwood Homestead Museum and Birdsacre Sanctuary is the former home of Cordelia Stanwood, a pioneer ornithologist. The museum was built in the 1850's and looks the part of its period. Birdsacre, a 170 acre wildlife preserve, provides rehabilitation facilities for hawks, ducks, songbirds, owls, and over 100 other bird species.

Holiday Inn

215 High Street
Ellsworth, ME 04605
207-667-9341

Type of Lodging: Motor Inn

Room Rates: $70–$145. AAA and AARP discounts.

Pet Charges and Deposits: None.

Pet Policy: All Pets Welcome.

Amenities: Extended cable TV, movies (fee), hair dryers, heated pool, whirlpool, sauna, exercise room, indoor tennis courts (fee), coin laundry, meeting, restaurant, cocktails, radios, coffee makers, data port/modem telephones, 2 stories, interior corridors.

Rated: 3 Paws — 103 rooms.

The Holiday Inn is centrally located, adjacent to a shopping plaza. Guest units are very comfortable and well-appointed. The lodging boasts a fine recreation facility, and there are numerous upscale amenities. The Black House, a Federal-style home built in the 1820's, looks exactly as it did when it was occupied by three generations of the Black family. The grounds extend over 180 acres and include formal gardens, nature trails, and a carriage house that features 19th century carriages and sleighs. Ellsworth is surrounded by numerous lakes and streams that offer opportunities for boating, canoeing, and fishing.

Jasper's Motel

200 High Street
Ellsworth, ME 04605
207-667-5318

Type of Lodging: Motor Inn

Room Rates: $49–$86. AAA and AARP discounts.

Pet Charges and Deposits: $10 per day per pet.

Pet Policy: All Pets Welcome.

Amenities: Cable TV, restaurant, cocktails, radios, data port/modem telephones, 1-2 stories, exterior corridors.

Rated: 2 Paws — 33 rooms.

Jasper's Motel is situation in a commercial area, opposite a shopping mall. Its units are nicely maintained and are set back from the highway. Jasper's Restaurant is very popular—you'll find lobster prepared ten different ways! Families and seniors have reported excellent service at this congenial place. Ellsworth began as a lumbering center in 1763. Water power from the Union River fueled its industrial growth. Lamoine State Beach Park, 6½ miles southeast, offers scenic views of Mount Desert Island and Frenchman Bay.

Freeport Inn & Café

31 U.S. 1 South
Freeport, ME 04032
207-865-3106
www.freeportinn.com

Type of Lodging: Motor Inn
Room Rates: $65–$125. AAA discounts.
Pet Charges and Deposits: None.
Pet Policy: By reservation only.
Amenities: Extended cable TV, movies, voice mail, some irons, some hair dryers, playground, canoes (fee), outdoor pool, valet laundry, restaurant, cocktails, radios, some coffee makers, data port/modem telephones, some refrigerators, 3 stories (no elevator), interior/exterior corridors.
Rated: 3 Paws — 80 rooms.

Freeport Inn is off the I-95, Exit 17, one mile north of the town. You'll find a wide variety of room styles and sizes. Some of the rooms can be quite cozy, others are larger. There's a nice river view from the property, and 25 acres of salt marsh water views adjoin the property. You're minutes away from L.L. Bean. The Desert of Maine is an area of sand dunes that has expanded significantly since the early 1900's. Formerly the Tuttle Farm, the topsoil began to erode in 1897, exposing an ancient glacial plain. Mast Landing Sanctuary, at the tideway of the Harraseeket River, once served as a delivery point for Maine lumber, which was used to make masts for British ships. Today, it's 140 acres of open fields, apple orchards, and forests, where you can see porcupines, minks, deer, and the ruins of an historic mill along 2½ miles of marked trails.

Isaac Randall House

5 Independence Drive
Freeport, ME 04032
207-865-9295

Type of Lodging: Historic Bed & Breakfast
Room Rates: $55–$140, including full breakfast. AAA and AARP discounts.
Pet Charges and Deposits: None.
Pet Policy: All Pets Welcome.
Amenities: Cable TV, some video games, smoke-free premises, ice skating on private pond (seasonal), playground, free local telephone calls, data port/modem telephones, some VCRs, some refrigerators, some microwaves, 2 stories, interior/exterior corridors.
Rated: 3 Paws — 10 units, including rooms and some suites.

The historic Isaac Randall House, a Federal-style farmhouse built in 1823, features varied room styles. If you possibly can, try and get the converted caboose! There are also a few suites. Freeport is the birthplace of Maine. It was here that colonial legislators signed the charter that separated Maine from the Massachusetts Bay Colony and ultimately led to Maine's statehood in 1820. Today's best known attraction is undoubtedly L.L. Bean, which is open 24/7/365. Shoe manufacturing, tourism, crabbing, and crab meat packing add to the burgeoning economy of Freeport. Atlantic Seal Cruises leave Freeport wharf on three-hour sightseeing excursions to Eagle Island State Park, where Commodore Peary planned his historic expedition to the North Pole.

Admiral Peary House

9 Elm Street
Fryeburg, ME 04037
207-935-3365

Type of Lodging: Bed & breakfast
Room Rates: $91–$151, including full breakfast.
Pet Charges and Deposits: None.
Pet Policy: All Pets Welcome. Pet on premises.
Amenities: No TVs, whirlpool, tennis court, cross-country skiing, bicycles, complimentary evening beverages, smoke-free premises, sauna, exercise room, game room, airport transportation, 2 stories, interior corridors.
Rated: 3 Paws — 6 rooms.

This Nineteenth century farmhouse, situated on 10 acres in a residential area, is surrounded by perennial gardens, and features period antiques and reproductions. It's a glorious place that evokes memories of an earlier, simpler time. There's much to see and do in the area. It's close to Freeport, Eagle Island, and Sequin Island, and a plethora of fine dining venues, including the restaurant in the Oxford House Inn, a very popular eating establishment in a handsome, Edwardian-period inn.

Leen's Lodge

P.O. Box 40 (Gravel entry road)
Grand Lake Stream, ME 04637
207-796-5575

Type of Lodging: Cottages
Room Rates: $93. AAA discounts.
Pet Charges and Deposits: None.
Pet Policy: All Pets Welcome.
Amenities: No TVs, swimming, boat dock, fishing, boats (fee), canoes (fee), paddleboats (fee), restaurant, refrigerators, some microwaves.
Rated: 2 Paws — 10 rustic cottages of varying sizes

This small lodging is actually a fishing camp in a secluded area bordering the lake. Rustic cottages vary in size and style, but they're all equipped with a fireplace and covered porch. Don't expect TV's and such—you won't find them here. But it *is* a perfect place for a laid-back vacation, replete with swimming, fishing, boating, and like outdoors activities.

Greenwood Motel

SR 6 & 15, P.O. Box 307
Greenville, ME 04442
207-695-3321

Type of Lodging: Motel
Room Rates: $41-76. AAA and AARP discounts.
Pet Charges and Deposits: $5 per day per pet.
Pet Policy: All Pets Welcome.
Amenities: Cable TV, movies, nature trails, snowmobiling (fee), outdoor pool, refrigerators, data port/modem telephones, 2 stories, exterior corridors.
Rated: 2 Paws — 15 rooms.

The wood framed building housing the Greenwood Motel is set back from the highway in a wooded copse opposite Moosehead Lake. *Katahdin*, a restored 1914 lake steamboat, takes visitors on 3-hour sightseeing voyages on Moosehead Lake, 5-hour cruises to Mount Kineo, and, in fall, an unforgettable 8-hour foliage cruise. The Moosehead Marine Museum has two rooms of area memorabilia. From Thanksgiving weekend through late March, Big Squaw Mountain is the area's premier ski area.

Kineo View Motor Lodge

P.O. Box 514
Greenville, ME 04441
207-695-4470

Type of Lodging: Motel
Room Rates: $55–$79. AAA and AARP discounts.
Pet Charges and Deposits: $5 per day per pet.
Pet Policy: Designated units only.
Amenities: Cable TV, movies, whirlpool, nature trails, data port/modem telephones, free local telephone calls, 2 stories, exterior corridors.
Rated: 2 Paws — 13 units including rooms and two suites.

Kineo View is a small motel that affords a splendid view of Moosehead Lake and the surrounding hills. Each of the 13 comfortable units has its own balcony. The Lodge allows early check-in and late check-out, a convenient amenity. Greenville is at the south end of Moosehead Lake. It's a year-round recreational center. You can enjoy fishing, swimming, canoeing, hiking, mountain climbing, horseback riding, seaplane tours, and white water rafting in summer, hunting in fall, and cross-country and alpine skiing and snowmobiling in winter. Mount Kineo was an historic Native American gathering place.

Crocker House Country Inn

H.C. 77, Box 171
Hancock, ME 04640
207-422-6806
e-mail: crocker@acadia.net

Type of Lodging: Country Inn

Room Rates: $90–$150, including full breakfast.

Pet Charges and Deposits: None.

Pet Policy: All pets welcome.

Amenities: Cable TV, movies, gourmet restaurant, cocktails, data port/modem telephones, 3 stories, interior corridors.

Rated: 3 Paws — 11 rooms.

The Crocker House Country Inn, tucked away on a peninsula at Hancock Point, was built in 1884 and lovingly restored in 1986. Its quiet, out-of-the-way location, fine cuisine, and individually appointed guest rooms, each with private bath. All combine to make the Crocker House a refreshing and memorable experience. The last sound you hear before retiring is the bell buoy lazily ringing its warning to mariners in Frenchman Bay. Awake to a full gourmet breakfast with fresh, hearty homemade specialties. Bordered by Frenchman Bay on the south and east, and the Skillings River to the west, Hancock Point is small enough that all roads lead to the water. Moorings are available for guests who arrive by sea, and a few bicycles are on hand for guests' touring. The Inn is conveniently located for you to take advantage of sightseeing in Acadia National Park and Hancock County.

Scottish Inns

Bangor Road
Houlton, ME 04730
207-532-4206

Type of Lodging: Motel

Room Rates: $40–$60. AAA and AARP discounts.

Pet Charges and Deposits: $8 per day per pet.

Pet Policy: All Pets Welcome.

Amenities: Cable TV, movies, winter plug-ins, restaurant adjacent, cocktails adjacent, data port/modem telephones, some refrigerators, 1 story, interior/exterior corridors.

Rated: 2 Paws — 40 rooms.

You'll find a variety of mostly older unit styles and sizes, many with at-door parking, at the well-maintained Scottish Inn. You can check in early and check out late, an added convenience for travelers. Houlton, on the Meduxnekeag River, is the oldest town and the county seat of Aroostook County, which is greater in area than Rhode Island and Connecticut combined. Its best-known product is the Aroostook potato. Houlton, virtually on the Canadian border, high up in northern Maine, is often referred to as the "Garden of Maine." The Aroostook Historical and Art Museum displays tools, vintage clothing, and local archival materials. Pierce Park features a drinking fountain with a 1916 cast iron statue, "The Boy with the Leaking Boot." Similar statues exist in Italy and Germany.

Sky Lodge Motel & Cabins

P.O. Box 428
Jackman, ME 04945
207-668-2171

Type of Lodging: Motel-cottage complex

Room Rates: $44–$165. AAA discounts.

Pet Charges and Deposits: $25 per day per pet.

Pet Policy: All Pets Welcome.

Amenities: Cable TV, ice skating, nature trails, canoeing (fee), snowmobiling (fee), bicycles (fee), meeting rooms, restaurant in winter, smoke-free premises, radios, data port/modem telephones, some refrigerators, some microwaves, 1 story, exterior corridors.

Rated: 2 Paws — 18 units, including motel rooms and cottages.

The Sky Lodge Motel & Cabins is a traditional older motel property set back from the highway. The cottages are situated in a beautiful setting, 120 acres, which gives you and your pet an excess of roaming territory. Jackman is adjacent to Big Wood Lake. The area is a marvelous winter wonderland with alpine and cross-country skiing, abundant woodland, and a paucity of crowds.

The Lodge at Kennebunk

95 Alewive Road
Kennebunk, ME 04043
207-985-9010
www.lodgeatkennebunk.com

Type of Lodging: Motel

Room Rates: $49–$135, some suites, including Continental breakfast. AAA and AARP discounts.

Pet Charges and Deposits: $10 deposit per night.

Pet Policy: All Pets Welcome.

Amenities: Extended cable TV, outdoor pool, horseshoes, shuffleboard, game room, barbecue grills, picnic tables, free local telephone calls, data port/modem telephones, some coffee makers, some refrigerators, some microwaves, 1 story, exterior corridors.

Rated: 2 Paws — 40 units, including rooms and 3 two-bedroom units.

The Lodge at Kennebunk occupies a quiet, 7-acre wooded setting adjacent to State Route 35. It's minutes away from Kennebunkport, with its shopping, dining and beaches. A 40-foot heated pool, game room, horseshoes, volleyball, and barbecue grills add to the atmosphere. The Kennebunks—Kennebunk, Kennebunkport, and Kennebunk Beach—combine to form one of Maine's most popular beach resort communities. In the first half of the Nineteenth century, Kennebunk was a major shipbuilding center—more than 1,000 schooners, clippers, and cargo vessels came out of its shipyards. The Brick Store Museum occupies four 19th century commercial buildings, dating from 1810 through 1860. Architectural walking tours of the historic district are available from June through Labor Day.

The Colony Hotel

140 Ocean Avenue
Kennebunkport, ME 04046
207-967-3331

Type of Lodging: Hotel (Open May 18–October 21 only)

Room Rates: $ 129–$435. AAA discounts.

Pet Charges and Deposits: $25 per day per pet.

Pet Policy: All Pets Welcome.

Amenities: Smoke-free premises, cable TV, voice mail, irons, hair dryers, beach, swimming, heated saltwater pool, putting green, social program, shuffleboard, croquet, ping pong, bocce, badminton, bicycles (fee), gift shop, meeting rooms, restaurant, cocktails, radios, coffee makers, data port/modem telephones, 2-3 stories, interior corridors.

Rated: 4 Paws — 123 units, including rooms and some suites.

The Colony is a classic, turn-of-the-20th-century hotel with a variety of unit styles. Beautifully landscaped grounds overlook the ocean, and there are amenities galore in this luxurious lodging. Long a favorite of artists and writers, Kennebunkport combines rich history and a quaint setting to attract visitors from all over the world. Dock Square has restored buildings housing galleries and boutiques. Parson's Way begins at Dock Square and continues past Walker's Point. Consider taking one of several available sightseeing cruises on the Kennebunk River or the coastal islands. At Cape Arundel, near Walker's Point—the former summer home of President George Bush *père*, you'll find waterspouts at spouting rock and blowing cave.

The Inn at Goose Rocks

71 Dyke Road
Kennebunkport, ME 04046
207-967-5425

Type of Lodging: Country Inn

Room Rates: $65–$175.

Pet Charges and Deposits: None.

Pet Policy: All Pets Welcome. Pet on premises.

Amenities: Extended cable TV, smoke-free premises, outdoor pool, whirlpool, gift shop, meeting rooms, restaurant, radios, coffee makers, data port/modem telephones, some VCRs, some refrigerators, 2 stories, interior corridors.

Rated: 3 Paws — 32 rooms.

Located just a short walk from Goose Rocks Beach, The Inn at Goose Rocks is set on a wooded knoll above a salt marsh. It's decorated with colonial-style furnishings. A highlight is the Goose Fare Dining Room that offers seafood, chicken and beef dishes, garnished with fresh seasonal produce and herbs grown on the premises. Continuing "down east" from former President Bush's summer home, you'll come to picturesque Goose Rocks Beach. Come back toward Kennebunkport and you'll relish the rocky shore of Cape Arundel and the fishing village of Cape Porpoise. The Kennebunkport Historical Society offers guided walks of the historic village of Kennebunkport, where author Booth Tarkington wrote at dockside in his schooner *Regina*.

Lodge at Turbat's Creek

Turbat's Creek Road
Kennebunkport, ME 04046
207-967-8700
www.visitkennebunkport.com

Type of Lodging: Motel (Open May 1—
October 30 only)

Room Rates: $99–$199, including
Continental breakfast. AAA and AARP discounts.

Pet Charges and Deposits: None.

Pet Policy: Designated units only. By reservation only.

Amenities: Cable TV, movies, radios, data
port/modem telephones, some refrigerators, 2 stories, exterior corridors.

Rated: 3 Paws — 26 rooms.

The Lodge at Turbat's Creek bills itself as, "A Family Place, Just like Maine itself." Its manageable size—26 spacious, modern rooms—and reasonable prices make it an exceptional find in Kennebunkport. The Kennebunkport Maritime Museum and Gallery, housed in Booth Tarkington's renovated boathouse, contains maritime artifacts and marine paintings, and ship models. The Nott House is an 1853 Greek revival home with Victorian furnishings. Shop, browse, *schmooze* and enjoy the scenic public walkway, Parson's Way, which begins and Dock Square and meanders out to Walker's Point.

The Yachtsman Lodge & Marina

Ocean Avenue
Kennebunkport, ME 04046
207-967-2511
innkeeper@yachtsmanlodge.com

Type of Lodging: Motel (Open April 1—
December 15 only)

Room Rates: $169–$250, including
Continental breakfast.

Pet Charges and Deposits: $20 per day per
pet.

Pet Policy: By advance reservations only.

Amenities: Cable TV, movies, CD players,
voice mail, irons, hair dryers, canoeing,
bicycles, marina (fee), massage (fee), valet
laundry, restaurant adjacent, health club
adjacent, smoke-free premises, VCRs,
radios, coffee makers, data port/modem
telephones, refrigerators, 1 story, exterior
corridors.

Rated: 3 Paws — 30 rooms.

The Yachtsman Lodge boasts luxurious rooms, each with its own private patio, at the water's edge. Canoes and bikes are available, and you can enjoy afternoon teas overlooking the Marina. Nearby Grissini Restaurant, an Italian bistro with expansive stone hearth, welcomes you to enjoy authentic Tuscan food cooked in wood-burning ovens. Kennebunkport's Seashore Trolley Museum has one of the world's oldest and largest collections of electric trolley cars dating from the 19th century. You'll see more than 50 refurbished trolleys that plied the streets of New Orleans (the "Streetcar Named Desire"), Budapest, Nagasaki, Boston, Sydney, and, of course, New York.

Herbert Inn

P.O. Box 67, Main Street
Kingfield, ME 04947
800-843-4372 • 207-265-2000
e-mail: herbert@somtel.com

Type of Lodging: Classic Hotel

Room Rates: $69–$185, including
Continental breakfast.

Pet Charges and Deposits: None.

Pet Policy: All pets welcome.

Amenities: Extended cable TV, movies,
game room, Jacuzzis, hot tubs, valet
laundry, conference facilities, fax, restaurant, cocktails, data port/modem telephones, 2 stories, interior corridors.

Rated: 4 Paws – 40 rooms.

Many small historic hotels would lose their
distinctiveness—or even be lost to the
wrecking ball—if it weren't for entrepre-
neurs such as Bud Dick. The Herbert, a 40-
room beaux arts hotel, is such a place.
Following a million-dollar restoration, this
beautifully restored 1918 jewel is glistening
with fumed oak, brass, and terrazzo floors.
The rooms are comfortable. Most have
Jacuzzi spas, brass beds, and antiques, with
cozy comforters and warm apple cider après
ski. The dining room emphasizes healthy
food, accompanied by nearly 100 wines
hand-selected and imported by the owner.
The Inn is located 20 minutes from world-
renowned Sugarloaf Mountain, home of
world-class skiing in winter and one of the
most striking mountain golf courses during
summer. There's great hiking, mountain
biking and white-water thrills on the
Kennebec and Dead Rivers.

Enchanted Nights Bed & Breakfast

29 Wentworth Street
Kittery, ME 03904
207-439-1489

Type of Lodging: Bed & Breakfast

Room Rates: $44–$150, some suites and
some whirlpool units, $115–$250, including full breakfast.

Pet Charges and Deposits: None.

Pet Policy: All Pets Welcome.

Amenities: Smoke-free premises,
extended cable TV, radios, data
port/modem telephones, some VCRs,
some refrigerators, some microwaves,
3 stories, interior/exterior corridors.

Rated: 3 Paws – 8 units, including
rooms and some suites.

Charm and enchantment personified,
Enchanted Nights Bed & Breakfast is an
1890 Queen Ann Victorian, complete with
turret. It's equidistant from the Kittery's
outlet malls—more than 1 mile of outlet
shops, including Factory Stores of America,
Manufacturers' Outlet, Tanger Factory
Outlet, and Tidewater Outlet Mall, as well
as Portsmouth, New Hampshire. Kittery,
at the extreme southwest corner of Maine,
was settled in 1623. One of the oldest shipyards in the nation, Portsmouth Naval
Shipyard on Seavey's Island, was established
in 1800. The first ship to fly the stars and
stripes, *The Ranger,* was launched at Kittery
under the command of John Paul Jones in
1777. In 1917, the first American submarine was launched from Kittery. Kittery
Historical and Naval Museum portrays
more than 350 years of Kittery's maritime
and cultural heritage.

Motel 6

516 Pleasant Street
Lewiston, ME 04240
207-782-6558

Type of Lodging: Motel
Room Rates: $37–$59. AARP discounts.
Pet Charges and Deposits: None.
Pet Policy: Small pets only.
Amenities: Extended cable TV, movies, coin laundry, restaurant adjacent, data port/modem telephones, 2 stories, interior/exterior corridors.
Rated: 2 Paws — 66 rooms.

Motel 6 has gone upscale in Lewiston, with pleasant, nicely decorated rooms. Lewiston started slowly—the first settler erected a cabin here in 1770, and was still a tiny town when the first woolen mill began its operations. In 1850, the water power of the Androscoggin River was harnessed, and things started to happen. Today, Lewiston, on the east bank of the Androscoggin, across from Auburn, is the second largest city in Maine. Bates College was founded here in 1864. You can see 50 miles west to the Presidential Range in New Hampshire from Bates' most notable landmark, 340-foot high Mount David. The Bates College Museum of Art displays changing exhibits if 18th and 19th century prints. Throncrag Bird Sanctuary contains more than 310 acres of forest, ponds, and hardwood stands. Cross-country skiing and snow-shoeing are popular winter activities here.

Pine Grove Cottages

RR 3
Lincolnville, ME 04849
207-236-2929

Type of Lodging: Cottages (Open May 1—October 31 only)
Room Rates: $51–$136.
Pet Charges and Deposits: $7 per day per pet.
Pet Policy: All Pets Welcome.
Amenities: Extended cable TV, nature trails, smoke-free premises, coffee makers, data port/modem telephones, some radios, some refrigerators, some microwaves, 1 story, exterior corridors.
Rated: 2 Paws — 11 units, some whirl-pool units available.

Pine Grove Cottages contain well-maintained individual cottages, some with water views, all with barbecues and decks. Lincolnville is located right in the middle of Maine's south coast, adjacent to Camden and Rockport. The view of Penobscot Bay is awe inspiring. Lincolnville is a year-round seaside resort. Bicycling, sailing, kayaking, and canoeing, either on the ocean or on one of many lakes is prevalent in summer. In winter, ice skating, cross-country skiing, and alpine skiing predominate.

The Eastland Motel

RR 1, Box 6915
Lubec, ME 04652
207-733-5501

Type of Lodging: Motel
Room Rates: $35–$65.
Pet Charges and Deposits: $5 per day per pet.
Pet Policy: Small pets only.
Amenities: TV, data port/modem telephones, 1 story, interior/exterior corridors.
Rated: 2 Paws — 19 rooms.

The Eastland Motel, small, manageable, and comfortable, is set back from the highway and afford a variety of lodgings, from spacious modern units, to cozy, older style rooms. Lubec, settled in 1780, is about as far east as you can go in "down east" Maine. It is the first spot where the sun rises in the continental United States. Across the Lubec Narrows in New Brunswick, Canada, lies Campobello Island. President Franklin D. Roosevelt first came here when he was a year old in 1883. Until 1921, FDR spent most of his summers on the island. Quoddy Head State Park consists of 600 acres of boardwalk, peat bog, picnic facilities, and the West Quoddy Lighthouse, built in 1808, which is closed to the public.

The Bluebird Motel

US 1, Box 45
Machias, ME 04654
207-255-3332

Type of Lodging: Motel
Room Rates: $49–$65; AAA and AARP discounts.
Pet Charges and Deposits: None.
Pet Policy: All pets welcome.
Amenities: Extended cable TV, free local telephone calls, data port/modem telephones, 1 story, exterior corridors.
Rated: 2 Paws — 40 rooms.

The Bluebird Motel is an older, very well-kept property, built in the traditional, one-story, at-door parking. Machias is Maine's oldest town east of the Penobscot River, founded in 1763. It is located in a major blueberry growing and processing area, and it's a starting point for hunting and fishing trips into the interior lake country. The first naval battle of the Revolutionary War was fought in Machias Bay on June 12, 1775—5 days before the Battle of Bunker Hill. Shortly after the formal beginning of that war, Fort Machias was built on a bluff overlooking the Machias River—you can still visit its earthworks today.

Machias Motor Inn

26 E. Main Street
Machias, ME 04654
207-255-4861

Type of Lodging: Motel

Room Rates: $56–$67; AAA and AARP discounts.

Pet Charges and Deposits: $5 per day per pet.

Pet Policy: Dogs only, sorry, no cats.

Amenities: Extended cable TV, heated pool, restaurant adjacent, free local telephone calls, radios, data port/modem telephones, 2 stories, exterior corridors.

Rated: 2 Paws — 35 rooms.

The Machias Motor Inn occupies a pleasant location overlooking Tidal Bay. Many of the 35 units have individual balconies to enhance your viewing pleasure. The Burnham Tavern Museum, at Main and Free Streets, is situated in the meeting place where Revolutionaries made plans for the first naval battle of the Revolutionary War. You can find numerous Revolutionary and Civil War artifacts here. The Gates House, built in 1807, contains several items of restored furnishings and models of the *Margareta* and the *Unity,* the two ships that fought the first naval battle of the Revolutionary War.

Gateway Inn

Route 157
Medway, ME 04460
207-746-3193

Type of Lodging: Motel

Room Rates: $50–$105; AAA and AARP discounts.

Pet Charges and Deposits: None.

Pet Policy: All pets welcome.

Amenities: Extended cable TV, movies, heated pool, whirlpool, sauna, exercise room, radios, data port/modem telephones, some refrigerators, some microwaves, 3 stories, interior/exterior corridors.

Rated: 3 Paws — 30 rooms, 8 suites.

Located at the foot of Mount Katahdin, with breathtaking views and a country setting, the Gateway Inn offers travelers spacious modern facilities. Rooms are clean, quiet, and equipped with comfortable queen- and king-sized beds. Some have private decks where guests can relax and enjoy the view. After a hard day on the road or in Maine's beautiful wilderness, enjoy the fully equipped weight and exercise room, or take a couple of laps in the heated pool. Finish unwinding in the bubbling hot tub. The Inn is located directly on a trail for snowmobilers and is minutes away from Baxter State Park.

Milford Motel

Route 2, P.O. Box 850
Milford, ME 04461
207-827-3200

Type of Lodging: Motel
Room Rates: $45–$61
Pet Charges and Deposits: None.
Pet Policy: All pets welcome.
Amenities: Extended cable TV, movies, coin laundry, data port/modem telephones, 2 stories, exterior corridors.
Rated: 2 Paws — 22 rooms.

The Milford Motel is a compact place, featuring comfortable, exceptionally clean units of varying size, which was built in 1989. It sits right on the Penobscot River, 15 minutes from Bangor, 10 minutes to the University of Maine. Well situated for travel in any direction, Milford is within a 1½ hour drive of a lot of the down east state's many attractions: Bar Harbor, Acacia National Park, Camden/Rockport, and Moosehead Lake to name a few. Whale watching, snow skiing, lake fishing and more are at your fingertips, and can all be reached within an easy day's drive there and back.

Best Western Heritage Motor Inn

935 Central Street
Millinocket, ME 04462
207-723-9777

Type of Lodging: Motor Inn
Room Rates: $65–$95, some whirlpool units
Pet Charges and Deposits: None.
Pet Policy: All pets welcome.
Amenities: Extended cable TV, whirlpools, meeting rooms, restaurant, cocktails, data port/modem telephones, 2 stories, interior corridors.
Rated: 2 Paws — 49 rooms.

Best Western Heritage Motor Inn is in a commercial location, set back from the highway. Its comfortable guest units vary in size. Millinocket is somewhat west of I-95, and is one of the more northerly towns in the state. Baxter State Park, which contains ten separate areas, is a huge spread (201,000 acres) that has canoeing, primitive camping, picnicking, hiking trails, fishing, swimming, and winter sports. Moosehead Lake, a center of year-round outdoor activities, is somewhat to the west of this university town.

The Katahdin Inn

740 Central Street
Millinocket, ME 04462
207-723-4555

Type of Lodging: Motel

Room Rates: $61–$91, some whirlpool units: $95–$110, including Continental breakfast; AAA discounts.

Pet Charges and Deposits: None.

Pet Policy: All pets welcome.

Amenities: Extended cable TV, heated pool, wading pool, whirlpool, exercise room, coin laundry, cocktails, coffee makers, data port/modem telephones, some refrigerators, some VCR's (fee), 3 stories, interior corridors.

Rated: 2 Paws — 82 rooms.

You'll find comfortable, clean guest units at the Katahdin Inn. Some of them overlook the property's atrium. Millinocket moves north and west to forests and mountain country. It's just beyond the headwaters of the Penobscot River. Continuing north from Millinocket, you'll come to Gero Island, 3,000 acres of parkland, pets on leash permitted, and Scraggly Lake, consisting of 10,000 acres filled with north woods-style outdoor activities.

Island Inn

P.O. Box 128
Monhegan Island, ME 04852
207-596-0371
islandin@midcoast.com

Type of Lodging: Inn

Room Rates: $110–$125, including full breakfast.

Pet Charges and Deposits: $10 per day per pet.

Pet Policy: All pets welcome.

Amenities: Cable TV, movies, restaurant, café, bakery, radios, data port/modem telephones, 3 stories, interior corridors.

Rated: 3 Paws — 32 rooms and 6 suites.

Located on beautiful Monhegan Island, overlooking the harbor, the Island Inn provides comfortable accommodations, ocean views, and evening sunsets. Though barely a mile square, the island boasts more than 600 species of wildflowers, laced with 17 miles of footpaths that run along the highest cliffs on the New England shore. The island lies 9 miles off the Maine coast. With more than 400 years of intriguing history, the island today is an art colony, with many working studios open to the public. Lobster and fishing boats keep the harbor busy all year. The island contains Cathedral Woods, a haven for deer, and a lighthouse built in 1824. There's regular passenger service daily from May through October, Monday, Wednesday, and Friday the rest of the year. The Inn's truck meets each boat and is available to carry luggage.

Augustus Bove House

Corner of State Route 302 & 114
Naples, ME 04055
207-693-6365

Type of Lodging: Historic Bed & Breakfast

Room Rates: $51–$176, including full breakfast. AAA and AARP discounts.

Pet Charges and Deposits: None.

Pet Policy: Pets by advance reservation only.

Amenities: Smoke-free premises, extended cable TV, movies, hair dryers, some irons, whirlpool, valet laundry, radios, data port/modem telephones, some VCR's, some coffee makers, 3 stories, interior corridors.

Rated: 3 Paws — 10 rooms.

This wonderful bed & breakfast is decorated with a mix of antiques and bric-a-brac in Victorian style. The dining room and the parlor have been renovated to complete the style of another era. The Augustus Bove House is situated between Long Lake and Sebago Lake in the southwest corner of the state. Songo Lock, in Naples, was opened in 1830 for transportation along the 41-mile canal system between Naples and Portland. A hand-operated gate is the only remnant of a system that once connected the lake district with the coast.

The Inn At Long Lake

Lake House Road
Naples, ME 04055
207-693-6226

Type of Lodging: Bed & Breakfast

Room Rates: $72–$145, some suites: $115–$165, including full breakfast. AAA and AARP discounts.

Pet Charges and Deposits: None.

Pet Policy: All pets welcome. (Pet on premises).

Amenities: Free local telephone calls, smoke-free premises, free newspaper, some data port/modem telephones, some radios, 4 stories (no elevator), interior corridors.

Rated: 3 Paws — 16 rooms.

The Inn at Long Lake is a turn-of-the-20th century country inn, located in the heart of Maine's lake region. The inn has an elegantly furnished parlor and a traditional front porch. The Songo River Queen II, berthed in the center of town, affords 1-2½ hour sightseeing cruises on an old-fashioned river boat. Naples is a recreational center for boating, windsurfing, seaplane rides, and mail boat runs. Rolling hills and lovely blue lakes share striking views of Mount Washington in the White Mountains of New Hampshire.

Lovley's Motel

P.O. Box 147
Newport, ME 04953
207-368-4311

Type of Lodging: Motel

Room Rates: $35–$90; AAA and AARP discounts.

Pet Charges and Deposits: None.

Pet Policy: All pets welcome.

Amenities: Extended cable TV, movies, some hair dryers, heated pool, whirlpool, playground, coin laundry, free local telephone calls, restaurant adjacent, coffee makers, data port/modem telephones, some microwaves, 2 stories, exterior corridors.

Rated: 2 Paws — 63 rooms.

At Lovley's Motel, you'll find a variety of new and older units in several sections. Situated in a commercial location, set back from the highway, you'll find a peaceful, restful time here. Newport may sound like one of those lovely little coastal towns on south end of the state. It's not. It's actually a lovely little town abutting Sebasticook Lake, off the I-95 about thirty west of Bangor—quite north as Maine goes. You traverse a particularly lovely stretch of highway with numerous lakes within a half hour's drive. All in all, it's a wonderful place for outdoor recreation.

Sign of the Owl

243 Atlantic Highway
Northport, ME 04849
207-338-4669

Type of Lodging: Farmhouse

Room Rates: $65–$85, including full breakfast.

Pet Charges and Deposits: None.

Pet Policy: Manager's advance approval required.

Amenities: Cable TV, radios, 2 stories, interior corridors.

Rated: 2 Paws — 3 rooms.

The Sign of the Owl is a 1794 Maine farmhouse, located nine miles north of Camden, that offers three guest rooms. Visitors are invited to explore the private beach just a short walk along a wooded path or to browse the gift and antique shop, filled with an ever-changing selection of fine furniture and accessories. Nearby Camden Hills State Park offers scenic vistas spanning Acadia National Park or the Camden-Rockport area.

The Captain Thomas Resort Motel

305 US 1
Ogunquit, ME 03907
207-646-4600
www.captainthomas.com

Type of Lodging: Suite Motel

Room Rates: $81–$251. AAA and AARP discounts.

Pet Charges and Deposits: None.

Pet Policy: Small pets only, by reservation only.

Amenities: Extended cable TV, heated pool, sauna, meeting rooms, restaurant, data port/modem telephones, some refrigerators, some coffee makers, some microwaves, 2 stories, exterior corridors.

Rated: 3 Paws — 76 units including rooms and some suites.

The Captain Thomas boasts modern, comfortable rooms as well as a number of luxury suites. The local trolley stops right in front of the lodging. It's only a 5-minute walk to Footbridge Beach. Ogunquit, which the Abenaki Native Americans called, "beautiful place by the sea," is 15 miles north of the New Hampshire frontier. A 3-mile sandy beach stretches to the north, and more than a mile of dramatic rocky shores lead south. Ogunquit is justifiably one of Maine's most popular summer resorts.

Studio East Motor Inn

43 Main Street
Ogunquit, ME 03907
207-646-7297

Type of Lodging: Motel

Room Rates: $58–$123.

Pet Charges and Deposits: $5 per day per pet.

Pet Policy: Small pets only.

Amenities: Extended cable TV, hair dryers, whirlpool, restaurant, radios, data port/modem telephones, refrigerators, some microwaves, 2 stories, exterior corridors.

Rated: 2 Paws — 26 rooms.

Studio East Motor Inn is situated right in the center of Ogunquit town, close to the shops and a short walk to the beach. The Ogunquit River, a tidewater river, parallels the beach. Shore Road leads to 100-foot high Bald Head Cliff, a monolith that goes 300 feet out into the ocean. Marginal Way, a mile long footpath to Perkins Cove, contains charter boats, restaurants, shops, and art galleries. The Ogunquit Museum if American Art, located in a meadow overlooking the Atlantic Ocean, features the work of superlative 20th century American artists.

White Rose Inn

P.O. Box 2227
Ogunquit, ME 03907
207-646-3432

Type of Lodging: Bed and Breakfast

Room Rates: $75–$175, including full breakfast; AAA discounts.

Pet Charges and Deposits: Extra charge, inquire.

Pet Policy: Small pets only in limited units only.

Amenities: Extended cable TV, hair dryers, whirlpool, smoke-free premises, refrigerators, data port/modem telephones, some microwaves, 2 stories, interior/exterior corridors.

Rated: 3 Paws — 8 rooms.

The White Rose Inn is surrounded by lovely landscaped grounds. Guest rooms are newly decorated and are located in both the main inn and the carriage house. The inn is situated in the center of the village. Two of the more popular companies operating scenic cruises are Finestkind Scenic Cruises (breakfast and evening cocktail cruise trips, lobster boat trips), and the Silverlining, a 1938 Hickley sloop yacht, which takes visitors on a 2-hour excursion along Maine's Ogunquit coastline.

Beau Rivage Motel

54 E. Grand Avenue
Old Orchard Beach, ME 04064
207-934-4668

Type of Lodging: Motel

Room Rates: $57–$175, some suites: $160–$200,

some whirlpool units: $150–$190; AAA and AARP discounts.

Pet Charges and Deposits: $10 per day per pet.

Pet Policy: Small pets only, in limited units only.

Amenities: Extended cable TV, heated pool, whirlpool, sauna, coin laundry, restaurant adjacent, data port/modem telephones, refrigerators, some VCR's, some coffee makes, some microwaves, several buildings in varying sizes.

Rated: 2 Paws — 82 units including rooms and suites.

Beau Rivage Motel is housed in several buildings. There are modern motel units, as well as older style cottages and apartments. In all, it's an eclectic mix of styles and sizes, which make it a wonderfully appropriate place to stay in this old beach resort. There are miles of sandy Atlantic beaches in Old Orchard Beach, and it's a great anchor for the surrounding areas. Portland, Maine is 15 miles north and Freeport is another half hour beyond Portland. Old Orchard Beach has got all the hokey, old-time fun you'd expect of a summer seaside resort town: amusement parks, arcades, a municipal pier, harness racing, even pari-mutuel betting. Barefoot Boy Restaurant, a block from the beach, is a standard steak-and-seafood place, with fabulous blueberry pancakes in the morning. Other notable eateries: Joseph's by the Sea and the Village Inn.

Old Colonial Motel

61 W. Grand Avenue
Old Orchard Beach, ME 04064
207-934-9862
Email: oldcol@gwi.net

Type of Lodging: Motel
Room Rates: $65–$190.
Pet Charges and Deposits: None.
Pet Policy: Small pets only, by reservation only.
Amenities: Extended cable TV, movies, heated pool, whirlpool, sauna, beach, swimming, exercise room, restaurant adjacent, babysitting services (fee), VCR's radios, refrigerators, data port/modem telephones, some coffee makers, some microwaves, 2 stories, exterior corridors.
Rated: 2 Paws — 30 units, including rooms and suites.

The Old Colonial Motel affords pleasant, very well-maintained units on an oceanfront location. Old Orchard Beach is located 15 minutes south of Portland. Freeport is a scant 35 miles away. Old Orchard Beach is one of the oldest seashore resorts in Maine. It has a 7-mile long white sand coastline, and low surf makes this a favored swimming area. Golf, tennis, and deep sea fishing, amusement parks and arcades, make this a fine, old-fashioned beach town.

Seaview Motel

65 W. Grand Avenue
Old Orchard Beach, ME 04064
207-934-4180
www.seaviewgetaway.com

Type of Lodging: Motel
Room Rates: $53–$204; AAA discounts.
Pet Charges and Deposits: $100 refundable deposit.
Pet Policy: All pets welcome.
Amenities: Extended cable TV, movies (fee), heated pool, beach, restaurant adjacent, refrigerators, data port/modem telephones, some VCR's, come coffee makers, some microwaves, 3 stories (no elevator), exterior corridors.
Rated: 2 Paws — 49 units, including rooms and some suites.

The Sea View Motel offers spectacular views of the ocean, which is just a few steps away from the property. There are new oceanfront and oceanside rooms, as well as two-bedroom suites. Summer in Old Orchard Beach is more than swimming. Beech Ridge Speedway hosts automobile racing and Scarborough Downs lets you bet on the trotters and pacers during the harness racing season. Ferry Beach, adjacent to nearby Saco, has 117 acres of fine nature trails, where pets on leashes are allowed to roam and romp.

Waves Oceanfront Resort

87 W. Grand Avenue
Old Orchard Beach, ME 04064
207-934-4949
www.wavesoceanfront.com

Type of Lodging: Motel

Room Rates: $65–$170.

Pet Charges and Deposits: None.

Pet Policy: All pets welcome.

Amenities: Extended cable TV, beach access, swimming, coin laundry, restaurant, radios, refrigerators, 2 stories, exterior corridors.

Rated: 2 Paws — 139 rooms.

Many of the rooms at Waves Oceanfront Resort have on ocean view, and there are some beachfront units as well. The rooms have kitchenettes and balconies. There's a beach, a nearby pier, and it's less than two hours to Boston. Scarborough Beach, 12 miles away and just south of Portland, has camping facilities, fishing, and swimming. Old Orchard Beach is a fine, feisty center for exploring Maine's down east coast.

Sweet Water Inn

H.C. 61, Box 4750
Orient, ME 04471
207-532-6840

Type of Lodging: Country home

Room Rates: $45–$110, including full breakfast. AARP and professional musicians' discounts.

Pet Charges and Deposits: $50 refundable deposit.

Pet Policy: All pets welcome.

Amenities: Cable TV, movies, game room with table tennis, billiards, chess, and darts, 1-2 stories, interior corridors.

Rated: 3 Paws — 6 rooms.

Sweet Water Inn, an unusual country home, was built to satisfy a large variety of aesthetic needs in the quiet of a spruce forest and apple orchard, high up in the eastern corner of north Maine on U.S. Highway 1, just over the border from Fosterville, New Brunswick, Canada. Guests enjoy abundant, healthy home cooking with organically grown vegetables and fruits. Visitors can even participate in pressing cider from the extensive wild apple orchards or pick fresh berries in season. Your host and hostess are multi-talented artists, musicians, and chefs, and they offer live performances nightly as well as original art and cuisine in the gift gallery. Stroll or ski over miles of wooded trails or enjoy guided all-terrain vehicle tours.

Best Western Black Bear Inn

and Conference Center
4 Godfrey Drive
Orono, ME 04473
207-866-7120

Type of Lodging: Motel

Room Rates: $58–$112, some whirlpool units: $125–$150. AAA and AARP discounts.

Pet Charges and Deposits: None.

Pet Policy: All pets welcome.

Amenities: Extended cable TV, irons, some hair dryers, sauna, exercise room, conference facilities, radios, coffee makers, data port/modem telephones, 3 stories, interior corridors.

Rated: 3 Paws — 68 rooms.

Best Western Black Bear Inn offers comfortable, well-appointed rooms with a view of the surrounding countryside. It's conveniently located at I-95, Exit 51. The University of Maine, which consists of eight colleges, has 11,000 students and is the main draw of Orono, a pleasant Penobscot Valley city. The Maine Center for the Arts, situated in Orono, houses the 1,628-seat Hutchins Concert Hall and the Jordan Planetarium and Observatory. Self-guided walking tours of the university and of the town it dominates, are available at the Rangely Road entrance to U of M.

University Motor Inn

5 College Avenue
Orono, ME 04473
207-866-4921

Type of Lodging: Motel

Room Rates: $45–$69.

Pet Charges and Deposits: None.

Pet Policy: Small pets only, in smoking rooms on ground floor only.

Amenities: Extended cable TV, movies, conference facilities, data port/modem telephones, 2 stories, interior corridors.

Rated: 2 Paws — 48 rooms.

Bordering the Penobscot River, the University Motor Inn is set back from the highway, eight miles north of Bangor. The back units offer a pleasant river view and a patio or balcony. While there are no views from the front rooms, they are nonetheless pleasant. In Orono, the Hudson Museum, in the Maine Center for the Arts Building on the University campus, houses exhibits relating to Native Americans from the northeastern woodlands, the northwest coast, the plains, the southwest, and the Arctic. Its Palmer Gallery displays pre-Hispanic, Mexican, and Central American artifacts.

Holiday Inn—West

81 Riverside Street
Portland, ME 04103
207-774-5601
www.portlandholidayinn.com

Type of Lodging: Motor Inn

Room Rates: $95–$165; AAA and AARP discounts.

Pet Charges and Deposits: None.

Pet Policy: Small pets only, in smoking units.

Amenities: Extended cable TV, movies (fee), video games, voice mail, irons, hair dryers, heated pool, whirlpool, sauna, exercise room, valet and coin laundry, conference facilities, free local telephone calls, restaurant, cocktails, radios, coffee makers, data port/modem telephones, some refrigerators (fee), 2 stories, interior corridors.

Rated: 3 Paws — 200 rooms.

Holiday Inn Portland West features a spacious garden courtyard, a health spa/fitness center, and evening entertainment. Rooms are spotlessly clean and comfortable. Poet Henry Wadsworth Longfellow lived in the Wadsworth-Longfellow House, the first brick home in Portland, which was built during the Revolutionary War, with a third story added in 1815. The Children's Museum of Maine, housed in an historic brick building, contains hands-on exhibits designed to interest children up to 14 years of age. There are numerous companies operating specialty cruises and tours in the Portland area, including Bay View Cruises, Casco Bay Lines, Olde Port Mariner Fleet, and Prince of Fundy Cruises. The Maine Narrow Gauge Railroad Co. & Museum takes you back to a different era and a fun means of transport.

Howard Johnson Hotel

155 Riverside Street
Portland, ME 04103
207-774-586

Type of Lodging: Motor Inn

Room Rates: $79–$153. AAA and AARP discounts.

Pet Charges and Deposits: $50 deposit.

Pet Policy: All pets welcome.

Amenities: Extended cable TV, movies (fee), some irons, hair dryers, heated pool, whirlpool, exercise room, valet and coin laundry, conference facilities, two restaurant, cocktails, coffee makers, data port/modem telephones, some VCR's (fee), some radios, some refrigerators, some microwaves, 3 stories, interior corridors.

Rated: 3 Paws — 120 units including rooms, suites and whirlpool units.

You'll find lots of welcome amenities at the Riverside Street venue of the Howard Johnson Hotel chain. Henry Wadsworth Longfellow described Portland, the city where he was born, as "The beautiful town seated by the sea." Today, it's Maine's largest city by far. The Portland Museum of Art, designed by I. M. Pei, houses a collection of works by Andrew Wyeth, Winslow Homer, Rockwell Kent, Claude Monet, Edgar Degas, and Pablo Picasso. The Victoria Mansion on Danforth Street between State and High Streets, is an Italianate villa built in 1858 and sumptuously furnished with period pieces. The Southworth Planetarium, on the University of Southern Maine campus, has changing, intriguing planetarium shows.

Radisson Eastland Hotel

157 High Street
Portland, ME 04101
800-333-3333 • 207-775-5411

Type of Lodging: Hotel

Room Rates: $109–$159 AAA and AARP discounts.

Pet Charges and Deposits: $100 refundable deposit.

Pet Policy: All pets welcome.

Amenities: Extended cable TV, movies, voice mail, exercise room, area transportation, valet laundry, conference facilities, fax, two restaurants, cocktails, data port/modem telephones, some refrigerators, some microwaves, 4 stories, interior corridors.

Rated: 3 Paws — 204 rooms and suites

A visit to Portland means a visit to the Radisson Eastland Hotel, a charming place to stay that combines the ambience of old New England with all the comforts and amenities that today's traveler expects. Guest rooms and spacious luxury suites are beautifully appointed with splendid harbor views. The Radisson Eastland is conveniently located in downtown Portland, within easy walking distance of nearby shops and restaurants, the Old Port, the Portland Museum of Art, theaters, and the civic center. Factory outlet shopping and the Maine Mall are a short drive away.

Tradewinds Motor Inn

2 Park Drive
Rockland, ME 04841
207-596-6661

Type of Lodging: Motor Inn

Room Rates: $61–$110. AAA and AARP discounts.

Pet Charges and Deposits: None.

Pet Policy: Small pets only.

Amenities: Extended cable TV, heated pool, whirlpool, sauna, exercise room (fee), gift shop, coin laundry, conference facilities, free local telephone calls, restaurant, cocktails, data port/modem telephones, some radios, some refrigerators, some microwaves, 3-5 stories, interior/exterior corridors.

Rated: 3 Paws — 142 rooms, some whirlpool units.

Some units at the Tradewinds Motor Inn come with harbor views and balconies. There are 142 rooms, ranging from spacious to compact and cozy. Rockland is known as the "Lobster Capital of the World," and the "Schooner Capital of Maine." A granite breakwater leads to the Rockland Breakwater Lighthouse, built in 1888. The town's historic Main Street district is a great shopping area. Farnsworth Art Museum houses American and European art, while the Owl's Head Transportation Museum has antique aircraft, automobiles, motorcycles, bicycles, and carriages, all in operating condition. Shore Village Museum, America's lighthouse museum, contains a large exhibit of lighthouse equipment—working lights, horns, bells, and lifesaving devices, as well as Civil War uniforms, carved ivory, and ship models.

Linnell Motor & Rest Inn Conference Center

986 Prospect Avenue
Rumford, ME 04276
207-364-4511

Type of Lodging: Motel

Room Rates: $55–$79, including Continental breakfast. AAA and AARP discounts.

Pet Charges and Deposits: $5 per day per pet.

Pet Policy: Small pets only.

Amenities: Extended cable TV, some hair dryers, coin laundry, conference facilities, free local telephone calls, restaurant adjacent, radios, data port/modem telephones, some refrigerators, 2 stories, interior/exterior corridors.

Rated: 2 Paws — 50 rooms.

The Linnell Motel boasts impressive meeting facilities and a great variety of sizes and types of rooms, all of which are clean, inviting, and comfortable. We often hear tales of going from "Maine to Mexico." That's easily possible in Rumford, because Mexico's just across the Androscoggin River from the town. Thirty-seven miles to the west, you'll find Grafton Notch State Park and Bald Pate Mountain, great outdoor and ski country, and not far from the New Hampshire border.

The Madison Motor Inn

1257 U.S. Route 2
Rumford, ME 04276
207-364-7973

Type of Lodging: Motor Inn

Room Rates: $79–$99, some suites: $130–$155. AAA discounts.

Pet Charges and Deposits: None.

Pet Policy: All pets welcome.

Amenities: Extended cable TV, heated pool, whirlpool, sauna, canoeing, fishing, jogging, valet laundry, restaurant, health club adjacent, data port/modem telephones, refrigerators, some VCR's, some radios, some coffee makers, some microwaves, 2 stories, exterior corridors.

Rated: 2 Paws — 60 units, including rooms and some suites.

Many units at Madison Motor Inn command a view overlooking the Androscoggin River. You get large portions of food, very well-presented, at the Madison Restaurant on the premises of the Inn. Rumford is located in the western part of the state, where you'll find superb downhill skiing at such venues as Goose Eye Mountain, Success Mountain, Mount Abram, and Old Spec Mountain. Mount Blue State Park has loads of outdoor activities for enthusiasts of all kinds.

Small Point Bed & Breakfast

Route 216. H.C. 32, Box 250
Sebasco Estates, ME 04565
207-389-1716

Type of Lodging: Bed & Breakfast
Room Rates: $60–$99, including full breakfast.
Pet Charges and Deposits: None.
Pet Policy: Dogs only, sorry, no cats. Manager's prior approval required.
Amenities: 1-2 stories, interior/exterior corridors.
Rated: 3 Paws — 3 guest rooms and 1 guest suite

Small Point Bed & Breakfast is nestled among the trees of scenic Cape Small in a quaint 1890's farmhouse. Guests are invited to share the charm of old Maine with the comfort and hospitality of your hosts, Captain Dave and Jan Tingle. Guest rooms are comfortably furnished with queen-sized beds, with a choice of private or shared bath. Special blankets are provided for canine guests, there's a wraparound screened porch, and pet access to the beach. In the evening, the gentle sounds of the Maine coast lull you to sleep. You awaken to the sounds of birds and the smell of Jan's full country breakfast. Sea Captain Dave offers boating adventures on their boat, the *Rhodes 19*. Nearby attractions include Popham Beach State Park, Seawall Beach, Sebasco Golf Course, Phippsburg Land Trust, and hiking on Hermit Island.

The Lawnmeer Inn

65 Hendricks Hill Road
Southport, ME 04576
207-633-2544
www.lawnmeerinn.com

Type of Lodging: Complex
Room Rates: $79–$161. AAA discounts.
Pet Charges and Deposits: $10 per day per pet.
Pet Policy: Small pets only.
Amenities: Extended cable TV, hair dryers, boat dock, free local telephone calls, restaurant, cocktails, smoke-free premises, data port/modem telephones, 3 stories (no elevator), interior/exterior corridors.
Rated: 3 Paws — 32 units, including rooms and some suites.

Situated on Boothbay Harbor, just south of the bridge to Southport Island, this lovely turn-of-the-20th century inn has adjacent modern motel units overlooking the ocean. The Lawnmeer Inn has been doing business here since 1898, and here the term "wonderful amenities" means broad lawns, porches, and serenity. Boothbay Harbor, one of the premier summer resorts on the coast, features every variety of river cruise, ocean cruise, whale watching cruise, sailing, and deep sea fishing activity, as well as Boothbay Railway Village, which features an 1847 Boothbay Town Hall, general store, little red schoolhouse, and all manner of railroad memorabilia.

Amerisuites

303 Sable Oaks Drive
South Portland, ME 04106
207-775-3900

Type of Lodging: Suite Motel

Room Rates: $120–$180, including Continental breakfast. AAA and AARP discounts.

Pet Charges and Deposits: $20 per day per pet.

Pet Policy: Smoking units only.

Amenities: Extended cable TV, movies (fee), video games, voice mail, irons, hair dryers, heated pool, exercise room, valet and coin laundry, conference facilities, free newspaper, restaurant adjacent, VCR's, radios, coffee makers, data port/modem telephones, refrigerators, microwaves, 6 stories, interior/exterior corridors.

Rated: 3 Paws — 130 suites.

Amerisuites is close to the Maine Mall and to the airport. Suites are spacious, modern, and comfortable. South Portland is actually a part of the Portland area, situated on the south side of the Fore River. Many attractive 19th century buildings straddle both sides of the river, which debouches into Casco Bay. Prince of Fundy cruises offers you a real getaway—an 11-hour one-way cruise to Yarmouth, Nova Scotia on a mini-liner, complete with dining, dancing, and floor shows. In keeping with his importance as mast agent for the British before the Revolutionary War, George Tate built the Georgian-style Tate House in 1755. Part of the house has been reconstructed and there are fine 18th century furnishings throughout. The Victoria Mansion (Victorian–Italianate) and the Wadsworth-Longfellow House (1785, the first Philadelphia-style brick house in Portland) are two outstanding examples of Maine's evocative past.

Best Western Merry Manor Inn

700 Main Street
South Portland, ME 04106
207-774-6151
www.seenewengland.com/merryma nor

Type of Lodging: Motor Inn

Room Rates: $61–$152

Pet Charges and Deposits: None.

Pet Policy: All pets welcome.

Amenities: Extended cable TV, movies (fee), irons, hair dryers, heated pool, whirlpool, wading pool, valet and coin laundry, conference facilities, free local telephone calls, free newspaper, restaurant, health club adjacent, radios, coffee makers, data port/modem telephones, some VCR's (fee), some refrigerators, some microwaves, 2 stories, interior/exterior corridors.

Rated: 3 Paws — 151 rooms.

Best Western Manor Inn is conveniently located close to all Portland attractions. Rooms are spotless, modern, and the entire complex is very inviting and attractive. Fore River Sanctuary is a 76-acre preserve within the Portland city limits. It includes a 2½ mile trail leading to the towpath of the historic Cumberland and Oxford Canal. The Maine History Gallery displays paintings, costumes, political memorabilia, archeological materials, and manuscripts. The Neal Dow Memorial on Congress Street is a Federal-style mansion built in 1829 for abolitionist, prohibitionist, and former mayor of Portland Neal Dow. Among his memorabilia, you can ask to see Mr. Dow's death mask, taken immediately following his demise. The second floor houses Maine's headquarters of the Women's Christian Temperance Union.

Howard Johnson Hotel

675 Main Street
South Portland, ME 04106
207-775-5343 • 1-800-I-GO-HOJO

Type of Lodging: Motor Inn

Room Rates: $81–$152; AAA and AARP discounts.

Pet Charges and Deposits: None.

Pet Policy: By reservation only.

Amenities: Extended cable TV, movies (fee), voice mail, hair dryers, heated pool, area transportation, valet laundry, conference facilities, restaurant, cocktails, radios, coffee makers, data port/modem telephones, some refrigerators (fee), some microwaves (fee), 4 stories, interior corridors.

Rated: 3 Paws — 121 rooms.

Howard Johnson Hotel in South Portland was the chain's Gold Medal Award winner for 2000. Conveniently located off Exit 7 of I-95, on Highway 1, this clean, modern, comfortable lodging is minutes from the Maine Mall, the beaches, Portland Headlight, and L.L. Bean. Complimentary airport shuttle is an added plus. Culturally, Portland is Maine's showplace. The Portland Performing Arts Center is home to the Portland Stage Company, the Ram Island Dance Company, and the Center for Performance Studies. The Portland Symphony Orchestra is one of the countries major orchestras. The Calendar Islands— 365 of them to be exact, are located east of Portland in Casco Bay.

Portland Marriott Hotel

200 Sable Oaks Drive
South Portland, ME 04106
207-871-8000

Type of Lodging: Hotel

Room Rates: $149–$209; AAA and AARP discounts.

Pet Charges and Deposits: $20 per day per pet.

Pet Policy: Small pets only.

Amenities: Extended cable TV, movies(fee), dual phone lines, voice mail, irons, hair dryers, heated pool, whirlpool, sauna, exercise room, golf– 18 holes (fee), gift shop, area transportation, valet and coin laundry, conference facilities, restaurant, radios, coffee makers, data port/modem telephones, some VCR's, some refrigerators, 6 stories, interior corridors.

Rated: 4 Paws — 227 rooms.

This wonderfully upscale Marriott property is close to a golf course, the Maine Mall, and the airport. The Portland Harbor Museum is housed in a former cannon repair building on historic Fort Preble. It's right next to the Spring Point Ledge Lighthouse, and, as might be expected, features all manner of nautical exhibits. Portland—then known as Falmouth—was founded in 1632. In 1676, a series of Native American raids sent residents fleeing back to Massachusetts, and left the town in ruins. After the city had rebuilt, disaster struck again in 1775 when, after the Colonists refused to surrender, the British bombarded and destroyed some 400 buildings. Nearly a century later, in 1866, fire leveled most of the city. Yet, it rose once again, and today Portland is Maine's major metropolis.

The Craignair Inn At Clark Island

533 Clark Island Road
Spruce Head, ME 04859
207-594-7644

Type of Lodging: Historic Country Inn

Room Rates: $41–$125..

Pet Charges and Deposits: $8.50 per day per pet per day.

Pet Policy: All pets welcome.

Amenities: Extended cable TV, nature trails, radios, restaurant, smoke-free premises, 2-3 stories (no elevator), interior/exterior corridors.

Rated: 3 Paws — 21 rooms.

The Craignair Inn is certainly one of the more unique lodgings in this book—a 1930 former quarrymen's boarding house on the ocean. It overlooks Clark Island and offers rooms of varying styles, many with an ocean view. Clark Island truly is an island off the south coast of Maine, adjacent to Spruce Head, which, itself is on a peninsula jutting south from Rockland. It's at the easternmost end of a series of rocky peninsulas. There are numerous inter-island ferries. Spruce Head is just enough "off the beaten path" to be peaceful (sometimes it seems you travel from town to town to town along Maine's south coast), yet close enough to catch Highway 1 north or south to the more crowded venues.

Waterford Inne

Box 149, Chadbourne Road
Waterford, ME 04088
207-583-4037

Type of Lodging: Inn

Room Rates: $110–$139, including full breakfast and dinner.

Pet Charges and Deposits: $10 per day per pet plus $50 refundable deposit.

Pet Policy: Advance reservations and manager's prior approval required.

Amenities: Dining room, data port/modem telephones, 2 stories, interior corridors.

Rated: 3 Paws — 8 rooms and 1 suite

The Waterford Inne is a 19th century farmhouse situated on a country lane amidst 25 acres of fields and woods. The interior is finished with hand-hewn beams and wide pine floors, creating a distinctive true country inn. Wander through the gardens, which provide a colorful array of flowers and a bounty of fresh fare for the dining table. Guest rooms are uniquely decorated with the warmth of early pine furnishings combined with contemporary comforts. An air of quiet, simple elegance pervades the common rooms. Awake to freshly brewed coffee and a full Maine breakfast featuring home baked goods and garden-fresh delights. Dinner is a leisurely affair, consisting of four courses created to complement one another in taste, color, and texture, elegantly served on fine china. The Waterford Inne is located in the Oxford Hills and Lakes Region, one of Maine's best-kept secrets.

Best Western—Waterville

356 Main Street
Waterville, ME 04901
207-873-3335

Type of Lodging: Motor Inn
Room Rates: $72–$144; AAA and AARP discounts.
Pet Charges and Deposits: None.
Pet Policy: All pets welcome.
Amenities: Extended cable TV, irons, whirlpool, valet laundry, conference facilities, complimentary newspaper, restaurant, radios, coffee makers, data port/modem telephones, some VCR's (fee), some refrigerators, some microwaves, 2 stories, interior corridors.
Rated: 3 Paws — 86 rooms.

Best Western Waterville borders the freeway, but there's plenty of wooded area at the rear of the property. Rooms are spotless, spacious, and the King rooms are newly renovated. Colby College, which was founded in 1813 and occupies a 714 acres campus on Mayflower Hill, is two miles away. Its Lorimer Chapel houses an organ designed by Albert Schweitzer. Abenaki Native Americans once met for tribal councils at the Kennebec River's Ticonic Falls near Waterville. Five miles west, near Oakland, is a large concentration of children's summer camps.

Econo Lodge

455 Kennedy Memorial Drive
Waterville, ME 04901
207-872-5577

Type of Lodging: Motel
Room Rates: $55–$85.
Pet Charges and Deposits: None.
Pet Policy: All pets welcome.
Amenities: Extended cable TV, free local telephone calls, restaurant adjacent, outdoor pool, data port/modem telephones, some VCR's (fee), come coffee makers, 2 stories, interior/exterior corridors.
Rated: 2 Paws — 50 rooms.

Econo Lodge features comfortable, clean units in the main section and in the annex wing. The motel is close to the freeway, but backs on to a wooded area. By the mid-19th century, Waterville was a prosperous freight and passenger port. Today, the city is an important center for timber and concrete products. West of the city lies the Belgrade Lakes region. Its largest lake, Great Pond, inspired the play and the movie "On Golden Pond." The Redington Museum in Waterville contains displays about the early history of the town.

Holiday Inn

375 Main Street
Waterville, ME 04901
207-873-0111

Type of Lodging: Motor Inn
Room Rates: $89–$129; AAA and AARP discounts.
Pet Charges and Deposits: None.
Pet Policy: All pets welcome.
Amenities: Extended cable TV, movies (fee), irons, hair dryers, heated pool, whirlpool, sauna, exercise room, coin laundry, conference facilities, restaurant, cocktails, radios, coffee makers, data port/modem telephones, some refrigerators (fee), 3 stories, interior corridors.
Rated: 3 Paws — 138 rooms.

Holiday Inn-Waterville, situated in a commercial location on the highway, features a variety of guest units, some of which border the attractive courtyard area. The Waterville Theater, a professional touring group, presents plays in the Waterville Opera House. Waterville, one of Maine's larger cities, is surrounded by the Kennebec River as well as numerous lakes. A particularly lovely stretch of I-95 runs south 20 miles to the state capital, Augusta.

Kawanhee Inn Lakeside Lodge & Cabins

Route 142, Box 119
Weld, ME 04285
207-585-2000
info@lakeinn.com

Type of Lodging: Lodge and cabins
Room Rates: $85–$175
Pet Charges and Deposits: None.
Pet Policy: Manager's prior approval required.
Amenities: Cable TV, movies, boat rentals (fee), restaurant, data port/modem telephones, some refrigerators, some microwaves, 1-2 stories, exterior corridors.
Rated: 3 Paws — 9 rooms and 12 cabins.

Kawanhee Inn Lakeside Lodge is nestled in the cathedral pines on a knoll overlooking Webb Lake, in the western Maine mountains. On entering the lobby, you are impressed with the rustic and refined décor. A huge fieldstone fireplace, accommodating four-foot logs, crackles a warm welcome. On the second floor of the Lodge are nine comfortable bedrooms—five with private baths, four with shared bath. The cabins face the lake and mountains and vary in size to accommodate parties from two to seven. Kawanhee Inn is noted for its home cooking, which is served either in the main dining room or on the porch. Picnic lunches are available for guests to take while exploring spots accessible by canoe or while climbing Tumbledown Mountain, or panning for gold on the Swift River.

Ne'r Beach Motel

395 Post Road, Route 1
Wells, ME 04090
207-646-2636

Type of Lodging: Motel
Room Rates: $38–$125.
Pet Charges and Deposits: $5 per day per pet.
Pet Policy: All pets welcome.
Amenities: Extended cable TV, heated pool, shuffleboard, restaurant adjacent, data port/modem telephones, some refrigerators, some coffee makers, smoke-free premises, 1-2 stories, exterior corridors.
Rated: 2 Paws — 44 units, room and some suites.

N'er Beach Motel is an economical, comfortable find in Wells, situated between the Kennebunks to the north and Ogunquit on the south. Wells, founded in 1640, was one of only four English communities to survive the second French and Indian War (1688-1697). Wells remained a fishing and farming community until tourists discovered Wells Beach—a seven-mile-long strand—in the early 20th century. Highlights of a trip to the area include the Rachel Carson National Wildlife Refuge (4,800 acres) of wetlands, the Wells National Estuarine Research Reserve, a, 1,600 acre wetland preserve located on a 19th century saltwater farm, and the Wells Auto Museum, which displays more than 80 antique and classic cars from the early 1900's to the 1960's.

Whispering Pines Motel

183 Lake Road
Wilton, ME 04Whispering Pines Motel
183 Lake Road
Wilton, ME 04294
207-645-3721

Type of Lodging: Motel
Room Rates: $49–$96; AAA and AARP discounts.
Pet Charges and Deposits: $3 per day per pet.
Pet Policy: All pets welcome.
Amenities: Extended cable TV, movies, swimming, boating, canoeing, boat dock, fishing (state fishing license required), gift shop, coin laundry, free local telephone calls, radios, refrigerators, data port/modem telephones, some VCR's (fee), some coffee makers, some microwaves, 2 stories, exterior corridors.
Rated: 2 Paws — 40 rooms and suites.

Whispering Pines Motel invites you to check in early or check out late. It's a comfortable, easy-to-take place, which gives you fine value for the money. Wilton is in the northwest part of Maine. The nearest town of any size, Farmington (4,200), eight miles away, is the county seat of Franklin County. You'll find rolling hill farms and apple orchards in the south, lakes and forested mountains in the north. University of Maine—Farmington boasts rotating Maine artists' exhibits in its art gallery. Nordica Homestead Museum was the birthplace of opera singer Lillian Nordica, who gained world renown in the late 19th century.

Down-East Village Motel

705 Route 1
Yarmouth, ME 04096
207-846-5161

Type of Lodging: Motor Inn

Room Rates: $59–$99; AAA and AARP discounts.

Pet Charges and Deposits: $5 per day per pet.

Pet Policy: All pets welcome.

Amenities: Extended cable TV, smoke-free premises, some hairdryers, heated pool, free local telephone calls, free newspaper, conference facilities, restaurant, radios, coffee makers, data port/modem telephones, some refrigerators, 1-story, exterior corridors.

Rated: 2 Paws — 31 rooms.

Down-East Village Motel is an older property dating from 1949, which has a variety of sizes and styles of rooms in a collection of different buildings. The grounds extend all the way to a mill pond on the Royal River. It's situated just south of Freeport (L.L. Bean) and only ten miles north of Portland, so you're truly in the center of everything "Maine." The well-known Down-East Village Restaurant's dining rooms have a rustic air, with stone fireplaces and a casual atmosphere. Although Yarmouth was first settled in 1636, permanent habitation only occurred in 1713. There are four nearby waterfalls on the Royal River, which provided power to fuel the town's early industry. A 41-foot-high rotating globe, Eartha, is on view in the lobby of the DeLorme Mapping Company. The Yarmouth Historical Society and Museum of History displays photographs, clothing, furniture, and other historical items.

Dockside Guest Quarters

P.O. Box 205
Harris Island
York, ME 03909
207-363-2868

Type of Lodging: Country Inn

Room Rates: $89–$214.

Pet Charges and Deposits: None.

Pet Policy: All pets welcome. Pet on premises.

Amenities: Extended cable TV, some irons, boating, canoeing, fishing, bicycles, marina (fee), restaurant, radios, data port/modem telephones, some refrigerators, some coffee makers, some microwaves, some suites, 2 stories, interior/exterior corridors.

Rated: 3 Paws — 25 units, rooms and some suites.

Dockside Guest Quarters, made up of an attractive inn and cottages, is right in York's harbor. Many of the guest rooms have a patio or a balcony and a water view, and the rooms are comfortable and spotless. The Old York Historical Society maintains several restored house museums representing four centuries of life in the coastal village of York. Among the historical highlights of York are the Elizabeth Perkins House (Colonial Revival period), the Emerson-Wilcox House, in the center of town, which has been a tavern, general store, tailor shop, post office, and private residence; Jefferd's Tavern, built in Wells, Maine in 1750, the John Hancock Warehouse, and the Old Schoolhouse, which dates from 1745 and is one of the oldest surviving one-room schoolhouses in the state.

York Commons Inn

P.O. Box 427
York, ME 03909
207-363-8903

Type of Lodging: Motel

Room Rates: $74–$150; including Continental breakfast; AAA and AARP discounts.

Pet Charges and Deposits: $6–$19 per day per pet.

Pet Policies: Small pets only.

Amenities: Extended cable TV, free local telephone calls, heated pool, data port/modem telephones, some refrigerators (fee), some microwaves (fee), 2 stories, interior corridors.

Rated: 2 Paws — 90 rooms.

The York Commons Inn is a manageable, mid-size facility with sizeable, comfortable rooms, a heated pool, and a most pleasant ambience. York, one of Maine's oldest, most historic towns, was settled in 1624. It started its life as Agamenticus, changed to Bristol in 1638, became Gorgeana in 1642 and finally morphed into York in 1652. Reminders of York's past include residential areas dating from the 18th century, Colonial churches, farmsteads, and the like. Ancient traditions are strong here—inhabitants are rock-ribbed New Englanders. The Old Gaol (jail) is one of the oldest English public buildings in the United States (1719), and was used as a jail until 1860. The John Hancock Warehouse, on the York River, was owned by John Hancock until 1794, and is one of the oldest surviving commercial buildings in Maine.

Inn At Harmon Park

415 York Street
York Harbor, ME 03911
207-363-2031

Type of Lodging: Bed & Breakfast

Room Rates: $59–$119, some suites, includes full breakfast.

Pet Charges and Deposits: None.

Pet Policy: All pets welcome. Pet on premises.

Amenities: Extended cable TV, VCR's, data port/modem telephones, some radios, smoke-free premises, 2 stories, interior corridors.

Rated: 3 Paws — 5 units.

The Inn at Harmon Park is a gracious 1899 Victorian home set in a pleasant residential area. Not only is the place totally charming, but the hospitality is everything you'd hope and expect it to be. York Harbor is the fashionable, upscale resort member of the Yorks (York, York Beach, York Harbor). Well-to-do residents of Boston, Philadelphia, New York, etc., built rambling three-story "cottages" and grand hotels. The summer colony once rivaled that of Bar Harbor and Newport, Rhode Island. Wiggey Bridge, a restored suspension bridge, spans the York River. The Sayward-Wheeler House, built in 1718, contains family pictures, booty brought back from the expedition against the French in 1745, and Queen Anne and Chippendale furniture.

MASSACHUSETTS

Nickname: Bay State; Old Colony
Population: 6,349,097 (13th)
Area: 10,555 sq. miles (44th)
Climate: Temperate, colder and drier in west
Capital: Boston
Entered Union: February 6, 1788 (6th)
Motto: By the sword we seek peace, but peace only under liberty.
Song: All Hail to Massachusetts
Flower: Mayflower
Tree: American elm
Bird: Chickadee

Famous "Bay Staters": John Adams, John Quincy Adams, Samuel Adams, Louisa May Alcott, Horatio Alger, Susan B. Anthony, Clara Barton, Alexander Graham Bell, Stephen Breyer, George Bush, John Cheever, E.E. Cummings, Emily Dickinson, Ralph Waldo Emerson, John Hancock, Nathaniel Hawthorne, Oliver Wendell Holmes, John F. Kennedy, Jack Lemmon, Samuel F.B. Morse, Edgar Allen Poe, Paul Revere, Dr. Seuss, Henry David Thoreau, Barbara Walters, James McNeil Whistler, John Greenleaf Whittier

History: The Algonquians and several other tribes of Native Americans were on hand to greet the Pilgrims, when they settled Plymouth in 1620, and celebrated the first Thanksgiving Day with them in 1621. During the next two decades, some 25,000 new settlers arrived. By the 1670's, relations between Native Americans and English settlers had deteriorated. In 1675-76, the little known King Phillip's War ended Native American resistance. It was followed by a more gruesome episode in American history, the Salem Witch Trials. Demonstrations against the British restrictions set off the Boston Massacre in 1770, the Boston Tea Party in 1773, and, in 1775 "the shot heard 'round the world" was fired in Lexington, precipitating the Revolutionary War. Boston ranks with Philadelphia as one of America's most significant historic cities, and today it is a living American "history book." Plimouth Plantation is a *must see.* America's first university, Harvard (1636), where the first digital computer was developed, is located in Cambridge. John F. Kennedy, one of the nation's most beloved presidents, was born and raised here.

Geography: Highest Point: 3,491 feet, Mt. Greylock. Lowest Point: Sea level, Atlantic Ocean. Time Zone: Eastern. Capital: Boston. Major cities: Boston (Population: 575,000, Metropolitan area, 3,000,000), Worcester (170,000), Lowell (170,000), Springfield (157,000). The most populous state in New England, the large cities hug the Atlantic seaboard. South and east is the magnificent "hook" of Cape Cod and the outlying islands of Martha's Vineyard and Nantucket. The jagged, indented coast gives way to stony upland pastures near the center of the state, and then to gentle, rolling hills in the west. Except for the west, the land is rocky, sandy, and not fertile.

Tourist Information: 1-800-227-MASS; Website: www.massvacation.com.

Recreation Areas
For You and Your Pet

All of these areas permit pets on a leash.

State Recreation Areas

Ames Nowell State Park: 607 acres, northwest of Abingdon via State Route 123, Horse rental, picnicking, hiking trails, boating, fishing, winter sports.

Ashland State Park: 47 acres, 2 miles southwest of Ashland on State Route 135. Picnicking, hiking trails, boating, fishing, swimming, winter sports.

Beartown State Park: 10,897 acres, 3 miles southeast of Stockbridge on State Route 23. Camping, picnicking, hiking trails, fishing, swimming, winter sports.

Boston Harbor Islands: In Boston Harbor:

  Bumpkin Island: Camping, picnicking, hiking trails, boating, fishing.

  Grape Island: Camping, picnicking, hiking trails, boating, fishing.

  Great Brewster Island: Camping, picnicking, hiking trails, boating, fishing.

  Lovell's Island: Camping, picnicking, hiking trails, boating, fishing, swimming.

  Paddock's Island: Camping, picnicking, hiking trails, boating, fishing.

  Thompson's Island: Picnicking, hiking trails, boating, fishing, food service.

Bradley Palmer State Park: 721 acres, southwest of Topsfield of US 1. Hiking trails, boating, fishing, winter sports.

Brimfield State Park: 3,250 acres, 2 miles south of Brimfield, off US 20. Horse rental, picnicking, fishing, swimming, winter sports.

Buffumville State Park: 400 acres, 4 miles south of North Oxford on State Route 12. Picnicking, boating, boat ramp, fishing, swimming.

Chester-Blandford State Park: 2,308 acres, 4 miles southeast of Chester on US 20. Camping, picnicking, hiking trails, boating, fishing, winter sports.

Chicopee State Park: 574 acres on Burnett Road in Chicopee. Picnicking, fishing, swimming, bicycle trails, winter sports.

Clarksburg State Park: 3,431 acres, 3 miles north of North Adams on State Route 8. Camping, picnicking, hiking trails, boating, fishing, swimming, winter sports.

Cochituate State Park: 1,126 acres, 3 miles east of Framingham off State Route 30. Picnicking, hiking trails, boating, boat ramp, fishing, swimming, food service.

Conway State Park: 1,946 acres, south of Conway via State Route 116. Horse rental, hiking trails, fishing, winter sports.

D.A.R. State Park: 1,517 acres, 3 miles north of Goshen off State Route 9. Horse rental, camping, picnicking, hiking trails, boating, fishing, swimming, winter sports.

Demarest Lloyd State Park: 222 acres, 3 miles south of Dartmouth off US 6 on Slocum Neck. Picnicking, fishing, swimming.

Douglas State Park: 4,595 acres, 2 miles west of Douglas off State Route 16. Horse rental, picnicking, hiking trails, boating, boat ramp, fishing, swimming, winter sports.

Erving State Park: 4,479 acres, 2 miles northeast of Erving on State Route 2A. Hose rental, camping, picnicking, hiking trails, boating, boat ramp, fishing, swimming, winter sports.

Granville State Park: 2,376 acres, 1 mile southwest of West Granville off State Route 57. Horse rental, camping, picnicking, hiking trails, fishing, swimming, winter sports.

Hampton Ponds State Park: 42 acres, northeast of Southampton of State Route 10. Picnicking, hiking trails, boating, boat ramp, fishing, swimming.

Harold Parker State Park: 3,500 acres, 2 miles northwest of Middleton off State Route 114. Horse rental, camping, picnicking, hiking trails, boating, fishing, swimming, winter sports.

Holland Pond State Park: 35 acres, 2 miles north of Holland off State Route 20. Horse rental, picnicking, boating, boat ramp, fishing, swimming.

Hopkinton State Park: 1,450 acres, 3 miles north of Hopkinton on State Route 85. Horse rental, picnicking, hiking trails, boating, fishing, swimming, winter sports.

Horseneck Beach State Park: 537 acres, 14 miles south of Fall River on State Route 88 at Horseneck Beach. Camping, picnicking, boating, boat ramp, fishing, swimming, food service.

J. A. Skinner State Park: 390 acres, 3 miles north of South Hadley on State Route 47. Snowmobiling, horse rental, picnicking, hiking trails, winter sports, visitor center.

Kenneth M. Dubuque Memorial Park: 7,822 acres off State Route 8A near Hawley. Horse rental, camping, hiking trails, boating, fishing, winter sports.

Leominster State Park: 4,126 acres, 7 miles south of Fitchburg on State Route 31. Horse rental, picnicking, hiking trails, boating, fishing, swimming, winter sports.

Massasoit State Park: 1,500 acres, 3 miles west of Middleboro off State Route 18, Horse rentals, camping, picnicking, hiking trails, boating, fishing, swimming, winter sports.

Mohawk Trail: 6,457 acres, 3 miles west of Charlemont on State Route 2. Camping, picnicking, hiking trails, fishing, swimming, winter sports, lodge/cabins.

Mount Grace State Forest: 1,689 acres, off State Route 78 in Warwick. Horse rentals, picnicking, hiking trails, winter sports.

Mount Greylock State Park: 12,500 acres, south of North Adams off State Route 2. Horse rentals, camping, picnicking, hiking trails, fishing, winter sports, visitor center, lodge/cabins, food service.

Mount Washington State Park: 4,169 acres, southwest of Egremont off State Route 41 on Mount Washington Road. Bash Bish Falls, horse rentals, camping, hiking trails, boating, fishing, winter sports.

Myles Standish State Park: 14,651 acres, 6 miles west of Plymouth off US 3. Horse rentals, camping, picnicking, hiking trails, boating, fishing, swimming, bicycle trails, winter sports.

October Mountain State Park: 16,127 acres, 3 miles north of Lee on a county road. Horse rentals, camping, hiking trails, boating, fishing, winter sports.

Otter River State Park: 12,788 acres, 1 miles north of Baldwinsville on US 202. Camping, picnicking, hiking trails, fishing, swimming, winter sports.

Pittsfield State Park: 10,000 acres, 4 miles northwest of Pittsfield. Horse rentals, Camping, picnicking, hiking trails, boating, fishing, swimming, winter sports, visitor center.

Quinsigamond State Park: 51 acres, 2 miles east of Worcester off State Route 9. Picnicking, boating, boat ramp, fishing, swimming.

Robinson State Park: 811 acres, 3 miles west on State Route 187 at Feeding Hills. Horse rentals, picnicking, hiking trails, fishing, swimming, bicycle trails, winter sports.

Roland C. Nickerson State Park: 1,955 acres, 1 mile east of East Brewster off State Route 6A. Horse rentals, camping, picnicking, hiking trails, boating, boat ramp, fishing, swimming, bicycle trails, winter sports, lodging/cabins, food service.

Rutland State Park: 396 acres, 3 miles southwest of Rutland on State Route 122A. Horse rentals, boating, boat ramp, fishing, swimming, winter sports.

Salisbury Beach State Park: 520 acres, 2 miles east of Salisbury off State Route 1A. Camping, boating, boat ramp, fishing, swimming, food service.

Sandisfield State Park: 7,785 acres, 1 miles west of Sandisfield off State Route 57. Horse rental, camping, picnicking, hiking trails, boating, boat ramp, fishing, swimming, winter sports.

Savoy Mountain State Park: 11,118 acres, 6 miles southeast of North Adams off State Route 2. Horse rentals, camping, picnicking, hiking trails, boating, boat ramp, fishing, swimming, winter sports, lodge/cabins.

Scusset Beach State Park: 380 acres, 3 miles east of Bournedale on Cape Cod Bay off US 6 and State Route 3A. Camping, picnicking, hiking trails, fishing, swimming, bicycle trails, food service.

Spencer State Park: 965 acres, ½ mile south of Spencer on State Route 31. Historic park, picnicking, hiking trails, boating, fishing, swimming, winter sports.

Streeter Point State Park: 10 acres, 1 miles west of Sturbridge off State Route 20. Picnicking, boating, boat ramp, fishing, swimming.

Tolland State Park: 4,893 acres, 3 miles north of New Boston off State Route 8. Horse rentals, camping, picnicking, hiking trails, boating, boat ramp, fishing, swimming, winter sports.

Wachusett Mountain State Park: 2,842 acres, southwest of Shirley. Downhill skiing, horse rentals, picnicking, hiking trails, winter sports, visitor center, food service.

Wells State Park: 1,470 acres, 2 miles north of Sturbridge off State Route 49N. Camping, hiking trails, boating, boat ramp, fishing, swimming, winter sports.

Wendell State Park: 7,900 acres, east of Farley, off State Route 2 on Wendell Road. Horse rentals, picnicking, hiking trails, boating, boat ramp, fishing, swimming, winter sports.

Willard Brook State Park: 2,380 acres, 3 miles east of Ashby off State Route 119. Scenic, horse rentals, camping, picnicking, hiking trails, fishing, swimming, winter sports, lodge/cabins.

Windsor Forest: 1,743 acres off State Route 116 in Windsor. Camping, picnicking, hiking trails, boating, fishing, swimming, winter sports.

Wompatuck: 3,500 acres off State Route 228 southeast of Hingham. Horse rentals, camping, hiking trails, fishing, bicycle trails, winter sports, visitor center.

University Lodge

345 North Pleasant Street
Amherst, MA 01002
413-256-8111

Type of Lodging: Motel
Room Rates: $74–$110.
Pet Charges and Deposits: None.
Pet Policy: All pets welcome.
Amenities: Extended cable TV, radios, coffee makers, data port/modem telephones, 2 stories, exterior corridors.
Rated: 2 Paws — 20 rooms.

University Lodge is a small, cozy lodging, less than a mile north of the center of town. It's a traditional older motel, well kept and appealing. Amherst, named for Lord Jeffrey Amherst, a British general in the French and Indian War, tried several times during the early years to industrialize. Ultimately, the two realized that cattle farming was Amherst's future. Massachusetts Agricultural College sprang up in the 1860's and subsequently became the University of Massachusetts. Earlier, in 1821, Amherst College was dedicated to preparing young men for missionary work. By the mid-19th century, it took a more liberal attitude, graduating such notables as Henry Ward Beecher and Calvin Coolidge. The National Yiddish Book Center at 1021 W. Street, on the campus of Hampshire College preserves more than 1.3 million books written in Yiddish in a building designed to resemble a 19th century *shtetl.*

Jenkins Inn

7 West Street
Barre, MA 01005
800-378-7373 • 978-355-6444

Type of Lodging: Historic Country Inn
Room Rates: $125–$175. AAA and AARP discounts.
Pet Charges and Deposits: $5 per day per pet. 1 night's refundable deposit.
Pet Policy: Manager's prior approval required.
Amenities: Extended cable TV, VCR's, free local telephone calls, 4-star restaurant on premises, cocktails, smoke-free premises, some coffee makers, data port/modem telephones, exercise area for pets, 2 stories, interior corridors.
Rated: 3 Paws — 5 rooms.

Whether your visit is a fall foliage retreat, a winter ski vacation, an antiquing weekend, or simply a getaway, the Jenkins Inn in historic Barre provides all the comfort and amenities of a home away from home. This wonderful find is situated on the town green. It's an 1834 residence with lovely English gardens surrounding the house. Some rooms have private bath, others share a bath. Guests will find shopping and theaters nearby, or consider sightseeing in Old Sturbridge Village. For the outdoor enthusiast, Mount Wachusett, Rutland State Park, and the Quabbin Reservoir provide beautiful hiking trails in summer and ski vacations in winter.

❖❖❖❖❖

Boston Harbor Hotel

70 Rowes Wharf
Boston, MA 02110
617-439-7000

Type of Lodging: Hotel
Room Rates: $400–$2,000.
Pet Charges and Deposits: None.
Pet Policy: All pets welcome.
Amenities: Extended cable TV, movies (fee), dual phone lines, voice mail, honor bar, hair dryers, heated pool, whirlpool, sauna, steam rooms, health club adjacent, boat dock (fee), massage (fee), gift shop, afternoon tea, area transportation, valet laundry, conference facilities, administrative services, fax, PC (fee), restaurant, cocktails, radios, data port / modem telephones, some refrigerators, some microwaves, 16 stories, interior corridors.
Rated: 5 Paws — 230 units, including rooms and suites.

Boston Harbor Inn is an extraordinarily luxurious hotel overlooking Boston Harbor. You'll find gracious hospitality and every amenity here. It's one of a handful of five-paw lodgings in this book, and the rating is deserved. More than any other American city, Boston is where our nation began. From Faneuil Hall to Paul Revere's house, the spirit of the Revolution lives on. Despite its being a large, sophisticated metropolis, Boston has a reputation as a smug refuge for stuffy intellectuals, stemming from its Puritan roots and the self-important air of

"Boston Brahmins," who referred to their town as "the Hub of the Universe." There are so many standout things to see, one hardly knows where to begin. But one thing's for certain: you'd better pack your walking shoes before you start, because Boston truly is a "walking city," best seen on foot—for everywhere you go is like opening a history textbook.

Colonnade Hotel

120 Huntington Avenue
Boston, MA 02116
800-962-3030 • 617-42407000
www.colonnadehotel.com

Type of Lodging: Hotel

Room Rates: $245–$450. AAA and AARP discounts.

Pet Charges and Deposits: None.

Pet Policy: All pets welcome.

Amenities: Extended cable TV, movies, rooftop heated pool, whirlpool, sauna, exercise room, conference facilities, fax, restaurant, cocktails, data port/modem telephones, some refrigerators, some microwaves, 16 stories, interior corridors.

Rated: 4 Paws — 285 rooms and 15 suites

The Colonnade, located in Boston's Back Bay, is an independent luxury hotel in the European tradition, catering to the discriminating traveler. Lauded for its bold, modern architecture, the building's façade is defined by a series of exterior columns that provide a look of contemporary grace and elegance. The guest rooms are classically furnished and thoughtfully designed with seating areas and comfortable work desks. The amenities range from plush bathrobes to telephones in the bathrooms. The suite feature Jacuzzi baths, stereo CD systems, and wide screen telephones. The resort-style swimming area commands stunning views of Boston and includes lounge chairs, tables for poolside dining, and changing rooms. For indoor recreation, enjoy the fully equipped fitness room. The award-winning cuisine of Café Promenade delights every taste and mood with its innovative seasonal fare.

Eliot Suite Hotel

370 Commonwealth Avenue
Boston, MA 02215
617-267-1607

Type of Lodging: Historic Hotel

Room Rates: $275–$415.

Pet Charges and Deposits: None.

Pet Policy: Small pets only.

Amenities: Extended cable TV, movies (fee), video games, dual phone lines, fax, honor bars, voice mail, irons, hair dryers, some CD players, valet laundry, massage (fee), conference facilities, restaurant, radios, data port/modem telephones, some microwaves, some VCR's, 9 stories, interior corridors.

Rated: 4 Paws — 95 units, including rooms and suites.

An intimate European luxury hotel in the center of Boston, the Eliot Suite Hotel, situated at the corner of Commonwealth and Massachusetts, provides understated elegance and highly personalized service. Boston's "Central Park"—The Boston Common—is the oldest public park in the United States. The area was set off in 1634 for common use as a cow pasture and training field. The Puritans kept stocks and pens for the punishment of those who profaned the Sabbath, and the British gathered in the park before the Battle of Bunker Hill. The Boston Public Library, at 700 Boylston Street, was established in 1848 and was the nation's first public library, allowing individuals to borrow books and materials. Today, it also features wonderful art and architectural exhibits, including John Singer Sargent's "Triumph of Religion," and the works of other American artists.

❀ ❀ ❀ ❀ ❀

Fairmont Copley Plaza–Boston

Copley Square
138 St. James Avenue
Boston, MA 02116
617-267-5300

Type of Lodging: Classic Hotel
Room Rates: $265–$425; AAA and AARP discounts.
Pet Charges and Deposits: None.
Pet Policy: Small pets only.
Amenities: Extended cable TV, voice mail, fax, honor bars, irons, hair dryers, exercise room, gift shop, valet laundry, conference facilities, administrative services, PC, airport transportation (fee), restaurant, movies (fee), radios, data port / modem telephones, some refrigerators, some VCR's (fee), 6 stories, interior corridors.
Rated: 5 Paws — 379 units.

The Fairmont Copley Plaza is a classic historic luxury hotel. You'll find everything you expect at this 5-paw standout. Huge ballrooms and crystal chandeliers for this elegant queen. You are surrounded by class from the moment you enter the front door—indeed, the doorman service has won several awards. There's a famous cigar bar and steakhouse. You are pampered with luxury at the Fairmont. Since it's conveniently situated in busy Copley Square, you can take the trolley around Boston, or simply walk across the street into an upscale mall with shops that go on for several blocks. The best on-foot "overlook" of Boston is to follow the Freedom Trail (marked by a red line, so it's easy to see). Just a few of the things you'll see include Boston Common, the Old North Church, Paul Revere's house, and Bunker Hill—but there's so very much more to gawk at on this trail.

Four Seasons Hotel Boston

*200 Boylston Street
Boston, MA 02116
617-338-4400*

Type of Lodging: Hotel

Room Rates: $550–$750, some suites: $750–$3,750; AAA discounts.

Pet Charges and Deposits: None.

Pet Policy: Small pets only.

Amenities: Extended cable TV, movies (fee), dual phone lines, voice mail, safes, honor bars, hair dryers, some CD players, fax, irons, gift shop, afternoon tea, area transportation within 5 miles, valet laundry, massage (fee), conference facilities, administrative services, PC, restaurant, cocktails, babysitting (fee), indoor pool, health club, radios, data port / modem telephones, some VCR's, 16 stories, interior corridors.

Rated: 5 Paws — 288 units, including rooms and suites.

The Four Seasons is one of the most elegant luxury hotels in the entire northeastern United States. You overlook extensive public gardens and the guest rooms ensconce you in unimagined charm, taste, and comfort. This is an easy choice five paw hotel, and the Aujourd'hui Restaurant, a smoke-free venue, by the way, is a five star dining experience, situated right in the hotel. Everything about the Four Seasons is *beyond* first class. Faneuil Hall, once a meeting house for Revolutionary masterminds, and the adjacent Quincy Market constitute the entertainment and food "center" of town—everything from 150 or so restaurants, to almost every brand name store you can think of, to a constant stream of street performers, makes this one of the liveliest venues in the Northeast.

Hilton Boston Back Bay

40 Dalton Street
Boston, MA 02115
617-236-1100

Type of Lodging: Hotel
Room Rates: $250–$500.
Pet Charges and Deposits: None.
Pet Policy: Small pets only.
Amenities: Extended cable TV, movies (fee), dual phone lines, voice mail, honor bars, hair dryers, irons, heated pool, exercise room, gift shop, valet laundry, conference facilities, administrative services, fax, airport transportation (fee), restaurant, radios, coffee makers, data port/modem telephones, some refrigerators (fee), 26 stories, interior corridors.
Rated: 3 Paws — 385 units.

This wonderful skyscraper Hilton Hotel is adjacent to Copley Place at the corner of Dalton and Belvedere Streets. Not only does it boast a "power location," but it is a first class lodging in comfort, luxury, and welcome amenities. Everything is tastefully done. Boston's roots were established in 1630, when Massachusetts Bay Puritans sailed to the New World, seeking freedom of worship—for themselves. Eleven ships landed at Salem. Their inhabitants moved to the hilly peninsula above the Charles River. By the end of the 17th century, Boston was one of the busiest ports in the British Empire and the largest town in North America. The 265-acre Arnold Arboretum on the Arborway in Jamaica Plain, contains 4,000 kinds of trees—all from the northern temperate regions.

Hotel LeMeridien

250 Franklin Street
Boston, MA 02110
617-451-1900

Type of Lodging: Hotel
Room Rates: $375–$550.
Pet Charges and Deposits: None.
Pet Policy: Small pets only.
Amenities: Extended cable TV, movies (fee), voice mail, honor bars, hair dyers, irons, some CD players, heated pool, whirlpool, sauna, gift shop, area transportation, valet laundry, massage (fee), conference facilities, administrative services, PC, fax, restaurant, radios, coffee makers, data port/modem telephones, some VCR's, 9 stories, interior corridors.
Rated: 4 Paws — 326 rooms.

The Hotel Le Meridien, a European-style luxury hotel, is set in the center of town on Post Office Square. The building is old and historic, but once inside, you are treated to a superb lodging experience, replete with every comfort you can imagine. The Bull & Finch Pub at 84 Beacon Street, inspired the setting for the TV show "Cheers." The front entrance of the bar was used for the opening scene for 11 seasons. The Boston Tea Party Ship & Museum recreates the notorious protest of tax on tea. The museum includes a full-scale working replica of the brig *Beaver II*, one of the three tea party ships. Boston National Historical Park consists of seven sites along the Freedom Trail. Only two of these sites, Bunker Hill Monument and the Charlestown Navy Yard are owned by the federal government.

Howard Johnson Lodge Fenway

1271 Boylston Street
Boston, MA 02215
617-267-8300

Type of Lodging: Motor Inn

Room Rates: $105–$199; AAA and AARP discounts.

Pet Charges and Deposits: None.

Pet Policy: All pets welcome.

Amenities: Extended cable TV, movies (fee), voice mail, some irons, hair dryers, small outdoor pool, area transportation, airport transportation (fee), valet laundry, free newspaper, restaurant, cocktails, coffee makers, data port/modem telephones, some refrigerators, some microwaves, 2 stories, interior corridors.

Rated: 2 Paws — 94 rooms.

The Howard Johnson Lodge Fenway is a compact, comfortable travelers' hotel in a busy section of town, next to Fenway Park and near Hynes Auditorium, Boston University, and Copley Place, It's 2 miles to downtown, 5 miles to Logan International Airport. The USS *Constitution*—*"Old Ironsides"*—was launched in 1797 and was the nemesis of French privateers. It is the oldest commissioned ship in the world. The 54-gun frigate was constructed of seasoned live oak and red cedar timbers, secured by bolts and copper sheathing made by Paul Revere. It's located at Pier 1, just a short distance from Edmund Hartt's Shipyard, from where it was launched. It gained immortality in the War of 1812. The adjacent USS Constitution Museum contains exhibits that allow visitors to command *Old Ironsides* in battle.

Millennium Bostonian Hotel

Faneuil Hall Marketplace
Boston, MA 02109
617-523-3600

Type of Lodging: Hotel

Room Rates: $310–$425.

Pet Charges and Deposits: None.

Pet Policy: Small pets only.

Amenities: Extended cable TV, movies (fee), dual phone lines, voice mail, safes, honor bars, hair dryers, irons, some CD players, exercise room, valet laundry, conference facilities, restaurant, cocktails, radios, data port/modem telephones, 8 stories, interior corridors.

Rated: 3 Paws — 201 rooms.

If you're touring downtown Boston, the Millennium Bostonian couldn't be more conveniently located. Faneuil Hall Marketplace and Quincy Marketplace are two of the premier fun places to be in the "land of the bean and the cod." Guest rooms are cozy and attractive, and top floor units have a view of the city skyline. There are some suites and some units with whirlpool baths. The Bunker Hill Monument, located on Breed's Hill in Charlestown, commemorates the site of the Battle of Bunker Hill (June 17, 1775). The 221-foot tall granite obelisk contains a spiral staircase to the top, from which you get a splendid view of the "Hub of the Universe." The Charles River Reservation is an outdoor recreation area extending along both sides of the Charles River (961 acres), where you'll find bicycle paths, six swimming pools, 12 tennis courts, a fitness course, and other such facilities.

❀ ❀ ❀ ❀ ❀

The Ritz-Carlton–Boston

15 Arlington Street
Boston, MA 02117
617-536-5700

Type of Lodging: Hotel
Room Rates: $550–$2,000.
Pet Charges and Deposits: $75 deposit, $20 per day per pet.
Pet Policy: All pets welcome.
Amenities: Extended cable TV, movies (fee), dual phone lines, voice mail, safes, honor bars, hair dryers, irons, exercise room, gift shop, afternoon tea, area transportation, airport transportation (fee), valet laundry, massage (fee), conference facilities, administrative services, PC, fax, three restaurants, two cocktail lounges, pet exercise area, radios, data port / modem telephones, 17 stories, interior corridors.
Rated: 5 Paws — 275 units.

The Ritz-Carlton is a property that richly deserves its five-paw award. Situated at Arlington and Newbury Streets, it overlooks the Public Gardens. This traditional, formal hotel, which offers gracious guest services as well as old world charm and elegance, has just undergone a multimillion dollar renovation, and you may rest assured that you will be one of the first to find comfort in this superlative old-new luxury lodging. Guest rooms and suites are furnished with French Provincial furnishings, complemented by imported fabrics and distinctive works of art. Casual or elegant dining is available in one of the three restaurants. An acclaimed seasonal menu offering innovative contemporary French cuisine greets you in the Dining Room. The Café is elegantly simple, with soft harp music providing a romantic backdrop. The Roof offers fine cuisine with spectacular views and dancing to the Ritz Carlton Orchestra.

Sheraton-Boston Hotel

39 Dalton Street At Prudential Center
Boston, MA 02199
617-236-2000

Type of Lodging: Hotel

Room Rates: $375–$650, some suites: $550–$2,500; AAA and AARP discounts.

Pet Charges and Deposits: None.

Pet Policy: All pets welcome.

Amenities: Extended cable TV, movies (fee), video games, voice mail, irons, hair dryers, some safes, heated pool, whirlpool, sauna, gift shop, valet laundry, area transportation (fee), conference facilities, administrative services, PC, fax, restaurant, cocktails, radios, coffee makers, data port/modem telephones, some refrigerators, 29 stories, interior corridors.

Rated: 3 Paws — 1,215 units, including rooms and suites.

The Sheraton-Boston Hotel, situated at Prudential Center, features wonderful, demonstratively luxurious public facilities and rooms ranging from compact to spacious. The hotel is huge—over 1,200 units—and sky-tall, 29 stories. The Children's Museum of Boston at Museum Wharf offers three floors of hands-on exhibits featuring Arthur's World, giant building toys, raceways, and a climbing maze. Boston National Historical Park's visitor center, at 15 State Street, across from the old State House, gives you an overview of Boston's Colonial history through audiovisual presentation. Rangers conduct free walking tours and programs throughout this magnificent historic park. Fort Warren, on Georges Island in Boston Harbor, can be reached by ferry from Hewitt's Cove.

Swissotel Boston

One Avenue Lafayette
Boston, MA 02111
617-451-2600

Type of Lodging: Hotel

Room Rates: $350–$485, some suites: $475–$2,500; AAA discounts.

Pet Charges and Deposits: None.

Pet Policy: Signed waiver.

Amenities: Extended cable TV, movies (fee), data port/modem telephones, dual phone lines, voice mail, honor bars, hair dryers, irons, heated pool, whirlpool, sauna, exercise room, gift shop, valet laundry, massage (fee), conference facilities, administrative services, fax, PC (fee), free newspaper, restaurant, cocktails, radios, coffee makers, 21 stories, interior corridors.

Rated: 4 Paws — 501 units, including rooms and suites.

Swissotel, located in the heart of downtown Boston, just east of the Boston Common at Lafayette Place, offers an atrium-like setting on several floors, and 501 superlative guest units. The "must see" Isabella Stewart Gardner Museum exhibits masterpieces by Titian, Rembrandt, James McNeil Whistler, John Singer Sargent, and others, in a setting resembling a Venetian palace. The Museum of Afro-American History was dedicated in 1806, and was the center for African-American community activities for over 100 years. The Museum includes the African Meeting House, purportedly the oldest standing African-American church building in the United States, and Abiel Smith School, the first publicly funded grammar school in the country for African-American children.

The Westin Hotel–Copley Place Boston

Copley Square—10 Huntington Avenue
Boston, MA 02116
617-262-9600

Type of Lodging: Hotel

Room Rates: $250–$500. AAA and AARP discounts.

Pet Charges and Deposits: $350 deposit.

Pet Policy: Manager's prior approval required.

Amenities: Extended cable TV, movies (fee), video games, dual phone lines, voice mail, safes, honor bars, hair dryers, irons, heated pool, whirlpool, sauna, gift shop, valet laundry, massage (fee), conference facilities, administrative services, fax, PC, airport transportation (fee), restaurant, cocktails, radios, coffee makers, data port/modem telephones, some VCR's (fee), 36 stories, interior corridors.

Rated: 3 Paws – 800 rooms.

The contemporary Westin Copley Place Boston is located in the city's charming and fashionable Back Bay, Boston's finest location. Eight hundred newly renovated guest rooms offer breathtaking views of Boston. Sample some of Boston's favorite restaurants within the Westin Copley Place, or enjoy 24-hour room service. The full service health club includes and indoor swimming pool, Jacuzzi, stairmasters, treadmill, and Nautilus equipment—all complimentary to hotel guests. The hotel is linked via skybridge to the upscale Copley Place Shopping Galleries, the new Prudential Center Fashion Court, and the Hynes Convention Center. The Westin is within walking distance of the historic Boston Common and Public Gardens, Beacon Hill, the Financial District, Faneuil Hall-Quincy Market Place, and the quaint historic north end and waterfront.

Hilton–Boston Logan Airport

85 Terminal Road
Boston, MA 02128
617-568-6700

Type of Lodging: Hotel

Room Rates: $300–$475; AAA discounts.

Pet Charges and Deposits: None.

Pet Policy: All pets welcome.

Amenities: Extended cable TV, movies (fee), video games, dual phone lines, voice mail, honor bars, hair dryers, irons, some CD players, heated pool, whirlpool, sauna, steam rooms, jogging, exercise room, gift shop, valet laundry, massage (fee), conference facilities, administrative services, restaurant, cocktails, radios, coffee makers, data port/modem telephones, some refrigerators, 10 stories, interior corridors.

Rated: 3 Paws – 599 rooms.

The Hilton is a carefully conceived, nicely executed airport hotel with expansive public areas and richly decorated guest units and baths. Once inside, you would not have any idea that this was an airport facility—it's that elegant *and* that quiet. Faneuil Hall, donated to the city in 1742 by wealthy industrialist Peter Faneuil, was burned in 1761, restored in 1763, and enlarged in 1805. British officers used the building as a theater during their occupation of Boston during the Revolutionary War. Three signers of the Declaration of Independence—John Hancock, Samuel Adams, and Robert Treat Paine—as well as Paul Revere, Peter Faneuil, Boston Massacre victims, and Benjamin Franklin's parents—found their final interment at the Granary Building Burial Ground, Tremont Street at the head of Bromfield Street.

Ramada Inn–Boston

800 Morrissey Boulevard
Boston, MA 02122
617-287-9100

Type of Lodging: Motel

Room Rates: $125–$200, including Continental breakfast. AAA and AARP discounts.

Pet Charges and Deposits: Inquire.

Pet Policy: Manager's prior approval required.

Amenities: Extended cable TV, movies (fee), voice mail, some irons, some hair dryers, outdoor pool, health club adjacent, area transportation—designated locations, coin laundry, conference facilities, fax, free local telephone calls, restaurant adjacent, radios, data port/modem telephones, some refrigerators (fee), some microwaves (fee), 2-3 stories, interior/exterior corridors.

Rated: 2 Paws — 174 units.

The Ramada Inn boasts 174 newly renovated guest rooms and an outdoor swimming pool, three adjacent restaurants and lounge, and multipurpose business meeting rooms. Historic downtown Boston is 3½ miles away. There's a caring and professional team ready to meet your every need. A CityPass, valid for 9 days once you visit the first attraction on your agenda, available from most visitor information centers and major hotels, offers great savings on admission to the Isabella Stewart Gardner Museum, the Museum at the John F. Kennedy Library, the John Hancock Observatory, the Museum of Fine Arts, and the New England Aquarium.

Seaport Hotel

One Seaport Lane
Boston, MA 02210
617-385-4000

Type of Lodging: Hotel

Room Rates: $275–$425; AAA and AARP discounts.

Pet Charges and Deposits: $35 deposit.

Pet Policy: All pets welcome.

Amenities: Extended cable TV, movies (fee), video games, dual phone lines, voice mail, safes, honor bars, irons, hair dryers, sauna, lap pool, gift shop, area transportation, valet laundry, massage (fee), conference facilities, administrative services, fax, PC (fee), restaurant, cocktails, non-smoking facility, radios, coffee makers, data port/modem telephones, 18 stories, interior corridors.

Rated: 3 Paws — 426 units (some suites, some whirlpool units).

The Seaport Hotel is a non-tipping and non-smoking hotel, giving it a clean, fresh atmosphere. It's located at the World Trade Center/Commonwealth Pier. Along with comfortable rooms, you'll find friendly, helpful service, and a pet-friendly attitude. The Museum at the John F. Kennedy Library is the nation's official memorial to its 35th president. In 21 exhibits, including 3 theaters and 20 videotape presentations, you'll learn about the life and times of President Kennedy and first lady Jacqueline Kennedy Onassis. The Museum of Fine Arts, Boston, contains nearly 200 galleries of Asiatic, Egyptian, Classical, European, and American paintings and sculpture. Impressionist works by Monet, Manet, Picasso, and Renoir mesh with works by Rembrandt, John Singer Sargent, and James McNeil Whistler.

THE
Boston

VICINITY

Including

Andover	Danvers	Newton
Bedford	Dedham	North Chelmsford
Billerica	Framingham	Revere
Braintree	Franklin	Rockport
Brookline	Gloucester	Salem
Burlington	Lawrence	Tewksbury
Cambridge	Marblehead	Waltham
Concord	Marlborough	Woburn

ANDOVER, MASSACHUSETTS (Pop. 29,200) (Boston Vicinity)

Hawthorn Suites—Andover

4 Riverside Drive—Andover Research Park
Andover, MA 01810
978-475-6000

Type of Lodging: Extended Stay Motel
Room Rates: $135–$175; AAA discounts.
Pet Charges and Deposits: $50 fee, plus $10 extra charge per day per pet.
Pet Policy: All pets welcome.
Amenities: Extended cable TV, movies (fee), video games, dual phone lines, voice mail, irons, heated pool, whirlpool, exercise room, sports court, coin laundry, conference facilities, administrative services, VCR's, radios, coffee makers, microwaves, refrigerators, data port/modem telephones, 3 stories, interior corridors.
Rated: 3 Paws — 84 units.

Hawthorn Suites—Andover is a wonderful long-term place to stay. It's right near the Andover Research Park. 81 of the units ate efficiencies and 3 come with complete kitchen. Furniture is comfortable and the mini-suites are spacious, clean, and modern. The Robert S. Peabody Museum of Archaeology has exhibits about cultures indigenous to the Americas, while the Andover Historical Society features 18th and 19th century exhibits, period rooms, and an 1819 barn. In Boston, the Museum of Science displays nearly 575 interactive exhibits about natural history, physical science, medicine, and astronomy. The Museum includes the Charles Hayden Planetarium (shows about stars, planets, and other phenomena of the universe), and the Magar Omni Theater, a 5-story domed screen that creates a wraparound effect.

Wyndham Andover

123 Old River Road
Andover, MA 01810
978-975-3600

Type of Lodging: Hotel

Room Rates: $149–$179; AAA and AARP discounts.

Pet Charges and Deposits: None.

Pet Policy: Small pets only.

Amenities: Extended cable TV, movies (fee), voice mail, irons, hair dryers, heated pool, whirlpool, sauna, exercise room, valet laundry, conference facilities, restaurant, cocktails, airport transportation (fee), radios, coffee makers, data port/modem telephones, some refrigerators (fee), 5 stories, interior corridors.

Rated: 3 Paws — 293 rooms.

The Wyndham hotel is a moderate high-rise with a beautiful lobby, replete with marble and brass accents. Rooms carry out the theme and are inviting, spacious, and comfortable. The Wyndham is a classy place indeed, and it includes both a restaurant and cocktail lounge. Andover's Addison Gallery of American Art features a collection of ship models and American artwork from the 18th century to the present. The New England Aquarium displays more than 24,000 specimens representing more than 550 species of fish and marine animals ranging from penguins to piranhas. The Nichols House Museum, a Federal-style house on Beacon Hill, was owned by prominent Bostonian Rose Standish Nichols. The house preserves Nichols' 16th through 19th century furnishings, which were characteristic of Boston's "Brahmin" class.

Renaissance Bedford Hotel

44 Middlesex Turnpike
Bedford, MA 01730
781-275-5500

Type of Lodging: Hotel

Room Rates: $249–$289; AAA and AARP discounts.

Pet Charges and Deposits: $100 deposit.

Pet Policy: Small pets only.

Amenities: Extended cable TV, movies (fee), video games, voice mail, honor bars, irons, hair dryers, heated pool, whirlpool, sauna, jogging, exercise room, basketball, tennis courts (fee), gift shop, airport transportation (fee), valet laundry, conference facilities, administrative services, restaurant, radios, coffee makers, data port/modem telephones, 3 stories, interior corridors.

Rated: 3 Paws — 285 rooms.

The Renaissance Bedford's buildings are set in rolling grounds and those grounds are very attractively landscaped. While there are few cozy units with two beds, most of the units are spacious and boast comfortable king-sized beds. There are some suites, and numerous first-class amenities in this fine property. Boston's Old North Church was built in 1723 and is the oldest church building in Boston. On the evening of April 18, 1775, a sexton displayed two lanterns in the steeple to signal the British advancing on Lexington ("One if by land, two if by sea, and I on the opposite shore will be"). The steeple has been destroyed and replaced twice as a result of violent storms. The most recent renovation was 1954. President Ford initiated the nation's Bicentennial from a pew in the Old North Church.

Homewood Suites By Hilton

35 Middlesex Turnpike
Billerica, MA 01821
978-670-7111

Type of Lodging: Extended Stay Motel

Room Rates: $199–$209; AAA and AARP discounts.

Pet Charges and Deposits: $25 fee.

Pet Policy: All pets welcome.

Amenities: Extended cable TV, movies (fee), video games, dual phone lines, voice mail, hair dryers, irons, heated pool, whirlpool, exercise room, airport transportation (fee), coin laundry, conference facilities, administrative services, VCR's, radios, coffee makers, refrigerators, microwaves, data port/modem telephones, 4 stories, interior corridors.

Rated: 3 Paws — 147 suites.

Homewood Suites is an extended-stay hotel that is clean, roomy, and comfortable. Billerica is on the Middlesex Turnpike, well north of Boston, between Burlington and Lowell. Even so, Boston is the magnet to which visitors always return. The Old South Meeting House was built in 1729 as a Puritan church. It was the site of many town meetings, including those that led to the Boston Tea Party. The Old State House started its life as the Old Town House in 1657. It was rebuilt and renamed in 1713, and is Boston's oldest public building. The Boston Massacre occurred at its eastern front in 1770. It was from the Old State House balcony that the Declaration of Independence was read to Bostonians on July 18, 1776.

Days Inn–Braintree

190 Wood Road
Braintree, MA 02184
781-848-1260

Type of Lodging: Motel

Room Rates: $109–$139, including Continental breakfast. AAA and AARP discounts.

Pet Charges and Deposits: $6 per day per pet.

Pet Policy: All pets welcome.

Amenities: Extended cable TV, movies (fee), dual phone lines, voice mail, hair dryers, irons, exercise room, coin laundry, conference facilities, free local telephone calls, radios, coffee makers, data port/modem telephones, some refrigerators, some microwaves, 3 stories, interior corridors.

Rated: 2 Paws — 104 rooms.

Days Inn is a clean, attractive, and reasonable choice for accommodations if you're in Braintree—just a few miles southeast of Boston. The Paul Revere House, built in 1680, is the oldest house in downtown Boston. The restored home, which Paul Revere owned from 1770 to 1800, contains 17th and 18th century furnishings and Revere memorabilia. You'll find a Colonial herb garden and a Revere-made bell on the grounds. The Park Street Church, built in 1809, was the scene of William Lloyd Garrison's first antislavery address in 1829. The 52-story Prudential Center, between Huntington Avenue and Boylston Street, is Boston's first unified business, civic, and residential development. Nearby, the Public Garden opened in 1837 and is said to have been the first public botanical garden in the country.

Bertram Inn

92 Sewall Avenue
Brookline, MA 02146
800-295-3822 • 617-556-2234

Type of Lodging: Bed & Breakfast Inn

Room Rates: $79–$208, including expanded Continental breakfast.

Pet Charges and Deposits: $150 refundable deposit.

Pet Policy: Manager's prior approval required.

Amenities: Common living room with fireplace, 2 stories, interior corridors.

Rated: 3 Paws — 14 rooms.

A stay at the Bertram Inn offers the opportunity to step back into another era. The handsome building was constructed by fine artisans, with oak panels and a sweeping stairway, masterpieces of lead and glass, and fireplaces in the tradition of the Old World. Typical of a large Victorian home, no two rooms are alike. Each of the guest rooms has its own character and size, with accommodations that offer king-sized, queen-sized, double, or twin beds. The large living room with fireplace provides a relaxing environment to read or rest and enjoy afternoon tea. In the morning, this cozy retreat becomes a cheerful breakfast room, where a hearty continental breakfast of fresh-baked muffins and fruits is served. The elegant Victorian home is located near the Commonwealth Mall, Boston Common, and the Charles River Esplanade.

Homestead Village Guest Studios–Boston/Burlington

40 South Avenue
Burlington, MA 01803
781-359-9099

Type of Lodging: Extended Stay Motel

Room Rates: $119–$159,

Pet Charges and Deposits: $75 fee.

Pet Policy: All pets welcome.

Amenities: Extended cable TV, movies (fee), voice mail, hair dryers, irons, coin laundry, health club adjacent, restaurant adjacent, radios, coffee makers, data port/modem telephones, refrigerators, microwaves, some VCR's, 3 stories, interior corridors.

Rated: 2 Paws — 141 mini-suites.

Homestead Village Guest Studios affords you all the spaciousness and comfort of a small, modern mini-apartment at a very affordable price for the Burlington-Boston area. An added plus: an attendant is available 24-hours a day for security. In Boston, the Shirley-Eustis House, built in 1747 in the Palladian style for Royal Colonial Governor William Shirley, also served as the residence of former Massachusetts State Governor William Eustis around the turn of the 19th century. The mansion had been restored to reflect Georgian and Federal architecture and furnishings. The Soldiers' Monument, on Dorchester Heights, is the place from which George Washington drove the British from Boston on March 17, 1776.

Staybridge Suites–Boston/Burlington

11 Old Concord Road
Burlington, MA 01803
781-221-2233

Type of Lodging: Extended Stay Motel

Room Rates: $179–$199; AAA and AARP discounts.

Pet Charges and Deposits: $10 per day per pet.

Pet Policy: All pets welcome.

Amenities: Extended cable TV, movies, dual phone lines, voice mail, hair dryers, irons, heated pool, exercise room, sports court, area transportation, complimentary laundry, conference facilities, VCR's, radios, coffee makers, data port/modem telephones, refrigerators, microwaves, 4 stories, interior corridors.

Rated: 3 Paws — 169 units.

Staybridge Suites are upscale, spacious, clean and inviting. There are 141 efficiencies and 28 two-bedroom units. Complimentary laundry is only one of a large assortment of welcome amenities. Boston's Freedom Trail is a living American History textbook and includes the Boston Common, State House, Park Street Church, Granary Burying Ground, King's Chapel, Old South Meeting House, Old State House, Faneuil Hall, the Paul Revere House, the Old North Church, Charlestown Navy Yard, USS *Constitution*, and Bunker Hill Monument. Boston is a sports town: the Boston Red Sox play at Fenway Park (baseball), the Boston Celtics, one of the most successful basketball franchises in the United States, plays at Fleet Center, and the 2002 Super Bowl Champion New England Patriots, is at home in Foxboro, about 45 minutes south of Boston.

Summerfield Suites By Wyndham

2 Van de Graaff Drive
Burlington, MA 01803
781-270-0800

Type of Lodging: Suite Motel

Room Rates: $249–$329; AAA and AARP discounts.

Pet Charges and Deposits: $50 fee, plus $10 per day per pet.

Pet Policy: All pets welcome.

Amenities: Extended cable TV, movies, dual phone lines, voice mail, hair dryers, irons, heated pool, exercise room, sports court, complimentary evening beverages on Monday-Thursday, area transportation, complimentary laundry, conference facilities, radios, coffee makers, data port/modem telephones, refrigerators, microwaves, VCR's, 3 stories, interior corridors.

Rated: 3 Paws — 151 suites.

Summerfield Suites by Wyndham is the top-of-the-line choice of accommodations in Burlington. The suites are relaxing, attractive, restful, and most accommodating. The Liberty Fleet of Tall Ships is at 67 Long Wharf in Boston. Climb aboard the 80-foot schooner *Liberty* and enjoy the sights of Boston Harbor. You can also set sail on a 2½ hour Sunday brunch cruise on the 125-foot *Liberty Clipper*. The *Spirit of Boston*, which departs from Boston's Commonwealth Pier, offers narrated lunch cruises in Boston Harbor and dinner entertainment cruises. Symphony Hall is home to the world-renowned Boston Symphony Orchestra, as well as the Boston Pops Orchestra. In July and August, the orchestra appears at Tanglewood Music Center in Lenox, Massachusetts.

The Charles Hotel In Harvard Square

One Bennett Street
Cambridge, MA 02138
617-864-1200

Type of Lodging: Hotel

Room Rates: $250–$315; some suites: $315–$3,000. AAA and AARP discounts.

Pet Charges and Deposits: None.

Pet Policy: Small pets only.

Amenities: Extended cable TV, movies (fee), dual phone lines, voice mail, safes, honor bars, hair dryers, irons, heated pool, whirlpool, sauna, steam room, gift shop, valet laundry, massage (fee), conference facilities, fax, restaurant, cocktails, radios, data port/modem telephones, some refrigerators, some VCR's (fee), 10 stories, interior corridors.

Rated: 4 Paws – 293 rooms.

The Charles Hotel, located just south of Harvard Square on the corner of Eliot and Bennett streets, is a charming place, with cozy, country-style rooms in the learning center of the world, literally at the gates of America's first and foremost university. The Charles does not scrimp on amenities, service, or attitude. In 1636, one John Harvard left his library and half his estate to a new college in what was then known as Newtowne...and the rest is history. Harvard, the oldest and most prestigious institution of learning in the United States, shaped the future of what became known as Cambridge. In and around the famous "yard" at Harvard Square, buildings represent the history of architecture in America. You'll find Harvard's collections of Asiatic, Islamic, and ancient art at Harvard's Arthur M. Sackler Museum, while masterpieces of Central and Northern European art, created from the Middle Ages to the present, will be found at Busch-Resinger Museum on the Harvard campus.

Radisson Hotel–Cambridge

777 Memorial Drive
Cambridge, MA 02139
617-492-7777
www.radisson.com

Type of Lodging: Hotel

Room Rates: $149–$339; AAA and AARP discounts.

Pet Charges and Deposits: None.

Pet Policy: All pets welcome.

Amenities: Extended cable TV, movies, dual phone lines, voice mail, hair dryers, irons, small heated indoor pool, valet laundry, conference facilities, restaurant, radios, coffee makers, data port/modem telephones, some refrigerators, some microwaves, 16 stories, interior corridors.

Rated: 3 Paws – 205 rooms.

The Radisson, a proud example of a marvelous chain, overlooks the Charles River. Two highlights of this wonderful property are the Bisuteki Japanese Steak House / Sushi Bar, and the Dionysus, which features fine Greek/American cuisine. This is the newest Radisson in the greater Boston area. It's near Harvard, MIT, Harvard Square. Boston is only a mile away. The Harvard Museum of Natural History houses three museums. Oh, yes, there's "that other Cambridge university"...it's called Massachusetts Institute of Technology—MIT for short—and it's got several attractions of its own, including the Hart Nautical Gallery, the List Visual Arts Center, and the MIT chapel. Old Cambridge goes on for several blocks. The best-known mansion in Cambridge is probably the Longfellow House.

Best Western At Historic Concord

740 Elm Street
Concord, MA 01742
978-369-6100

Type of Lodging: Motel
Room Rates: $114–$159; AAA and AARP discounts.
Pet Charges and Deposits: $10 per day per pet.
Pet Policy: All pets welcome.
Amenities: Extended cable TV, movies, irons, outdoor pool, whirlpool, exercise room, coin laundry, conference facilities, restaurant adjacent, radios, data port/modem telephones, some refrigerators (fee), 2 stories, interior corridors.
Rated: 2 Paws — 106 rooms.

The prototypical Best Western, the Concord venue is situated on the green in the center of town. It's a manageable, two story structure with attractive, mid-size, well-furnished units. Concord exploded on the world's literary scene in the 19th century. The "superstars" included Ralph Waldo Emerson, Henry David Thoreau, and Louisa May Alcott. The standout Concord Museum contains 5 period rooms, 13 historical and decorative arts galleries, the lanterns from Paul Revere's famous ride, the contents of Ralph Waldo Emerson's study, arranged as they were in 1882, and a large collection of Thoreau's possessions, including his bed, desk, and chair from Walden Pond. The Old Manse, next to the North Bridge, was built in 1770 by Ralph Waldo Emerson's grandfather. Nathaniel Hawthorne lived here from 1842-1845 and gave the house its name.

Towneplace Suites By Marriott

238 Andover Street
Danvers, MA 01985
978-777-6222

Type of Lodging: Extended Stay Motel
Room Rates: $99–$149, some suites; AAA and AARP discounts.
Pet Charges and Deposits: $50 fee, plus $10 per day per pet.
Pet Policy: All pets welcome.
Amenities: Extended cable TV, movies, dual phone lines, voice mail, hair dryers, irons, heated pool, exercise room, coin laundry, radios, coffee makers, data port/modem telephones, refrigerators, microwaves, 4 stories, interior corridors.
Rated: 3 Paws — 157 suites.

This well-regarded extended stay apartment hotel boasts the typical high quality and good value of the Marriott chain. There are 127 units with kitchen and 30 two-bedroom units. There are also a plethora of welcome amenities. While nearby Boston is better known for its history than its nightlife, you'll spend plenty to do if you're planning a night on the town. Brew pubs are popular gathering places in the city of Samuel Adams. At the Black Rose in Quincy Market, Irish memorabilia lines the walls, stout flows freely, and genuine Celts watch their basketball-playing namesakes on TV. There are also myriad comedy clubs (Comedy Connection, Nick's Comedy Stop, Dick Doherty's Comedy Vault, ImprovBoston) and dance clubs. All in all, it's a heckuva town.

Hilton Dedham Place

25 Allied Drive
Dedham, MA 02026
781-329-7900

Type of Lodging: Hotel

Room Rates: $229–$269; AAA and AARP discounts.

Pet Charges and Deposits: None.

Pet Policy: All pets welcome.

Amenities: Extended cable TV, movies (fee), dual phone lines, voice mail, hair dryers, irons, heated pool, whirlpool, sauna, jogging, volleyball, lighted tennis courts (fee), racquetball courts (fee), gift shop, airport transportation, valet laundry, massage (fee), conference facilities, administrative services, restaurant, cocktails, radios, coffee makers, data port/modem telephones, some refrigerators (fee), 4 stories, interior corridors.

Rated: 3 Paws — 249 rooms.

The Hilton is located in a quiet location adjacent to a conservation area—a perfect place for your pet to roam. It boasts elegant public areas and very attractively landscaped grounds, in addition to the quality and comfort you always expect of a Hilton. The Fairbanks House, East Street and Eastern Avenue, was built in 1636 and is one of the oldest wooden frame houses in North America. The house contains furniture, textiles, and other objects that belonged to the family. Dedham Historical Society contains a genealogical research library and history museum that includes Dedham and Chelsea pottery, paintings, artifacts, and furniture from the 16th, 17th, and 18th centuries.

Red Roof Inn

650 Cochituate Road
Framingham, MA 01701
508-872-4499

Type of Lodging: Motel

Room Rates: $79–$119; AAA discounts.

Pet Charges and Deposits: None.

Pet Policy: Small pets only.

Amenities: Extended cable TV, movies, video games, voice mail, free local telephone calls, free newspaper, restaurant adjacent, radios, data port/modem telephones, some refrigerators, some microwaves, some coffee makers, 2 stories, exterior corridors.

Rated: 2 Paws — 170 rooms.

Red Roof Inn—Framingham is an excellent budget choice in the greater Boston area. Rooms are mid-size, furnishings are comfortable, clean, and sturdy. Framingham was settled in 1650. By 1700, the town had grown to 70 families. One resident, Crispus Attucks, was killed for inciting a mob against British soldiers on March 5, 1770, an incident that later became known as the Boston Massacre. Attucks was the first African-American killed in the country's battle for independence. The Danforth Museum of Art houses seven galleries, including a children's interactive gallery. The Garden In the Woods, 45 acres, houses one of the largest landscaped collections of wildflowers in the Northeast. There are more than 1,700 species and varieties of native American plants and flora.

Hawthorn Suites, Ltd.

835 Upper Union Street
Franklin, MA 02038
508-553-3500

Type of Lodging: Extended Stay Motel

Room Rates: $109–$229, some suites and whirlpool units, including hot buffet breakfast; AAA and AARP discounts.

Pet Charges and Deposits: $100 deposit.

Pet Policy: All pets welcome.

Amenities: Extended cable TV, movies (fee), dual phone lines, voice mail, hair dryers, irons, heated pool, whirlpool, exercise room, coin laundry, conference facilities, free local telephone calls, radios, coffee makers, data port/modem telephones, refrigerators, microwaves, some VCR's, 3 stories, interior corridors.

Rated: 3 Paws — 100 suites.

Hawthorn Suites boasts "It's so comfortable you'll think you're home," and that claim is not far off the mark. After all, you not only get a good night's sleep in a studio, one-, or two-bedroom suite, but you also have a convenience store, a full hot buffet breakfast, and a wonderful selection of amenities. It's only 45 minutes to Cape Cod, and an easy day trip to Boston via commuter rail. In the years following the American Revolution, Boston transformed itself from a haphazard seaport to an aesthetically refined city through the efforts of architect Charles Bullfinch. As the face of Boston changed, so did its people. Irish immigrants settled in the city's North and South ends. Among them was Patrick Kennedy, John F. Kennedy's great-grandfather. Italians were the next wave. By 1850, Boston was America's third most populous city.

Cape Ann Motor Inn

33 Rockport Road
Gloucester, MA 01930
978-281-2900

Type of Lodging: Motel

Room Rates: $69–$139, some whirlpool units: $159–$200.

Pet Charges and Deposits: None.

Pet Policy: All pets welcome.

Amenities: Extended cable TV, beach, swimming, radios, refrigerators, some microwaves, data port/modem telephones, 3 stories, (no elevator), exterior corridors.

Rated: 2 Paws — 31 rooms.

Every unit at Cape Ann Motor Inn has a balcony, double bed, and sleeper sofa, making it a roomy, comfortable, clean property that you'll return to again and again. Gloucester, on Cape Ann, is a summer resort town, with a rocky coastline and a safe harbor. Originally settled in 1623, it has remained a fishing center as well. Cape Ann Whale Watch. Harbor Tours, Seven Seas Whale Watch, Yankee Whale Watch, Schooner *Thomas E. Lannon,* and Leisure Casino Cruises offer 2-4 hour whale watch and specialty cruises. Hammond Castle Museum, built by inventor John Hay Hammond between 1926 and 1929, is a medieval-style castle with furniture and architectural pieces from dwellings and churches abroad, as well as Roman, medieval, and Renaissance artifacts.

Hampton Inn Boston–North Andover

224 Winthrop Avenue
Lawrence, MA 01843
978-975-4050

Type of Lodging: Motel
Room Rates: $99–$139; AAA and AARP discounts.
Pet Charges and Deposits: None.
Pet Policy: All pets welcome.
Amenities: Extended cable TV, movies, voice mail, irons, hair dryers, exercise room, valet laundry, conference facilities, restaurant adjacent, radios, coffee makers, data port/modem telephones, some refrigerators, 5 stories, interior corridors.
Rated: 3 Paws — 126 rooms.

Each Hampton Inn gives you great value for the price. The Lawrence venue is modern, clean, spacious, and inviting, with a restaurant immediately adjacent to the property. Lawrence was established in 1845 to support the growing industries along the Merrimack River. Its Great Stone Dam was built between 1845 and 1848 to generate electrical power. Constructed with hand-hewn granite blocks hauled by oxen and laid stone by stone, this massive dam can be viewed today from Falls Bridge. Lawrence's mills once produced 800 miles of cloth a day through the labor of thousands of immigrants. The Bread and Roses Strike of 1912 sparked the American labor movement. Today, you can visit a restored workers' boarding house and other exhibits at Lawrence Heritage State Park.

Seagull Inn

106 Harbor Avenue
Marblehead, MA 01945
781-631-1893

Type of Lodging: Bed & Breakfast Inn
Room Rates: $125–$250 including Continental breakfast.
Pet Charges and Deposits: None.
Pet Policy: All pets welcome.
Amenities: TVs, refrigerators, microwaves, 3 stories, interior corridors.
Rated: 3 Paws — 4 suites

Seagull Inn on Marblehead Neck affords ocean and harbor views from every room. Enjoy the casual elegance of this remarkable Bed & Breakfast. The suites are all impressive, with many unique features. They're furnished with antiques and Shaker-style furniture, cherry floors, private baths, and original paintings. Breakfasts include fresh fruits and juices, homemade granolas, oven-warm baked goods, bagels, muffins, and breads. There are many cultural and recreational activities, including golf at one of several nearby courses, ice skating, museums, yachting, and exercising your pet on one of the many beaches. Marblehead is on a particularly attractive neck(cape) northeast of Boston. Marblehead, founded in 1629, flourished as a major commercial fishing center and by the mid-18th century was a major northeast port.

Embassy Suites – Boston Marlborough

123 Boston Post Road West
Marlborough, MA 01752
508-485-5900

Type of Lodging: Suite Motel

Room Rates: $199–$229; AAA and AARP discounts.

Pet Charges and Deposits: $50 deposit.

Pet Policy: All pets welcome.

Amenities: Extended cable TV, movies (fee), video games, voice mail, hair dryers, irons, heated pool, whirlpool, exercise room, gift shop, airport transportation (fee), coin laundry, conference facilities, administrative service, PC, restaurant, cocktails, radios, coffee makers, data port/modem telephones, refrigerators, microwaves, 6 stories, interior corridors.

Rated: 3 Paws – 229 suites.

Embassy Suites is a hallmark of comfort in the greater Boston area. Sensibly priced, the building has a wonderfully open, attractive, "atrium" feel and large, well-furnished guest suites. As always, the insulation is particularly good, giving you a quiet, restful stay. In nearby Lowell, visit the American Textile History Museum—300 years of American textile production with a large assortment of hand powered tools and equipment, as well as spinning and waving demonstrations. Lowell National Historical Park includes cotton textile mills, workers' housing, and a 5½ mile power canal system. The Boott Cotton Mills Museum, housed within a cotton mill built in 1873, chronicles the Industrial Revolution. Of great interest is a 1920's weave room containing 88 looms operated by belts, shafts, and pulleys.

Homestead Village Guest Studios

19 Northborough Road
Marlborough, MA 01752
508-490-9911

Type of Lodging: Extended Stay Motel

Room Rates: $109–$119.

Pet Charges and Deposits: $75 fee.

Pet Policy: All pets welcome.

Amenities: Extended cable TV, movies, voice mail, irons, coin laundry, health club adjacent, radios, coffee makers, data port/modem telephones, refrigerators, microwaves, 3 stories, interior corridors.

Rated: 2 Paws – 135 suites.

Homestead Village Guest Studios afford you the space of a mini-suite at a price that's even lower than a comparable hotel room. It's inviting, well-sized, and very comfortable. In nearby Lynn, founded in 1629, the Lynn Heritage State Park Visitor's Center, downtown, traces the history of this sub-city near Boston, depicting important events from its shoe manufacturing roots to its present day production of jet engines. The Lynn Museum is a 19th century house with four period rooms used to trace Lynn's history from 1776-1876. Horizon's Edge Casino Cruises offers gaming variations on the cruise theme—cruises leave the dock at 76 Marine Avenue, Lynn, at 11: 00 a.m. and 7: 00 p.m.

Sheraton Newton Hotel

320 Washington Street
Newton, MA 02158
617-969-3010

Type of Lodging: Hotel

Room Rates: $99–$339, suites whirl-pool units; AAA and AARP discounts.

Pet Charges and Deposits: None.

Pet Policy: All pets welcome.

Amenities: Extended cable TV, movies (fee), voice mail, irons, hair dryers, small heated indoor pool, exercise room, valet laundry, conference facilities, fax, restaurant, radios, coffee makers, data port/modem telephones, some refrigerators, some microwaves, 12 stories, interior corridors.

Rated: 3 Paws — 272 rooms.

The Sheraton-Newton, situated in a high-rise, 12-story building, is a first class lodging with finely-furnished, inviting rooms and a large assortment of amenities designed to make your stay as enjoyable as possible. Jackson Homestead, a stop on the Underground Railroad, is a Federal-style farmhouse built in 1809. It houses a permanent collection of historical artifacts and items depicting Newton's history. Newton is immediately adjacent to Cambridge, which means Harvard, Harvard Square, the Longfellow House, and all of the Harvard and MIT Museums, which make this such a one-of-a-kind place. It's also within easy striking distance of Boston and the plethora of activities that make "Bean Town" the "Hub of the Universe."

Hawthorn Suites, Ltd.

25 Research Place
North Chelmsford, MA 01863
978-256-5151

Type of Lodging: Extended Stay Motel

Room Rates: $129–$159; AAA and AARP discounts.

Pet Charges and Deposits: $50 fee, plus $10 per day per pet.

Pet Policy: All pets welcome.

Amenities: Extended cable TV, movies (fee), video games, dual phone lines, voice mail, irons, outdoor pool, exercise room, gift shop, coin laundry, convenience store, VCR's radios, coffee makers, data port/modem telephones, refrigerators, microwaves, VCR's, 3 stories, interior corridors.

Rated: 3 Paws — 105 suites.

Hawthorn Suites—North Chelmsford affords you 13 efficiencies and 92 units with kitchen in mini-suites designed to make your stay in North Chelmsford pleasant and restful. North Chelmsford is practically on the New Hampshire border, closer to Nashua, N.H. than it is to Boston, even though it's still considered an exurb of Boston. The city is situated on the Merrimack River, adjacent to Lowell, Lowell Dracut State Forest, and Lowell National Historical Park. Top sights in Lowell include not only the National Historical Park, but also the American Textile History Museum, the New England Quilt Museum, the Sports Museum of New England, and the Whistler House Museum of Art, the 1834 birthplace of James Abbott McNeil Whistler, said by some to be the Thomas Kincade of his day because of his skills not only of painting, but of promoting as well.

Howard Johnson Hotel

407 Squire Road
Revere, MA 02151
781-284-7200

Type of Lodging: Motor Inn
Room Rates: $99–$179; AAA and AARP discounts.
Pet Charges and Deposits: Inquire.
Pet Policy: All pets welcome.
Amenities: Extended cable TV, movies, outdoor pool, airport transportation, restaurant, cocktails, coffee makers, data port/modem telephones, some refrigerators, some microwaves, valet laundry, conference facilities, 4 stories (no elevator), interior corridors.
Rated: 2 Paws — 107 rooms.

The newly-renovated Howard Johnson Hotel in Revere reopened for business in 2001. In addition to its "fresh out of the box" feel, it has a restaurant and cocktail lounge on the premises. Just northeast of Boston, Revere is close to a standout Massachusetts attraction. The Saugus Ironworks began in 1646. Its success launched the American iron and steel industry. Saugus Ironworks National Historic Site contains a reconstructed blast furnace, working water wheels, a forge, and a rolling and slitting mill. The museum displays a 500-pound hammer used in the original forge, and you'll also enjoy a blacksmith demonstration. The Iron Works House, a 17th century house, contains early American furnishings and exhibits.

Sandy Bay Motor Inn

173 Main Street
Rockport, MA 01966
978-546-7155

Type of Lodging: Motel
Room Rates: $79–$159; AAA discounts.
Pet Charges and Deposits: $50 deposit. Designated units only.
Pet Policy: All pets welcome.
Amenities: Extended cable TV, some hair dryers, heated pool, whirlpool, sauna, putting green, two tennis courts, coin laundry, conference facilities, restaurant, radios, data port/modem telephones, some refrigerators, 2 stories, interior/exterior corridors.
Rated: 2 Paws — 79 units, including rooms and suites.

Sandy Bay Motor Inn has excellent recreational facilities on nicely landscaped grounds. There are 79 units, including 6 two-bedroom units and 25 efficiencies. Rooms are quiet and restful. Rockport's artist colony is justifiably famous through the northeast. Hour-long Footprints Walking Tours include historic buildings and other sites. The James Babson Cooperage Shop, built in 1658, is the oldest building on Cape Ann (where Rockport is situated). The shop displays early American tools and furniture. The Paper House in nearby Pigeon Cove, is built of 215 thicknesses of newspaper. The furniture is also made of newspaper and a desk made of papers concerning Charles Lindbergh's historic flight is a highlight.

Hawthorne Hotel

18 Washington Square West
Salem, MA 01970
978-744-4080
www.hawthornehotel.com

Type of Lodging: Classic Hotel

Room Rates: $129–$319; AAA and AARP discounts.

Pet Charges and Deposits: None.

Pet Policy: Small pets only.

Amenities: Extended cable TV, movies, dual phone lines, voice mail, exercise room, gift shop, valet laundry, conference facilities, restaurant, radios, data port/modem telephones, some refrigerators, some coffee makers, 6 stories, interior corridors.

Rated: 3 Paws — 89 units, including rooms and suites.

The Hawthorne Hotel is one of the nicest places to say in historic Salem. Luxury accommodations, award-winning dining, and a central location, right on the common, make this lodging a wonderful choice. An added plus is the cozy tavern, complete with fireplace. You're within easy walking distance to museums, shopping, and the waterfront. Salem was the capital of Massachusetts Bay Colony from 1626 to 1630. Built in 1642, the Witch House at 310½ Essex Street, was the site of preliminary witchcraft examinations in the infamous Salem Witch Trials of 1692. In all, 19 people were hanged and one was crushed to death. The House of the Seven Gables Historic Site includes the oldest surviving mansion in Salem (1668), the Hathaway House (1682) and Nathaniel Hawthorne's birthplace (1804). The Peabody Essex Museum is a hallmark of 30 galleries, a research library, and 11 historic houses.

The Salem Inn

7 Summer Street
Salem, MA 01970
800-446-2995 • 978-741-0680
www.SalemInnMA.com

Type of Lodging: Historic Bed and Breakfast

Room Rates: $139–$299, including breakfast; AAA discounts.

Pet Charges and Deposits: None.

Pet Policy: All pets welcome.

Amenities: Extended cable TV, hair dryers, irons, restaurant adjacent, radios, coffee makers, data port/modem telephones, some microwaves, 4 stories (no elevator), interior corridors.

Rated: 3 Paws — 39 rooms.

The Salem Inn was converted from 1834 townhouses and historic buildings, including the West House (1834), the Curwen House (1854), and the Peabody House (1874). Of the 39 units, there is 1 two-bedroom unit and 11 units with kitchen. You're surrounded by restful old-time charm. Each of the individually decorated rooms and suites reflects the fine craftsmanship of the Federal period. Guest rooms are spacious and comfortable. Many have equipped kitchens and working fireplaces. A complimentary light breakfast is available in the Breakfast Room each morning. In warmer weather, the private rose garden brick patio is the perfect place to enjoy your breakfast, or a quiet moment at the end of the day. The Inn is a short walk from the National Park Maritime Historical Site, the Essex and Peabody Museums, fine restaurants, and the waterfront.

Residence Inn By Marriott

1775 Andover Street
Tewksbury, MA 01876
978-640-1003

Type of Lodging: Suite Motel

Room Rates: $149–$219.

Pet Charges and Deposits: $10 extra charge, plus $5 per day per pet.

Pet Policy: All pets welcome.

Amenities: Extended cable TV, movies (fee), voice mail, irons, hair dryers, heated pool, whirlpool, exercise room, sports court, coin laundry, conference facilities, radios, coffee makers, data port/modem telephones, refrigerators, microwaves, 3 stories, exterior corridors.

Rated: 3 Paws — 163 suites.

Residence Inn is situated in a quiet, rural setting with 11 New England-style buildings. The units are very spacious and some have fireplaces. There are 130 units with kitchen and 33 two-bedroom units. Wamesit Native American Monument on Main Street is a 7-foot-high cast bronze sculpture set on a 9-foot high granite boulder designed by Mico Kaufman, Tewksbury resident and world-class sculptor. Kaufman also created the Anne Sullivan-Helen Keller Monument, "Water." A young girl, deaf and blind, feels water at the pump and, with three extended fingers, understands the sign language for the letter "W" and water. The monument is a tribute to Helen Keller's dedicated teacher Anne Sullivan, a long-time resident of Tewksbury.

Townplace Suites By Marriott

20 International Place
Tewksbury, MA 01876
978-863-9800

Type of Lodging: Extended Stay Motel

Room Rates: $114–$179.

Pet Charges and Deposits: $75 fee, plus $5 per day per pet.

Pet Policy: All pets welcome.

Amenities: Extended cable TV, movies, dual phone lines, voice mail, irons, heated pool, exercise room, coin laundry, restaurant adjacent, radios, coffee makers, data port/modem telephones, refrigerators, microwaves, some VCR's, 3 stories, interior corridors.

Rated: 3 Paws — 117 suites.

Townplace Suites has 95 units with kitchen and 22 two-bedroom units. The units are stylish and comfortably furnished—a true home away from home. Get up and wander over to the Cracker Barrel Restaurant for an all-American breakfast that certainly won't leave you hungry. Tewksbury, considerably north of Boston, is situated between Lawrence and Lowell, both historical mill textile mill towns on the Merrimack River. It's also located between Harold Parker State Forest and Warren H. Manning State Park. Lest you're wondering why Tewksbury is listed as a suburb of Greater Boston, it's less than a twenty minute drive to the Boston-Cambridge area and all the cultural, educational, recreational, and, above all, historical wonders you'll find there.

Homestead Village Guest Studios

52 Fourth Avenue
Waltham, MA 02254
781-890-1333

Type of Lodging: Extended Stay Motel

Room Rates: $119–$139; AAA and AARP discounts.

Pet Charges and Deposits: $75 fee.

Pet Policy: All pets welcome.

Amenities: Extended cable TV, movies, voice mail, irons, coin laundry, health club adjacent, restaurant adjacent, airport transportation (fee), radios, coffee makers, data port/modem telephones, refrigerators, microwaves, 3 stories, interior corridors.

Rated: 2 Paws — 140 mini-suites.

You'll find a large number of uniform, comfortable mini-suites in Homestead Village Guest Studios, located right behind the Westin Hotel. Sleep secure: there's always an attendant on duty. This is a clean, restful place indeed. Waltham, a western suburb of Boston, is only minutes from the "Hub of the Universe," even closer to Lexington, the site of the first conflict of the Revolutionary War. The entire city is a living history monument. One of the highlights of a trip to this area includes Minute Man Historical Park, encompassing lands in Concord, Lexington, and Lincoln. The Park commemorates the opening battles of the Revolutionary War in April, 1775. There were not one but several battles along the 20 mile hilly road between Lexington and Concord.

Summerfield Suites Hotel

54 Fourth Avenue
Waltham, MA 02154
781-290-0026

Type of Lodging: Suite Motel

Room Rates: $229; AAA and AARP discounts.

Pet Charges and Deposits: $200 fee, plus $10 per day per pet.

Pet Policy: All pets welcome.

Amenities: Extended cable TV, movies, dual phone lines, voice mail, irons, hair dryers, heated pool, whirlpool, exercise room, gift shop, coin laundry, conference facilities, VCR's radios, coffee makers, data port/modem telephones, refrigerators, microwaves, 3 stories, interior corridors.

Rated: 3 Paws — 187 suites.

The units at Summerfield Suites are among the most spacious we've seen anywhere. Nicely furnished, clean and comfortable, there are 136 units with kitchen and 51 two-bedroom suites. Lexington's famed Battle Green was the site of the first skirmish of the Revolutionary War on April 19, 1775, between Minutemen and the Concord-based British troops. The Minuteman Statue at the head of Battle Green, represents Captain John Parker, who commanded the Minutemen gathered on the Green. He said to his troops, "Stand your ground. Don't fire unless fired upon, but if they mean to have a war, let it begin here." It did. So did our country. And there are several historical structures commemorating that heroic period in our nation's history.

The Westin Hotel, Waltham

70 Third Avenue
Waltham, MA 02154
781-290-5600

Type of Lodging: Hotel

Room Rates: $149–$299, some suites: $179–$339. AAA and AARP discounts.

Pet Charges and Deposits: None.

Pet Policy: All pets welcome.

Amenities: Extended cable TV, movies (fee), dual phone lines, voice mail, honor bars, irons, hair dryers, heated pool, whirlpool, sauna, steam room, exercise room, airport transportation (fee), gift shop, valet laundry, conference facilities, administrative services, PC, restaurant, cocktails, radios, coffee makers, data port/modem telephones, some VCR's, 8 stories, interior corridors.

Rated: 4 Paws — 346 rooms.

Top marks go to the luxurious Westin Hotel. It's a high-rise blue reflective glass landmark on a hillside overlooking Cambridge Reservoir. It goes without saying that you are bathed in elegance from the moment you enter the posh public areas, until the last time you leave the door of your own tastefully furnished room. Situated in five beautiful acres of landscaped lawns and garden overlooking the scenic Cambridge Reservoir, the newly redecorated guest rooms and suites are filled with amenities catering to your business and personal comforts. The hotel offers 24-hour room service and a variety of dining and entertainment options. The hotel is less than 10 miles from historic Lexington-Concord Battleground, DeCordova Museum, and the Burlington Mall.

Hampton Inn Boston–Woburn

315 Mishawum Road
Woburn, MA 01801
781-935-7666

Type of Lodging: Motor Inn

Room Rates: $109–$179' AAA and AARP discounts.

Pet Charges and Deposits: None.

Pet Policy: Small pets only.

Amenities: Extended cable TV, movies, dual phone lines, irons, valet laundry, restaurant, health club adjacent, radios, coffee makers, data port/modem telephones, 5 stories, interior corridors.

Rated: 2 Paws — 99 rooms.

Hampton Inn always assures you a great value for the money. The Woburn venue is a semi-high-rise 5-story building, and a great place to stay when you're in Woburn, a northern suburb of Boston, located between Cambridge and Burlington. Head west from Woburn toward historic Lexington and Concord. Just before Concord, turn to the left and you'll come to Walden Pond, immortalized by Henry David Thoreau. Literary and historic niceties aside, it's a beautiful, tranquil, peaceful place where, despite the crowds that come in the summer and on weekends, you can find space to wander and, perhaps, even time to contemplate, as Thoreau did, on the wonders of nature. The Concord Museum contains five period rooms, thirteen historical and decorative arts galleries, and numerous surprise exhibits.

Ramada Inn

15 Middlesex Canal Park Road
Woburn, MA 01801
781-935-8760

Type of Lodging: Motor Inn
Room Rates: $139–$189; AAA and AARP discounts.
Pet Charges and Deposits: None.
Pet Policy: Small pets only.
Amenities: Extended cable TV, movies, voice mail, irons, hair dryers, heated pool, exercise room, airport transportation, valet laundry, conference facilities, restaurant, cocktails, radios, coffee makers, data port/modem telephones, some refrigerators (fee), some microwaves (fee), 4 stories, interior corridors.
Rated: 2 Paws — 195 rooms.

Ramada Inn is a well-maintained, well-traveled lodging, with clean, comfortable rooms and pleasant motel-style furniture. It's a fine rest stop on the way between Boston and points north. Lexington's Buckman Tavern, 1 Bedford Street, was built in 1709 and has pre-Revolutionary War furnishings. The Hancock-Clarke House in Lexington, built in 1698 and enlarged in 1734, was where Samuel Adams and John Hancock were sitting when Paul Revere brought news of the British advance. The Munroe Tavern in the same town served as the British headquarters and hospital during the Battle of Lexington. The Old Belfry, near the Common in Lexington, is a reproduction of the original belfry whose bell sounded the alarm that assembled the Minutemen.

Cape Cod

Including

Buzzards Bay
Centerville
Falmouth
Hyannis
Hyannis Port
Orleans
Provincetown
Sandwich
South Yarmouth
Yarmouth Port

Bay Motor Inn

223 Main Street
Buzzards Bay, MA 02532
508-759-3989

Type of Lodging: Cottage

Room Rates: $59–$119; AAA and AARP discounts.

Pet Charges and Deposits: None.

Pet Policy: Pets must not be left unattended at any time.

Amenities: Extended cable TV, movies, outdoor pool, free local telephone calls, data port/modem telephones, some coffee makers, some refrigerators, 1 story, exterior corridors.

Rated: 2 Paws — 17 units.

Travel back to the early 1950's at Bay Motor Inn. There are free-standing cottages and duplex units—also a small motel section—on gently sloping, grassy grounds that surround the owner's home and the pool. If you've ever wondered what it was like back then, this is nostalgia personified. Cape Cod—a style, a cuisine, or changing moods and patterns of light, depending on whether you're an architect, a gourmet, or an artist, is a long elbow of land—a huge peninsula—that juts out into the Atlantic southeast of Boston and Plymouth. Buzzard's Bay is at the beginning of the Cape, technically still on the mainland. The Cape Cod Canal on Academy Drive is a 17½-mile link between Buzzards Bay and Cape Cod Bay designed to save 135 miles of coastline travel around the tip of Cape Cod.

Centerville Corners Motor Lodge

369 South Main Street
Centerville, MA 02632
508-775-7223
email: ccorners@cape.com.

Type of Lodging: Motel

Room Rates: $79–$159.

Pet Charges and Deposits: $5 per day per pet.

Pet Policy: All pets welcome.

Amenities: Extended cable TV, movies, heated pool, sauna, coffee makers, data port/modem telephones, some refrigerators (fee), 2 stories, exterior corridors.

Rated: 2 Paws — 48 rooms.

Centerville Corners Motor Lodge has an old-fashioned village setting and a down-home feel. Most of the units have two double beds, some units have a queen bed in the room. Of the 48 units, 2 have efficiencies. The place looks like a comfortable New England-style home and is a pleasing place to stay. There are endless beaches on Cape Cod—you can people watch at one of several popular beaches, or you can find a secluded strand and listen to the waves crash on nearby rocks. Centerville, on Nantucket Sound, was the home of wealthy ship captains who built stately homes in the early 1800's. Centerville Historical Society Museum is housed in an 1840's home with added wings. You can visit a Colonial Revival kitchen, Victorian period rooms, gowns, accessories, and Civil War artifacts.

Mariner Motel

555 Main Street
Falmouth, MA 02540
508-548-1331

Type of Lodging: Motel

Room Rates: $69–$169; AAA discounts.

Pet Charges and Deposits: $15 per day per pet.

Pet Policy: Limited to one dog only per unit.

Amenities: Smoke-free premises, extended cable TV, heated pool, playground, picnic tables, restaurant adjacent, refrigerators, 1 story, exterior corridors.

Rated: 2 Paws — 30 rooms.

The Mariner is spacious and very comfortable. All rooms are at ground level and smoke free. From the motel's superb location, enjoy a short stroll to the harbor, island ferry, beaches, shops, and restaurants. You can purchase discount tickets to Martha's Vineyard, Whale Watching, Plymouth attractions and meals in the area at the motel. Quakers settled Falmouth in 1661 and was one of the first New England towns that sanctioned religious tolerance. Falmouth today is a picturesque beach resort centered on the historic village green. It's a point of departure for ferries to Nantucket and Martha's Vineyard. The Falmouth Historic Society Museum, two restored houses on the village green, contains a whaling exhibit and historic period furnishings.

Quality Inn

291 Jones Road
Falmouth, MA 02540
508-540-2000

Type of Lodging: Motel

Room Rates: $85–$285. AAA, AARP, AKC, ABA, and *ask about Pets Welcome™* discounts.

Pet Charges and Deposits: None.

Pet Policy: All pets welcome.

Amenities: Extended cable TV, movies, heated pool, sauna, exercise room, game room, conference facilities, fax, restaurant, pub, free local newspapers, data port/modem telephones, some refrigerators, some microwaves, 2 stories, interior/exterior corridors.

Rated: 3 Paws — 93 rooms and 5 suites

Located near the ferry to Martha's Vineyard, the Inn features contemporary guest accommodations, ranging from junior to king-sized suites. Connecting suites are available upon request. Guests are invited to enjoy the large indoor heated pool, sauna, and game room. The Garden Room Restaurant serves hearty, family-style meals, and the Bizz Street Pub invites casual and friendly socializing. The Inn is convenient to the wonders of Massachusetts, such as Martha's Vineyard and the Woods Hole Oceanographic Institute and Aquarium. The area is home to scenic beaches, deep-sea fishing, and whale watching. Golfers will be delighted to find six local golf courses within five miles.

Comfort Inn

1470 Route 132
Hyannis, MA 02601
508-771-4804

Type of Lodging: Motel

Room Rates: $69–$229; AAA and AARP discounts.

Pet Charges and Deposits: $6 per day per pet.

Pet Policy: All pets welcome.

Amenities: Extended cable TV, movies (fee), video games, dual phone lines, voice mail, hair dryers, irons, heated pool, whirlpool, sauna, exercise room, valet laundry, conference facilities, radios, data port/modem telephones, some refrigerators, some microwaves, 2-3 stories (no elevator), interior/exterior corridors.

Rated: 3 Paws — 104 rooms.

Comfort Inn is situated in a quiet, natural hillside location. It's utterly charming with attractive, tastefully furnished rooms, and it's spotlessly clean to boot. Craigville Beach, the largest on the cape, is right near Hyannis. Cape Cod Melody Tent presents theater-in-the-round concerts and comedy shows nightly during the summer. Downtown, the John F. Kennedy Hyannis Museum contains photographs and oral histories pertaining to the times Kennedy spent in the area with his family and friends. There's also a memorial to John F. Kennedy, Jr., as well as a videotape reflecting on the "Summer White House," where JFK went to get away from it all.

Harbor Village

160 Marston Avenue
Hyannis Port, MA 02647
508-775-7581

Type of Lodging: Cottages

Room Rates: $119–$149; weekly rates only—June 26–September 3: $1,375–$1,675; AAA discounts.

Pet Charges and Deposits: $100 per week extra charge.

Pet Policy: All pets welcome.

Amenities: Extended cable TV, irons, beach, swimming, VCR's, radios, coffee makers, refrigerators, microwaves, data port/modem telephones, 2 stories, exterior corridors.

Rated: 2 Paws — 26 cottages.

Harbor Village has a fine location in a wooded setting along a tidal river and adjacent to the ocean. Here you'll fine one-to-three bedroom cottages with kitchen, living room, and fireplace. Fourteen units have kitchens, 9 are two-bedroom units, and 3 are three-bedroom units. Hyannis Port, on Nantucket Sound, is only a few blocks from Hyannis—the hub of Cape Cod. Barnstable County Airport, the famed Hyannis beaches, and the ferries to Nantucket and Martha's Vineyard (summer only, for the most part) are adjacent. Ocean Avenue, Hyannis Port's "Main Street" goes from Craigville Beach in the west, to Lewis Bay in the east. This is the area of superelegant private homes and estates. Martha's Vineyard, like Nantucket, was an early refuge and supply point for coastal traffic that rounded Cape Cod. Today, it remains one of the quaintest areas near the Cape.

Skaket Beach Motel

203 Cranberry Highway
Route 6A
Orleans, MA 02653
508-255-1020
www.skaketbeachmotel.com

Type of Lodging: Motel

Room Rates: $69–$169; AAA discounts.

Pet Charges and Deposits: $9 per day per pet.

Pet Policy: Off-season only, inquire.

Amenities: Extended cable TV, movies, heated pool, horseshoes, coin laundry, restaurant adjacent, radios, coffee makers, data port/modem telephones, refrigerators, some microwaves, 2 stories, exterior corridors.

Rated: 3 Paws — 46 units, including efficiencies.

Skaket Beach Motel combines charming hospitality, a unique location, distinctive amenities, and undivided attention into a holiday paradise. Minutes from the door of Skaket Beach Motel, you'll find beaches, boating, golf shops, and restaurants. The motel features freshly baked cranberry and blueberry muffins, along with comfortable rooms and efficiencies on spacious, wooded grounds. Orleans, situated between the Atlantic Ocean and Cape Cod Bay, has a quaint town center surrounded by pristine shores and forest. During the 19th century, windmill powered salt works processed sea water into salt. Today, the water draws tourists to beaches and fishing areas on both sides of the town. Skaket Beach, on the bay, has a 150-car parking lit, showers, picnic tables, and a snack bar.

Bayshore Condominiums

493 Commercial Street
Provincetown, MA 02657
508-Bayshore Condominiums
493 Commercial Street
Provincetown, MA 02657
508-487-9133

Type of Lodging: Condominium

Room Rates: $79–$209, weekly rates only, 6/23–9/7: $1,125–$2,195.

Pet Charges and Deposits: $15 per day per pet.

Pet Policy: All pets welcome.

Amenities: Extended cable TV, irons, beach, swimming, radios, refrigerators, microwaves, 2-3 stories (no elevator), exterior corridors.

Rated: 3 Paws — 22 units.

Less than a mile east of the Town Hall, Bayshore Condominiums feature studios, one- and two-bedroom suites with living room and kitchen. The units, some of which are on the bay and others of which are across the street, are delightful and unique. Some have private decks and patios. "P-Town," at the very tip of the cape, is the ultimate travelers' destination on the Cape. The Mayflower Pilgrims landed here in November, 1620. Today, a monument on High Pole Hill commemorates the event. Since it's so far out, Provincetown's isolation has always made it dependent on the sea for its livelihood. Once a major whaling port, the town is now an art colony and tourist mecca.

Best Inn

698 Commercial Street
Provincetown, MA 02657
508-487-1711

Type of Lodging: Motor Inn

Room Rates: $79–$169, including Continental breakfast; AAA and AARP discounts.

Pet Charges and Deposits: None.

Pet Policy: All pets welcome.

Amenities: Extended cable TV, movies, irons, hair dryers, restaurant, pool bar and barbeque, wading pool, meeting rooms, free local telephone calls, radios, coffee makers, data port/modem telephones, refrigerators, microwaves, some VCR's (fee), 2 stories, exterior corridors.

Rated: 2 Paws — 78 rooms.

Best Inn is located directly across the street from the ocean and a sandy beach. The guest units, which are somewhat older and have a less-than-new décor ('70's vintage), are nevertheless clean and well-maintained. Miles of beaches line both sides of the peninsula at Provincetown, and even the names of the areas around Provincetown—Long Point Light, Wood End Light, Pilgrim Landing, Race Point Light, Cape Cod Light, and Pilgrim Heights—evoke the nautical history of this special place. P-Town even has its own airport, as well as numerous restaurants, galleries, and perfect tourist venues.

White Wind Inn

174 Commercial Street
Provincetown, MA 02657
508-4ind Inn
174 Commercial Street
Provincetown, MA 02657
508-487-1526

Type of Lodging: Bed and Breakfast

Room Rates: $79 –$229, including full breakfast; (5 night minimum stay from July 1 through August 31).

Pet Charges and Deposits: $10 per day per pet.

Pet Policy: Manager's prior approval required.

Amenities: Extended cable TV, movies, restaurant adjacent, VCR's, radios, refrigerators, data port/modem telephones, 2 stories, interior corridors.

Rated: 3 Paws — 13 rooms.

This incredibly charming, gracious bed & breakfast lodging lives in a New England mansion that was built in the mid-1800's and was once the home of a prosperous shipbuilder. Today, this inn is home to visitors from around the world. The large veranda overlooks Commercial Street. It's a perfect place to people watch. Guest units are beautifully furnished. The bathrooms may be a tad on the small side, but overall it's a wonderful place to stay when you're in "P-Town." Provincetown marks the end of the Cape Cod National Seashore, 40 miles of coastline, marshland, glacial cliffs, dunes, and dense forest surrounding the eastern turn-up of the Cape. The area, marked by weathered cottages, villages, and lighthouses, has been spared the scars of industrialization.

The Earl of Sandwich Motel

378 Route 6A
Sandwich, MA 02537
508-888-1415
www.earlofsandwich.com

Type of Lodging: Motel,

Room Rates: $65–$119, including Continental breakfast.

Pet Charges and Deposits: None.

Pet Policy: All pets welcome.

Amenities: Extended cable TV, heated pool, playground, refrigerators, data port/modem telephones, 1 story, exterior corridors.

Rated: 3 Paws — 23 rooms.

The Earl of Sandwich bills itself as, "One of those nicest little places this side of heaven," and that's not an understatement. It's a quiet, peaceful place, built around a duck pond in a country setting. Immaculate rooms, lush grounds, and a homemade Continental breakfast daily make this a perfect holiday venue. Sandwich, the site of one of the 19th century's largest glass factories, was founded in the mid-1600's and is one of the Cape's oldest towns. Standout Heritage Plantation contains 76 acres of landscaped grounds and several buildings dedicated to depicting early American life. Wing Fort House, built in 1642, was occupied continuously by the Wing family until it became a museum in 1942. The Sandwich Glass Museum preserves Sandwich's 19th century heyday.

Motel 6

1314 Main Street
South Yarmouth, MA 02664
508-394-4000
www.vacationinnproperties.com

Type of Lodging: Motel

Room Rates: $99–$249; AAA and AARP discounts.

Pet Charges and Deposits: None.

Pet Policy: Small pets only, 1 per room limit, must be attended.

Amenities: Extended cable TV, movies, irons, heated pool, whirlpool, sauna, beach, exercise room, activity center, complimentary laundry, free newspaper, coffee makers, data port/modem telephones, refrigerators, some microwaves, VCR's, 2 stories, interior corridors.

Rated: 2 Paws — 89 rooms.

A Motel 6 on Cape Cod? Yes, and it's a particularly nice example of Accor's budget chain. You get free morning coffee and an outdoor pool, a heated indoor pool and sauna. Of the units, two of them are 2-bedroom mini-suites. It's an easy trip from Cape Cod to Nantucket Island, celebrated in story and song. Nantucket was purchased from Native Americans for 30 British pounds and two beaver hats. Much of Nantucket's charm is based on its cobblestone main street and its narrow country lanes. The Nantucket Whaling Museum contains ship models, whaling tools, a whale skeleton, scrimshaw, and a 16-foot lens from a nearby lighthouse. The Peter Foulger Museum on Broad Street depicts the history of Nantucket through exhibitions of furniture, baskets, portraits, and artifacts.

Colonial House Inn

Route 6A
Yarmouth Port, MA 02675
800-999-3416 • 508-362-4348

Type of Lodging: Bed & Breakfast Inn

Room Rates: $99–$125, including breakfast and dinner. AAA, AARP, AKC, ABA, and *ask about Pets Welcome*™ discounts.

Pet Charges and Deposits: $5 per day per pet.

Pet Policy: Manager's prior approval required.

Amenities: Restaurant, lounge, fitness area, indoor swimming pool, Jacuzzi, free movies, handicapped accessible, 3 stories, interior corridors.

Rated: 3 Paws — 4 guest rooms and 1 suite.

Located on historic Old King's Highway on the north shore of Cape Cod, the Colonial House Inn has been carefully preserved and the tradition of gracious dining and hospitality carried forward. Constructed in the 1730's, with a long list of well-known owners and several renovations, the charm of Cape Cod shines through the Colonial House Inn today. The large guest rooms are individually decorated and furnished with antiques. Each room has its own private bath and a charming view of the grounds. In addition to the Main House, the renovated Carriage House offers a conference center and additional guest rooms. The menu at the Inn is continental fare in an elegant, yet casual, atmosphere. There are three intimate dining rooms, with Cape Cod's fresh seafood forming the basis of the salt-air selections. There's also an extensive wine cellar and a lounge with full bar.

Wainright Inn

518 South Main Street
Great Barrington, MA 01230
413-528-2062
www.wainrightinn.com

Type of Lodging: Inn

Room Rates: $80–$190, including full breakfast.

Pet Charges and Deposits: 1 night's rate refundable deposit.

Pet Policy: Dogs only, sorry, no cats. Manager's prior approval required.

Amenities: 3 stories, handicapped accessible, interior corridors.

Rated: 3 Paws — 7 rooms and 1 suite.

Originally opened as a tavern in 1766, the Inn has been offering New England hospitality for generations. Located in the heart of the southern Berkshire region (southwest corner of Massachusetts), the Inn is a four-season destination easily accessible from Boston and New York. All the charming guest rooms and suites have private baths and are furnished with comfortable beds and décor. Guests are welcome to take full advantage of the many common areas, including the cozy living room and distinctive wraparound porches. While enjoying homemade breads at breakfast, feel free to discuss dinner plans with the chef. Tanglewood is just minutes away, with summer concerts and picnics on the lawn. Enjoy performances by top-name performers at the Berkshire Theater Festival.

The Brandt House

29 Highland Avenue
Greenfield, MA 01301
413-774-3329

Type of Lodging: Historic Bed and Breakfast

Room Rates: $109–$209, some whirlpool units, including Continental breakfast; AAA discounts.

Pet Charges and Deposits: $20 per day per pet.

Pet Policy: Dogs only, sorry, no cats.

Amenities: Extended cable TV, tennis court, bocce ball, croquet, billiard room, radios, smoke-free premises, data port/modem telephones, some VCR's, some refrigerators, 3 stories (no elevator), interior corridors.

Rated: 3 Paws — 9 rooms.

The Brandt House is a stately, turn-of-the-20th century Colonial Revival mansion, featuring a wraparound porch with wonderful mountain views. All rooms have plush beds, fluffy down comforters, warm, thick robes, fresh flowers, and lovely period or reproduction furniture. Some rooms have fireplaces. The House is located on 3½ acres of sweeping lawns surrounded by lush vegetation that provides quiet privacy. Guest rooms include pet treats, featherbeds, complimentary bathrobes, and wonderful amenities. Guests are invited to walk, hike, bike, or cross-country ski in the adjacent woods, play tennis on the clay tennis courts, fish or ice skate on a neighboring pond. The Brandt House is a short drive from historic Deerfield.

Howard Johnson

401 Russell Street
Hadley, MA 01035
413-586-0114

Type of Lodging: Motel

Room Rates: $79–$169, including Continental breakfast. AAA and AARP discounts.

Pet Charges and Deposits: None.

Pet Policy: All pets welcome.

Amenities: Extended cable TV, movies, some irons, some hair dryers, exercise room, outdoor pool, coin laundry, conference facilities, coffee makers, data port/modem telephones, some refrigerators, 2-3 stories, interior corridors.

Rated: 3 Paws — 100 rooms, including some whirlpool units.

Howard Johnson Motel in Hadley—in the Amherst area—is inviting, nicely maintained, and well-priced. Meeting rooms house up to 35 people, and the lodging is centrally located near the five colleges. The Hadley Farm Museum, housed in a restored 1782 barn, displays a 15-seat stagecoach, an oxcart, a peddler's wagon, early broommaking machinery, and household and farm implements. The Porter-Phelps-Huntington Historic House Museum, set in a 1752 Georgian house, remains virtually unchanged since its last "remodeling" in 1799. It displays seven generations' worth of collectabilia. Concerts are presented here from June through August.

Jericho Valley Inn

2541 Hancock Road
Hancock, MA 01267
413-458-9511
www.jerichovalleyinn.com

Type of Lodging: Motel

Room Rates: $89–$159, including Continental breakfast. AAA and AARP discounts.

Pet Charges and Deposits: None.

Pet Policy: Designated units (cottages) only.

Amenities: Winter plug-ins, extended cable TV, movies, hair dryers, heated pool, hiking trails, coin laundry, free local telephone calls, radios, coffee makers, data port/modem telephones, some coffee markers, some refrigerators, smoke-free premises, 1-2 stories, interior/exterior corridors.

Rated: 3 Paws — 24 units, including rooms and suites.

Jericho Valley Inn boasts newly decorated motel units and cottages with some luxury amenities. Cottages have the original knotty pine walls. All of this is contained in a quiet, wooded environment with lovely mountain views. It's a great bargain in the Berkshires, with over 350 mountain acres of hiking trails. Hancock Shaker Village is a 1,200 acre restoration of the Shaker community founded in 1783, which was dedicated to simplicity, celibacy, and equality. The village includes 21 buildings with original Shaker furniture and artifacts, a round, stone barn, a working farm, and an heirloom herb and vegetable garden. Members of the staff demonstrate 19th century crafts, including woodworking, weaving, and oval box-making. Plan on a minimum of 2½ hours here.

Seven Hills Country Inn & Restaurant

40 Plunkett Street
Lenox, MA 01240
800-869-6518 • 413-637-0060

Type of Lodging: Historic Country Inn

Room Rates: $79–$339, some whirlpool units.

Pet Charges and Deposits: $20 per day per pet.

Pet Policy: Designated units only. Small pets only.

Amenities: Smoke-free premises, extended cable TV, movies, some hair dryers, some irons, heated pool, 2 tennis courts, nature trails, shuffle board, volleyball, conference facilities, restaurant, data port/modem telephones, 2 stories, interior/exterior corridors.

Rated: 3 Paws — Berkshire Cottage and 38 motel units.

Seven Hills Country Inn, ensconced on 27 acres, consists of an original Berkshire cottage and 38 recently renovated motel units. One of the original Berkshire cottages, Seven Hills offers you an invitation to enjoy the romantic luxuries of traditional elegance. Furnishings consist of care-worn antiques, hand-carved fireplaces, leaded-glass windows, and high-ceilinged charm. You'll be delighted when you sample the exceptional cuisine. The menu's European influences are complemented by seasonal graciousness. The region is a recreational paradise. There are dozens of lakes and rivers perfect for boating, swimming, and fishing, with miles of country lanes for biking and walking. Berkshire Public Theater, Hancock Shaker Village, and the William Cullen Bryant Homestead are among the wonderful historic and entertainment venues.

Red Roof Inn

60 Forbes Blvd.
Mansfield, MA 02048
508-339-2323

Type of Lodging: Motel
Room Rates: $89–$139.
Pet Charges and Deposits: None.
Pet Policy: Small pets only.
Amenities: Extended cable TV, movies (fee), video games, voice mail, coin laundry, heated pool, radios, data port/modem telephones, 5 stories, interior corridors.
Rated: 2 Paws – 135 rooms.

Red Roof Inn—Mansfield is an outstanding budget choice, with large, cheery rooms, a welcoming atmosphere, and comfortable amenities. Mansfield is in southeastern Massachusetts, near the Rhode Island border. Gilbert Hills State Park and Taunton are nearby. The latter city, founded in 1639 by Puritan Elizabeth Pole, is a major manufacturing center for clothing, tools, plastics, hardware, and ceramic products. The Gertrude M. Boyden Wildlife Refuge, west of Taunton, features many varieties of plants and animals, from the great blue herons of the marsh to the predatory red-tailed hawks. Taunton's Old Colony Historical Society, housed in an 1852 building, contains a museum of American decorative arts, a silver collection, military room, and genealogical library.

Days Inn–Plymouth / Middleboro

30 E. Clark Street
Middleboro, MA 02346
508-946-4400

Type of Lodging: Motel
Room Rates: $69–$119, including Continental breakfast; AAA and AARP discounts.
Pet Charges and Deposits: $3 per day per pet.
Pet Policy: Small pets only.
Amenities: Extended cable TV, movies, hair dryers, some irons, complimentary laundry, free local telephone calls, airport transportation (fee), conference facilities, radios, data port/modem telephones, some refrigerators, some microwaves, some coffee makers, 2 stories, interior corridors.
Rated: 2 Paws – 113 rooms.

Days Inn is a wonderful find in the Plymouth/ Middleboro area. The rooms are spacious and very comfortable. It's minutes from Plymouth and Cape Cod and only half a mile to the MBTA Train Station with direct service to Boston. The cities of Newport, R.I. and Boston are less than an hour away. Children stay free with their parents. Middleboro is less than twenty miles from Plymouth. While most people head immediately to Plymouth Rock, our author's most memorable stop in Massachusetts—if not all of New England—is Plimoth Plantation (yes, the spelling is correct), a living history museum of the 17th century, where costumed interpreters portray residents of the colony. This is a *full* living village, with activities ranging from planting, house building, harvesting, military exercises (complete with muskets), and preserving foods. You'll spend the better part of a day in the 17th century—and love it.

Days Inn Taunton

164 New State Highway
Raynham, MA 02767
508-824-8647

Type of Lodging: Motel

Room Rates: $69–$89; AAA and AARP discounts.

Pet Charges and Deposits: None.

Pet Policy: All pets welcome.

Amenities: Extended cable TV, movies, heated pool, restaurant adjacent, radios, data port/modem telephones, 2 stories, interior/exterior corridors.

Rated: 2 Paws — 70 rooms.

Days Inn is a typical modern budget motel. It's easy on the wallet, convenient, comfortable, and possessed of everything necessary to afford you a restful night's sleep. Raynham is convenient to historic Plymouth, where you'll find a plethora of activities. The *Mayflower II* is a reproduction of the ship that brought the Pilgrims to the New World. Plymouth Rock itself is protected by a granite portico. It's much smaller than you think. Pilgrim Hall Museum, at Court and Chilton Streets in Plymouth, was first opened in 1824 and is one of the oldest public museums in America. It houses a collection of Pilgrim furniture, armor, decorative arts, and early American painting, as well as the remains of the *Sparrow Hawk,* a trans-Atlantic ship dating from 1626.

Five Bridge Inn Bed & Breakfast

154 Pine Street
Rehoboth, MA 02769
508-252-3190

Type of Lodging: Bed and Breakfast

Room Rates: $94–$109, including full breakfast, some whirlpool units, $115–$140; AARP discounts.

Pet Charges and Deposits: $10 per day.

Pet Policy: Small pets only. Manager's prior approval required.

Amenities: Extended cable TV, outdoor pool, tennis court, data port/modem telephones, radios, some refrigerators, some microwaves, some coffee makers, 3 stories (no elevator), interior corridors.

Rated: 3 Paws — 4 rooms and 1 suite.

The Five Bridge Inn is a striking, stately Georgian Colonial retreat, situated on over 60 acres of forests and fields in a quiet, but easily accessible, area. Stroll the English herb or flower garden, or hike the miles of trails. Enjoy the private tennis court and pool, or avail yourself of horseback riding next door. Guest rooms are comfortable and quiet, each promising a scenic view, and offer king-sized or queen-sized beds with a private or shared bath. Here you'll find warm country comfort and elegance. The living areas are spacious—there's a great room with cathedral ceilings, and a formal dining room where a hearty breakfast awaits you each morning. The price is startlingly reasonable for so much comfort and atmosphere. Five Bridge Inn is a 45-minute drive from Plymouth, Newport, Boston, or New London, and only 10 minutes from Providence.

Holiday Inn Express

909 Hingham Street
Rockland, MA 02370
781-871-5660

Type of Lodging: Motel
Room Rates: $99–$109, including Continental breakfast. AAA and AARP discounts.
Pet Charges and Deposits: None.
Pet Policy: All pets welcome.
Amenities: Extended cable TV, movies, coffee makers, data port/modem telephones, some refrigerators, some microwaves, 3 stories, interior/exterior corridors.
Rated: 3 Paws — 72 rooms and 11 suites.

Holiday Inn Express in Rockland is centrally located between Boston and Plymouth. It offers 72 spacious guest rooms and 11 fully equipped guest suites. The rooms are furnished with contemporary décor and feature king-sized or double queen-sized beds in each room. A buffet style continental breakfast is served and includes freshly brewed coffee and fruit juices. Holiday Inn Express is conveniently located 23 miles from Boston's Logan International Airport. In Boston, you'll enjoy touring the U.S.S. Constitution (Old Ironsides), Freedom Trail, Faneuil Hall, and the Boston Aquarium. In nearby Plymouth, Plimouth Plantation is a standout. You might also want to stop by Plymouth Rock (smaller than you think), Mayflower II, and the Ocean Spray Cranberry World Visitor Center.

Ivanhoe Country House

254 South Undermountain Road,
Route 41
Sheffield, MA 01257
413-229-2143

Type of Lodging: Inn
Room Rates: $80–$130, including Continental breakfast. AAA discounts.
Pet Charges and Deposits: $10 per day per pet.
Pet Policy: Dogs only, sorry, now cats. Manager's prior approval required.
Amenities: Heated pool, kitchenettes, 3 stories, interior corridors.
Rated: 3 Paws — 9 rooms.

Built in 1780 at the foot of Mount Race, on 25 acres of wooded splendor, Ivanhoe Country House welcomes travelers to the southern Berkshires. Guest rooms are comfortable and feature private baths. Some rooms are fully equipped with kitchenettes. Enjoy the refreshment of the pool. The Chestnut Room, a common area, has a fireplace, library, television, piano, and game tables to offer guests a choice of indoor recreation or relaxation. Start your day with a continental breakfast, served outside each bedroom, offering a choice of beverages and baked goods. Plan your visit to include the unmatched spectacle of fall foliage, or challenger the novice-to-expert slopes at nearby Catamount or Butternut Ski Basin. Bike through the rural countryside or hike the Appalachian Trail. An evening at the Berkshire Playhouse or Jacob's Pillow is a summer treat for everyone.

Race Brook Lodge

c/o Nutmeg Bed & Breakfast Agency
P.O. Box 1117
West Hartford, CT 06127-1117
800-727-7592 • 860-236-6698

Type of Lodging: Inn

Room Rates: $109–$150, including Continental breakfast.

Pet Charges and Deposits: $10 per day per pet.

Pet Policy: Manager's prior approval required.

Amenities: 3 stories, interior corridors.

Rated: 3 Paws — 15 guest rooms and 3 suites in restored barn.

Race Brook Lodge is housed in a restored 19th century barn in the Berkshires' scenic south county, complete with a babbling brook. Guest rooms and suites are individually decorated and reflect the country style of textured fabrics, quilts, original artwork, hand-stenciling, and hand-hewn beams. The three bungalows will each accommodate a family of five. Every third Sunday of the month, the Race Brook Lodge hosts lively jazz sessions, accompanied by gourmet seasonal lunches. Discover more than 40 antique shops in historic Sheffield, or hike from the Lodge to the Race Brook waterfalls and then on the Appalachian Trail along the breathtaking crest of Mount Race. Visitors also enjoy the Norman Rockwell Museum in Stockbridge, the Boston Symphony at Tanglewood, plus many fine restaurants, museums, and outdoor activities.

Red Roof Inn

367 Turnpike Road
Southborough, MA 01772
508-481-3904

Type of Lodging: Motel

Room Rates: $69–$99; AAA discounts.

Pet Charges and Deposits: None.

Pet Policy: Small pets only.

Amenities: Extended cable TV, movies (fee), voice mail, free local telephone calls, newspaper, data port/modem telephones, some refrigerators, 2 stories, exterior corridors.

Rated: 2 Paws — 108 rooms.

Another clean, convenient, comfortable, and attractive motel in a wonderful budget chain, Red Roof Inn gives you everything you need for a good night's rest—and a free newspaper when you awake in the morning. Southborough, adjacent to Marlborough, is halfway between Boston and Worcester (pronounced Woo' ster), and no more than a half hour from each. In nearby Sudbury, a very exclusive exurb of Boston, you'll find Longfellow's Wayside Inn of Sudbury, immortalized in Henry Wadsworth Longfellow's poem "Tales of a Wayside Inn." It is one of the country's oldest inns, and Longfellow spent his summers here during the mid-1800's and Henry Ford refurbished the inn in 1923-24. Today, the inn houses a 13-room museum, formal gardens, a stone bridge, and a working gristmill. Redstone Schoolhouse, attended by Mary Sawyer, was the inspiration for the immortal nursery rhyme, "Mary Had a Little Lamb."

Holiday Inn

711 Dwight Street
Springfield, MA 01104
413-781-0900
www.holiday-inn.com.

Type of Lodging: Hotel

Room Rates: $99–$179; AAA and AARP discounts.

Pet Charges and Deposits: None.

Pet Policy: All pets welcome.

Amenities: Extended cable TV, movies (fee), voice mail, irons, hair dryers, heated pool, exercise room, valet laundry, conference facilities, restaurant, cocktails, radios, coffee makers, data port/modem telephones, some refrigerators, some microwaves, 12 stories, interior corridors.

Rated: 3 Paws — 242 rooms.

High-rise Holiday Inn is a standout lodging in Massachusetts' third largest city. There are 242 very comfortable, well-furnished guest rooms, kids stay free in their parents' rooms. Zaffino's Restaurant and Lounge, on the 12th floor, gives you a spectacular view of the city. It's close to Six Flags New England, the Basketball Hall of Fame, Sturbridge, Big E, Yankee Candle, the Berkshires, and Enfield & Hartford, Connecticut—central to every place in New England. While here, be sure to visit the Springfield Library and Museums, which includes several museums and exhibits, including the Connecticut Valley Historical Museum, the George Walker Vincent Smith Art Museum, the Museum of Fine Arts, and the Springfield Science Museum. The Indian Motorcycle Museum has a collection of the first gasoline-powered motorcycles built in the United States.

American Motor Lodge–Best Western

350 Main Street
Sturbridge, MA 01566
508-347-9121

Type of Lodging: Motor Inn

Room Rates: $69–$99, including Continental breakfast. AAA and AARP discounts.

Pet Charges and Deposits: None.

Pet Policy: Small pets only.

Amenities: Extended cable TV, movies, irons, hair dryers, heated pool, sauna, coin laundry, conference facilities, free local telephone calls, restaurant, cocktails, data port/modem telephones, 2 stories, interior corridors.

Rated: 2 Paws — 55 rooms.

Best Western American Motor Lodge is a 2-story motel with traditional motel décor. It boasts the largest indoor pool in town, in-room hair dryers and irons, a pleasant restaurant-lounge, and a play area for children. It's minutes to antique and gift shops and to historic Sturbridge Village. Just as Plimoth Plantation in eastern Massachusetts takes you on a living history journey through the 17th century, Old Sturbridge Village is a complete, re-created village of the early 19th century. The spectacular 200-acre living museum contains more than 40 restored buildings, relocated from various parts of New England. By far the standout attraction in these parts, costumed staff members demonstrate the daily life and work of early New Englanders. You can count on spending at least most of a day here.

Comfort Inn & Suites

215 Charlton Road
Sturbridge, MA 01566
508-347-3306
www.sturbridgecomfortinn.com

Type of Lodging: Motel

Room Rates: $99–$199, including Continental breakfast. AAA and AARP discounts.

Pet Charges and Deposits: None.

Pet Policy: Designated units only.

Amenities: Extended cable TV, movies (fee), dual phone lines, voice mail, irons, hair dryers, heated pool, whirlpool, exercise room, coin laundry, conference facilities, restaurant adjacent, cocktails, massage (fee), free newspaper, radios, coffee makers, data port/modem telephones, some refrigerators, some microwaves, 3 stories, interior/exterior corridors.

Rated: 3 Paws — 77 rooms.

Comfort Inn is an exceptionally well-kept motor inn. It features a modern three-story motel with a single-story building adjacent. This wonderful 77-room hotel overlooks Pistol Pond. You get a free Continental breakfast. Pistol's Lounge and the Cracker Barrel Restaurant are on the premises. Old Sturbridge Village houses—among so many other buildings and activities—homes, a tin shop, a shoe shop, a printing office, a bank, a law office, a center meeting house, and a general store. Paths lead to a gristmill, a sawmill, a wool-carding mill, a blacksmith shop, a cooper's shop, and a working historical farm. The Cheney Wells Clock Gallery displays more than 100 clocks and timepieces from the period.

Days Inn

66-68 Old Route 15
Haynes Street
Sturbridge, MA 01566
508-347-3391

Type of Lodging: Motel

Room Rates: $59–$139, including Continental breakfast. AAA and AARP discounts.

Pet Charges and Deposits: $7 per day per pet.

Pet Policy: All pets welcome.

Amenities: Extended cable TVs, hair dryers, outdoor pool, radios, coffee makers, data port/modem telephones, 2 stories, interior/exterior corridors.

Rated: 2 Paws — 32 rooms.

Days Inn features 32 units in a wooded setting. It's located 1½ miles from Old Sturbridge Village. At-the-door parking and free Continental breakfast are added, welcome amenities. When you've finally had your fill of Old Sturbridge Village, Worcester, the "heart of the Commonwealth," is only minutes away, northeast, via the Massachusetts Turnpike and I-395. The city, located in the very center of the state, was known for its 19th century dramatic, musical, and civic events. Dr. Robert Goddard, father of U.S. rocketry, was born in Worcester and fired his first rocket in nearby Auburn. The Worcester Art Museum contains more than 35,000 objects, representing 5,000 years of art and culture, from Egyptian and Roman antiquities to Impressionist paintings and pop art.

Green Acres Motel

2 Shepard Road, Route 131
Sturbridge, MA 01566
508-347-3496

Type of Lodging: Motel

Room Rates: $59–$119; AAA and AARP discounts.

Pet Charges and Deposits: None.

Pet Policy: Small pets only.

Amenities: Extended cable TV, movies, restaurant adjacent, data port/modem telephones, some refrigerators (fee), 2 stories, exterior corridors.

Rated: 2 Paws — 16 rooms.

Green Acres Motel, a wonderful small lodging, is in a quiet area, back from the road. Five of the 16 rooms have efficiencies (but no utensils). It's quiet, comfortable, and very well priced for the area. In nearby Worcester, Mechanics Hall was built in 1857 and soon became *the* arena for concerts and other popular social events. Try to attend the once-a-week lecture tour of the restored Victorian-style building. Broad Meadow Brook Wildlife Sanctuary, at 272 acres, is reputedly the largest urban wildlife sanctuary in New England. Trails and wooden walkways traverse the oak woods, fields, streams, and wetlands of the Sanctuary. The Goddard Exhibition in Clark University's Goddard Library, contains a display of Dr. Robert Goddard's patents, notebooks, manuscripts, and memorabilia.

Publick House Historic Inn

295 Main Street
Sturbridge, MA 01566
508-347-3313
www.publickhouse.com

Type of Lodging: Complex

Room Rates: $89–$179; AAA and AARP discounts.

Pet Charges and Deposits: $5 per day per pet.

Pet Policy: All pets welcome.

Amenities: Extended cable TV, some hair dryers, 2 swimming pools, tennis court, nature trails, playground, gift shop, valet laundry, conference facilities, free local telephone calls, free newspaper, restaurant, cocktails, radios, data port/modem telephones, some refrigerators, some coffee makers, 2 stories, interior/exterior corridors.

Rated: 3 Paws — 115 rooms and 11 suites.

The Publick House gives you three lodging options: Historic Inn, Bed & Breakfast, or Motor Lodge, situated on 60 acres of countryside. It's listed in the National Register of Historic Places, and it's only a mile from Old Sturbridge Village. In the early days of our country's independence, there was an inn on Sturbridge Common that was so cozy and dependable, such a haven for tired and hungry travelers, that it was famed far and wide. Today, the same is essentially true at the Publick House. The sheep still graze in the meadow just beyond the Bake Shoppe. Recipes for dishes like lobster pie and breakfast muffins are the same as in 1771, though the ingredients are better and more people come to eat them. Visit endless venues such as Old Sturbridge Village, antique shops, museums, galleries, and playhouses.

Rodeway Inn

172 Main Street
Sturbridge, MA 01566
508-347-9673

Type of Lodging: Motel
Room Rates: $49–$159, including Continental breakfast. AAA and AARP discounts.
Pet Charges and Deposits: $10 deposit, $5 per day per pet.
Pet Policy: Small pets only.
Amenities: Extended cable TV, movies, hair dryers, free local telephone calls, coffee makers, data port/modem telephones, some refrigerators, 1 story, exterior corridors.
Rated: 2 Paws — 17 rooms.

Rodeway Inn affords some cozy (translation: small) rooms and some larger ones in a compact, one-story structure. It's well-maintained and quite comfortable. It's walking distance to Sturbridge Plaza, only 1½ miles to Old Sturbridge Village. In nearby Worcester, the Higgins Armory Museum displays weapons and armor from medieval and Renaissance Europe, feudal Japan, and ancient Greece and Rome in a Gothic castle setting. The Ecotarium is a 60-acre environmental exploration museum offering three floors of interactive exhibits, a planetarium and observatory, nature trails, a tree-canopied walkway, 60 species of wildlife, a telecommunications center, and a narrow gauge railroad.

Sturbridge Host Hotel / Conference Center

366 Main Street
Sturbridge, MA 01566
508-347-7393

Type of Lodging: Motor Inn
Room Rates: $129–$209, some suites: $259–$359. AAA and AARP discounts.
Pet Charges and Deposits: None.
Pet Policy: Small pets only.
Amenities: Extended cable TV, movies (fee), irons, hair dryers, heated pool, whirlpool, sauna, beach, swimming, tanning booth, fishing, tennis court, exercise room, boats (fee), paddle boats (fee), miniature golf (fee), racquetball courts (fee), gift shop, valet laundry, conference facilities, restaurant, cocktails, radios, coffee makers, data port/modem telephones, some refrigerators (fee), 2-3 stories, interior corridors.
Rated: 3 Paws — 222 units, including rooms and suites.

Sturbridge Host is situated at the crossroads of New England. Rooms are newly renovated, with New England décor. It's located directly across from Old Sturbridge Village. Sturbridge Host is a full resort hotel on beautiful Cedar Lake. Here, you'll find the historic Oxhead Tavern as well as P. Bella's Trattoria—"Italian with an attitude." Go northeast to Worcester, or travel west to Springfield, where you'll enjoy the Basketball Hall of Fame, a state-of-the-art museum, and Forest Park, a 735-acre municipal park where you'll find baseball fields, tennis courts, lawn bowling, a playground, picnic facilities, and band concerts. The Springfield Armory National Historic Site was commissioned by General George Washington as one of the first two national armories in the country. Today, it houses one of the most extensive collections for firearms in the world.

Wyndham Westborough Hotel

5400 Computer Drive
Westborough, MA 01581
508-366-5511

Type of Lodging: Hotel
Room Rates: $109–$199; AAA and AARP discounts.

Pet Charges and Deposits: None.
Pet Policy: Small pets only.
Amenities: Extended cable TV, movies (fee), video games, voice mail, irons, hair dryers, heated pool, saunas, whirlpool, exercise room, gift shop, valet laundry, conference facilities, airport transportation (fee), restaurant, radios, coffee makers, data port/modem telephones, some refrigerators, 4 stories, interior corridors.
Rated: 3 Paws — 223 rooms.

The Wyndham Westborough has touches of great elegance. Rooms are large and comfortably furnished, and there are more amenities here than in almost anyplace in town. Westborough is a scant seven miles east of Worcester. In winter, it's a fine cross-country ski area. Westborough is also the nearest community to Quinsigamond Lake and Quinsigamond State Park, a manageable 51 acre park 2 miles east of Worcester that allows pets on leash. The Worcester Historical Museum pays tribute to the city's industrial accomplishments and its proud history. The Salisbury Mansion, at 40 Highland Street in Worcester, was built in 1772 and has been restored to its 1830's appearance, including period furniture.

Wachusett Village Inn

9 Village Inn Road
Westminster, MA 01473
978-874-2000

Type of Lodging: Motor Inn
Room Rates: $99–$199, some suites: $199–$299; AAA and AARP discounts.

Pet Charges and Deposits: $25 deposit.

Pet Policy: Designated units only.
Amenities: Extended cable TV, movies, dual phone lines, voice mail, 2 pools, (1 heated, 1 indoor), whirlpool, sauna, steam room, 2 tennis courts, cross-country skiing, ice-staking, playground, exercise room, game rooms, sleigh rides (fee), dog sledding (fee), hay rides (fee), valet laundry, massage (fee), conference facilities, restaurant, cocktails, radios, coffee makers, data port/modem telephones, refrigerators, some microwaves, 1-2 stories, interior/exterior corridors.
Rated: 3 Paws — 74 units, including rooms and suites.

At Wachusett Village Inn, you'll find colonial style cottages, some with fireplace, and motel units. This is a full service hotel with a plethora of amenities and a strong accent on comfort and service. Westminster is located in the extreme north-central part of Massachusetts, near the New Hampshire border, adjacent to Wachusett Lake and Leominster State Forest. John Chapman, better known as Johnny Appleseed, was born in Leominster in 1774. Leominster's National Plastics Center and Museum, house din an early 1900's school building, is dedicated to the past, present, and future of plastics. Nearby Fitchburg is home to the Fitchburg Art Museum (American, European, and Asian paintings and drawings, as well as antiquities from Mesoamerica, Egypt, Greece, and Robe), and the Fitchburg Historical Society Museum (Victorian, Colonial specialties).

Red Roof Inn

1254 Riverdale
West Springfield, MA 01089
413-731-1010

Type of Lodging: Motel
Room Rates: $69–$109; AAA discounts.
Pet Charges and Deposits: None.
Pet Policy: Small pets only.
Amenities: Extended cable TV, movies (fee), voice mail, some irons, some hair dryers, free local telephone calls, free newspapers, restaurant adjacent, health club adjacent, data port/modem telephones, 2 stories, exterior corridors.
Rated: 2 Paws — 111 rooms.

Red Roof Inn is a well-kept budget property with spacious, but modest, units. The attitude is decidedly pet-friendly and you can rest assured of a good night's sleep. West Springfield, just over the Connecticut River from Springfield, is the key to the Southern Berkshires, even though it's immediately adjacent to its much larger sister city to the east. The Josiah Day House, at 70 Park Street, was built in 1754 and is thought to be the oldest brick saltbox house in the nation. Storrowtown Village, 1 mile west of town on State Route 147, is a restored Early American village, made up of seven New England buildings dating from 1767 to 1850. These relocated classics include a mansion, farmhouse, smithy, schoolhouse, tavern, and church. You can also enjoy craft demonstrations.

Pleasant Valley Motel

42 Stockbridge Road (Route 102)
West Stockbridge, MA 01266
413-232-8511

Type of Lodging: Motel
Room Rates: $49–$169; AAA and AARP discounts.
Pet Charges and Deposits: $10 per day per pet.
Pet Policy: All pets welcome.
Amenities: Extended cable TV, outdoor pool, data port/modem telephones, refrigerators, some microwaves, 1 story, exterior corridors.
Rated: 2 Paws — 16 rooms.

Pleasant Valley Motel is a wonderfully manageable, small motel in the traditional style. The rooms are updated and have refrigerators. It's located in the center of all major ski areas, minutes to the Norman Rockwell Museum and Tanglewood. West Stockbridge, on the western edge of the state, near the New York border, is located in the midst of impressive, if low elevation, mountains, and forest country, in the southern Berkshires and west of the Appalachian Trail. In addition to the Hancock Shaker Village, nearby Pittsfield features the Berkshire Artisans, the Albany Berkshire Ballet, and an engaging variety of cultural attractions. Pittsfield is credited with the creation of the country fair, first held on the village green in 1810. Arrowhead was, for thirteen years, the home of Herman Melville, and the place where he completed *Moby Dick*.

Cozy Corner Motel

284 Sand Springs Road
Williamstown, MA 01267
413-458-8006

Type of Lodging: Motel

Room Rates: $49–$129.

Pet Charges and Deposits: $20 deposit, $5 per day per pet.

Pet Policy: All pets welcome.

Amenities: Extended cable TV, movies, conference facilities, restaurant, adjacent, radios, data port/modem telephones, some refrigerators, some VCR's (fee), 2 stories, exterior corridors.

Rated: 2 Paws — 12 rooms.

Cozy Corner Motel is another of those wonderful little motels that seem to have evaporated when the big guys took over the traveler's trade. It's well worth your while to stop here. Housekeeping is exceptional and the units are well maintained. Williamstown, the western terminus of scenic State Route 2, is in the extreme northwest corner of the state, almost straddling the New York and New Hampshire borders. The Sterling and Francine Clark Art Institute, near the Williams College campus, houses works by Corot, Degas, Fragonard, Della Francesca, Gainsborough, Goya, Winslow Homer, Manet. Monet, Renoir, and Gilbert Stuart. Tucked away, as it is, in this relatively small New England town, it is an impressive collection indeed.

Jericho Valley Inn

2541 Hancock Road
Williamstown, MA 01267
413-458-9511

Type of Lodging: Inn

Room Rates: $89–$250, including Continental breakfast.

Pet Charges and Deposits: None.

Pet Policy: All pets welcome.

Amenities: Cottages have full kitchens with fireplaces, 1-2 stories, interior/exterior corridors.

Rated: 3 Paws — 12 rooms and 12 fully furnished cottages on 350 acres.

If you are planning a trip to the Berkshires, Jericho Valley Inn welcomes you and your pet as guests. Located on 350 acres, it is surrounded by the beauty and tranquility of the New England countryside, yet it's only minutes away from all of the area's major attractions. Spacious, comfortable guest rooms have been designed for quiet and comfort, offering individually-controlled heat and air conditioning, full private baths, fine bedding, and comfortable furniture. Charming, secluded one-, two-, and three-bedroom cottages offer full kitchens and spacious living rooms with fireplaces. Williamstown is a great place, offering visitors far-ranging cultural and recreational choices—close to the Jiminy Peak Ski Resort, Vermont's Green Mountains, and the Berkshire Hills.

The Villager Motel

953 Simonds Road
Williamstown, MA 01267
413-458-4046

Type of Lodging: Motel

Room Rates: $49–$109, including Continental breakfast. AAA and AARP discounts.

Pet Charges and Deposits: None.

Pet Policy: Small pets only. Prior approval required.

Amenities: Extended cable TV, free local telephone calls, data port/modem telephones, some refrigerators, 1 story, exterior corridors.

Rated: 2 Paws — 13 rooms.

The Villager Motel is an utterly charming older place. Many of the units have knotty pine walls. The location is semi-rural and very quiet, assuring you of a comfortable, restful stay. The Chapin Library of Rare Books, on the campus of Williams College, contains original copies of the Constitution, Bill of Rights, Declaration of Independence, and Articles of Confederation. Williamstown is the closest town to Mount Greylock, the highest point in Massachusetts. There are several state forests in this area of the southern Taconic Mountains, and it's a fall-and-winter wonderland from October through March. Traveling east, you'll be driving on Massachusetts State Route 2, one of the most scenic roads in New England.

The Regency Suites

70 Southbridge Street
Worchester, MA 01608
508-753-3512

Type of Lodging: Extended Stay Motel

Room Rates: $89–$149, including Continental breakfast. AAA and AARP discounts.

Pet Charges and Deposits: $100 deposit.

Pet Policy: Limit one pet.

Amenities: Extended cable TV, movies, voice mail, irons, hair dryers, heated pool, exercise room, coin laundry, conference facilities, free local telephone calls, restaurant, cocktails, radios, coffee makers, data port/modem telephones, some refrigerators, microwaves, 10 stories, interior corridors.

Rated: 2 Paws — 110 rooms.

Regency Suites offer the ultimate extended stay lodging in Worcester. Suites consist of studios, one-, or two- bedroom units. Although Regency Suites are situated in a busy downtown location, the suites are remarkably quiet, restful, and comfortable. Worcester (pronounced Woo'ster) is a remarkable city with impressive attractions. Most notable are the Worcester Art Museum, Broad Meadow Brook Wildlife Sanctuary, the largest urban wildlife sanctuary in New England, the Higgins Armory Museum, housed in a Gothic castle-like setting, the Goddard Exhibition of rocketry, the Ecotarium, the Worcester Historical Museum, and the Salisbury Mansion. Known as the "heart of the Commonwealth," it is Massachusetts' second city, and a commercial, industrial, and cultural center.

NEW HAMPSHIRE

Nickname: Granite State; White Mountain State

Population: 1,235,786 (41st)

Area: 9,350 sq. miles (46th)

Climate: Highly varied, due to proximity of high mountains and ocean

Capital: Concord

Entered Union: June 21, 1788 (9th)

Motto: Live free or die

Song: Old New Hampshire

Flower: Purple lilac

Tree: White birch

Bird: Purple finch

Famous Granite Staters: Salmon P. Chase, Ralph Adams Cram, Mary Baker Eddy, Daniel Chester French, Robert Frost, Horace Greeley, Sarah Buell Hale, Franklin Pierce, Augustus Saint-Gaudens, Adam Sandler, Alan Shepard, David H. Souter, Earl Tupper, Daniel Webster

History: The Algonquian Peoples inhabited not only New Hampshire, but virtually the whole of New England when England's Martin Pring (1603) and France's Samuel Champlain (1605) first visited the area. New Hampshire's first settlement, Rye, was founded in 1623. Prior to the start of the Revolutionary War, New Hampshire residents eized the fort at Portsmouth in 1774 and drove the royal governor out. In 1776, New Hampshire became the first colony in America to adopt its own constitution.

Geography: Highest Point: 6,288 ft., Mount Washington. Lowest Point: Sea level, Atlantic Ocean. Time Zone: Eastern. Capital: Concord. Major cities: Manchester (100,000), Nashua (79,700), Concord (36,000), Portsmouth (26,000). New Hampshire's low, rolling coast rises to the abundant hills and mountains as one moves west. The magic of fall's changing colors is legendary.

Tourist Information: 1-800-FUNINNH, ext. 169. Website: www.visitnh.com.

Recreation Areas
For You and Your Pet

All of these areas permit pets on a leash.

National Forest

White Mountain National Forest, 770,000 acres in Northern New Hampshire. Camping, picnicking, hiking trails, boating, boat ramp, fishing, swimming, bicycle trails, winter sports, visitor center.

Army Corps of Engineers

Blackwater Dam, 18 miles north of Concor off State Route 127. Boating, fishing, winter sports.

Edward McDowell Lake, 1,198 acres 4 miles north of Peterborough off State Route 101. Picnicking, boating, fishing, winter sports.

Franklin Falls Dam, 2,800 acres, 15 miles along the Pemigewassett River, 2 miles north of Franklin off State Route 127. Boating, fishing, winter sports.

State Recreation Areas

Bear Brook State Park, 9,800 acres, 2 miles east of Allenstown off State Route 28. Museums, camping, picnicking, hiking trails, boat rentals, fishing, swimming, winter sports, visitor center, food service.

Coleman State Park, 1,605 acres 12 miles east of Colebrook off State Route 26. Camping, picnicking, boating, boat ramp, fishing, winter sports.

Crawford Notch, 5,950 acres 12 miles west of Bartlett on US 302. Camping, picnicking, hiking trails, fishing, visitor center, food service.

Franconia Notch, 6,440 acres 5 miles north of North Woodstock off US 3. Camping, picnicking, hiking trails, boating, boat ramp, fishing, swimming, bicycle trails, winter sports, visitor center, food service.

Greenfield State Park, 401 acres 1 mile west of Greenfield, off State Route 136. Canoe rental, camping, picnicking, hiking trails, boating, boat ramp, fishing, swimming, winter sports, food service.

Lake Francis State Park, far northeast, 1,684 acres 7 miles north of Pittsburg off US 3. Camping, picnicking, boating, boat ramp, fishing, swimming, winter sports, food service.

Moose Brook State Park, 755 acres, 2 miles west of Gorman off US 2. Camping, picnicking, hiking trails, fishing, swimming, winter sports.

Mount Sunapee State Park, 2,893 acres, 3 miles south of Sunapee at the junction of State Routes 103 and 103B. Picnicking, hiking trails, boating, boat ramp, fishing, swimming, winter sports, visitor center, food service.

Pillsbury State Park, 3,702 acres, 3½ miles north of Washington on State Route 31. Camping, picnicking, hiking trails, fishing, winter sports

Pisgah State Park, 13,500 acres off State Route 63 in Chesterfield. Hunting, picnicking, hiking trails, fishing, swimming, bicycle trails, winter sports.

Other Notable Recreation Areas

Moore Reservoir, 3,500 acres 8 miles west of Littleton off I-93 via State Routes 18 and 135. Picnicking, hiking trails, boating, boat ramp, fishing, swimming, bicycle trails, visitor center.

The Villager Motel

Route 302
Bartlett, NH 03812
603-274-2742

Type of Lodging: Motel

Room Rates: $41–$129; some suites, $120–$179; AAA and AARP discounts.

Pet Charges and Deposits: $7 per day per pet.

Pet Policy: Advance reservations only.

Amenities: Extended cable TV, heated pool, swimming, fishing, nature trails, playground, coin laundry, free local telephone calls, data port/modem telephones, refrigerators, some microwaves, some coffee makers, 1 story, exterior corridors.

Rated: 3 Paws — Variety of units.

The Villager Motel is located in a pleasant mountain setting. Units are very well maintained and the landscaping is particularly attractive. It's 10 minutes and a million miles from North Conway, situated on 15 wooded acres. Swim in the pool or in the Saco River. You're two minutes to Story Land and to Attitash Bear Peak. You have a choice of dining and over 150 tax-free outlets nearby. With Bear Mountain to the south, Mount Parker to the north, and Mount Carrigain to the west, Bartlett is a year-round recreation center. The village was incorporated in 1790, when the land along the Saco River east of Crawford Notch, was granted to William Stark and several other settlers for their service in the French and Indian War. A scenic road runs from Bartlett to the White Mountain National Forest.

Adair Country Inn

80 Guider Lane
Bethlehem, NH 03574
603-444-2600

Type of Lodging: Historic Country Inn

Room Rates: $189–$369, some whirlpool units, $320–$369. AAA and AARP discounts.

Pet Charges and Deposits: None.

Pet Policy: All pets welcome. Pet on premises.

Amenities: No TV's, hair dryers, dining room, golf privileges, tennis court, snow shoes, nature trails, afternoon tea, radios, smoke-free premises, 3 stories (no elevator), interior corridors.

Rated: 4 Paws — 10 rooms.

Adair Country Inn, a 1927 Georgian Colonial, is situated on 200 wooded acres with ponds, hills, lawns, and perennial gardens. It's furnished with antiques and reproductions to make your stay even more colorful and relaxing. Bethlehem, in the northeast quadrant of New Hampshire, is situated just east of the Amonoosuc River, ten miles east of the Moore Dam on the wide Connecticut River, and less than fifteen miles west of the White Mountains. A particularly lovely stretch of U.S. Highway 302 runs east and south—indeed, the entire area is a mountain wonderland with cross-country and alpine skiing, unspoiled forest to roam with your pet, and picture postcard villages throughout.

Super 8 Motel

Route 3
Campton, NH 03264
603-536-3520

Type of Lodging: Motel

Room Rates: $52–$144; AAA and AARP discounts.

Pet Charges and Deposits: $10 per day per pet.

Pet Policy: All pets welcome.

Amenities: Extended cable TV, heated pool, sauna, steam bath, coin laundry, conference facilities, data port/modem telephones, 2 stories, interior corridors.

Rated: 2 Paws — 101 rooms.

Actually located in nearby Plymouth, New Hampshire, clean, pleasant Super 8 Motel is near all area attractions and skiing. It's open all year and is a fine bargain. Campton, situated at the southwest corner of the White Mountain National Forest, is a year-round playground, surrounded by some of the most gorgeous scenery in New England. It's fifteen miles to Plymouth, just off I-93, which, in this area, is one of the loveliest stretches of Interstate in the United States. If huge Lake Winnipesaukee is too far of a drive for you (it's about 30 miles away), there are several smaller lakes within a radius of ten miles. Skiing? Try Sandwich Mountain, Stinson Mountain, or Mount Kineo, all in close proximity.

Corner House Inn

22 Main Street
Center Sandwich, NH 03227
800-501-6219 • 603-284-6219

Type of Lodging: Inn

Room Rates: $100, including full breakfast.

Pet Charges and Deposits: None.

Pet Policy: All pets welcome.

Amenities: Restaurant, radios, 3 stories (no elevator), interior corridors.

Rated: 3 Paws — 4 rooms.

Center Sandwich, an unspoiled 19th century village nestled between the White Mountains and Squam Lake, provides the setting for the historic Corner House Inn. The Inn, built in 1849, has been in continuous operation for over 100 years. Its second floor still provides lodging for the traveler. Three of the four guest rooms have shared bath facilities; one includes a private bath. The rooms reflect a lovely Victorian influence, with antiques and handmade quilts. Downstairs, four separate dining rooms serve guests in an intimate, candlelit atmosphere. The restaurant serves lunch and dinner, featuring New England seafood and homemade desserts, An art gallery, weaving designery, numerous antique and craft shops, and an historical museum are all within walking distance.

Chesterfield Inn

399 Crossroad
Chesterfield, NH 03466
603-256-3211

Type of Lodging: Country Inn

Room Rates: $155–$ 280; some suites $200–$225; some whirlpool units, $255–$275.

Pet Charges and Deposits: None.

Pet Policy: Managers prior approval required.

Amenities: Extended cable TV, CD players, honor bars, irons, hair dryers, valet laundry, conference facilities, dining room, smoke-free premises, radios, coffee makers, data port/modem telephones, refrigerators, some VCRs, 2 stories, interior/exterior corridors.

Rated: 3 Paws — 15 units, including rooms and some suites.

Rooms at the Chesterfield Inn are clean, cheerful, and comfortable. All rooms come with iron and ironing board. The candlelit dining room in this elegant, romantic inn creates a feast for your eyes *and* for your palate. You'll enjoy the beautiful views of rolling hills and spectacular sunsets, as well as the crab cakes with remoulade and chocolate cake with crème Anglais. Chesterfield, in the extreme southern part of New Hampshire, is close to excellent skiing, the Connecticut River, and Brattleboro, just over the border in Vermont. Undeveloped Pisgah State Park is an excellent place for roaming and romping with your pet.

Best Budget Inn

24 Sullivan Street
Claremont, NH 03743
603-542-9567

Type of Lodging: Motel

Room Rates: $39–$69; AAA and AARP discounts.

Pet Charges and Deposits: $5–$10 per day per pet.

Pet Policy: All pets welcome.

Amenities: Extended cable TV, movies, data port/modem telephones, some refrigerators, some microwaves, 1 story, exterior corridors.

Rated: 2 Paws — 21 rooms.

Best Budget Inn is a small, comfortable motel in the center of town. Early check-in and late check-out are welcome conveniences. Claremont, a sizeable town situated between Sunapee Lake and Mount Sunapee to the east, and the Connecticut River and the Vermont frontier to the west, is situated in southwestern New Hampshire. Just south of Sunapee Lake, you'll find great cross-country and alpine skiing at Mount Sunapee and nearby Wadleigh State Park. To the northwest, consider visiting Saint-Gaudens National Historical Site, the 1885-1907 home and studio of sculptor Augustus Saint-Gaudens, which was originally a country tavern built in the early 1800's, near Cornish. Two miles south of the site, on State Route 12A, you'll find one of the longest covered bridges in the United States, built in 1866, measuring 460 feet in length and spanning the Connecticut River.

Southern Comfort Motel

RR 1, Box 520
Colebrook, NH 03576
603-237-4440

Type of Lodging: Motel

Room Rates: $55–$75, some suites $69–$85, including Continental breakfast; AAA discounts.

Pet Charges and Deposits: None.

Pet Policy: Small pets only.

Amenities: Extended cable TV, heated pool, playground, basketball, free local telephone calls, radios, data port/modem telephones, refrigerators, some microwaves, some coffee makers 1 story, exterior corridors.

Rated: 2 Paws — 19 units.

Northern Comfort Motel boasts pleasant, well-maintained units with rustic, knotty pine interior. Way up north, in the northeast corner of New Hampshire, lies Colebrook—one mile across the Connecticut River from Vermont, ten miles to the province of Quebec, Canada. Dixville Peak, 3,482 feet high, offers fine alpine and cross-country skiing. Dixville Notch and Coleman State Park are nearby, as are Lake Francis, First Connecticut Lake, and Second Lake. The only thing missing here is a lot of people—at 1,200 souls, Coleman is the metropolis of a pretty hefty segment of Northeast New Hampshire. But, when you and your pet are on holiday, maybe that's not such a bad thing, is it?

Best Western Concord Inn & Suites

97 Hall Street
Concord, NH 03301
603-228-4300

Type of Lodging: Motel

Room Rates: $69–$209, some suites–$114–$204; AAA and AARP discounts.

Pet Charges and Deposits: $10 per day per pet.

Pet Policy: All pets welcome.

Amenities: Extended cable TV, movies (fee), voice mail, irons, hair dryers, heated pool, whirlpool, sauna, exercise room, valet and coin laundry, conference facilities, radios, coffee makers, data port/modem telephones, refrigerators, microwaves, 3 stories, interior corridors.

Rated: 3 Paws — 66 units.

One thing you can always be sure of—you'll get a fine, modern room with all of the comforts at Best Western Concord Inn & Suites. Concord, the state capital since 1808, is also the financial center of the state. The State House on Main Street is the country's oldest statehouse where the legislature continues to meet in its original chambers. The Christa McAuliffe Planetarium is a memorial to America's first teacher to be chosen for the Space Program, who died tragically in the Challenger explosion in 1986. The planetarium offers a variety of shows and exhibits. The Museum of New Hampshire history, across from the State House, features an overview of the state's history, highlighted by exhibits of Native American Chief Passaconaway, Revolutionary War General John Stark, Daniel Webster, Robert Frost, and Command Alan B. Shepard, Jr., the first American in space.

Concord Comfort Inn

71 Hall Street
Concord, NH 03301
603-226-4100

Type of Lodging: Motel

Room Rates: $59–$189; some whirlpool units–$100–$250, including Continental breakfast. AAA and AARP discounts.

Pet Charges and Deposits: None.

Pet Policy: All pets welcome.

Amenities: Extended cable TV, movies (fee), video games, irons, hair dryers, heated pool, whirlpool, sauna, conference facilities, radios, coffee makers, data port/modem telephones, some refrigerators (fee), some microwaves, some VCR's, 3 stories, interior corridors.

Rated: 3 Paws — 100 units.

Concord's Comfort Inn affords well-appointed, pleasant units, and a quiet residential location. Nevertheless, it's convenient to downtown and the Interstate. The Inn is near historic Concord, McAuliffe Planetarium, and the New Hampshire International Speedway. It's an easy drive to beaches, lakes, mountains, and skiing. Canterbury Shaker Village, established in 1792, is now a museum and historic site. Twenty-five of the original buildings in this religious colony have been restored. Skilled artisans re-create Shaker crafts of broom making, dovetailing, oval box making and weaving. The Pierce Manse was home to President Franklin Pierce from 1842-1848. This restored mid-19th century house if furnished in period style.

White Deer Motel

379 White Mountain Highway
Conway, NH 03818
603-447-5366

Type of Lodging: Motel

Room Rates: $41–$131; AAA and AARP discounts.

Pet Charges and Deposits: $35 deposit, $10 per day per pet.

Pet Policy: All pets welcome.

Amenities: Extended cable restaurant adjacent, coffee makers refrigerators, data port / model telephones, some radios, 2 stories, interior/exterior corridors.

Rated: 2 Paws — 14 rooms.

Independently owned and operated White Deer Motel, located just north of the village center, boasts pleasant, well-maintained, comfortable motel units. Conway, just outside the southeastern entrance to the White Mountain National Forest, and right between Oea Porridge Pond and Conway Lake, is part of the diverse three Conways (Conway, North Conway, Center Conway), which lies in the easternmost part of New Hampshire, just west of the Maine border. Obviously, its location makes it a year-round recreation place—skiing, hiking, boating, fishing—and an almost uncountable array of outdoor activities. It's one of the most scenic places in the Granite State. The Conway Scenic Railroad, located in the center of town, takes you on a one hour, 11 mile antique steam train ride through the Mount Washington Valley.

Days Inn

481 Central Avenue
Dover, NH 03820
603-742-0400

Type of Lodging: Motel

Room Rates: $89–$169; AAA and AARP discounts.

Pet Charges and Deposits: $50 deposit.

Pet Policy: All pets welcome.

Amenities: Extended cable TV, movies (fee), some irons, some hair dryers, heated pool, whirlpool, conference facilities, restaurant adjacent, health club adjacent, radios, data port/modem telephones, some coffee makers, some refrigerators, some microwaves, 2 stories, interior/exterior corridors.

Rated: 2 Paws — 54 units.

Days Inn-Dover is an inviting motel with pleasant, comfortable rooms. Dover, situated between Portsmouth to the south and Rochester to the north, is in the southeastern quadrant of the state, just a few miles from the border with Maine. The oldest permanent settlement in the state, Dover was founded in 1623 by tidewater fishermen and traders. By the late 1600's, the village had grown so quickly that it had to be moved from Dover Point on State Route 4 at the Piscataqua River, to its present location. Renovations in the downtown area and along the riverfront feature Colonial and early Victorian buildings.

Payne's Hill Bed & Breakfast

141 Henry Law Avenue
Dover, NH 03820
603-740-9441
www.bestinns.net/usa/nhpayneshill.html

Type of Lodging: Historic Bed & Breakfast

Room Rates: $65–$85, including Continental breakfast.

Pet Charges and Deposits: None.

Pet Policy: Dogs only, sorry, no cats. Manager's prior approval required.

Amenities: Cable TV, music room, 3 stories (no elevator), interior corridors.

Rated: 3 Paws — 4 rooms.

Conveniently located near the town of Dover, Payne's Hill Bed & Breakfast is a recently restored 120-year-old New England charmer, situated on two acres. You and your pet are encouraged to stroll the grounds, which contain annual, perennial, and vegetable gardens. Each room is individually decorated with comfortable, unique furnishings and cable TV. Guests are invited to enjoy the music room, which has several instruments including a piano, as well as audio equipment. Unwind in the gazebo and enjoy the surrounding natural beauty during any season. Payne's Hill B&B is within walking distance to downtown, shopping, parks, restaurants, movies, and the newly constructed Riverwalk. Scenic and historic Portsmouth, the beautiful eastern coastal areas, and the new Whittemore Recreational Complex are all conveniently nearby.

Silver Street Inn

103 Silver Street
Dover, NH 03820
603-743-3000

Type of Lodging: Historic Bed & Breakfast

Room Rates: $89–$149; AAA discounts.

Pet Charges and Deposits: None.

Pet Policy: All pets welcome. Pet on premises.

Amenities: Extended cable TV, dietary food preparation for breakfast on request, smoke free premises, radios, 3-stories (no elevator), interior corridors.

Rated: 3 Paws — 10 rooms.

Silver Street Inn is certainly the lodging of choice if you're looking for charm and ambience in Dover. This 1880's home features attractive guest rooms with original, hand-painted canvas wallpaper and fine plaster ceilings and moldings. A meal plan is available. The Woodman Institute, 182-190 Central Avenue, consists of three display building, the hand-hewn 1675 Dame Garrison House, furnished in the earliest American style, the 1818 Woodman House, which has exhibits about natural history and science; and the 1813 Hale House, the home of abolitionist Senator John P. Hale. Dover is at the northeast corner if Great Bay, which ultimately meets the Atlantic Ocean at Portsmouth.

Hickory Pond Inn & Golf Course

One Stage Coach Road
Durham, NH 03824
603-659-2227

Type of Lodging: Historic Bed & Breakfast

Room Rates: $62–$104; AAA and AARP discounts.

Pet Charges and Deposits: None.

Pet Policy: In designated rooms only.

Amenities: Extended cable TV, cross-country skiing, bicycles, exercise room, conference facilities, radios, data port/modem telephones, some VCR's, 2 stories, interior corridors.

Rated: 3 Paws — 18 rooms.

This wonderful 18th century farmhouse boasts modern amenities for your comfort. It's close to the University of New Hampshire and only a short drive to Portsmouth and the New Hampshire beaches. Some rooms come with shared baths, others with private baths. Durham, in the southeast corner of New Hampshire, is on Little Bay, southwest of Dover. Settled in 1635 and separated from Dover in 1732, the town was the home of Revolutionary War hero and three-time governor of New Hampshire Major General John Sullivan. A commemorative tablet marks the site of the old meetinghouse where, in 1774, Sullivan and his band of Durham patriots stored the gunpowder they had taken from the British in Newcastle. Rural and maritime activity gave way to "town and gown" in 1893, when a bequest moved what became the University of New Hampshire from Hanover to Durham.

Best Western Hearthside Motor Inn

137 Portsmouth Avenue
Exeter, NH 03833
603-772-3794

Type of Lodging: Motel
Room Rates: $129–$154.
Pet Charges and Deposits: $10 per day per pet.
Pet Policy: All pets welcome.
Amenities: Extended cable TV, outdoor pool, data port/modem telephones, some refrigerators, some microwaves, 3 stories (no elevator), interior corridors.
Rated: 2 Paws — 33 rooms.

Even though the Best Western Hearthside Motor Inn is located in a busy commercial area, then property is set back from the highway and the units are quiet, comfortable, and relaxing. Situated at the falls of the Squamscott River, Exeter began its life in 1638, when the Reverend John Wheelwright, whose radical views and religious nonconformity led to his expulsion from Boston, established a settlement here. From that time forward, Exeter has been a center of outspoken dissent. Exeterians defied royal commands, flouted talk of liberty, and burned Lord North and Lord Bute in effigy. When the Revolutionary War began, the capital of the colony was moved from Portsmouth, which was then controlled by Tories, to the Patriot stronghold of Exeter. The American Independence Museum is situated in the Ladd-Gilman house, built in the early 1700's.

The Unique Yankee B&B Lodge

354 Upper Troy Road
Fitzwilliam, NH 03447
603-242-6706

Type of Lodging: Bed & Breakfast
Room Rates: $79–$142; some whirlpool units–$114–$124; including full breakfast; AAA and AARP discounts.
Pet Charges and Deposits: None.
Pet Policy: Designated rooms only—cottage or annex.
Amenities: Extended cable TV, sauna, valet laundry, movies, VCR's, radios, coffee makers, data port/modem telephones, some refrigerators, some microwaves, smoke-free premises, 2 stories, interior corridors.
Rated: 2 Paws — 7 rooms.

The Unique Yankee B&B Lodge is a very small lodging with a great number of amenities and comfortable, timeless rooms. Fitzwilliam is the classic New England community—a village green framed by a meeting house, historic residences, antique shops, and a 1797 inn. Small woodworking operations give Fitzwilliam a stable economy. Rhododendron State Park, offers views of Mount Monadnock and other mountains in the region, as well as 16 acres of native rhododendron maxima. The bushes, some as high as 24 feet, bloom in mid-July. Fitzwilliam, located in the extreme southern portion of the state, is only about six miles to the Massachusetts frontier.

Franconia Village Hotel & Conference Center

87 Wallace Hill Road
Franconia, NH 03580
603-823-7422

Type of Lodging: Motor Inn
Room Rates: $69–$139; AAA and AARP discounts.
Pet Charges and Deposits: $10 per day per pet.
Pet Policy: All pets welcome.
Amenities: Extended cable TV, hair dryers, heated pool, whirlpool, sauna, exercise room, game room, conference facilities, fax (fee), restaurant, cocktails, radios, coffee makers, refrigerators, microwaves, data port/modem telephones, 2 stories, interior corridors.
Rated: 2 Paws – 60 rooms.

Franconia Village Hotel & Conference Center has quite acceptable rooms, very nice public facilities, and a plethora of fine amenities. Franconia, a few miles north of Franconia Notch, is a pleasant New England town. Its most famous attraction is The Frost Place. Born in San Francisco, Robert Frost, one of America's greatest and best-loved poets, moved to Massachusetts with his mother after his father's death. After a sojourn of several years in England, he purchased the house and farm here in 1915. Some of his best known works, including *The Road Not Taken* and *Stopping by the Woods on a Snowy Evening* were written here. The New England Ski Museum, beside Cannon Mountain Aerial Tramway, details the history of Nordic and alpine skiing in the area. The Cannon Mountain Aerial Tramway extends from Valley Station to the top of Cannon Mountain (2,022 feet ascent, 7½ minutes), from where you'll have a spectacular view of the area's mountains and valleys.

Gale River Motel

One Main Street
Franconia, NH 03580
603-823-5655
www.galerivermotel.com

Type of Lodging: Motel
Room Rates: $52–$84; AAA and AARP discounts.
Pet Charges and Deposits: $5 per day per pet.
Pet Policy: All pets welcome.
Amenities: Extended cable TV, heated pool, whirlpools, playground, horseshoes, shuffleboard, volleyball, barbeques, free local telephone calls, radios, coffee makes, refrigerators, data port/modem telephones, some microwaves, 1 story, exterior corridors.
Rated: 2 Paws – 12 rooms.

Located on I-93, Exit 38, Gale River Motel is a bargain-hunter's paradise, with economy motel units and cottages. The grounds are well-kept, with picnic tables and grill, and the location is very pleasant, with beautiful views of the White Mountains. Unquestionably, the standout attraction in the area is Franconia Notch, the most celebrated mountain gap in the East. It has more scenic spots than any other White Mountain notch. By the mid-1800's, it was a renowned tourist destination, with huge hotels. The hotels no longer exist, but the scenery is still here to be enjoyed by all. The Flume, at the south end of the notch, is a chasm extending 800 feet along the flank of Mount Liberty. Within the Flume, you'll find two covered bridges as well as waterfalls and cascades. The Profile, also called the Old Man of the Mountain and the Great Stone Face, consists of a 40-foot high "head" formed by five separate ledges.

Horse and Hound Inn

205 Wells Road
Franconia, NH 03580
800-450-5501 • 603-823-5501

Type of Lodging: Bed & Breakfast

Room Rates: $99–$110, including full breakfast.

Pet Charges and Deposits: $10 per stay, $50 refundable deposit.

Pet Policy: All pets welcome. (Several pets on premises).

Amenities: Restaurant, 2 stories (no elevator), interior corridors.

Rated: 3 Paws — 8 rooms.

The Horse and Hound Inn, which started as a 19th century farmhouse around 1830, is now one of New England's finest traditional bed & breakfast inns. Rooms are comfortably furnished with king- and queen-sized beds, some with adjoining rooms furnished with single or double beds. All rooms offer peaceful views of the surrounding landscape. Gus and Max, the house cocker spaniels, welcome four-legged guests, and twin cats, Boris and Igor, may make an appearance. Complimentary full breakfast includes the chef's choice of pancakes, eggs, and omelets. The dining room serves continental cuisine each evening at very reasonable prices. Located "off the beaten path" on the north side of Cannon Mountain, the Inn is adjacent to the White Mountain National Forest and Franconia Notch State Park. Cross-country ski right out the front door in season.

Lovett's Inn

1474 Profile Road
Franconia, NH 03580
800-356-3802 • 603-823-7761

Type of Lodging: Historic Inn

Room Rates: $140–$210, including full breakfast and four course dinner.

Pet Charges and Deposits: None.

Pet Policy: All pets welcome.

Amenities: Heated pool, whirlpool, spas, two dining rooms, cocktail lounge, data port/modem telephones, 2 stories (no elevator), interior corridors.

Rated: 3 Paws — 22 rooms and 3 suites.

Enjoy a peaceful getaway pampered by true New England hospitality in this beautiful, historic 1794 home. Sample the many seasons of New Hampshire's north country, where recreation and relaxation go hand in hand. The Inn offers comfortable single, double, and suite arrangements, all with private baths. Each room is furnished with antique and period decorations. Comfortable bungalows with fireplaces dot the property, offering woodland privacy or poolside charm. The candlelit dining room provides a soothing atmosphere and a unique menu. Situated on ten scenic acres only moments from Franconia Notch State Park, Lovett's offers convenient access to many area attractions. Visit the Old Man of the Mountain, the Basin, the Flume, or Cannon Mountain Aerial Tramway. Enjoy golfing, hiking, bicycling, downhill, and cross-country skiing.

Atwood Inn

71 Hill Road
Franklin, NH 03235
603-934-3666

Type of Lodging: Historic Bed & Breakfast

Room Rates: $69–$99, including full breakfast.

Pet Charges and Deposits: None.

Pet Policy: All pets welcome. Pet on premises.

Amenities: No TVs, smoke-free premises radios, data port/modem telephones, 3 stories (no elevator), interior corridors.

Rated: 3 Paws — 7 rooms.

The Atwood Inn, an historic bed & breakfast, is housed in an 1830 inn. Four of the seven guest rooms have a fireplace. The attractive guest rooms and surroundings make this lovely little inn a memorable place indeed. Daniel Webster, the immortal orator and statesman, was born in a two-room house off State Route 127, 3½ miles south of Franklin, in 1782. Now restored, the house contains period antiques and relics. Upon separating from the town of Salisbury in 1828, citizens wanted to name their town after native son Daniel Webster, but since the state already had a town called Webster, they decided, instead, to honor Benjamin Franklin. The 1820 Congregational Church, Franklin's first church, displays a bust of Daniel Webster in front of the church, the work of sculptor Daniel Chester French, who later sculpted of the seated Abraham Lincoln in the Lincoln Memorial in Washington, D.C.

Temperance Tavern

P.O. Box 369, Old Province Road
Gilmanton, NH 03237
603-267-7349

Type of Lodging: Historic Bed & Breakfast

Room Rates: $69–$159, including Continental breakfast. AAA and AARP discounts.

Pet Charges and Deposits: None.

Pet Policy: Manager's prior approval required.

Amenities: No TVs, exercise room, data port/modem telephones, some radios, smoke-free premises, 3 stories (no elevator), interior corridors.

Rated: 3 Paws — 5 units.

What a remarkable historic find is the Temperance Tavern! This 1793 homestead has served as an inn for more than 200 years. You'll find many fireplaces and original 18th center stenciling. Don't expect TVs here. You'll have to do without your usual shot of the boob tube. Gilmanton is the westernmost of the "Gilmantons" (Gilmanton, Lower Gilmanton, Gilmanton Iron Works). This small town is just southwest of New Hampshire's largest lake, Lake Winnipesaukee ("Smile of the Great Spirit"), which has 183 miles of coastline, over 300 islands, and, despite being landlocked, excellent salmon fishing. The New Hampshire Intrernational Speedway is less than 14 miles away, and Laconia, the largest town and population center of the Lakes Region, is less than ten miles distant.

Mount Madison Motel

365 Main Street
Gorham, NH 03581
603-466-3622
www.mtmadisonmotel.com

Type of Lodging: Motel
Room Rates: $39–$89; AAA and AARP discounts.
Pet Charges and Deposits: None.
Pet Policy: Small pets only.
Amenities: Winter plug-ins, extended cable TV, heated pool, restaurant adjacent, radios, coffee makers, data port/modem telephones, some refrigerators, some microwaves, some VCR's, 1-2 stories, exterior corridors.
Rated: 2 Paws — 33 rooms.

Mount Madison Motel features bright, comfortable units, with some very small bathrooms. It's near Storyland, Santa's Village, and Mount Washington. Rooms are immaculate and well-appointed. Gorham, gateway to the Great North Woods, has several miles of scenic and challenging trails, including a part of the Appalachian Trail. This is moose country, and you're sure to see roads by the side of the road reading, "Brake for Moose—It could save your life—211 collisions," and the like. Gorham, at the top of the largest section of White Mountain National Forest, is about ten miles from the Maine border on an incredibly beautiful stretch of two of New Hampshire's most scenic highways, U.S. 2 and State Highway 16, in the midst of mountains and forest.

Royalty Inn

130 Main Street
Gorham, NH 03581
603-466-3312
www.royaltyinn.com

Type of Lodging: Motor Inn
Room Rates: $49–$99
Pet Charges and Deposits: $5 per day per pet.
Pet Policy: All pets welcome.
Amenities: Extended cable TV, movies (fee), voice mail, 2 heated pools, whirlpool, sauna, racketball courts, basketball, game room, coin laundry, conference facilities, restaurant, cocktails, radios, data port/modem telephones, some refrigerators (fee), some coffeemakers, some microwaves (fee), some VCR's, 1-2 stories, interior/exterior corridors.
Rated: 3 Paws — 88 rooms.

Royalty Inn has bright, cheerful rooms of varying sizes, some with private balcony. Three generations of the King family have offered warm hospitality, excellent service, and health-oriented recreation facilities. The Birches Restaurant serves breakfast and dinner daily, and the cocktail lounge is open every evening. Royalty Inn is located in the charming small town of Gorham, within walking distance to shopping, the town common, tennis courts, and a playground. Golfers will appreciate the 18-hole golf course three minutes away, as well as nearby Mount Washington and the majestic Presidential Range, offering challenging hiking, climbing, and skiing, and a host of year round activities.

Top Notch Motor Inn

265 Main Street
Gorham, NH 03581
603-466-5496
www.top-notch.com

Type of Lodging: Motor Inn

Room Rates: $46–$144, AAA and AARP discounts.

Pet Charges and Deposits: None.

Pet Policy: Small pets only.

Amenities: Extended cable TV, outdoor pool, whirlpool, coin laundry, free local telephone calls, restaurant adjacent, radios, coffee makers, data port/modem telephones, some refrigerators, some microwaves, some VCR's, 1-2 stories, exterior corridors.

Rated: 2 Paws — 36 rooms.

The pleasantly decorated units in Top Notch Motor Inn have paneled walls and small bathrooms. It's centrally located in Gorham, near Mount Washington, Storyland, and Santa's Village. Kids stay free in their parents' room. In addition to being at the northern end of a large portion of White Mountain National Forest, Gorham is also at the *southern* end of a smaller, northern portion of the forest. Moose Brook State Park is nearby, as are several mountains, such as Mount Crescent, 3,230 feet, Cascade Mountain, 2,606 feet, Mount Madison, 5,362 feet, and Mount Washington, at 6,288 feet the highest point in New Hampshire. There's lots of fabulous skiing in the immediate area.

Town & Country Motor Inn

U.S. Route 2
P.O. Box 220
Gorham, NH 03581
603-466-3315
www.townandcountryinn.com

Type of Lodging: Motor Inn

Room Rates: $52–$84, some suites $89–$112,

some whirlpool units: $89–$112.

Pet Charges and Deposits: $6 per day per pet.

Pet Policy: All pets welcome.

Amenities: Winter plug-ins, extended cable TV, some hair dryers, heated pool, whirlpool, sauna, steam room, snowmobiling, nature trails, exercise room, golf—18 holes (fee), restaurant, cocktails, radios, data port/modem telephones, some refrigerators, some VCR's, 2 stories, interior/exterior corridors.

Rated: 2 Paws — 160 units, including rooms and suites.

Town & Country Motor Inn has a beautiful mountain setting, with attractively landscaped grounds and various sized units. It's nestled in the heart of the world-renowned Shelburne Birches. With 160 units, it's the largest facility in the area. The Androscoggin River widens perceptibly as it makes a ninety degree bend at Gorham. There are more than half a dozen mountains over 5,000 feet in altitude, perhaps not much by Rockies and Sierra standards, but truly mountainous in this part of the world, within easy reach. That means skiing, and lots of it in the vicinity. Wildcat Mountain Gondola Tramway, Glen Ellis Falls, and Pinkham Notch are only a few of the fascinating locales just south of Gorham.

Hampton Falls Inn

11 Lafayette Road
Hampton Falls, NH 03844
800-356-1729 • 603-926-9545

Type of Lodging: Motel

Room Rates: $74–$174; AAA and AARP discounts.

Pet Charges and Deposits: $10 per day, $50 refundable deposit.

Pet Policy: Small dogs only (sorry, no cats). Manager's prior approval required.

Amenities: Extended cable TV, hair dryers, heated pool, whirlpool, valet laundry, conference facilities, free local telephone calls, restaurant, radios, microwaves, refrigerators, data port/modem telephones, some VCR's (fee), 3 stories (no elevator), interior corridors.

Rated: 3 Paws — 33 rooms and 14 suites.

Hampton Falls Inn, strategically located along New Hampshire's seacoast, offers comfortable and affordable accommodations. Guest rooms are equipped with queen-sized or double queen-sized beds, cable TV, refrigerators, and private balconies. Enjoy a day of recreation and then unwind in the large indoor heated swimming pool and hot tub. Other guest amenities include the in-house coffee shop offering both breakfast and lunch. The Inn is located minutes away from year-round recreation—whether it be the sea, mountains, top entertainment, fine dining, ski slopes, tennis, or golf.

Notchland Inn

Route 302
Harts Location, NH 03812
603-374-6131

Type of Lodging: Historic Country Inn

Room Rates: $114–$289, some suites: $200–$289, some whirlpool units: $230–$289.

Pet Charges and Deposits: None.

Pet Policy: All pets welcome, pet on premises.

Amenities: Smoke-free premises, no TVs, irons, hair dryers, some CD players, smoke-free premises, whirlpool, river swimming, cross-country skiing, ice skating, nature trails, hiking trails, gift shop, restaurant, cocktails, radios, data port/modem telephones, 2 stories, interior corridors.

Rated: 3 Paws — 13 units.

The Notchland Inn is an impressive 1862 granite mansion. Its location is exceptional—in the midst of the White Mountain National Park, close to Crawford Notch and Crawford Notch State Park. It's sixteen miles south of Bretton Woods. With the opening of the Mount Washington Hotel in 1902, Bretton Woods became a well-known resort. Fifty trains arrived *daily*, and private railway cars sat on a siding by the golf course, waiting to take their passengers home. In July, 1944, President Roosevelt selected Bretton Woods as the site of the World Monetary Fund Conference, which established the American dollar as the cornerstone of international finances. Mount Washington Cog Railway is a fascinating part of New Hampshire's history: a coal-fired, steam-powered locomotive follows a 3½-mile track along a steep trestle to the top of Mount Washington.

The Meeting House Inn

35 Flanders Road
Henniker, NH 03242
603-428-3228

Type of Lodging: Historic Country Inn

Room Rates: $69–$119, some suites: $119; AAA discounts.

Pet Charges and Deposits: None.

Pet Policy: All pets welcome. Pet on premises.

Amenities: No TVs, private whirlpool and sauna rental, restaurant, data port/modem telephones, some refrigerators, some coffee makers, smoke-free premises, 2 stories, interior corridors.

Rated: 3 Paws — 6 rooms.

The Meeting House Inn, an 18th century house rebuilt in 1840, has an attached barn that houses a restaurant. It's adjacent to the Pat's Peak ski area. It possesses a great deal of history and charm. Henniker and its twin town of West Henniker, are situated very close to Hopkinton-Everett Lake, a large, hoseshoe-shaped body of water in south central New Hampshire. Henniker lies at the west vertex of a triangle, the other vertices of which are Concord, 20 miles to the northeast, and Manchester, 27 miles to the southeast. The Pat's Peak Ski Area is within a hop, skip, and jump of Henniker.

The Manor on Golden Pond

Shepard Hill Road
Holderness, NH 03245
603-968-3348
www.manorongoldenpond.com

Type of Lodging: Historic Country Inn

Room Rates: $179–$429; AAA and AARP discounts.

Pet Charges and Deposits: None.

Pet Policy: All pets welcome. Pet on premises.

Amenities: Extended cable TV, irons, hair dryers, some CD players, beach, swimming, canoeing, paddle boats, boat dock, fishing (state fishing license required), lighted tennis court, afternoon tea, smoke-free premises, meeting rooms, restaurant, cocktails, radios, data port/modem telephones, some refrigerators, some coffee makers, some VCR's, 1-2 stories, interior/exterior corridors.

Rated: 4 Paws — 25 units.

This lodging is a superb English-style mansion, set on spacious, landscaped grounds overlooking Squam Lake. You'll stay in the mansion's inn rooms or in the carriage house. Not only is the lodging luxury class, but the dining is first rate, elegantly presented, with impeccable service. Squam Lakes Natural Science Center at the junction of State Routes 3 and 113, has nature trails and live animal enclosures. Owls, bears, deer bobcats, otters, and birds of prey are housed in setting resembling their natural habitats. Holderness, just southwest of the Squam Mountains, is very close to the southern entrance to White Mountain National Forest.

Carter Notch Inn

Carter Notch Road, S.R. 16B
Jackson, NH 03846
603-383-9630

Type of Lodging: Bed and Breakfast

Room Rates: $71–$159, some whirlpool units: $129–$179, including full breakfast.

Pet Charges and Deposits: None.

Pet Policy: All pets welcome. Pet on premises.

Amenities: Extended cable TV, some hair dryers, heated pool, whirlpool, two tennis courts (one lighted), nature trails, cross-country skiing (fee), radios, smoke-free premises, 3 stories (no elevator), interior corridors.

Rated: 3 Paws — 7 rooms.

Picture romance personified. Picture Carter Notch Inn, a 19th century cottage-style inn on a mountain road near the village, with a wraparound porch overlooking the Wildcat River Valley. Picture a cozy, romantic room with the one you love most—and maybe your *second* most loved one, your pet—there. Jackson, nestled between several peaks in the White Mountain National Forest, offers visitors numerous year-round recreational opportunities in one of the most picturesque settings in New England. Forests and streams surround the White Mountains, which rise to the north of New Hampshire's central plateau. The Presidential Range—Mounts Washington, Adams, Jefferson, Madison, and Monroe—exceed 5,000 foot elevations, while notches—passes through the mountains—such as Crawford, Dixville, Franconia, Kinsman, and Pinkham—afford you some of the most dramatic scenery in the state.

Dana Place Inn

Route 16, Pinkham Notch
Jackson, NH 03846
800-537-9276 • 603-383-6822
e-mail: danaplace@ncia.net

Type of Lodging: Inn

Room Rates: $99–$165, including full breakfast and afternoon tea or après ski refreshment. AAA and AARP discounts.

Pet Charges and Deposits: None.

Pet Policy: Dogs only, sorry, no cats. Manager's prior approval required.

Amenities: Extended cable TV, movies, heated indoor pool, whirlpool, outdoor swimming hole, clay and asphalt tennis courts, restaurant, cocktail lounge, data port/modem telephones, 3 stories, interior/exterior corridors.

Rated: 3 Paws — 35 rooms.

Experience more than 100 years of hospitality at historic Dana Place Inn, situated on 300 acres in Pinkham Notch, nestled at the base of the highest mountain in the northeast, Mount Washington. Surrounded by the 750,000 acre White Mountain National Forest, this rural retreat is dotted with apple orchards and mountain pools on the sparkling Ellis River. The Inn is situated in a charmingly updated Colonial farmhouse. The Inn features fine dining, a spirited pub, heated pool and Jacuzzi, a library with fireplace, and superb hospitality. Enjoy classical dining in one of four dining rooms. Cross-country ski from the doorsteps in winter or choose from four downhill ski mountains within fifteen miles. The Inn is located minutes from the White Mountain attractions that offer year-round recreational fun.

Ellis River House

P.O. Box 656, Route 16
Jackson, NH 03846
800-233-8309 • 603-383-9339

Type of Lodging: Country Inn

Room Rates: $95–$235, including full breakfast.

Pet Charges and Deposits: $15 per day per pet.

Pet Policy: Manager's prior approval required.

Amenities: Cable TV, heated pool, whirlpool, sauna, restaurant, pub, data port/modem telephones, 2 stories, interior corridors.

Rated: 3 Paws — 20 rooms and 4 suites.

The Ellis River House is an enchanting country inn offering romance and rejuvenation to the discriminating traveler. The house is situated on three acres of sparkling riverfront property, where you can fish for trout right from the riverbank. Each beautifully appointed guest room is filled with the spirit of old New England, featuring period antiques, private bath, fireplace, and scenic balconies. Awake to a hearty breakfast, and be sure to come back in the evening to enjoy River House's renowned candelight dinners. Cross-country ski right out your door on the beautifully groomed Ellis River Trail running across the Inn's grounds, or choose a downhill run suited for the first-time skier or the world-class expert. Whether you're on family vacation of a romantic weekend getaway, the White Mountains offer everything you could possible ask for.

Village House

P.O. Box 359, Route 16A
Jackson, NH 03846
800-972-8343 • 603-383-6666

Type of Lodging: Country Inn

Room Rates: $80–$160, including seasonal breakfast and afternoon beverages. Special rates for returning guests.

Pet Charges and Deposits: $10 per day per pet.

Pet Policy: All pets welcome.

Amenities: Heated pool, whirlpool, Jacuzzi, tennis court, 3 stories, interior corridors.

Rated: 3 Paws — 14 rooms.

Just behind the famous Jackson Covered Bridge, you'll find the Village House, where guests are welcomed with a tradition that is more than 100 years old. This affordable country inn offers the luxuries of a resort and the atmosphere of a small bed and breakfast. Put your feet up, read a book on the porch or gazebo, or stroll around the six lovely acres of rolling riverfront landscape. Other amenities include a swimming pool, tennis court, and a year-round Jacuzzi, which is delightful after a day of hiking or skiing. Breakfast is served on the wraparound porch on warm mornings. Jackson is a picturesque village where you can spend your time relaxing in peace and serenity or explore the White Mountains' adventure and activity. Enjoy ice skating or sleigh rides under the stars and fine dining and cozy pubs with entertainment and hot chocolate by the fireplace.

Whitneys' Inn–Jackson

Route 16B, P.O. Box 822
Jackson, NH 03846
603-383-8916
www.whitneysinn.com

Type of Lodging: Country Inn

Room Rates: $69–$169, some suites: $150–$215.

Pet Charges and Deposits: $25 per day per pet.

Pet Policy: Designated rooms only.

Amenities: Extended cable TV, heated pool, beach, swimming in pond, paddle boats, fishing, tennis court, ice staking, nature trails, playground, cross-country skiing (fee) coin laundry, conference facilities, restaurant, cocktails, coffee makers, data port/modem telephones, some refrigerators, some microwaves, 2 stories, interior/exterior corridors.

Rated: 2 Paws – 30 rooms.

Whitney's Inn lies at the foot of Black Mountain, on wonderfully spacious, meticulously landscaped grounds. Rooms run from cozy to spacious, and you'll find one that's just right for you in the main inn, the cottages, or the annex. Nestlenook Farm offers year-round recreational activities on a picturesque 65-acre Victorian estate. In summer, you can go fly fishing, or you can feed the reindeer. In winter, the place truly comes alive, with snowshoeing, ice skating, and horse-drawn sleighrides. You'll find great alpine and cross-country skiing at Balck Mountain, Jackson Ski Touring Foundation, and Wildcat Mountain.

Best Western Sovereign Hotel

401 Winchester Street
Keene, NH 03431
603-357-3038

Type of Lodging: Hotel

Room Rates: $94–$169; AAA and AARP discounts.

Pet Charges and Deposits: None.

Pet Policy: All pets welcome.

Amenities: Extended cable TV, movies (fee), irons, hair dryers, heated pool, valet laundry, conference facilities, restaurant, radios, coffee makers, data port/modem telephones, some refrigerators, some microwaves, 2 stories, interior corridors.

Rated: 3 Paws – 131 rooms.

Clean, modern, comfortable, attractive, and well-furnished. These adjectives amply describe the inviting Best Western Sovereign Hotel in Keene, one of New Hampshire's larger cities. In 1772, the well-known Wyman Tavern was the scene of the first meeting of the trustees of newly-formed Dartmouth College. Five years later, Captain Isaac Wyman led 29 Minutemen from the tavern to Lexington at the onset of the Revolutionary War. Four covered bridges can be found between Keene and nearby Winchester. Horatio Colony Wildlife Preserve is a 450-acre refuge for many species of birds, animals, and plants. The Horatio Colony House Museum (1806) has unusual heirlooms, ornamental tin ceilings, and decorative tiles and is well worth seeing.

Days Inn

175 Key Road
Keene, NH 03431
603-352-7616

Type of Lodging: Motel

Room Rates: $74–$149; AAA and AARP discounts.

Pet Charges and Deposits: None.

Pet Policy: Small pets only, in designated rooms only.

Amenities: Extended cable TV, movies (fee), irons, hair dryers, heated pool, whirlpool, exercise room, valet laundry, coffee makers, data port/modem telephones, some refrigerators, some microwaves, 2 stories, interior corridors.

Rated: 3 Paws — 80 rooms.

Located in the Monadnock region of New Hampshire known for its rich history and "Currier & Ives" appeal, the Days Inn—Keene offers guests both service and comfort at affordable rates. Sit back and relax in one of the 80 spacious guest rooms, all designed with rich, traditional furnishings, or choose of the two exclusive executive suites with private Jacuzzi. Guests will find many memorable adventures awaiting them, including a scenic drive through quaint New England villages, a visit to the romantic covered bridges, or an exhilarating hike up Mount Monadnock. Nearby Wheelock Park provides an ideal environment for romping or relaxing with your pet.

Days Inn

135 State Route 120
Lebanon, NH 03766
603-448-5070

Type of Lodging: Motel

Room Rates: $90–$130; AAA and AARP discounts.

Pet Charges and Deposits: None.

Pet Policy: Designated units only.

Amenities: Extended cable TV, movies (fee), winter plug-ins, irons, hair dryers, valet laundry, radios, data port/modem telephones, some refrigerators, some microwaves, 2 stories, interior/exterior corridors.

Rated: 2 Paws — 49 rooms.

Days Inn—Lebanon is modern and attractive, with clean, spacious rooms and numerous welcome amenities. Lebanon, on the west side of New Hampshire, sits practically astride the Connecticut River, just east of the Vermont border. Although a relatively large city for New Hampshire, it's adjacent to the Moose Mountains, Mescoma and Crystal Lakes, and it's within an houe of Mount Sunapee and Sunapee Lake (southeast), Lyme Center Ski Area (northeast), and numerous mountain peaks.

Parker's Motel

Route 3, Box 100
Lincoln, NH 03251
603-745-8341

Type of Lodging: Motel

Room Rates: $39–$89; AAA and AARP discounts.

Pet Charges and Deposits: $25 deposit, $5 per day per pet.

Pet Policy: All pets welcome.

Amenities: Winter plug-ins, extended cable TV, heated pool, whirlpool, sauna, game room, data port/modem telephones, some refrigerators, some microwaves, 1-2 stories, exterior corridors.

Rated: 2 Paws — 27 units.

Parker's Motel is a most reasonably priced small motel with quite attractive grounds, and some units with balcony. You'll find specials in the off-season and midweek. Lincoln is at the western end of the Kancamagus Highway (State Route 112), one of New Hampshire's most scenic drives, which starts just southwest of Conway and winds its way through the White Mountain National Forest. Clark's Trading Post features erlin's Mystical Mansion, Tuttle's Rustic House, water bumper boats, rides on the White Mountain Central Railroad, performing black bears and the 1884 Pemigewasset Hook & Ladder Fire Station. At Loon Mountain Resort, a four-passenger gondola travels 7,000 feet from base to summit, affording you a grand view of mountain, valley, and forest scenery. The star attractions at Whale's Tale Water Park include a wave pool with ocean size breakers, waterslides, flumes, tube slides, and more.

Ammonoosuc Inn

641 Bishop Road
Lisbon, NH 03585
603-838-6118

Type of Lodging: Historic Country Inn

Room Rates: $49–$135; AAA and AARP discounts.

Pet Charges and Deposits: None.

Pet Policy: Small pets only, in designated units only.

Amenities: No TVs, fishing, cross-country skiing, nature trails, golf–9 holes (fee), conference facilities, fax, restaurant, cocktails, 3 stories (no elevator).

Rated: 3 Paws — 9 rooms.

Ammonoosuc Inn is an wonderful 1880's country inn, situated in the midst of woodland, overlooking the Ammonoosuc River. Rooms range from compact and cozy to spacious and quite attractive. A public golf course surrounds the inn, meaning lots of room for you and your pet to roam. Lisbon lies halfway between White Mountain National Forest and the Connecticut River frontier with Vermont, in a valley surrounding by low-lying mountains. This means great cross-country skiing in winter—Bronson Hill and Cooley Hill afre nearby—and great summer hiking for you and your pet.

East Gate Motor Inn

335 Cottage Street
Littleton, NH 03561
603-444-3971
www.eastgatemotorinn.com

Type of Lodging: Motor Inn

Room Rates: $49–$89.

Pet Charges and Deposits: None.

Pet Policy: In designated units only.

Amenities: Winter plug-ins, extended cable TV, movies, heated pool, wading pool, snowmobiling, playground, conference facilities, restaurant, radios, data port/modem telephones, 1 story, interior/exterior corridors.

Rated: 2 Paws — 55 rooms.

The East Gate Motor Inn boasts well-kept facilities in a quiet location close to Littleton Hospital. Rooms are bright, cheery, and inviting. Littleton is a fair-sized town 16 miles northwest of the northwestern entry to White Mountain National Forest. Prior to the Civil War, Littleton was a station on a branch of the Underground Railroad that led northward to Vermont and Canada. One of New England's largest water harnessing projects, Moore Station, eight miles west of Littleton, now impounds the Moore Reservoir. Littleton Grist Mill in the center of town was built along the Amonoosuc River in 1798 and has been restored to its original appearance. The mill produces stone ground flours, just as it did in the 18th century,

Lovejoy Farm Bed & Breakfast

268 Lovejoy Road
Loudon, NH 03301
603-783-4007

Type of Lodging: Bed and Breakfast

Room Rates: $74–$99, including full breakfast.

Pet Charges and Deposits: None.

Pet Policy: By reservation only.

Amenities: Smoke-free premises; no TVs, cross-country skiing, hiking trails, radios, data port/modem telephones, 2 stories, interior corridors.

Rated: 3 Paws — 7 rooms.

The Lovejoy Farm Bed & Breakfast is a rare, wonderful find. It's located in a 1790 Georgian Colonial and carriage house, in a country setting. Your hosts insure that your every need is met and exceeded. Tiny Loudon is almost an eastern suburb of Concord, located on the Soucock River in southern New Hampshire. It's just "down the road" from New Hampshire International Speedway, located within an hour or so of New Hampshire's Lakes Region. Shaker Village is 12 miles away. First established in 1792, it is a living history museum, with 25 of the original buildings in the colony having been restored. Artisans recreate Shaker crafts, such as oval box making and weaving.

Center of New Hampshire–Holiday Inn

700 Elm Street
Manchester, NH 03101
603-625-1000

Type of Lodging: Hotel

Room Rates: $94–$174; AAA and AARP discounts.

Pet Charges and Deposits: None.

Pet Policy: All pets welcome.

Amenities: Extended cable TV, movies (fee), voice mail, irons, hair dryers, heated pool, whirlpool, sauna, gift shop, valet laundry, conference facilities, fax, airport transportation, restaurant, cocktails, health club, radios, coffee makers, data port/modem telephones, some refrigerators (fee), some microwaves (fee), 12 stories, interior corridors.

Rated: 3 Paws — 250 rooms.

The Holiday Inn in New Hampshire's largest city is a large, impressive high-rise, with a big-city number of rooms, amenities galore, and all the comforts, luxury, and convenience of a first class hotel. Although Manchester in dedicated to business rather than tourism, there are some standout attractions here. Chief among them is the Currier Gallery of Art, housed in a 1929 Beaux-Arts building, which displays European and American painting, sculpture, and decorative arts from the 13th century to the present. In addition to New Hampshire artists and craftsmen, Winslow Homer, Henri Matisse, Claude Monet, Georgia O'Keeffe, Pablo Picasso, and Andrew Wyeth are well represented in this wonderful gallery. The Zimmerman House, reached by van from the Currier Gallery, is a small-but-elegant Usonian house designed by Frank Lloyd Wright.

Comfort Inn–Manchester

298 Queen City Avenue
Manchester, NH 03102

Type of Lodging: Motel

Room Rates: $75–$120, including Continental breakfast. AAA and AARP discounts.

Pet Charges and Deposits: $100 refundable deposit.

Pet Policy: All pets welcome.

Amenities: Extended cable TV, movies, heated pool, whirlpool, sauna, exercise room, valet and coin laundry, airport shuttle service, free morning newspaper, conference facilities, fax/data port/modem telephones, some refrigerators, some microwaves, 5 stories, interior corridors.

Rated: 3 Paws — 100 rooms and 4 suites.

Conveniently located near Interstate 293 and offering airport shuttle service, Comfort Inn is situated in the heart of Manchester. Whether the nature of your visit is business, pleasure, or just passing through, you'll find a cheerful staff and comfortable accommodations. Guest rooms offer queen-size or king-sized rooms, with refrigerators and microwaves available upon request. A continental breakfast is served each morning along with the current edition of USA Today. When in Manchester, visit the Currier Gallery of Art, Anheuser-Busch Brewery, home of the world-famous Clydesdale horses, and Canterbury Shaker Village. You'll also enjoy the Palace Theater's drama, orchestras, Broadway musicals, and comedy shows.

Econo Lodge

75 W. Hancock Street
Manchester, NH 03102
603-624-0111

Type of Lodging: Motel

Room Rates: $59–$129; AAA and AARP discounts.

Pet Charges and Deposits: $100 deposit, $10 per pet, per day.

Pet Policy: All pets welcome.

Amenities: Extended cable TV, coin laundry, data port/modem telephones, some refrigerators, some microwaves, some VCR's, 5 stories, interior corridors.

Rated: 2 Paws — 113 rooms.

An Econo Lodge in a converted mill building? That's exactly what you'll find in this 5-story behemoth (for an Econo Lodge), overlooking the Merrimack River in New Hampshire's largest metropolis. The giant brick Amoskeag Mills stretch on the riverbank along Commercial Street for more than a mile. The large Anheuser-Busch Brewery, in nearby Merrimack, gives you (but, alas, not your pet) a free tour. The Lawrence L. Lee Scouting Museum features a collection of Boy Scout memorabilia, while the See Science Center explores electricity, geology, aviation, and reptiles. The Manchester Historic Association exhibits Native American artifacts, 19th century firefighting apparatus, and images and articles recording Manchester's social and industrial history.

Peep-Willow Farm

51 Bixby Street
Marlborough, NH 03455
603-876-3807
e-mail: naderer@top.monad.net

Type of Lodging: Farm lodging

Room Rates: $50–$75, including Continental breakfast.

Pet Charges and Deposits: $5 per day per pet, plus 1 night's rate deposit, refundable.

Pet Policy: All pets welcome.

Amenities: 1-2 stories, interior corridors.

Rated: 3 Paws — 3 rooms.

Peep-Willow Farm is an 18-acre working horse farm, where thoroughbreds are born, raised, and trained to be top competition horses. Guests are welcome to help with chores, wander around, and talk to, feed, or pet the livestock. Imagine sitting on the terrace and enjoying a view all the way to the Connecticut River Valley, while newborn foals and their moms frolic before you. The ambience at the farm is casual, comfortable, and homey. The 25-year-old Colonial farmhouse is charming, evoking relaxation and enjoyment of the great outdoors. Located at the foot of Mount Monadnock, known for great climbing and hiking adventures, this area offers a myriad of activities nearby. Enjoy riding, canoeing, swimming, tennis and nature walks in the state parks or golf at any of several renowned courses. A variety of exceptionally fine dining and cultural offerings abound.

Radisson Hotel & Conference Center

Four Executive Park Drive
Merrimack, NH 03054
603-424-8000

Type of Lodging: Motor Inn

Room Rates: $74–$194; AAA and AARP discounts.

Pet Charges and Deposits: $10 per day per pet.

Pet Policy: All pets welcome.

Amenities: Extended cable TV, movies, irons, hair dryers, heated pool, whirlpool, steam room, valet laundry, conference facilities, airport transporation, restaurant, cocktails, radios, coffee makers, data port/modem telephones, some refrigerators (fee), some microwaves (fee), 4 stories, interior corridors.

Rated: 3 Paws — 200 rooms.

This Radisson is typical of the breed—fine value, upscale, luxurious accommodations, inviting public areas. Although this is a large motor hotel, you get the feel of an inn, once you're here. The big draw in this Manchester exurb is the Anheuser-Busch Brewery, where you get tours, tasting, and a chance to visit the Clydesdale stables (those big horses you see on the TV commercials). Merrimack sits astride the Merrimack River, almost exactly halfway between Manchester and Nashua, New Hampshire's largest cities. It's also within striking distance of New Hampshire's staggering 30 miles of Atlantic seacoast.

Residence Inn By Marriott

246 Daniel Webster Highway
Merrimack, NH 03054
603-424-8100

Type of Lodging: Apartment Hotel

Room Rates: $115–$175; AAA and AARP discounts.

Pet Charges and Deposits: $50 deposit, $5 per day per pet.

Pet Policy: All pets welcome.

Amenities: Winter plug-ins, extended cable TV, movies (fee), video games, voice mail, irons, hair dryers, whirlpool, exercise room, sports court, valet laundry, conference facilities, administrative services, outdoor pool, radios, coffee makers, data port/modem telephones, refrigerators, microwaves, 2-3 stories, interior/exterior corridors.

Rated: 3 Paws — 129 apartment units.

Residence Inn by Marriott is a long-term apartment-hotel, where you'll find everything that could possibly make your stay smooth, restful, and homelike. If you're in southern New Hampshire, you could hardly be more centrally located. Merrimack is convenient to skiing, a number of good-sized lakes, rivers, the Atlantic seacoast and the Massachusetts border. You're not that far from Monadnock Mountain, one of the most climbed and photographed places in the Northeastern United States. It's a great place to spend a few days.

Ram in the Thicket

24 Maple Street
Milford, NH 03055
603-654-6440

Type of Lodging: Bed & Breakfast

Room Rates: $75–$100, including Continental breakfast.

Pet Charges and Deposits: $10 per day per pet.

Pet Policy: Manager's prior approval required.

Amenities: Swimming pool, hot tub, restaurant, cocktail lounges, radios, 3 stories (no elevator), interior corridors.

Rated: 3 Paws — 9 rooms and 2 suites.

Located in the rolling eastern foothills of the Monadnock Mountain region, Ram in the Thicket is the fruition of a longtime yearning and dream of the owners. The dream began with restoring and completely renovating this grand old Victorian mansion, which now consists of four dining rooms featuring a great crystal chandelier, a hand-carved fireplace, and other subdued Victorian touches. Weather permitting, guests are invited to enjoy the large screened summer garden dining porch. Almost every menu item is made from scratch and cooked to order, using fresh quality seasonal ingredients. Ram in the Thicket is minutes away from the finest summer theater and year-round outdoor activities. Enjoy excellent summer hiking trails and swimming beaches in southern New Hampshire. The woods turn into beautiful color foliage trails in autumn and ski areas in winter.

Matterhorn Motor Inn

340 Route 25
Moultonborough, NH 03254
603-253-4314

Type of Lodging: Motel

Room Rates: $89–$139; AAA discounts.

Pet Charges and Deposits: None.

Pet Policy: Manager's prior approval required, by reservation only.

Amenities: Winter plug-ins, extended cable TV, movies, heated pool, snowmobiling, free local telephone calls, data port/modem telephones, 2 stories, exterior corridors.

Rated: 2 Paws — 28 rooms.

Matterhorn Motor Inn is a very manageable small motel that provides comfortable, restful rooms and an atmosphere commensurate with a mountain town. Moultonborough is perched at the very top of Lake Winnipesaukee, about 25 miles south of the White Mountain National Forest, and in the heart of the Lakes Region. Need we say more? Actually, yes. It's a short drive to White Lake State Park, Squam Lake, numerous ski areas, and the Maine Border. The area is a magnificent holiday venue.

Olde Orchard Inn

108 Lee Road
Moultonborough, NH 03254
603-476-5004

Type of Lodging: Historic Bed and Breakfast

Room Rates: $79–$179

Pet Charges and Deposits: None.

Pet Policy: All pets welcome. Pet on premises.

Amenities: Smoke-free premises, whirlpool, sauna, fishing, cross-country skiing, ice skating, hiking trails, restaurant adjacent, smoke-free premises, data port/modem telephones, some radios, some coffee makers, 2 stories, interior corridors.

Rated: 3 Paws — 9 rooms.

Housed in an early 1800's restored farmhouse, surrounded by fields and a large apple orchard, the Olde Orchard Inn is a singularly inviting place, decorated with antiques, period furniture, and Oriental carpets. Take any highway into or out of Moultonborough and you can be sure it will be among the most scenic in the northeastern United States. State Routes 16 (North-South, about 15 miles to the east), and the legendary Kancamagus Highway, up the 16 to State Route 112, are especially gorgeous, even more so when the leaves start to change color in the fall.

Best Western Sunapee Lake Lodge

1403 Route 103
Mt. Sunapee, NH 03255
800-606-5253 • 603-763-2010

Type of Lodging: Motel

Room Rates: $99–$169, including Continental breakfast; AAA and AARP discounts.

Pet Charges and Deposits: $8 per day per pet.

Pet Policy: Small pets only.

Amenities: Extended cable TV, hair dryers, heated pool, tanning booth (fee), exercise room, coin laundry, conference facilities, free local telephone calls, restaurant adjacent, radios, data port/modem telephones, some refrigerators, some microwaves, some VCR's, 3 stories, interior corridors.

Rated: 3 Paws — 55 rooms and 2 suites.

Best Western Sunapee Lodge is centrally located at Mounty Sunapee State Park in Newbury. Guests may choose suites with microwaves, wet bars, and refrigerators; some have whirlpool baths. The Lodge offers a restaurant and lounge, an indoor pool, mini-gym, and lobby with a fireplace. The Lodge is located minutes from Newport, Claremont, and Interstate 89. Guests will appreciate the Lodge's location, just a four-minute walk to the state park beach on Lake Sunapee, or, in the winter, ride the free shuttle to Mount Sunapee Ski Area. Four seasons of natural beauty and recreation await you in this special region.

Nashua Marriott

2200 Southwood Drive
Nashua, NH 03063
603-880-9100

Type of Lodging: Motor Inn
Room Rates: $99–$169; AAA discounts.
Pet Charges and Deposits: None.
Pet Policy: All pets welcome.
Amenities: Extended cable TV, movies (fee), voice mail, irons, hair dryers, heated pool, whirlpool, playground, exercise room, basketball, volleyball, gift shop, valet laundry, conference facilities, administrative services, PC, fax, restaurant, cocktails, radios, coffee makers, data port/modem telephones, some VCR's (fee), some refrigerators, 4 stories, interior corridors.
Rated: 3 Paws — 245 rooms.

Leave it to the Marriott chain to locate in a pleasant, wooded location that's convenient to area businesses in one of New Hampshire's largest cities. Guest rooms are Marriott-modern and Marriott-comfortable, which, as usual, says a lot. Nashua, New Hampshire's second city, is also its southernmost, on the border of Massachusetts. Everything's amazingly close— Manchester's 15 minutes away, Lowell, Massachusetts about the same. Silver Lake State Park is close by, as are some pretty substantial (by New Hampshire standards) mountains. That means skiing, the nearby lakes mean swimming, and the enter conurbation means "close enough to the *country* to go anywhere.

Red Roof Inn

77 Spitbrook Road
Nashua, NH 03060
603-888-1893

Type of Lodging: Motel
Room Rates: $54–$84; AAA discounts.
Pet Charges and Deposits: None.
Pet Policy: All pets welcome.
Amenities: Extended cable TV, movies (fee), video games, voice mail, coin laundry, radios, data port/modem telephones, some refrigerators (fee), some microwaves (fee), 3 stories, exterior corridors.
Rated: 2 Paws — 115 rooms.

As always, Red Roof Inn provides great value for a relatively small amount of money. Rooms are modern, spacious, and attractive and the location, just east of the city center, is perfect. Nashua sits astride the west bank of the Merrimack River. Largely industrial Nashua is about an hour east of Jaffrey, a town near Monadnock. It's a quiet village which surrounds the 1775 white clapboard Meeting House, site of the Amos Fortune Forum, an annual lecture series established in 1958 to honor Amos Fortune, a slave who was granted freedom and later became a prominent Jaffrey citizen. Silver Ranch and Silver Ranch Airpark in Jaffrey offer scenic airplane rides and hose drawn carriage and sleigh rides.

Lakeview Motor Lodge

1349 Route 103
Newbury, NH 03255
603-763-2701

Type of Lodging: Motel
Room Rates: $59–$109; including Continental breakfast. AAA and AARP discounts.
Pet Charges and Deposits: None.
Pet Policy: All pets welcome.
Amenities: Extended cable TV, canoeing (fee), bicycles (fee), free local telephone calls, VCR's, radios, coffee makers, refrigerators, data port/modem telephones, some microwaves, 1-2 stories, exterior corridors.
Rated: 2 Paws — 12 rooms.

Lakeview Motor Lodge is a perfectly sized small motel near Mount Sunapee. The area is gorgeous, the rooms cozy, bright and comforting, the ambience inviting, in short, all you need to enjoy a fine sojourn in New Hampshire's mountain wonderland. The Fells at John Hay National Wildlife Refuge was the summer home of John M. Hay, a diplomat and writer who was President Lincoln's private secretary. He was also ambassador to Great Britain and secretary of state under presidents William McKinley and Theodore Roosevelt. The grounds, which overlook Lake Sunapee, contain a Japanese water lily pool and early 20th century gardens planted with roses, rhododendron, azaleas, dogwoods, and wildlflowers. There are five miles of hiking trails for you and your pet.

The Farm By The River B&B

2555 Westside Road
North Conway, NH 03860
603-356-2694
www.farmbytheriver.com

Type of Lodging: Bed and Breakfast
Room Rates: $84–$165, some suites: $165–$225,
some whirlpool units: $150–$225; AAA discounts.
Pet Charges and Deposits: None.
Pet Policy: All pets welcome. Pet on premises.
Amenities: No TVs, swimming, fishing (state fishing license required), cross-country skiing, winter sleigh rides in horse drawn sled, smoke-free premises, snow shoeing, hiking trails, horseback riding, 65 acres of walking trails, fall foliage wagon ride, complimentary evening beverages, free local telephone calls, 2 stories, interior corridors.
Rated: 3 Paws — 9 units.

Nestled on a pasture land and maple sugar orchards abutting a the Saco River, this 70-acre property was originally a land grant from King George III. Today, The Farm By the River B&B is an extraordinary lodging, housed in an 18th century home. The activities are unique, and you're able to experience New England the way you always dreamed it would be. Artist Benjamin Champney was so entranced with the view of Mount Washington from North Conway's Main Street that he set up his easel in the middle of the road in August, 1850, and painted what he saw. Lithographs of that picture were circulated nationwide. North Conway is at the very center of the Mount Washington Valley. The community is a year-round holiday ground—sports and sightseeing, theater and nightlife, shopping and fine dining—make it a very successful one.

Isaac E. Merrill House Inn

720 Kearsarge Road
North Conway, NH 03847
800-328-9041 • 603-356-9041
www.nhinns.com

Type of Lodging: Inn

Room Rates: $79–$179, including full breakfast, cheese trays, and afternoon tea. AAA and AARP discounts.

Pet Charges and Deposits: None.

Pet Policy: Manager's prior approval required.

Amenities: Data port/modem telephones, children under 18 stay free in parents' room, some refrigerators, some microwaves, 3 stories, interior corridors.

Rated: 3 Paws — 17 rooms and 3 suites.

Located in picturesque North Conway, dotted with a variety of classic New England restaurants and shops to explore, this 226-year-old historic inn extends White Mountains hospitality. The Isaac Merrill House has room to stretch out, with plenty of blossoming garden paths to stroll. Rooms are uniquely decorated with queen-sized and king-sized beds, fluffy comforters, and private baths. The quiet country setting offers a full breakfast with a menu ranging from Texas-style French toast topped with strawberries to Eggs Benedict. Nearby Mount Washington Valley provides year-round recreation for the whole family—including moose tours.

North Conway Mountain Inn

2114 White Mountain Highway
North Conway, NH 03860
603-356-2803

Type of Lodging: Motel

Room Rates: $64–$174; AAA and AARP discounts.

Pet Charges and Deposits: $50 deposit.

Pet Policy: All pets welcome.

Amenities: Extended cable TV, some hair dryers, smoke-free premises, data port/modem telephones, some VCR's, 2 stories, exterior corridors.

Rated: 3 Paws — 34 rooms.

North Conway Mountain Inn is an exceptionally well-furnished lodging, featuring very attractive rooms with private porches. The Conway Scenic Railroad offers narrated, round-trip train rides, pulled along by restored steam or early diesel locomotives. The 5½ hour trip to Crawford Notch is especially enjoyable, and dining service is available. Echo Lake State Park covers 396 acres. A scenic road near the top of Cathedral Ledge offers a superb view of the White Mountains and the Saco River Valley. The park offers swimming, picnicking, hiking, and climbing opportunities. South of the park, White Horse Ledge provides a spectacular backdrop.

Stonehurst Manor

Route 16
North Conway, NH 03860-1937
800-525-9100 • 603-356-3113
www.stonehurstmanor.com

Type of Lodging: Manor house

Room Rates: $99–$189, including Continental breakfast and dinner.

Pet Charges and Deposits: $10 per day per pet plus $50 refundable deposit.

Pet Policy: All pets welcome.

Amenities: Cable TV, movies, heated pool, Jacuzzi, tennis courts, restaurant, 3 stories, interior corridors.

Rated: 4 Paws — 24 suites.

Set on a secluded hillside among thirty-three acres of tall pines, Stonehurst Manor invites you to enjoy the luxury of this elegant, turn-of-the-20th-century mansion. English country manor in style, the architectural highlights feature hand-carved oak woodwork, leaded glass windows, a multitude of stone fireplaces, and a screened tile porch. Guest rooms, many with fireplaces, are beautifully and comfortably decorated. Natural and man-made attractions and activities are abundant in the Mount Washington Valley. In winter, there is cross-country skiing at the doorstep on 40 miles of groomed trails. Six major alpine ski areas are minutes away. You'll also find horse-drawn sleigh rides, ice skating, ice climbing, and après ski pubs at locations throughout the valley.

The Glen

77 The Glen Road
Pittsburg, NH 03592
603-538-6500

Type of Lodging: Lodge

Room Rates: $84–$199.

Pet Charges and Deposits: None.

Pet Policy: All pets welcome.

Amenities: No TV's, swimming, boat dock, fishing, hiking trails, boats (fee), restaurant, radios, data port/modem telephones, some coffee makers, some refrigerators, 1-2-story cottages and lodge units.

Rated: 3 Paws — 16 units, including cottages and lodge units.

The Glen, made up of 1-to-4 bedroom cottages and lodge units, is a sportsman's paradise. Surroundings are rustic and quiet. The lodge houses a cozy sitting room with fireplace, and you can fish or go bird-watching on First Connecticut Lake. Pittsburg is the northeasternmost community of any size in New Hampshire. You can walk due west for about four miles and cross the Canadian border, or, if you prefer, you can drive 11 miles *south* or 26 miles north, to enter our northern neighbor. Pittsburg is convenient to Lake Francis State Park, Lake Francis, Second Lake, and tiny Third Lake, which abuts the frontier. The forested area around Pittsburg contains Shatney Mountain, Deer Mountain, and the Connecticut Lakes State Forest. But don't expect to find many people around here.

Residence Inn By Marriott

One International Drive
Portsmouth, NH 03801
603-436-8880

Type of Lodging: Suite Motel

Room Rates: $159–$249; AAA and AARP discounts.

Pet Charges and Deposits: $250.00 fee.

Pet Policy: All pets welcome.

Amenities: Extended cable TV, movies, dual phone lines, voice mail, irons, hair dryers, heated pool, whirlpool, exercise room, sports court, complimentary evening beverages—Monday-Thursday, valet and coin laundry, conference facilities, radios, coffee makers, data port/modem telephones, refrigerators, microwaves, 3 stories, interior corridors.

Rated: 3 Paws — 90 units.

Residence Inn by Marriott features 90 units with kitchen, of which 18 are two-bedroom suites. Clean, comfortable, and modern, the only downside of this property is its rather pet-*un*friendly $250 fee. If you stay for a lengthy period, you can amortize this stiff fee, dividing it by the number of nights you're there. Portsmouth, called Strawberry Banke when it was first settled in 1623, justifiably claims to be the birthplace of New Hampshire, and has much history to prove it. Strawberry Banke Museum, set in a ten ace park, is a living history museum with 35 buildings. Prescott Park lies to the east, along the water; its formal gardens have fountains and over 500 varieties of annuals. Several of Portsmouth's grand historic houses, including the Governor John Langdon House (1784), the John Paul Jones House (1758), and the Wentworth Gardner House (1760) have been beautifully preserved.

Woodbound Inn

62 Woodbound Road
Rindge, NH 03461
800-688-7770 • 603-532-8341

Type of Lodging: Inn

Room Rates: $89–$149, including full breakfast. AAA and AARP discounts.

Pet Charges and Deposits: None.

Pet Policy: All pets welcome.

Amenities: Extended cable TV, movies, golf, tennis, gift shop, restaurant, cocktail lounge, radios, modem telephones, 1-3 stories, interior/exterior corridors.

Rated: 4 Paws - 44 rooms and cabins.

Located on the shores of Lake Contoocook, with breathtaking views of Mount Monadnock, the Woodbound Inn offers accommodations to meet every need. Choose from the charm of the historic Main Inn, contemporary rooms in the Edgewood Building, or charming lakefront cottages. The cabin are one- and two-bedroom, with either a king-sized bed or two twins, with day beds in the living rooms. Each cabin is equipped with a fireplace and is situated just a few feet from the Inn's private beach. Each day begins with a hearty breakfast. The property consists of 165 wooded acres, which includes a golf course, clay tennis courts, private beach for swimming or fishing, and a netwotk of marked hiking and cross-country ski trails. The entire Monadnock region is filled with year-round activities, including summer concerts on the Common, regional festivals, a marionette theater, and sporting events.

Anchorage Inn

80 Main Street
Rochester, NH 03839
603-332-3350

Type of Lodging: Motel
Room Rates: $44–$99, including Continental breakfast; AAA and AARP discounts.
Pet Charges and Deposits: $5 per day per pet.
Pet Policy: All pets welcome.
Amenities: Extended cable TV, movies, outdoor pool, horseshoes, picnic area with grills, data port/modem telephones, some refrigerators, some microwaves, 1 story, exterior corridors.
Rated: 2 Paws — 31 rooms.

Anchorage Inn is an older property, with small units and baths. It is well-maintained and comfortable. Rochester, three miles from the Maine border, is just up the Spalding Turnpike from Portsmouth—but far enough up the Turnpike to be convenient to the entire Lakes Region (Lake Winnipesaukee is only half an hour's drive away). It's equally convenient to Ogunquit, Maine, and the standout Ogunquit Museum of American Art. The Governor's Inn Dining Room in Rochester provides a pleasant dining experience in a traditional New England country inn—regional cuisine with the emphasis on seafood. Rochester is a fine central anchor for your New Hampshire holiday.

Red Roof Inn

15 Red Roof Lane
Salem, NH 03079
603-898-6422

Type of Lodging: Motel
Room Rates: $54–$99
Pet Charges and Deposits: None.
Pet Policy: Small pets only.
Amenities: Extended cable TV, movies (fee), video games, voice mail, coin laundry, free local telephone calls, free newspaper, data port/modem telephones, 2 stories, exterior corridors.
Rated: 2 Paws — 108 rooms.

Red Roof Inn is modern, uniform in quality, and an excellent value for the money. It's located just southeast of the center of town, off I-93, exit 2. The Canobie Lake amusement park offers more than 85 rides, games, and activities. There are four roller coasters, an 1890's carousel, a Ferris wheel, a lake cruise on a paddle wheeler, a replica of a Spanish galleon, and two log flume water rides. Salem is in the southeast corner of the state, walking distance to the Massachusetts frontier, and convenient to Manchester, Nashua, Lowell, Mass., and Methuen, Mass, four miles away.

Snowvillage Inn

Stewart Road, P.O. Box 68
Snowville, NH 03832
603-447-2818

Type of Lodging: Country Inn
Room Rates: $99–$259; AAA discounts.
Pet Charges and Deposits: None.
Pet Policy: All pets welcome. Pet on premises.
Amenities: No TVs, sauna, beach, swimming, fishing, cross-country skiing, nature trails, hiking trails, restaurant, smoke-free premises, radios, data port/modem telephones, smoke-free premises, 2 stories, interior/exterior corridors.
Rated: 3 Paws — 18 rooms.

Snowvillage Inn is quiet, secluded, and possessed of wonderful mountain views. You can choose from many styles—turn-of-the-20th century to modern, and several sizes of rooms. Since there's a resident pet on the premises, you may rest assured that this is a pet-friendly establishment. Snowville is in the heart of ski country, at the south end of Conway Lake, four miles from the Maine border. It's less than ten miles to the eastern terminus of the Kancamagus Highway, one of the most scenic and best known in New England. Snowville is a wonderful place to hunker down for a supremely satisfying holiday.

The Hilltop Inn

1348 Main Street
Sugarhill, NH 03585
603-823-5695

Type of Lodging: Bed and Breakfast
Room Rates: $84–$199, including full breakfast.
Pet Charges and Deposits: $10 per day per pet.
Pet Policy: Dogs only, sorry no cats.
Amenities: No TVs, smoke-free premises, cross-country skiing, hiking trails, conference facilities, radios, data port/modem telephones, some refrigerators, 2 stories, interior corridors.
Rated: 3 Paws — 6 rooms.

Hilltop Inn is the perfect New England venue—a turn-of-the-20th-century home in the center of a picture postcard village. Small and very manageable, with only six units, if you simply *have* to get your TV "fix," you can go to the common room, where there is one (1) cable TV. Guest rooms are beautifully furnished with unusual antiques and feature immaculate full private baths with lots of fluffy towels and amenities. Breakfast specialties include con-smoked bacon, ham, and salmon soufflés, farm fresh eggs, and homemade jams, breads, and muffins. Enjoy year-round recreation at White Mountain National Forest or on the many pet-friendly hiking trails right on the property. Stroll along quiet country lanes or relax on the porches and enjoy nature's show. Golden maremmas Beemer and Bogie are gracious four-legged hosts.

Dexter's Inn

258 Stagecoach Road
Sunapee, NH 03782
603-763-5571

Type of Lodging: Bed and Breakfast

Room Rates: $99–$189, including full breakfast.

Pet Charges and Deposits: $10 per day per pet.

Pet Policy: All pets welcome.

Amenities: Smoke-free premises, three tennis courts, horseshoes, shuffleboard, volleyball, conference facilities, outdoor pool, data port/modem telephones, some coffee makers, some refrigerators, some microwaves, 2 stories, interior/exterior corridors.

Rated: 3 Paws — 18 rooms.

Dexter's Inn is situated on extensive grounds with a breathtaking panoramic view. It's sandwiched between Lake Sunapee and Mount Sunapee. You can have a room in the main inn or in the converted barn annex. Guests are invited to enjoy tastefully prepared meals complemented by a select wine list. Beautifully groomed lawns, flowering gardens, meadows, and woods surround the Inn. Three top-condition, all-weather tennis courts are available for play or a lesson from the resident pro. Relax in the pool, stroll along country lanes, read on the terrace, or enjoy croquet, horseshoes, or shuffleboard. Dexter's has a significant array of outdoor recreation activities. The area will keep you and your pet entertained for days on end.

Loafer Inn At The 1792 Whitecomb House

27 Main Street
Swanzey, NH 03446
603-357-6624

Type of Lodging: Historic Bed and Breakfast

Room Rates: $59–$89.

Pet Charges and Deposits: $20 per day per pet.

Pet Policy: Small pets only.

Amenities: Smoke-free premises, no TVs, gift shop, radios, coffee makers, 3 stories, interior corridors.

Rated: 3 Paws — 6 rooms.

Loafer Inn is another wonderful find, situated in a converted 18th century house. A meal plan is available if you prefer. Swanzey is a tiny community in the southwestern part of New Hampshire. It's close to Swanzey Lake and undeveloped Pisgah State Park. The largest city in the area, Keene, is a ten minute drive away. "The Old Homestead" a drama adaptation of the Prodigal Son story set in Swanzey during the 1880's, was first presented at Swanzey's Colonial Center in 1886. It is still presented for three nights in late July of each year. Four covered bridges can be found on side roads off State Route 10 between Keene and Winchester. The Center at Keene, a collection of shops in a restored railroad depot, and the Colony Mill Marketplace in a restored woolen mill, are the two major shopping sites in the area.

The Tamworth Inn

15 Cleveland Hill Road
Tamworth, NH 03886
603-323-7721
e-mail: inn@tamoworth.com

Type of Lodging: Historic Country Inn

Room Rates: $169–$299.

Pet Charges and Deposits: $10 per day per pet.

Pet Policy: Small pets only.

Amenities: No TVs, some CD players, outdoor pool, fishing, cross-country skiing, nature trails, hiking trails, meeting rooms, restaurant, data port/modem telephones, some radios, 3 stories (no elevator), interior corridors.

Rated: 4 Paws — 9 rooms, 7 suites.

Surround yourself with the essence of New England hospitality. Each guest room is tastefully decorated with a country flavor and the Inn's public areas offer a warm invitation to relax and enjoy the comforts of an authentic New England village inn. Built in 1833, the Tamworth Inn today retains its charm of yesterday—good food with comfortable lodging. There are picturesque mountains with miles of hiking trails and acres of green lawns. Located within a short drive are the high peaks of the White Mountain National Forest and the beautiful Lake Winnipesaukee waterfront. Excellent cross-country skiing is at the front door and the oldest professional theater in the United States is down the lane. A river borders the back lawn, with some of the best fishing to be found in the state.

Tilton Manor

40 Chestnut Street
Tilton, NH 03276
603-286-3457

Type of Lodging: Bed & Breakfast

Room Rates: $70–$85, including full breakfast.

Pet Charges and Deposits: None.

Pet Policy: Dogs only, sorry, no cats. Manager's prior approval required.

Amenities: Common area with books, games, TV, 3 stories, interior corridors.

Rated: 3 Paws — 2 rooms and 1 suite.

Tilton Manor is a sixteen-room turn-of-the-20th-century Victorian nestled in a tranquil 3½ acre setting. Specializing in extraordinary service and ensuring guest comfort, your hosts, Chip and Diane, look forward to sharing this four-season vacation land with you. Guest quarters are furnished with antiques and handmade afghans that will warm your spirits. The common area features a relaxing fire, books, games, and a color TV. Start your day with as hearty a country breakfast as you'll find in New Hampshire, as you awaken to the aroma of home cooking and freshly baked delicacies. The Manor's close proximity to the Gunstock and Highland ski resorts, as well as the lake regions, allows you to enjoy the beauty of both winter and summer. And, of course, when fall comes, you'll gasp at the sheer beauty of Mother Nature's fireworks, the autumn foliage.

Fieldstone Country Inn

125 Fieldstone Lane
Twin Mountain, NH 03595
603-846-5646

Type of Lodging: Bed and Breakfast
Room Rates: $79–$99; AAA discounts.
Pet Charges and Deposits: None.
Pet Policy: All pets welcome. Pet on premises.
Amenities: Smoke-free premises, ice skating, hiking trails, free local telephone calls, 2 stories, interior corridors.
Rated: 3 Paws — 7 units.

Fieldstone Country Inn, just off State Route 302, east of its junction with US 3, dates back to 1925. Its pleasant rooms range in size from compact to spacious, and the décor is attractive and inviting. Twin Mountain, six miles north of Bretton Woods, is in the very heart of the most mountainous portion of White Mountain National Forest. It's a year-round holiday spot. Just south of Bretton Woods is Crawford Notch, a standout attraction in the state of New Hampshire. Created when the Pleistocene ice sheet pushed through a narrow preglacial pass, majestic Crawford Notch (pass) stretches from Bartlett in the south to Saco Lake on the north. Here you'll find Arethusa Falls, one of the highest waterfalls in New Hampshire (200 foot drop), and the Silver and Flume Cascades.

Best Western Silver Fox Inn

14 Snowsbrook Road
Waterville Valley, NH 03215
603-236-3699
Emai: wvlodges@together.net

Type of Lodging: Motel
Room Rates: $74–$194; AAA and AARP discounts.
Pet Charges and Deposits: None.
Pet Policy: All pets welcome. Pet on premises.
Amenities: Extended cable TV, area transportation, coin laundry, conference facilities, access to athletic club, resort shuttle, smoke-free premises, 3 stories, interior corridors.
Rated: 2 Paws — 32 rooms.

There's a pet on premises at the small, comfortable Best Western Silver Fox Inn. Guest rooms are newly decorated, with two double beds or one queen bed in each room. Children stay free in their parents' room. The motel is housed in a wonderfully evocative, typically New England building and it's spotlessly clean, charmingly restful. Waterville Valley is in the midst of White Mountain National Forest. It's a self-contained ski area, surrounded by more than six majestic peaks. Convenient to the Lakes Region, the Kancamagus Highway, and the Presidential Range, it makes a fine headquarters for vacation in the great forest.

Airport Economy Inn

45 Airport Road
West Lebanon, NH 03784
603-298-8888

Type of Lodging: Motel

Room Rates: $64–$144, including Continental breakfast. AAA discounts.

Pet Charges and Deposits: $10 per day per pet.

Pet Policy: All pets welcome.

Amenities: Winter plug-ins, extended cable TV, movies (fee), hair dryers, outdoor pool, coin laundry, free local telephone calls, radios, data port/modem telephones, refrigerators, 4 stories, interior corridors.

Rated: 3 Paws — 56 rooms.

You'll find luxury rooms at economy prices at this clean, modern lodging located at Lebanon Airport. You can walk to restaurants and shopping centers, and you'll find a large, impressive collection of sports memorabilia here. West Lebanon is two miles from the Vermont border, and is the site of the airport serving the main city of Lebanon. Six miles, or so, to the north, you'll find Hanover. When the Reverend Eleazar Wheelock arrived in Hanover in 1769, to establish a model school that would spread Christianity to the Abenaki Native Americans, little did he know or suspect it would become Dartmouth College, the ninth oldest college in the nation and the northernmost of the eight Ivy League institutions.

Fireside Inn & Suites

25 Airport Road
West Lebanon, NH 03784
603-298-5906
Email: info@afiresideinn.com

Type of Lodging: Motor Inn

Room Rates: $94–$130, including full breakfast buffet. AAA and AARP discounts.

Pet Charges and Deposits: None.

Pet Policy: All pets welcome.

Amenities: Extended cable TV, movies (fee), irons, hair dryers, heated pool, whirlpool, exercise room, gift shop, coin laundry, conference facilities, airport transportation, restaurant, radios, coffee makers, data port/modem telephones, some refrigerators, some microwaves, 2 stories, interior corridors.

Rated: 3 Paws — 126 rooms.

Located in the heart of New England, in the Lebanon-Hanover-White River Junction area, Fireside Inn & Suites is modern, quiet, clean, and comfortable property. It's minutes from Dartmouth College, Quechee Gorge, Woodstock Village, and many more attractions. Dartmouth Row consists of four classroom buildings, the oldest of which dates from 1784. Dartmouth features the Hood Museum of Art (ten galleries) and Hopkins Center, which was architect Wallace Harrison's prototype for what became the Metropolitan Opera House at Lincoln Center, New York. The Baker Library, also on the Dartmouth campus, containes nearly 2 million volumes. Murals painted by Mexican artist José Clemente Orozco cover 3,000 square feet and depict the story of civilization on the American continents.

Spalding Inn & Country Cottages

Mountain View Road
Whitefield, NH 03598
800-368-VIEW • 603-837-2572
Seasonal: Open June-October

Type of Lodging: Inn and Cottages

Room Rates: $165–$225, including full breakfast and full service dinner. AAA, AARP, AKC, and *ask about Pets Welcome*™ discounts.

Pet Charges and Deposits: None.

Pet Policy: All pets welcome.

Amenities: Cable TV, movies, heated pool, restaurant, cocktails, clay tennis courts, golf course, 1-2 stories, interior/exterior corridors.

Rated: 4 Paws — 36 rooms, 6 cottages, 1 guest house with fireplace.

The Spalding Inn and Country Cottages is located in the heart of the mountains, set amidst 200 acres of manicured orchards and perennial gardens. The broad front porch welcomes you to the inn, and on chilly evening a fire crackles in the stone fireplace of the main lobby. Guests will find spacious, romantic rooms with king-sized beds and handmade quilts, decorated with country cottage antiques. The private cottages have living rooms with fireplaces, service bars, and one or more connecting bedrooms—ideal for families. Fresh flowers, silver, crisp linens, and candlelight enhance the wonderful food served in elegant yet comfortable surroundings. Enjoy summer stock theater or a shopping spree at the nearby tax-free outlet. For the sports minded, there trout fishing, boating and enticing carriage roads for walking, as well as the Appalachian Trail.

Stepping Stones Bed & Breakfast

6 Bennington Battle Trail
Wilton Center, NH 03086
888-654-9048 • 603-654-9048

Type of Lodging: Bed & Breakfast

Room Rates: $65–$75, including full breakfast.

Pet Charges and Deposits: None.

Pet Policy: Manager's prior approval required.

Amenities: 2 stories, interior/exterior corridors.

Rated: 3 Paws — 3 rooms.

Stepping Stones is a fine bed & breakfast situated at the edge of one of southern New Hampshire's most charming villages. In friendly European tradition, hostess Ann Carlsmith invites her guests to share an unusually interesting 19th century house and garden. Furnishings are simply but abundantly comfortable. Each guest room contains handwoven throws, pillows, and rugs in natural fibers and gentle colors, all created on the looms in the weaving room. Outside, a network of terraces and pathways connects extensive lush gardens. Begin your day with a full breakfast served in the solar breakfast room. During colder months, enjoy wood fires, hot cocoa, and classical music. Stepping Stones is located in the Monadnock region, in the peaceful countryside, just behind the picture-book hamlet of Wilton Center. Enjoy hiking on the Wapack Trail, biking, antiquing, or simply gazing at the beautiful setting.

The Lake Motel

280 S. Main Street
Wolfeboro, NH 03894
603-569-1100

Type of Lodging: Motel
Room Rates: $99–$129.
Pet Charges and Deposits: None.
Pet Policy: Small pets only, by reservation only.
Amenities: Extended cable TV, beach, swimming, boat dock, fishing, tennis court, playground, boats (fee), canoes (fee), restaurant adjacent, data port/modem telephones, some refrigerators, some coffee makers, 1 story, interior/exterior corridors.
Rated: 2 Paws — 35 rooms.

The Lake Motel boasts very spacious grounds, extending all the way to Crescent Lake. At 35 rooms, this small motel is simple, clean, and comfortable, as well as pet-friendly. Wolfeboro, one of the oldest summer resorts in the United States, has been attracting visitors—and wealthy holidaymakers—since Governor John Wentworth of Massachusetts built the country's first summer home in 1768. By the time the governor's manor burned down in 1820, it was no longer unique. Highlights of the town include the Clark House Museum Complex (three historic buildings on the Village Green), the E. Stanley Wright Museum (details of life on the "home front" during World War II), the Hampshire Pewter Company, the Libby Museum (natural history and early life in Wolfeboro), and the *Winnipesaukee Belle,* which offers 1½ hour narrated sightseeing cruises of the eastern portion of New Hampshire's largest lake.

Nootka Lodge

36 Smith Street
Woodsville, NH 03785
603-747-2418

Type of Lodging: Motel
Room Rates: $44–$114; AAA and AARP discounts.
Pet Charges and Deposits: None.
Pet Policy: Small pets only, in designated rooms only.
Amenities: Extended cable TV, whirlpool, snowmobiling, exercise room, game room, outdoor pool, free local telephone calls, data port/modem telephones, some refrigerators, some microwaves, 2 stories, exterior corridors.
Rated: 2 Paws — 25 rooms.

Nootka Lodge is a Swiss-style log motel at the entrance to the White Mountains. It features a quiet, restful location, and clean, inviting rooms. Located at the western end of White Mountain National Forest, which, at this point, is the western edge of the state of New Hampshire, Woodsville sits on the eastern bank of the Connecticut River. It's just north of Bedell Bridge State Park, and is situated on particularly lovely confluences of several scenic highways. Cross-country and alpine skiing are nearby. Cannon Aerial Tramway and the sights, recreation facilities, and beauty of the White Mountain National Forest are just a few miles away.

RHODE ISLAND

Nickname: Little Rhody; Ocean State
Population: 1,048,319 (43rd)
Area: 1,545 sq. miles (50th)
Climate: Invigorating and changeable
Capital: Providence
Entered Union: May 29, 1790 (13th)
Motto: Hope
Song: Rhode Island
Flower: Violet
Tree: Red maple

Bird: Rhode Island Red
Famous Rhode Islanders: Ambrose Burnside, George M. Cohan, Nelson Eddy, Nathaniel Greene, Christopher LaFarge, Oliver LaFarge, Matthew C. Perry, Oliver Hazard Perry, Gilbert Stuart

History: Narragansett, Niantic, Nipmuc, and Wampanoag Native Americans occupied the area before European exploration. Verrazano visited the area as early as 1524, but it was another 112 years before Roger Williams founded the first permanent settlement at Providence in 1636, after he was expelled from the Massachusetts Bay Colony. Williams believed that *all* persons should have freedom of conscience and religion. Anne Hutchinson, who was also exiled, settled Portsmouth in 1638. Quaker and Jewish immigrants seeking freedom of worship arrived between 1650 and 1660. In 1764, Rhode Island became the first to prohibit the importation of slaves. British trade restrictions angered the colonists, and, on May 4, 1776, Rhode Island became the first colony to formally renounce allegiance to King George III. Rhode Island was initially opposed to joining the Union. It was the last of the original 13 Colonies to ratify the Constitution. In 1930, the first America's Cup race was held in Newport, which continues to this day as one of the premier Northeastern U.S. playgrounds for the rich and famous, and for those who enjoy a nautical lifestyle.

Geography: Highest Point: 812 feet, Jerimoth Hill. Lowest Point: Sea level, Atlantic Ocean. Time Zone: Eastern. Capital: Providence. Major cities: Providence (160,800), Warwick (85,400), Pawtucket (72,600), Newport (28,200). Eastern lowlands of the Narragansett Basin, flat and rolling hills in the west.

Tourist Information: 1-800-556-2484. Website: www.visitrhodeisland.com.

Recreation Areas
For You and Your Pet

All of these areas permit pets on a leash.

State Recreation Areas

Colt State Park, 455 acres 2 miles west of Bristol on Narragansett Bay. Historic, nature program, horse trails, picnicking, hiking trails, boating, boat ramp, fishing, winter sports, bicycle trails, food service.

Fort Adams State Park, 105 acres in west Newport adjoining Narragansett Bay. Historic, picnicking, boat ramp, boat rentals, fishing, swimming, visitor center, food service.

Goddard State Park, 472 acres east of East Greenwich on Ives Road, near Warwick. Golf, horse trails, picnicking, hiking trails, boating, boat ramp, fishing, swimming, winter sports, food service.

Lincoln Woods State Park, 627 acres 5 miles north of Providence on State Route 146. Horse rentals, horse trails, Camping, picnicking, hiking trails, boating, boat ramp, boat rentals, fishing, swimming, winter sports.

Pulaski Memorial, 100 acres 3 miles north of West Gloucester off U.S. 44. Cross-country skiing, picnicking, hiking trails, fishing, swimming, winter sports.

Bartram's Bed & Breakfast

94 Kane Avenue
Middletown, RI 02842
401-846-2259
E-mail: ebartram@juno.com

Type of Lodging: Bed & Breakfast
Room Rates: $80–$90, including full breakfast.
Pet Charges and Deposits: None.
Pet Policy: Dogs only.
Amenities: 1 story, interior corridors.
Rated: 2 Paws — 3 rooms.

In the true bed-and-breakfast tradition, Bartram's invites you to enjoy the hospitality of a private home, sharing facilities with the family and the family's yellow Lab, Ada. Summer mornings, breakfast is served on the patio overlooking the water, garden, and fountain. In winter, sit by the crackling fire and enjoy home-baked goods and piping hot beverages. Located two miles from downtown Newport, the town has historical mansions and a beautiful seacoast to explore. Visitors can enjoy the Newport Vineyards, the Norman Bird Sanctuary, and Prescott Farm, whose grounds include medicinal-culinary herb and edible flower gardens.

Howard Johnson Inn–Newport

351 W. Main Road
Middletown, RI 02842
401-849-2000

Type of Lodging: Motel
Room Rates: $45–$199; AAA and AARP discounts.
Pet Charges and Deposits: None.
Pet Policy: Designated units only.
Amenities: Extended cable TV, movies, voice mail, some honor bars, heated pool, whirlpool, sauna, 2 tennis courts, valet laundry, conference facilities, free newspaper, restaurant adjacent, radios, coffee makers, data port/modem telephones, some VCR's (fee), some refrigerators, some microwaves, 2 stories, interior corridors.
Rated: 2 Paws — 155 rooms.

Howard Johnson Inn provides pleasant accommodations a few miles from Newport. During almost three years of British occupation of Newport, Middletown served as the eastern terminus of the Newport defense lines. Purgatory Chasm, a narrow cleft between two rock ledges, has a fine scenic overlook. Norman Bird Sanctuary features 7 miles of trails through fields, swampland, and rocky cliffs. Prescott Farm affords a glimpse of early New England life. Farm sights include an 1811 windmill still used to grind grain, an 1815 country store, and the 1730 guardhouse where General Richard Prescott, commander of the British forces in Rhode Island, was held. The Whitehall Museum House, built in 1729 by noted British philosopher and educator Bishop George Berkeley (pronounced Barkley), houses furniture from the late 17th and early 18th centuries.

Motel 6

249 J.T. Connell Highway
Newport, RI 02840
401-848-0600

Type of Lodging: Motel

Room Rates: $49–$89; AARP discounts.

Pet Charges and Deposits: None.

Pet Policy: One pet per room.

Amenities: Extended cable TV, data port/modem telephones, 2 stories, interior corridors.

Rated: 2 Paws — 77 rooms.

Motel 6 is clean and convenient, only minutes from downtown Newport. Newport has a plethora of standout attractions, including Chateau-Sur-Mer, a huge, granite Victorian mansion built in 1852 for William S. Wetmore, who made his fortune in the China trade; The Elms, a neoclassical mansion built in 1901 and patterned after the 18th century Chateau d'Asnieres near Paris (lavish 18th century French antique furniture and Venetian paintings; Hunter House, an outstanding example of Colonial architecture built in 1748; Kingscote, an 1841 Gothic Revival-style house; Marble House, built in 1892 for William K. Vanderbilt, one of the most sumptuous of Newport's mansions—it is remarkably similar to 17th and 18th century palaces, such as the Petit Trianons of Versailles and the Louvre—said to cost $11 million *back then;* and Rosecliff, built in 1902 and designed after Louis XIV's Grand Trianon. The Touro Synagogue National Historic Site is the oldest Jewish house of worship in the nation, built in 1763.

Murray House Bed & Breakfast

One Murray Place
Newport, RI 02840
401-846-3337
E-mail: bikinicat@aol.com

Type of Lodging: Bed & Breakfast

Room Rates: $75–$165, including Continental breakfast, snacks, and soft drinks. AAA and AARP discounts.

Pet Charges and Deposits: $15 per stay per pet and $25 refundable deposit.

Pet Policy: Manager's prior approval required.

Amenities: 2 stories, exterior corridors.

Rated: 3 Paws — 3 rooms and 2 suites.

Sparkling beaches await you, water surrounds you on three sides, gourmet restaurants beckon you, and summer events vie for your attention. You are in Newport, the city by the sea. Nestled in this gem is the Murray House, where the mood is relaxing, the surrounding serene, and the location convenient. The décor is attractive and inviting as well as meticulously clean and comfortable. Murray House offers a fully furnished two-bedroom apartment on the first level, as well as a mini-suite on the second level. The apartment features a queen-sized bed, private bath, and a screened summer room with a beautiful view of Almy Pond. A swimming pool and flower gardens are on site, with the lovely beach of "Me Dog Park" a short walk away.

Sanford-Covell Villa Marina

72 Washington Street
Newport, RI 02840
401-847-0206

Type of Lodging: Inn

Room Rates: $85–$309, including Continental breakfast.

Pet Charges and Deposits: None.

Pet Policy: Dogs only, sorry, no cats.

Amenities: Swimming pool, Jacuzzi hot tubs, guest laundry facilities, 3 stories, interior/exterior corridors.

Rated: 4 Paws — 7 rooms and 2 suites.

Designed and built as a summer "cottage," the Sanford-Covell Villa Marina is an architectural landmark dating back to 1869. Among the extraordinary features are the grand staircase and multi-story entrance hall accented by projecting balconies at various levels. The woods used in this house include oak, ash, cherry, hard pine, maple, black walnut, butternut, and ebony. Located on an historic street in Newport, the setting invites guests to relax on the comfortable porch and enjoy spectacular sunsets over the bay, watching the boats sailing by. A delightful continental breakfast is served in the formal dining room, featuring a dining set once owned by the founder of the U.S. Naval Academy in Annapolis. Historic Newport offers many attractions and activities, including the Newport Mansion tours, the Newport Music Festival, and the International Boat Show. Shopping areas include the Brick Marketplace, America's Cup Avenue, and Thames Street.

The Westin Providence

One West Exchange Street
Providence, RI 02903
401-598-8000

Type of Lodging: Hotel

Room Rates: $379–$479, some suites: $500–$1,725, some whirlpool units. AAA and AARP discounts.

Pet Charges and Deposits: $50 per stay, $50 refundable deposit.

Pet Policy: Small pets only. Pets must be contained. Manager's prior approval required.

Amenities: Movies (fee), video games, dual phone lines, data port/modem telephones, voice mail, safes, honor bars, hair dryers, irons, heated pool, whirlpool, sauna, steam rooms, gift shop, valet laundry, massage (fee), conference facilities, administrative services, fax, free newspaper, 2 restaurants, 3 cocktail lounges, coffee makers, 25 stories, interior corridors.

Rated: 4 Paws — 364 rooms and 22 suites.

The Westin Providence, a landmark of luxury and neoclassical beauty, is in the heart of Providence. From the moment you enter the Rotunda, with its dramatic backdrop of the Capitol Building, you feel old-world class and modern comfort. Furnished with European style and graced with spectacular views of the city, you'll easily accommodate to the elegance surrounding you. You'll feel on top of the world in the glass-domed rooftop health spa. Schedule a massage or an exercise session with personal trainer. Enjoy a quiet interlude in the elegant Library Lounge. The Café affords fresh American cuisine or a delightful Sunday brunch, while inventive seafood and regional favorites can be found at Agora, the award-winning specialty restaurant.

The Kings' Rose Bed & Breakfast Inn

1747 Mooresfield Road
South Kingston, RI 02879
401-783-5222

Type of Lodging: Bed and Breakfast

Room Rates: $89–$139, including full breakfast.

Pet Charges and Deposits: None.

Pet Policy: All pets welcome.

Amenities: Extended cable TV, hair dryers, some irons, tennis court, afternoon tea, radios, smoke-free premises, 3 stories, interior corridors.

Rated: 3 Paws — 5 rooms.

The Kings' Rose Bed & Breakfast Inn is situated in a 1930's Colonial-style house with spacious lawns and English gardens. It's furnished with antiques and has one room with a working fireplace. You'll surely enjoy afternoon tea here. In 1765, Hannah Robinson, lovely young daughter of a prominent local citizen, fell in love with her French tutor. Hannah's father disapproved, and the couple was forced to meet at a large rock near the observation tower at what is today Hannah Robinson Park. They eventually eloped. Hannah was disinherited, and her new husband deserted her. Her health declined, and she was eventually brought home to die, for the last time passing by the rock where she and her beloved had met in happier days. The University of Rhode Island, established in 1892, occupies 1,200 acres in nearby Kingston Village.

Larchwood Inn

521 Main Street
Wakefield, RI 02789
800-275-5450 • 401-783-5454

Type of Lodging: Country Inn

Room Rates: $65–$125. AAA, AARP, AKC, ABA, and *ask about Pets Welcome*™ discounts.

Pet Charges and Deposits: $5 per day per pet.

Pet Policy: All pets welcome.

Amenities: Three dining rooms, 3 stories, interior corridors.

Rated: 3 Paws — 18 rooms.

Located in the quiet village of Wakefield, the Larchwood Inn has survived the necessities of modernization, while preserving the charm of its past. Century-old trees dot the ground of this 160-year-old country inn. The three story manor is surrounded by a wide expanse of landscaped grounds and by South County beaches. Each comfortable guest room has been individually decorated and all are furnished with carefully selected period pieces. Most of the rooms have private baths. Guests may enjoy fine dining throughout the day in one of the three dining rooms, which serve traditional fare along with many interesting daily specials and light suppers. Local attractions include beautiful surf and sheltered beaches, making Larchwood a perfect base for swimming, fishing, sailing, biking, or bird watching.

Comfort Inn–Airport

1940 Post Road
Warwick, RI 02886
401-732-0470

Type of Lodging: Motel

Room Rates: $109–$239, some whirlpool units: $169–$239, including Continental breakfast; AAA and AARP discounts.

Pet Charges and Deposits: $50 deposit.

Pet Policy: Designated units only.

Amenities: Extended cable TV, movies (fee), video games, voice mail, hair dryers, irons, airport transportation, valet laundry, conference facilities, free local calls, cocktails, radios, coffee makers, data port/modem telephones, some refrigerators, 4 stories, interior corridors.

Rated: 3 Paws – 200 units, including some whirlpool units.

Comfort Inn is clean, modern, and surprisingly quiet. The larger units are situated in the south wing of the motel. Warwick is actually the southern suburb of Providence and the location of its airport. Samuel Gorton, Warwick's founder and one of Rhode Island's most colorful characters, did not believe in civic or religious authority. He was exiled from Plymouth Colony, he was exiled from Portsmouth, and even Roger Williams, himself an exile, banished Gorton from Providence. Gorton then went off and bought what is today Warwick from the Narragansett Native Americans. The Massachusetts Bay Colony then arraigned Gorton and his followers before a tribunal, which condemned them to prison for blasphemy. When he was released, Gorton went to England to seek protection from Massachusetts. When he was promised such protection by the Earl of Warwick, he returned to the town and named it after the earl.

Mainstay Suites, Warwick

268 Metro Center Blvd.
Warwick, RI 02886
401-732-6667

Type of Lodging: Extended Stay Motel

Room Rates: $119–$169 (some suites), including Continental Breakfast. AAA and AARP discounts.

Pet Charges and Deposits: $10 per day per pet.

Pet Policy: All pets welcome.

Amenities: Extended cable TV, movies (fee), voice mail, hair dryers, irons, whirlpool, exercise room, sports court, complimentary evening beverages–Monday-Wednesday, coin laundry, radios, coffee makers, data port/modem telephones, refrigerators, microwaves, 3 stories, interior corridors.

Rated: 3 Paws – 94 units, including suites and efficiencies.

Mainstay Suites—"from the people who brought you Comfort Inn"—afford condominium privacy with full hotel amenities, including guest exercise room and laundry, guest barbecue, social hours, and outdoor hot tub. Providence, Rhode Island's capital and largest city, was founded in 1636 by Roger Williams, who had been banished from Massachusetts for his religious view. Brown University, relocated from Warren to Providence in 1770, is one of America's premier Ivy League schools. The Cathedral of St. John (1810) is the oldest Episcopal church in the city. The Cathedral of St. Peter and St. Paul dates from the late 19th century. This neo-Gothic Catholic church contains a rare 6,330-pipe Cassavant organ, with pipes ranging from 6 inches to 32 feet.

Master Hosts Inn

2138 Post Road
Warwick, RH 02886
401-737-7400

Type of Lodging: Motel

Room Rates: $119–$179; AAA and AARP discounts.

Pet Charges and Deposits: None.

Pet Policy: All pets welcome.

Amenities: Extended cable TV, movies, valet laundry, conference facilities, airport transportation, restaurant adjacent, radios, coffee makers, data port/modem telephones, some refrigerators, 3 stories, interior corridors.

Rated: 2 Paws — 103 rooms.

Master Hosts Inn is located opposite the airport runway. Not to worry, though—it has strong soundproofing. Some of the units are quite spacious, all are clean and comfortable. Providence's Culinary Archives and Museum features more than 300,000 culinary and hospitality related items, reflecting the food industry from ancient times to the present. The Museum of Art— Rhode Island School of Design houses more than 80,000 works of art, from ancient Greek and Roman to European, as well as works from China, India, Latin America, France, and Egypt. Roger Williams Park Zoo features 40 acres of animal exhibits, including the Tropical Rainforest Building, the Marco Polo Trail, and the Plains of Africa natural habitat.

Residence Inn By Marriott

500 Kilvert Street
Warwick, RI 02886
401-737-7100

Type of Lodging: Apartment Hotel

Room Rates: $179–$239; AAA discounts.

Pet Charges and Deposits: Inquire.

Pet Policy: Small pets only, in designated units only.

Amenities: Extended cable TV, movies, voice mail, hair dryers, irons, heated pool, whirlpool, exercise room, sports court, coin laundry, conference facilities, airport transportation, radios, coffee makers, data port/modem telephones, refrigerators, microwaves, some VCR's (fee), 2 stories, exterior corridors.

Rated: 3 Paws — 96 mini-suites.

Residence Inn is housed in Tudor-style brick and stucco buildings, with attractively landscaped walkways, inviting, spacious studio and two-level penthouse units, many with fireplaces, barbecues, and picnic facilities. Providence's Roger Williams Park is a 435-acre area with a chain of lakes, extensive flower gardens, and nine miles of winding drives. Carousel Village features a children's train, pony rides, miniature golf, and a replica of a Victorian carousel. The Roger Williams Park Museum of Natural History features not only animal skeletons, cultural collections, and natural history exhibits, but also the Cormack Planetarium, which offers planetarium shows on weekends.

Sheraton Providence Airport Hotel

1850 Post Road
Warwick, RI 02886
401-738-4000

Type of Lodging: Hotel
Room Rates: $159–$315; AAA and AARP discounts.
Pet Charges and Deposits: $25.
Pet Policy: All pets welcome.
Amenities: Extended cable TV, movies (fee), dual phone lines, voice mail, hair dryers, irons, heated pool, sauna, exercise room, area transportation, valet laundry, conference facilities, restaurant, cocktails, radios, coffee makers, data port/modem telephones, some refrigerators, 5 stories, interior corridors.
Rated: 3 Paws — 206 rooms.

There are several deluxe units in the Sheraton Providence Airport Hotel. All units are clean, comfortable, and tastefully furnished. Public areas are bright and attractive. The 1786 John Brown House Museum, a restored three-story Georgian house, was built by a wealthy China trader. The Roger Williams National Memorial is the site of the original 1636 Providence settlement. The First Baptist Church in America was established by Roger Williams in 1638 and is the oldest Baptist house of worship in the country. The First Unitarian Church, built in 1816, has the largest bell ever cast in Paul Revere's Foundry. The Providence Art Club offers changing exhibits in two houses dating from 1786 to 1791.

The Villa

190 Shore Road
Westerly, RI 02891
800-772-9240 • 401-596-1054

Type of Lodging: Bed & Breakfast
Room Rates: $85–$235, including Continental breakfast.
Pet Charges and Deposits: $25 per stay.
Pet Policy: Manager's prior approval required.
Amenities: Designer pool, Jacuzzi spa, hot tubs, fireplaces, private terrace, 1-3 stories, interior corridors.
Rated: 4 Paws — 6 suites.

An oasis of privacy and luxury, The Villa is a large, gracious home, situated on 1½ landscaped acres, surrounded by beautiful gardens and spacious lawns. Gracing this delightful setting is a Mediterranean designer pool and a delightful outdoor Jacuzzi spa. This deluxe bed and breakfast features six luxury suites, individually inspired and uniquely highlighted with romantic and inviting details. A pleasing breakfast, featuring home-baked goods, is served in the dining area at poolside or in the privacy of your suite. Located at the crossroads of historic Westerly and Watch Hill, The Villa is minutes from Rhode Island's pristine shoreline. The many nearby attractions include Misquamicut Beach, Foxwoods Resort and Casino, and the Mystic Aquarium. Guests can also enjoy shopping at Old Mystic Village, ocean view golf courses, and salt water fishing.

VERMONT

Nickname: Green Mountain State
Population: 608,827 (49th)
Area: 9,614 sq. miles (43rd)
Climate: Temperate, with considerable extremes, heavy snowfall in mountains
Capital: Montpelier
Entered Union: March 14, 1791 (14th)
Motto: Freedom and unity
Song: These Green Mountains
Flower: Red clover

Tree: Sugar Maple
Bird: Hermit thrush
Famous Vermonters: Ethan Allen, Chester A. Arthur, Calvin Coolidge, John Deere, George Dewey, John Dewey, Stephen A. Douglas, Dorothy Canfield Fisher, James Fisk, James Jeffords, Rudy Vallee

History: Abnaki and Mahican peoples lived in the region prior to the arrival of the first Europeans. Champlain explored the area in 1609. The French settled the area in 1666, but their settlement did not survive. The first English settlement, Fort Dummer, was founded in 1724. Just prior to the American Revolution, Ethan Allen and the Green Mountain Boys captured Fort Ticonderoga (New York) in 1775. Vermont was something of a wilderness. New York and New Hampshire disputed its ownership, but in 1777 Vermont proclaimed itself a free and independent nation, maintaining that status until 1791, when it was admitted to the United States. A land of self-sufficient farmers, Vermont turned to sheep raising in the mid-1800's, but the western lands, as well as Australia, produced agricultural goods more cheaply than Vermont could, and the state's economy declined. Today, the state is mostly rural and has the lowest population of any New England state. Dairy farming and tourism are its two most important industries.

Geography: Highest Point: 4,395 feet, Mount Mansfield. Lowest Point: 95 feet, Lake Champlain. Time Zone: Eastern. Capital: Montpelier. Major cities: Burlington (50,000), Bennington (18,000), Brattleboro (12,000), Montpelier (8,000). The Green Mountains, a range 20-36 miles wide, constitutes the north-south backbone of the state. The average altitude of the state is 1,000 feet above sea level. Try to be there in October, when the leaves change color and the state is one of the nation's most gorgeous. Or, consider winter at Stowe—so many north-easterners follow the trail blazed by the real-life Sound of Music's Maria von Trapp.

Tourist Information: 1-800-VERMONT. Website: www.1-800-vermont.com.

Recreation Areas
For You and Your Pet

All of these areas permit pets on a leash.

National Forest Area

Green Mountain National Forest, 370,000 acres, south-central through north-central Vermont. Camping, picnicking, hiking trails, boating, fishing, swimming, winter sports.

State Recreation Areas

Allis State Park, 487 acres 5 miles south of Northfield of State Route 12, Scenic, hunting, camping, picnicking, hiking trails.

Ascutney State Park, 1,984 acres 3 miles northwest of Ascutney off U.S. 5, Snowmobiling, camping, picnicking, hiking trails.

Bomoseen State Park, 2,739 acres (two areas), 5 miles north of West Castleton. Nature center, nature trails, Camping, picnicking, hiking trails, boating, boat ramp, boat rentals, fishing, swimming, food service.

Branbury State Park, 96 acres, 3 miles east of Salisbury off U.S. 7. Nature center, nature trails, Camping, picnicking, hiking trails, boating, boat ramp, boat rentals, fishing, swimming, lodge/cabins, food service.

Brighton State Park, 152 acres, 2 miles east of Island Pond off State Route 105. Marina, nature center, nature trails. camping, picnicking, hiking trails, boating, boat ramp, boat rentals, fishing, swimming.

Burton Island State Park, 253 acres in Lake Champlain, access by boat only from Kamp Kill Kare State Park. Marina, nature center, nature trails, camping, picnicking, hiking trails, boating, boat rentals, fishing, swimming, food service.

Button Nay State Park, 236 acres, 7 miles west of Vergennes. Nature center, nature trails, Camping, picnicking, hiking trails, boating, boat ramp, boat rentals, fishing, swimming.

Calvin Coolidge State Forest, 16,165 acres 2 miles north of Plymouth via State Route 100A. Snowmobiling, camping, picnicking, hiking trails, fishing, winter sports.

DAR State Park, 95 acres, 1 mile north of Chimney Point on State Route 17. Camping, picnicking, boating, fishing, swimming.

Elmore State Park, 709 acres at Elmore on State Route 12. Camping, picnicking, hiking trails, boating, boat rentals, fishing, swimming, food service.

Emerald Lake State Park, 430 acres at North Dorset on U.S. 7. Nature center, nature trails, camping, picnicking, hiking trails, boating, boat rentals, fishing, swimming, winter sports, food service.

Fort Dummer State Park, 217 acres, 2 miles south of Brattleboro off I-91, Exit 1 on Old Guilford Road. Playground, camping, picnicking, hiking trails.

Gifford Woods State Park, 114 acres, 2 miles north of Killington on State Route 100. Camping, picnicking, hiking trails, fishing.

Grand Isle State Park, 226 acres, 5 miles north of South Hero off U.S. 2. Camping, boating, boat ramp, boat rentals, fishing, swimming, lodge/cabins.

Groton Forest State Park, 25,625 acres (nine areas) midway between Montpelier and St. Johnsbury. Snowmobiling, nature center, nature trails, camping, picnicking, hiking trails, boating, boat ramp, boat rentals, fishing, swimming, winter sports, lodge/cabins, food service.

Half Moon Pond State Park, 1,570 acres, 11 miles northwest of Rutland off State Route 30. Nature programs, nature trails, camping, hiking trails, boating, boat rentals, fishing, swimming, lodge/cabins.

Jamaica State Park, 689 acres, 1 miles east of Jamaica on State Route 30. Camping, picnicking, hiking trails, fishing, swimming.

Lake Carmi State Park, 482 acres, 3 miles south of East Franklin off State Route 120. Nature trails, camping, picnicking, hiking trails, boating, boat ramp, boat rentals, fishing, swimming, winter sports, lodge/cabins, food service.

Lake St. Catherine State Park, 117 acres, 3 miles south of Poultney on State Route 30. Nature center, nature trails, camping, hiking trails, boating, boat ramp, boat rentals, fishing, swimming, food service.

Little River State Park, 12,000 acres, 1½ miles west of Waterbury on U.S. 2, then 3½ miles on Little River Road. Camping, picnicking, hiking trails, boating, boat ramp, boat rentals, fishing, swimming.

Maidstone State Park, 469 acres southwest of Bloomfield via State Forest Highway. Nature trails, camping, picnicking, hiking trails, boating, boat ramp, boat rentals, fishing, swimming, winter sports.

Molly Stark State Park, 158 acres, 15 miles west of Brattleboro off State Route 9. Camping, picnicking, hiking trails.

Mount Mansfield State Forest, 27,613 acres. Cross-country skiing, downhill skiing, snowmobiling, Camping, picnicking, hiking trails, boating, boat ramp, boat rentals, fishing, swimming, winter sports, lodge/cabins.

Mount Philo State Park, 648 acres, 14 miles south of Burlington off U.S. 7. Scenic, camping, picnicking, hiking trails, winter sports.

North Hero State Park, 399 acres, 8 miles north of North Hero off U.S. 2. Nature trails, camping, picnicking, boating, boat ramp, boat rentals, fishing, swimming.

Quechee Gorge State Park, 612 acres, 7 miles west of White River Junction off U.S. 4. Camping, picnicking, hiking trails, fishing.

Silver Lake State Park, 34 acres, 1 mile east of Barnard off State Route 12. Camping, picnicking, boating, boat rentals, fishing, swimming, food service.

Smuggler's Notch State Park, 25 acres 8 miles west of Stowe on State Route 108. Camping, picnicking, hiking trails, fishing.

Townshend State Forest, 856 acres, 17 miles northwest of Brattleboro via State Route 30. Camping, picnicking, hiking trails, fishing.

Wilgus State Park, 100 acres, 1 mile south of Ascutney on U.S. 5. Nature trails, Camping, picnicking, hiking trails, boating, fishing.

Woodford State Park, 400 acres, 10 miles east of Bennington off State Route 9. Nature trails, camping, picnicking, hiking trails, boating, boat rentals, fishing, swimming.

Woods Island State Park, 125 acres, 4 miles north of Burton Island State Park in Lake Champlain. Permit camping only, picnicking, boating, fishing, swimming.

The Ransom Bay Inn

4 Center Bay Road
Alburg, VT 05440
802-796-3399

Type of Lodging: Historic Bed & Breakfast

Room Rates: $64–$79, including full breakfast, AAA and AARP discounts.

Pet Charges and Deposits: None.

Pet Policy: Small pets only, cat on premises.

Amenities: No TVs, area transportation, data port/modem telephones, some microwaves, smoke-free premises, 1-2 stories, interior corridors.

Rated: 3 Paws — 4 rooms.

When it was first built, 200 years ago, the structure was designed to be an inn and tavern. Once again, it has opened its doors to welcome visitors to the Lake Champlain islands. Guest rooms are spacious and tastefully decorated, while bathrooms are more moderate, with antique fixtures retained when possible. Three fireplaces and a wood-burning stove warm the common rooms of this large stone house.

Inn at HighView

753 East Hill Road
Andover, VT 05143
802-875-2724

Type of Lodging: Inn

Room Rates: $109–$159, including Continental breakfast. AAA and AARP discounts.

Pet Charges and Deposits: $10 per day per pet.

Pet Policy: All pets welcome.

Amenities: Pool, sauna, conference room, restaurant, 2 stories, interior/exterior corridors.

Rated: 3 Paws — 6 rooms and 2 suites on 72 acres.

Nestled amidst the Green Mountains of Vermont lies the tiny village of Andover, home of The Inn at HighView. A spacious, rambling farmhouse, the Inn sits high on East Hill. From its handsome wide porch and lushly planted grounds, you are treated to a dazzling view of the mountains. Guest rooms are beautifully appointed, with antique furnishings and canopy beds with country quilts and goose-down comforters. The country dining room is well-known for excellent, imaginative cuisine. In addition to the traditional full breakfasts, the "guests only" weekend dining offers delicious Italian fare. Whether you prefer hiking, tennis, canoeing, browsing country stores and auctions, alpine skiing, or a peaceful afternoon snooze in the hammock, you will find it all here.

Hill Farm Inn

R.R. 2, Box 2015
Arlington, VT 05250
800-882-2545 • 802-375-2269
E-mail: hillfarm@vermontel.com

Type of Lodging: Country Inn

Room Rates: $89–$139, including full breakfast and a jar of homemade strawberry-rhubarb jam.

Pet Charges and Deposits: $5 per day per pet and one night's rate as a refundable deposit.

Pet Policy: All pets welcome.

Amenities: Some refrigerators, some wood stoves, 2 stories, interior/exterior corridors.

Rated: 3 Paws — 11 rooms and 2 suites.

Hill Farm Inn, one of Vermont's first country inns, still specializes in the warm hospitality that began more than 90 years ago. The Inn is surrounded by 50 acres of farmland, with a mile of frontage on the famed Battenkill River, offering spectacular mountain views in every direction. Seven guest rooms are located on the second floor of the 1830's main house, with an additional six units in the 1790's guest house next door. You'll find New England farmhouse décor throughout the guest accommodations, with each room individually and uniquely decorated. The suites have private porches and incomparable views of the Taconic and Green Mountains. Guests enjoy a full country breakfast each morning, and, for a minimal fee, can feast on a four-course dinner each night. The Hill Farm Inn specializes in soups, breads, and desserts—all made from scratch, of course—and vegetables fresh from the garden. The chef offers a choice of vegetarian, light, or hearty entrees.

The Hollow Inn & Motel

278 S. Main Street
Barre, VT 05644
802-479-9313

Type of Lodging: Motel

Room Rates: $65–$145, AAA and AARP discounts.

Pet Charges and Deposits: None.

Pet Policy: Designated rooms only, in motel units only.

Amenities: Extended cable TV, iron, hairdryers, heated pool, whirlpool, sauna, exercise room, video rentals, coin laundry, meeting rooms, fax, VCR's, radios, coffee makers, refrigerators, data port/modem telephones, some microwaves, 2 stories, interior/exterior corridors.

Rated: 2 Paws — 41 rooms.

Located in the heart of Barre off Interstate 89, the Hollow Inn boasts a hilltop setting and attractively landscaped grounds. There are lovely, spacious guest rooms within the main Inn, more modest units in the motel. Efficiency rooms and kitchenettes are available upon request. Local area attractions include the Vermont State Capitol building, located 8 miles from the Inn. Morse's Farms Sugar Shack offers maple sugar tours. The Rock of Ages features a scenic visit to a 100-year-old quarry. Local cultural activities include the Barre Opera House, Billings' Farm & Museum, the Pavilion, and the T.V. Wood Art Gallery.

Bennington Motor Inn

143 W. Main Street
Bennington, VT 05201
802-442-5479
Website/Email: zink@together.net

Type of Lodging: Motel

Room Rates: $64–$104, AAA and AARP discounts.

Pet Charges and Deposits: $15. per day per pet.

Pet Policy: Designated rooms only.

Amenities: Extended cable TV, movies, free local telephone calls, restaurant adjacent, coffee makes, data port/modem telephones, some refrigerators, 2 stories, interior/exterior corridors.

Rated: 2 Paws — 25 units.

Bennington Motor Inn is a quaint, family-run motel. The Zink family has been your innkeepers for over a quarter of a century. The Inn is across from Hemmings Motor News and Antique Auto Display. Bennington is set in a valley between Mount Anthony in the Taconic Range and the foothills of the Green Mountains. Bennington's three covered bridges are reminders of long ago. Plays and exhibits are presented April through October, while concerts are offered the rest of the year in Bennington Center for the Arts. Bennington Battle Monument was the tallest battle monument in the world when it was completed in 1891; it's still the tallest structure in Vermont (306 feet). A diorama and exhibit illustrate the Revolutionary War battle of 1777 that took place there.

Darling Kelly's Motel

357 State Route 7 South
Bennington, VT 05201
802-442-2232

Type of Lodging: Motel

Room Rates: $49–$109, including Continental breakfast, AAA and AARP discounts.

Pet Charges and Deposits: None.

Pet Policy: Designated units only.

Amenities: Extended cable TV, movies, outdoor pool, yard games, free local telephone calls, radios, data port/modem telephones, some refrigerators, 1 story, exterior corridors.

Rated: 3 Paws — 21 rooms.

Darling Kelly's is set 300 feet back from Route 7, on five acres of grounds with a mountain view and cozy rooms. It has an enticing country charm. It's only a mile from Main Street, near colleges, restaurants and museums. Bennington Museum houses the world's largest publicly displayed collection of folk artist Grandma Moses' paintings. Her worktable, equipment, and awards are also displayed. The Grandma Moses Schoolhouse, which the artist attended in her youth, displays her personal belongings. The Museum also houses the Bennington Flag, one of the oldest Stars & Stripes flags in existence, as well as uniforms, firearms, dolls, toys, and tools. The Wasp, a 1925 luxury touring car designed by local resident Karl Martin, is on display at this standout attraction.

Fife 'n Drum Motel

693 U.S. Route 7
Bennington, VT 05201
802-442-4074
Email: toberua@sover.net

Type of Lodging: Motel
Room Rates: $45–$105, AAA and AARP discounts.
Pet Charges and Deposits: $5. per day per pet.
Pet Policy: Small pets only, designated units only.
Amenities: Extended cable TV, movies, outdoor pool, whirlpool, playground, horseshoes, shuffleboard, picnic areas with grills, gift shop, free local telephone calls, coffee makers, data port/modem telephones, refrigerators, some microwaves, 1-2 stories, exterior corridors.
Rated: 3 Paws — 18 rooms.

Located in Bennington, the cradle of Vermont history, the Fife 'n Drum offers fun and relaxation, starting right at your doorstep. Guests will enjoy comfortable rooms with panoramic views, refrigerators, and king- or queen-sized beds. Situated on several acres, the motel features a heated pool with spa, a playground, shuffleboard, a horseshoe pit, and a badminton court. Enjoy all these amenities while barbecuing your favorite fare on the outdoor grill. If you are a history buff, or just eager to experience Vermont, historic Old Bennington is minutes away. Visit the church and cemetery where poet Robert Frost is buried, stroll Monument Avenue, rich with Revolutionary-period homes, or enjoy the Museum and Battle Monument. Add ten major ski areas located within a thirty-mile radius, and you have year-round enjoyment.

Knotty Pine Motel

130 Northside Drive
Bennington, VT 05201
802-442-5487

Type of Lodging: Motel
Room Rates: $49–$99
Pet Charges and Deposits: None.
Pet Policy: All pets welcome.
Amenities: Winter plug-ins, Extended cable TV, some irons, restaurant adjacent, outdoor pool, coffee makers, refrigerators, data port/modem telephones, some microwaves, 1 story, exterior corridors.
Rated: 2 Paws — 19 rooms.

Knotty Pine Motel is a small family-owned and operated motel, with extraordinarily friendly and hospitable owner-hosts. Guest units are housed in a New England country-style décor, with, you guessed it, knotty pine walls. Bennington is in the southwest corner of Vermont, practically on the New York border, at the southwest edge of Green Mountain National Forest. State Route 9, going from Brattleboro in the east to Bennington in the west, is a particularly scenic stretch of road. There's lots of place to ski, all within an hour's drive of Bennington. Old First Church, on Monument Avenue in Old Bennington Village, is among the oldest in Vermont (1805-1806). The church is widely regarded as one of the most beautiful in New England.

South Gate Motel

P.O. Box 1073/U.S. 7 South
Bennington, VT 05201
802-447-7525

Type of Lodging: Motel
Room Rates: $44–$89, AAA discounts.
Pet Charges and Deposits: $6 per day per pet.
Pet Policy: All pets welcome.
Amenities: Extended cable TV, winter plug-ins, movies, outdoor pool, data port/modem telephones, refrigerators, some microwaves, 1-2 stories, interior corridors.
Rated: 2 Paws — 19 rooms.

Cozy, comfortable, modest, and modestly priced rooms are the hallmark of the South Gate motel. Built in 1865, the Park-McCullough House in nearby North Bennington is a 35-room Victorian mansion, which contains original furniture and decorative art pieces, as well as period clothing once used by the Park and McCullough families. You'll enjoy the gardens, and a carriage house that contains a collection of antique carriages. Bennington's Old Burying Ground, behind the Old First Church, contains the graves of the founders of Bennington, five Vermont governors, and the poet Robert Frost, whose epitaph is, "I had a lover's quarrel with the world."

Greenhurst Inn

River Street, RR 2, Box 60
Bethel, VT 05032-9404
800-510-2553 • 802-234-9474

Type of Lodging: Country inn
Room Rates: $60–$110, including Continental breakfast. AAA and AARP discounts.
Pet Charges and Deposits: $50 refundable deposit.
Pet Policy: Manager's prior approval required.
Amenities: Outdoor exercise area, 3 stories (no elevator), interior corridors.
Rated: 3 Paws — 13 rooms.

Located midway between Boston and Montreal, in the center of Vermont, this charming country inn offers gracious hospitality and elegant comfort. The Greenhurst Inn is a lovely 1890's Victorian mansion overlooking the White River. This grand inn, with its turrets, porches, and gazebo, houses magnificent woodwork, carved staircases, high ceilings, and lovely, intricate light fixtures. Guest rooms are comfortably decorated with antiques and original artwork. Many offer fireplaces. Breakfast is served in the period dining room, offering home-baked goods with an array of jams and preserves. A crackling fire and strains of classical music accompany the sumptuous fare. Seasonal activities include Nordic and alpine skiing, golfing, boating, canoeing, and fishing. The historic countryside awaits your exploration, and the Appalachian Trail is minutes away.

Colonial Motel & Spa

889 Putney Road
Brattleboro, VT 05301
802-257-7733

Type of Lodging: Motor Inn

Room Rates: $54–$94, some suites, some whirlpool units, including Continental breakfast, AAA and AARP discounts.

Pet Charges and Deposits: $10 per day per pet.

Pet Policy: All pets welcome.

Amenities: Extended cable TV, movies, voice mail, two pools (one heated, one indoor), exercise room, meeting rooms, free local telephone calls, restaurant, radios, some coffee makers, data port/modem telephones, some refrigerators, 1-2 stories, exterior corridors.

Rated: 2 Paws — 73 rooms.

Colonial Motel & Spa is a spacious, comfortable place that affords you great value for the money. Brattleboro's slogan, "Where Vermont begins," is apt. It was here that the state's first permanent European settlement, Fort Dummer, was established in 1724. Rudyard Kipling built a house for his bride near here, and wrote *Captains Courageous, Just So Stories,* and the two *Jungle Book* stories while he lived in that house. Unfortunately, the house is not open to the public. The Brattleboro Museum and Art Center houses four galleries of changing exhibits. Brattleboro sits astride the Connecticut River at the southeastern edge of the state.

Firefly Ranch

P.O. Box 152
Bristol, VT 05443
802-453-2223

Type of Lodging: Inn

Room Rates: $89–$150, including full breakfast.

Pet Charges and Deposits: 30% of bill refundable deposit.

Pet Policy: All pets welcome.

Amenities: Hot tub, spring-fed pong, trail rides, 1-2 stories, interior/exterior corridors.

Rated: 2 Paws — 3 rooms.

Firefly Ranch offers relaxed, traditional New England hospitality in a peaceful Vermont setting. Located at the foot of beautiful Mount Abraham, Mount Lincoln, and Mount Grant, guests enjoy relaxing by the spring-fed pond or watching the horses graze in the pasture from a window in the spacious contemporary country rooms. Guest accommodations are comfortably furnished. If there are no vacancies at the Ranch, you are invited to set up a tent on the beautiful grounds and take advantage of the outdoor activities and meals as desired, with no charge for camping. Savor delectable gourmet continental cuisine, prepared with fresh Vermont-grown products in season. Saddle up and discover beautiful country roads and tree-lined trails, with breathtaking views in the foothills of Vermont's famous Green Mountains. Walk to the renowned New Haven River for fly-fishing, hike up the famous Long Trail, or mountain bike through the delightful surrounding rural areas.

Cavendish Pointe Hotel

State Route 103
Cavendish, VT 05142
802-226-7688
www.okemo/cavendishpointe.com

Type of Lodging: Motor Inn

Room Rates: $74–$214, some whirlpool units, $99–$214, AAA and AARP discounts.

Pet Charges and Deposits: None.

Pet Policy: Small pets only.

Amenities: Winter plug-ins, extended cable TV, movies, voice mail, hair dryers, heated pool, whirlpool, meeting rooms, free local telephone calls, restaurant, cocktails, game room, free ski shuttle to and from Okemo, hot tub, kids stay free with parents, radios, refrigerators, data port/modem telephones, 2 stories, interior corridors.

Rated: 3 Paws — 70 rooms.

Cavendish Pointe Hotel boasts 70 spacious rooms, where children can stay free with their parents. There's a restaurant and lounge, a hot tub, a game room, and a free ski shuttle to Okemo Mountain Resort, three miles away. Cavendish is located on the Black River, just east of Okemo State Park, amidst woods and mountains. Ski areas abound in every direction, and the Connecticut River, the border with New Hampshire, is less than twenty miles to the east. Wilgus State Park and Ascutney State Park, both at the eastern edge of the state, are excellent recreation areas for you and your pet to romp and roam in this sparsely populated segment of Vermont.

Hampton Inn Hotel/Conference Center

42 Lower Mountainview Drive
Colchester, VT 05446
802-655-6177

Type of Lodging: Motor Inn

Room Rates: $99–$149, some suites, $139–$165, AAA and AARP discounts.

Pet Charges and Deposits: None.

Pet Policy: All pets welcome.

Amenities: Winter plug-ins, cable TV, movies (fee), video games, voice mail, irons, hair dryers, heated pool, whirlpool, exercise room, area transportation, valet and coin laundry, conference facilities, fax, restaurant, radios, coffee makers, data port/modem telephones, some refrigerators (fee), some microwaves (fee), 4-5 stories, interior corridors.

Rated: 3 Paws — 188 rooms.

Enjoy all the charm of a Vermont country inn, ideally situated in Colchester. Hampton Inn features traditional New England décor and beautiful mountain views. Step into the large, inviting lobby within its sunken living room and cozy fireplace. Enjoy swimming year-round in the indoor pool. Soak yourself in a bubbling Jacuzzi or work out at the well-equipped fitness center. During warmer months, relax on the sunny deck, in the gazebo, or on the lush garden patio. The hotel is within five minutes of downtown Burlington, the airport, beautiful Lake Champlain, five shopping malls, five golf courses, and many area events and attractions. Considered part of Vermont's Vacation Valley, you'll find some of Vermont's finest attractions along Lake Champlain, including breathtaking scenery and lots of family fun venues. Day and night skiing is less than 45 minutes away.

Motel 6

*74 S. Park Drive
Colchester, VT 05446
802-654-6860*

Type of Lodging: Motel

Room Rates: $44–$85

Pet Charges and Deposits: None.

Pet Policy: All pets welcome.

Amenities: Winter plug-ins, cable TV, movies, heated pool, coin laundry, health club, data port/modem telephones, some refrigerators, some microwaves, 3 stories, interior corridors.

Rated: 2 Paws — 106 rooms.

Motel 6 affords comfortable, standard rooms at a great bargain price. Colchester is adjacent to Burlington on the northwest section of Vermont, on large, impressive Lake Champlain. The standout Shelburne Museum on US 7 consists of 37 historic structures, many of them dismantled and relocated from several parts of New England. Spread over 45 acres, the buildings are a wonderful exhibit of early New England life. The living history museum contains 18th and 19th century houses, a jail, country store, meetinghouse, stagecoach inn, railroad depot, a two-lane covered bridge, and a handcrafted model circus parade some 500 feet long. The Electra Havemeyer Webb Memorial houses European furnishings, sculpture, and paintings by Corot, Courbet, Degas, Goya, Manet, Monet, and Rembrandt.

The Inn on the Common

*1162 N. Craftsbury Road
Craftsbury Common, VT 05827
802-586-9619*

Type of Lodging: Historic Country Inn

Room Rates: $179–$315, some suites $285–$315

Pet Charges and Deposits: $15 per day per pet.

Pet Policy: All pets welcome.

Amenities: No TVs, hair dryers, outdoor pool, tennis court, cross-country skiing, nature trails, bicycles (fee), restaurant, cocktails, radios, data port/modem telephones, some coffee makers, some refrigerators, some microwaves, 2 stories, interior corridors.

Rated: 3 Paws — 14 rooms and 2 suites.

Inn on the Common is situated on a panoramic hilltop surrounded by 15 beautifully landscaped acres. It's located in Craftsbury Common, a village of white clapboard homes in Vermont's pristine Northeast Kingdom, where the roads run along ridges and brilliant green farmland falls away to the distant mountains. Sixteen guest units with private baths are spread out between three houses. All have sitting areas made for relaxing and are stylishly furnished with fine wallpaper, distinctive artwork, and antiques. The meals rival Boston's finest in both service and excellence. Guests are invited to enjoy the pool or clay tennis courts, or to simply explore the back roads throughout the scenic area. During winter, the Craftsbury Nordic Center trails crisscross the kind of red-barn-spotted farmscape that speaks Vermont. After a day on the trails, enjoy The Wellness Barn, a state-of-the-art fitness center featuring spas and saunas, which is located 10 minutes away.

Barrows House

P.O. Box 98, Route 30
Dorset, VT 05251
800-639-1620 • 802-867-4455
E-mail: barhouse@vermontel.com

Type of Lodging: Historic Inn

Room Rates: $139–$259, including full breakfast and gourmet dinner.

Pet Charges and Deposits: $15 per day per pet.

Pet Policy: Dogs only, sorry, no cats. Manager's prior approval required.

Amenities: Heated pool, sauna, badminton, croquet green, tennis courts, touring bikes, pub, 2 stories, interior/exterior corridors.

Rated: 4 Paws — 18 rooms and 10 suites.

The Barrows House is an historic inn, consisting of eight buildings nestled on 12 park-like acres. The white clapboard buildings, colorful gardens, manicured lawns, and stately trees evoke a history dating back to the 1700's. The unique facilities and extensive grounds feature modern conveniences, with each guest room or cottage uniquely furnished in its own restful style, with antiques, old family pieces, and modern bedding. Each house has its own sitting room, porch, or terrace. The main inn features a living room with a glowing hearth and a cozy tavern, which provide an opportunity for either companionship or privacy. The inn offers swimming, tennis, lawn games and touring bikes for leisurely rides around Dorset and down the Mettowee River Valley. Nearby Manchester offers an array of shopping adventures and an 18-hole golf course.

The Wilson Inn

10 Kellogg Road
Essex Junction, VT 05452
802-879-1515

Type of Lodging: Suite Motel

Room Rates: $99–$149

Pet Charges and Deposits: $10 per day per pet.

Pet Policy: All pets welcome.

Amenities: Winter plug-ins, extended cable TV, movies, voice mail, irons, heated pool, hairdryers, playground, valet and coin laundry, cocktails, radios, coffee makers, data port/modem telephones, refrigerators, microwaves, some VCR's, 3 stories (no elevator), interior corridors.

Rated: 3 Paws — 32 units.

The Wilson Inn features modern, very attractive, fully equipped one- and two-bedroom suites and loft units. Each of the units comes with kitchen and each suite is comfortable and spacious. Essex Junction, in northwest Vermont, is a suburb of the largest city in Vermont, Burlington, population 30,100. Burlington Square Mall features more than 40 stores. The area was first settled in 1775, but most folks left when the Revolution started, and they didn't return until after the war. The city's oldest section is along Battery Street, near the lakefront. Church Street Marketplace is a four block pedestrian mall in the historic district. The Ethan Allen Homestead was once the home of the famous Revolutionary, and Ethan Allen Park includes part of the farm he once owned. The Robert Hull Fleming Museum, on the University of Vermont campus, displays European, American, African, Ancient Egyptian, and Middle Eastern art.

The Inn At Buck Hollow Farm

2150 Buck Hollow Road
Fairfax, VT 05454
802-849-2400

Type of Lodging: Historic Bed & Breakfast

Room Rates: $59–$89, including full breakfast, AAA discounts.

Pet Charges and Deposits: None,

Pet Policy: Manager's prior approval required, pets on premises.

Amenities: Extended cable TV, irons, heated pool, whirlpools, cross-country skiing, hiking trails, playground, smoke-free premises, radios, data port/modem telephones, some VCR's, 2 stories, interior corridors.

Rated: 3 Paws — 4 units.

The Inn at Buck Hollow Farm is a restored 1790 carriage house, located on 400 acres. There are some suites, some shared baths, and an antique shop right on the premises of this friendly, comfortable place. Fairfax is a small town, halfway between Burlington and Mount Mansfield—somewhat north of either of them. It's near Arrowhead Mountain Lake, and about 25 miles west of the Cold Hollow Mountains. Within a brief drive, you'll find numerous ski areas, including Mt. Mansfield, the highest point in Vermont (4,393 feet). Fairfax is situated in a year-round pleasure and recreation zone, with miles of untrammeled trails, paths, woods, ski trails, and water. It's northern Vermont at its very best.

Silver Maple Lodge & Cottages

520 U.S. 5 South
Fairlee, VT 05045
802-333-4326

Type of Lodging: Historic Bed & Breakfast

Room Rates: $59–$99, including full breakfast. AARP discounts.

Pet Charges and Deposits: None,

Pet Policy: Small pets only, in cottages only. Manager's prior approval required.

Amenities: Bicycles (fee), data port/modem telephones, some coffee makers, some refrigerators, some microwaves, 2 stories, interior/exterior corridors.

Rated: 3 Paws — 15 units.

The Silver Maple Lodge & Cottages is one of Vermont's oldest continuously operating country inns. The centerpiece of this historic property is an antique farmhouse dating to the late 1700's, which was expanded in the Victorian style in the 1800's. Choose from eight clean and cozy rooms in the original farmhouse, or one of the six handsome knotty pine cottage rooms. Each morning, guests enjoy breakfast highlighted by home-baked breads served in the dining room. Weather permitting, you may choose to relax on the huge wraparound screened porch, or under a shade tree. Attractions and activities nearby include cycling, canoeing, hiking, golf, hot air ballooning, fishing, swimming, tennis, antique shops, museums, theaters, dining, and crafts stores. Enjoy a full range of winter activities, including alpine and cross-country skiing, snowmobiling, and snowshoeing.

Three Mountain Inn

100 Main Street
Jamaica, VT 05343
802-874-4140

Type of Lodging: Historic County Inn

Room Rates: $129–$239, some suites $239–$269.

Pet Charges and Deposits: $75 fee.

Pet Policy: Designated units only.

Amenities: Hair dryers, some CD players, meeting rooms, restaurant, outdoor pool, radios, smoke-free premises, data port/modem telephones, some VCR's, 3 stories, interior/ exterior corridors.

Rated: 3 Paws — 15 units.

Three Mountain Inn is located in the heart of the historic village of Jamaica. This 1790's country inn surrounds you with a romantic, rustic ambience, with fireplaces, original wood plank walls, and antique furnishings. The inn is distinctive, with its white picket fence and attractively landscaped grounds. Guest units bespeak a more modern country décor, yet you'll find thick comforters, decorative accent pillows, excellent artwork, and a mix of antique and modern furniture. Tiny Jamaica is situated on State Highway 100, one of the loveliest in the state, in Green Mountain National Forest and moments away from Townshend Lake, Jamaica State Park, and Townshend Lake State Forest. Stratton Mountain (3,936 feet) and its adjacent ski area are just west of Jamaica. In summer, be sure to catch the Stratton Mountain Arts Festival.

Deer Run Motor Inn

80 Deer Run Loop
Jeffersonville, VT 05464
802-644-8866

Type of Lodging: Motel

Room Rates: $64–$74, AAA and AARP discounts.

Pet Charges and Deposits: $10 per day per pet.

Pet Policy: All pets welcome.

Amenities: Winter plug-ins, cable TV, charcoal grill, free local telephone calls, outdoor pool, coffee makers, refrigerators, data port/modem telephones, some microwaves, some radios, 2 stories, interior/exterior corridors.

Rated: 2 Paws — 25 rooms.

Deer Run Motor Inn, in a rural area, boasts excellent housekeeping and a clean, comfortable, very hospitable establishment. Jeffersonville is in the northwestern quadrant of the state, at the southwestern edge of the Cold Hollow Mountains. 30 miles to the northwest is St. Albans, nestled between Lake Champlain and the Green Mountains. Henry Ward Beecher once called it, "place in the midst of a greater variety of scenic beauty than any other I can remember in America." But the town was not always peaceful. St. Albans was a notorious center for smuggling operations in Lake Champlain in the early 1800's, and later became an important link on the underground railroad. The St. Albans Historical Museum, at Church and Bishop Streets, exhibits quilts, clothing, china, glass, and all manner of Revolutionary and Civil War memorabilia.

Butternut On The Mountain

63 Weathervane Road
Killington, VT 05751
802-422-2000
butternt@together.net

Type of Lodging: Motor Inn

Room Rates: $79–$309, including Continental breakfast, AAA discounts.

Pet Charges and Deposits: None.

Pet Policy: Prior approval required. Summer only.

Amenities: Winter plug-ins, extended cable TV, area transportation, coin laundry, free local telephone calls, restaurant, cocktails, data port/modem telephones, some VCR's, some refrigerators (fee), 2 stories, interior/exterior corridors.

Rated: 2 Paws — 18 units.

Butternut on the Mountain combines the charm of a country inn with the amenities and privacy of a fine hotel. Here you'll find private baths, in-room phones and color cable TV, an indoor heated pool, whirlpool, and a fireside library lounge. The Motor Inn gives you guest discounts to Mrs. Brady's Steak & Seafood Restaurant, and summer and fall saver packages. There are two large sections of Green Mountain National Forest, and Killington, no more than a mile or two from Sherburne Pass, sits squarely at the southeastern edge of the northern segment. Killington, along with Stowe, has become one of the premier skiing venues, not only of New England, but of the entire eastern half of the United States. Needless to say, this is also a center of all-year outdoor activities and a scenic wonderland in the Green Mountain State.

The Cascades Lodge & Restaurant

58 Old Mill Road
Killington, VT 05751
800-345-0113 • 802-422-3731
www.cascadeslodge.com
info@cascadeslodge.com

Type of Lodging: Motor Inn

Room Rates: $84–$204, including Continental breakfast, AAA, AARP, AKC, ABA, and *ask about Pets Welcome™* discounts.

Pet Charges and Deposits: $25 per day per pet.

Pet Policy: Pets welcome summer and fall only.

Amenities: Winter plug-ins, extended cable TV, voice mail, hair dryers, exercise room, reading room, area transportation, valet and coin laundry, massage (fee), heated pool, sauna, whirlpool, golf and skiing adjacent, hiking trails, radios, data port/modem telephones, some VCR's (fee), some coffee makers, some refrigerators (fee), 2-3 stories, interior corridors.

Rated: 3 Paws — 47 units.

Enjoy Vermont from The Cascades, a classic lodge where winter comes alive. This New England venue offers alpine or cross-country skiing, snowmobiling, snowshoeing, or ice skating. Admire nature's majestic mountain views from your private suite or from the award-winning dining room. Visit the on-site exercise room, relax by the indoor pool, or enjoy a whirlpool, sauna, or soothing massage. Two golf courses, shopping, and antiquing are all within a short walk. The restaurant offers a feast of fine food from country breakfast or gourmet dinners, to late-night snacks and tantalizing desserts. For more casual fare, visit the pub, which has a lighter menu and more than 50 ales and lagers.

Val Roc Motel

8006 U.S. 4
Killington, VT 05751
802-422-3881
www.valroc.com

Type of Lodging: Motel
Room Rates: $54—139, including continental breakfast. AAA and AARP discounts.
Pet Charges and Deposits: $5 per day per pet.
Pet Policy: All pets welcome.
Amenities: Extended cable TV, heated pool, whirlpool, tennis court, playground, coffee makers, refrigerators, data port/modem telephones, some microwaves, 1-2 stories, interior/exterior corridors.
Rated: 2 Paws — 24 rooms.

Val Roc Motel, affordably priced, clean, comfortable, and wholesome, is situated in a mountain valley one minute from the Killington Skyeship Gondola, close to golf courses, skiing, and area attractions. The lodging features an outdoor heated pool, hot tub, tennis and basketball, a playground, and a game room. Children under 12 stay free in their parents' room. Killington Resort is in the Calvin Coolidge State Forest. On the summit of Killington Peak, the Reverend Samuel Peters, a clergyman from Connecticut, claimed to have named the state "Verdmont" because, as he said, "her mountains and hills shall be ever green and shall never die." Today, this premier recreational site provides skiing, biking, hiking, tennis, and golf in the shadow of Sherburne Pass.

Rabbit Hill Inn

Lower Waterford Road
Lower Waterford, VT 05848
807-748-5168

Type of Lodging: Historic Country Inn
Room Rates: $329—379, some suites and whirlpool units, $385–$459, AAA discounts.
Pet Charges and Deposits: None.
Pet Policy: All pets welcome. (Pet on premises).
Amenities: Smoke-free premises, no TV's, CD players, irons, hair dryers, swimming, canoeing, fishing, golf privileges, cross-country skiing, hiking trails, video room, video library, restaurant, radios, coffee makers, data port/modem telephones, 3 stories, (no elevator) interior/exterior corridors.
Rated: 4 Paws — 21 rooms.

Rabbit Hill Inn is a handsome old New England inn. Its main house was built in 1825 and its annex was built even earlier, in 1795. The Inn is beautifully furnished and offers gracious, elegant hospitality. Swimming, canoeing, fishing, golf privileges, cross-country skiing, hiking trails, and forests are right out your front door, and when the sun goes down, you are invited to avail yourself of the video room and video library. Looking for a splendid restaurant? Look no further than the Rabbit Hill Dining Room, in the Inn. Reservations are required. Dining is a luxurious experience and the chef makes it a point to insure that the seasonally changed *prix fixe* menu features many exciting food combinations, featuring beef, chicken, vegetarian, fresh seafood, pasta, and wild game, all garnished with local ingredients. The candlelit experience is indeed memorable.

Cavendish Pointe Hotel

Route 103, Box 525
Ludlow, VT 05149
800-438-7908 • 802-226-7688

Type of Lodging: Hotel

Room Rates: $89–$179. AAA, AARP, AKC, and *ask about Pets Welcome™* discounts.

Pet Charges and Deposits: None.

Pet Policy: Manager's prior approval required.

Amenities: Extended cable TV, heated pool, whirlpool, sauna, conference facilities, restaurant, cocktails, 2 stories, interior corridors.

Rated: 3 Paws — 70 rooms.

The cupola atop the Cavendish Pointe Hotel at Okemo Mountain serves as the beacon for southern Vermont's largest and newest country hotel. Set amid the Green Mountains, the hotel offers oversized guest rooms, featuring pairs of queen- or king-sized beds and full baths. Handicapped-accessible rooms, including whirlpool baths or suites with bunk beds, are available upon request. The restaurant serves hearty, sumptuous meals, including a variety of entrees and specialties for children. Experience all four seasons in Vermont. Enjoy spectacular blazing autumn foliage while hiking, biking, or gondola riding. Spend a winter day on the slopes, or shopping for that special holiday gift. Warmer weather brings out the delights of maple syrup and swimming holes, while crafts fairs, concerts, theater, and outdoor entertainments round out summer's pleasures.

Combes Family Inn

953 East Lake Road
Ludlow, VT 05149
800-822-8799 • 802-228-8799
www.combesfamilyinn.com

Type of Lodging: Inn

Room Rates: $65–$135, including full breakfast.

Pet Charges and Deposits: $75 refundable deposit.

Pet Policy: All pets welcome.

Amenities: Lounge area, 1-2 stories, interior/exterior corridors.

Rated: 2 Paws — 11 rooms.

As the name indicates, this is a true family inn situated on a quiet country back road in the heart of Vermont's mountain and lake region. There are 50 acres of rolling meadows for you and your pet to explore. Built in 1891, the dairy farm supplied Ludlow and surrounding towns, and the sugar bushes yielded untold gallons of maple syrup. The Inn now offers a quiet respite, with homey ambience, good food, friendly hosts, and spectacular scenery. Cozy, country-inspired guest rooms, all with private bath, are scattered between the farmhouse and adjoining units. Meals at the Inn are hearty, Vermont style, with fresh home-baked goods and jams. The dining room has exposed beams and a large bay window overlooking the pastures and Okemo Mountain. You'll find swimming, boating, and fishing on Lake Rescue and Echo Lake, bicycling on country roads, hiking, picnicking, golf, tennis, and horseback riding nearby.

Happy Trails Motel

321 Route 103 South
Ludlow, VT 05149
802-228-8888
Email: happytm@tds.net

Type of Lodging: Motel

Room Rates: $59–$209, AAA and AARP discounts.

Pet Charges and Deposits: $25 per day per pet.

Pet Policy: Pets welcome summer and fall only.

Amenities: Winter plug-ins, extended cable TV, voice mail, hair dryers, exercise room, reading room, area transportation, valet and coin laundry, massage (fee), heated pool, sauna, whirlpool, golf and skiing adjacent, hiking trails, radios, data port/modem telephones, some VCR's (fee), some coffee makers, some refrigerators (fee), 2-3 stories, interior corridors.

Rated: 3 Paws — 47 units.

Happy Trails Motel, a wonderful middle-sized choice, affords you enticing, attractive lodgings in Ludlow. The location couldn't be better: it's 1½ miles from Okemo Mountain (3,343 feet). It's just 25 minutes from Rutland, in the heart of Okemo Valley. Located along the Black River, Ludlow offers views of mountain ranges, lakes, and fertile farmland. After the Civil War, Ludlow residents pioneered the manufacture of reworked wool to combat cloth shortages. The Black River Academy opened in 1885 and closed in 1938. Calvin Coolidge was an 1890 graduate. Today, the Black River Academy Museum contains manuscripts, photographs, and tools depicting life in the late 19th century in rural Ludlow.

Timber Inn Motel

112 Route 103 South
Ludlow, VT 05149
802-228-8666
Email: timberinn@tds.net

Type of Lodging: Motel

Room Rates: $69–$209, AAA and AARP discounts.

Pet Charges and Deposits: None.

Pet Policy: Small dogs only, sorry, no cats. Seasonal only.

Amenities: Extended cable TV, movies, two pools (one heated, one small), whirlpool, sauna, fishing (state fishing license required), playground, free local telephone calls, radios, some coffee makers, data port/modem telephones, some refrigerators, some microwaves, 2 stories, exterior corridors.

Rated: 3 Paws — 17 rooms and 1 suite.

The Timber Inn sits on 3½ acres, backed by the Black River and landscaped with apple, spruce, and balsam trees. Step out of your room and saturate yourself in spectacular views of Okemo Mountain in all its ever-changing landscape—vibrant green in spring and summer; gold, red, and orange in autumn; and frosty white in winter. Guest rooms are finished in cedar and knotty pine, and feature two double beds with private bath and separate vanity areas. A two-bedroom suite features a queen-sized bed in the main room, a set of bunk beds in the back bedroom, and a private bath. The "Mountain View" apartment is also available seasonally. For family fun, enjoy year-round activities at Plymouth State Park, located 15 minutes away. The quaint towns of Woodstock and Weston, as well as larger Manchester, are all close by for shopping and sightseeing.

Cortina Inn & Resort

103 U.S. 4
Mendon, VT 05751
802-773-3333
Email: cortina1@aol.com

Type of Lodging: Motor Inn

Room Rates: $129–$199, some whirlpool units, $209–$289, AAA, AARP, AKC, ABA, and *ask about Pets Welcome*™ discounts.

Pet Charges and Deposits: $5 per day per pet. $50 refundable deposit.

Pet Policy: Manager's prior approval required.

Amenities: Winter plug-ins, extended cable TV, heated pool, whirlpool, sauna, fishing, 8 tennis courts, ice skating, nature trails, playground, snowmobiling (fee) bicycles (fee), area transportation, valet and coin laundry, massage (fee), meeting rooms, restaurant, radios, data port/modem telephones, some VCR's (fee), some coffee makers, some refrigerators (fee), some microwaves (fee), 2 stories, interior corridors.

Rated: 3 Paws — 91 rooms and 6 suites.

The Cortina Inn, located amidst Vermont's scenic beauty, blends hospitality and cozy charm with the luxury of a fine resort. Each room is decorated individually and offers fresh, fragrant flowers, brass beds, and handmade quilts. In some of the deluxe rooms, you can warm yourself by the fireplace or enjoy the scenic beauty surrounding your inn from your balcony or terrace. Center Court, where a fire blazes, is one of the common areas where guests can enjoy a game of backgammon or bridge. The restaurant serves a sumptuous array of foods rich in flavor, artfully prepared, and served in the elegant dining room. Stroll through the Mountain Art Gallery to view works of acclaimed regional artists. Besides golf and tennis, seasonal activities include snowmobiling, sleigh rides, ice skating, and snowshoeing in winter, and fabulous mountain biking, hiking, and fly fishing in summer.

Edelweiss Motel & Chalets

119 U.S. Route 4
Mendon, VT 05701
800-479-2863 • 802-775-5577

Type of Lodging: Motel

Room Rates: $50–$120. AAA and AARP discounts.

Pet Charges and Deposits: $5 per day per pet.

Pet Policy: Designated units only. Manager's prior approval required.

Amenities: Winter plug-ins, satellite TV, movies, heated pool, whirlpool, sauna, data port/modem telephones, some refrigerators, some microwaves, some coffee makers, 1 story, exterior corridors.

Rated: 2 Paws — 37 rooms and 8 suites.

Located in the Green Mountains, this year-round resort offers motel accommodations with a lodge atmosphere. The newly remodeled rooms feature in-room coffee, and private baths. Many units can accommodate five or six comfortably. Connecting units and efficiency apartments are available upon request. The large heated pool is a welcome pleasure after volleyball, badminton, or horseshoes. You'll also find a picnic area, complete with grill. Children will enjoy the large swing, slide, and trapeze on the grounds. During winter months, breakfast is served in the rustic lobby next to a cozy fire. The magnificent surrounding countryside offers hiking, golf, tennis, boating, fishing, and horseback riding. Be sure to take a ride on North America's longest ski lift, Killington's 3½-mile gondola, minutes from the lodge. The Pico Alpine Slide is a thrill for the whole family.

Econo Lodge–Killington Area

51 U.S. 4
Mendon, VT 05701
802-773-6644

Type of Lodging: Motel

Room Rates: $44–$109. AAA and AARP discounts.

Pet Charges and Deposits: None.

Pet Policy: All pets welcome.

Amenities: Winter plug-ins, extended cable TV, outdoor pool, whirlpool, game room, small library, gift shop, meeting rooms, data port/modem telephones, some coffee makers, some refrigerators, some microwaves, 2 stories, interior corridors.

Rated: 2 Paws — 30 rooms.

Econo Lodge, member of a worldwide chain, offers affordable, clean, dependable rooms in the fabled Killington-Mendon area. It's 11 miles from Killington in the east, to Mendon in the west, over the Sherburne Pass, but the entire "conurbation" (if you want to call it that) is a haven for skiers, sportsmen, and outdoor enthusiasts of every kind. Pico Peak (3,957 feet) and Killington Peak (4,235 feet) offer some of the best skiing in the eastern United States. Coolidge State Forest is just east of Mendon, and the "big city" of Rutland, population 18,200, is just west of Mendon. This is a year-round recreational wonderland, situated in the midst of the Green Mountain National Forest.

Mendon Mountainview Resort Lodge

78 U.S. 4
Mendon, VT 05751
802-773-4311

Type of Lodging: Motor Inn

Room Rates: $49–$159, some whirlpool units. AAA discounts.

Pet Charges and Deposits: $50 deposit.

Pet Policy: All pets welcome.

Amenities: Winter plug-ins, extended cable TV, heated pool, whirlpool, sauna, nature trails, restaurant, cocktails, radios, coffee makers, data port/modem telephones, some VCR's (fee), 3 stories, interior corridors.

Rated: 3 Paws — 40 rooms.

Mendon Mountainview Resort Lodge has 40 rooms, six of them boasting fireplaces. There are some whirlpool units and a fine restaurant that provides you with well-prepared, hearty mountain fare. You'll experience the refreshment of a heated pool after trekking nature trails in the immediate area, or, if that sounds too cool, immerse yourself in saunas or whirlpools on the premises. Mendon-Killington, located on scenic U.S. Route 4, provides something for everyone, unless you look forward to the crush of people. Of course, if that's your "thing," just wait around 'til winter when skiers dominate the landscape. It's a beautiful, year-round resort area—certainly one of the finest in New England.

Red Clover Inn

7 Woodward Road
Mendon, VT 05701
800-752-0571 • 802-775-2290
E-mail: redclovr@vermontel.com

Type of Lodging: Inn

Room Rates: $120–$375, including full breakfast and gourmet dinner.

Pet Charges and Deposits: $5 per day per pet and 50% refundable deposit.

Pet Policy: Manager's prior approval required.

Amenities: Heated pool, whirlpool, award-winning restaurant, cocktails, 2 stories, interior/exterior corridors.

Rated: 3 Paws — 14 rooms on 13 picturesque acres.

General John Woodward built the Red Clover Inn as a private retreat in 1840. Once inside, the Inn feels like a large, cozy home with comfortable furniture, exposed wood beams, and a roaring fire in the fieldstone fireplace. Guest rooms are beautifully appointed, with private baths. Many rooms boast fireplaces, whirlpools, and picturesque mountain views. Awake to a country breakfast of fresh fruits and home-cooked delights, such as Cinnamon Swirl French Toast, served in the sunlit breakfast room. Dinner offerings feature innovative and traditional American cuisine by candlelight, complemented by an award-winning wine list. The Red Clover Inn is convenient to Killington and the Pico Mountains, minutes away. Cross-country ski on well-groomed trails during winter. In the warmer months, swim in the knoll-top pool, hike, bike, or horseback ride the Appalachian or Long Trail.

The Middlebury Inn

14 Court Square
Middlebury, VT 05753
800-842-4666 • 802-388-4961
Email: midinnvt@sover.net

Type of Lodging: Historic Country Inn

Room Rates: $88–$260, some whirlpool units, including Continental Breakfast. AAA and AARP discounts.

Pet Charges and Deposits: $6 per day per pet. $50 refundable deposit.

Pet Policy: Small dogs and cats only. Manager's prior approval required.

Amenities: Winter plug-ins, extended cable TV, hairdryers, gift shop, afternoon tea, meeting rooms, free local telephone calls, restaurant, cocktails, health club adjacent, radios, data port/modem telephones, some coffee makers, some refrigerators, 1-4 stories, interior/exterior corridors.

Rated: 3 Paws — 75 rooms.

A fine old inn in a lovely, lively college town, the Middlebury Inn features wide hallways, high ceilings, cozy little libraries and sitting areas, hand-cut lampshades, and antique beds. The Middlebury Inn has presided over happenings in Addison County's shire town since 1827, welcoming guests for more than 170 years. There are 75 recently redecorated rooms from which to choose, ranging from historic to contemporary, all with private baths. Each area has its own charm, combining traditions of the past with present-day amenities. Located conveniently at a crossroads, visitors can enjoy Lake Champlain, the Green Mountains, and the nearby Shelbourne Museum.

Seymour Lake Lodge

RR 1, Box 61
Morgan, VT 05853
802-895-2752

Type of Lodging: Lodge
Room Rates: $54–$95.
Pet Charges and Deposits: None.
Pet Policy: All pets welcome.
Amenities: 2 stories, interior/exterior corridors.
Rated: 2 Paws — 7rooms.

Seymour Lake Lodge offers you the opportunity to relax, unwind, and listen to the loons. At day's end, sit on the large porch and enjoy the beautiful setting sun and peaceful views of the lake. The Lodge can accommodate 16 guests in 7 comfortable, private bedrooms, with either shared or private bath. Delicious home-cooked meals are served daily, and special dietary concerns are carefully noted. One of Vermont's most beautiful lakes, Seymour Lake has year-round activities with a boat launch nearby and guided fishing tours available. Recreational opportunities abound, with canoeing, hiking, even swimming during warm weather. Just above the lake is a wilderness area, where several waterways offer a glimpse into a wildlife fantasy, and you can see Vermont's loons, ducks, partridge, beaver, deer, and even the occasional moose.

Four Columns Inn

21 West Street
Newfane, VT 05345
802-365-7713

Type of Lodging: Historic Country Inn
Room Rates: $119–$179, some whirlpool units $195–$345. AAA and AARP discounts.
Pet Charges and Deposits: $10 per day per pet.
Pet Policy: All pets welcome.
Amenities: No TVs, hairdryers, hiking trails, outdoor pool, restaurant, radio's, smoke-free premises, 2-3 stories (no elevator), interior corridors.
Rated: 3 Paws — 15 rooms.

Housed in an 1832 Greek-revival style mansion, the Four Columns Inn is a wonderfully comfortable, welcoming place. There are miles of hiking trails all around the Inn. Its dining room is legendary in the area. Reservations are suggested and dressy casual is appropriate. Set in the confines of this charming country inn, the dining room exhibits a refined ambience, with a rustic French country theme, followed in its design. The food is internationally influenced cuisine, with features a refined ambience, with fresh Vermont produce used whenever possible. Each dish is skillfully presented and excellently prepared, with rich, mature sauces, and a variety of fresh herbs and spices. The menu includes fresh seafood, duck, lamb, venison, chicken, and prime steak.

Inn At The Hill

1724 E. Main Street
Newport, VT 05855
802-334-6611

Type of Lodging: Complex

Room Rates: $59–$89, including Continental breakfast. AAA and AARP discounts.

Pet Charges and Deposits: $10 per day per pet.

Pet Policy: Limited units only.

Amenities: Smoke-free premises, cross-country skiing, video library, valet and coin laundry, restaurant adjacent, VCR's data port/modem telephones, some refrigerators, 3 stories (no elevator), interior/exterior corridors.

Rated: 2 Paws — 15 units.

The attractive, cozy rooms at Inn At The Hill are contained in a Victorian-style inn, with separate motel and cottage units. The grounds are very well maintained, and the ambience is lovely. Newport, about as far north as you can get in central Vermont, is a gateway between New England and Canada. The city is situated on the southern shore of Lake Memphremagog, whose name is derived from the Abenaki Native American word for "beautiful waters." You can get impressive views of two countries from the summit of 3,360-foot high Owl's Head, on the western side of the 32-mile-long lake. On Prospect Hill, the granite towers of St. Mary's Star of the Sea Church rise above the city.

Shore Acres Inn

237 Shore Acres Drive
North Hero, VT 05474
802-372-8722

Type of Lodging: Motor Inn

Room Rates: $89–$169. AAA and AARP discounts.

Pet Charges and Deposits: $10 per day for first night, $5 per day for additional nights.

Pet Policy: All pets welcome.

Amenities: Beach swimming, boat dock, fishing, target golf course, two tennis courts, shuffleboard, croquet, lawn games, restaurant, radios, data port/modem telephones, some refrigerators, some microwaves, 1-2 stories, exterior corridors.

Rated: 2 Paws — 23 rooms.

Shore Acres Inn is located on an island in Lake Champlain, well back from the highway. Between November 1 and April 30, only four of the 23 units are available. It's a comfortable, well-located lodging that offers beach swimming, a boat dock, fishing, a target golf course, two tennis courts, and a miscellany of lawn games. The Shore Acres Restaurant specializes in fresh grilled fish, steak and chops, homemade bread, pastry, and dessert. The décor is cozy New England, and the site overlooks Lake Champlain. The drive from Burlington on the mainland to the Canadian frontier at Alburg, is intriguing. U.S. Highway 2 becomes a causeway as it leaves the mainland at Sand Bar State Park and heads into the Grand Isle area of the huge lake. The first "city" you hit is South Hero, then you traverse the lake to another island, where you'll find North Hero. It's more island before you hit the mainland once again, at South Alburg.

Johnny Seesaw's

State Route 11,
P.O. Box 68
Peru, VT 05152
802-824-5533

Type of Lodging: Lodge

Room Rates: $79–$199

Pet Charges and Deposits: $10 per day per pet.

Pet Policy: All pets welcome.

Amenities: Tennis court, restaurant, outdoor pool, data port/modem telephones, some refrigerators, 2 stories, interior/ exterior corridors.

Rated: 2 Paws — 22 rooms.

Johnny Seesaw's is about as country-rural as you can get, even in sparsely populated Vermont. You'll find simple, but comfortable rooms, an outdoor pool, and a tennis court. Peru is on State Route 11, in the southern section of Green Mountain National Forest. Less than ten miles to the east, in Londonderry, you'll yodel praises for the Swiss Inn Dining Room, with its friendly, knowledgeable service and excellent, flavorful food. The fare includes an assortment of fondues, and you must not miss the veal in white wine cream sauce. Ten miles west is Manchester, a year-round resort guarded on the west by Mount Equinox (3,816 feet), the highest peak in the Taconic Range. Hildene, a Georgian Revival mansion, was the summer home of Robert Todd Lincoln, the only son of Abraham Lincoln to live to maturity. His descendants lived here until 1975.

Pittsfield Inn

P.O. Box 685
Pittsfield, VT 05762
802-746-8943

Type of Lodging: Country Inn

Room Rates: $45–$70, including full breakfast.

Pet Charges and Deposits: $10 per day per pet. $50 refundable deposit.

Pet Policy: Manager's prior approval required.

Amenities: Restaurant, 2 stories, interior corridors.

Rated: 2 Paws — 8 rooms and 1 suite.

This classic country inn, nestled in the heart of the Green Mountains, offers guests comfortable accommodations complemented by delicious meals, always made from the freshest, finest ingredients. The recent restoration has recaptured the original grandeur, with comfortable beds, warm quilts, and private baths. Situated on 3½ acres of wilderness, the Inn provides an escape to outdoor fun and adventure. The year-round activities include skiing, sleigh rides, and snowshoeing in winter, and mountain biking, hiking, fly fishing, and golf in fair weather. If culture is your pleasure, you have the opportunity to visit numerous local historic sites or browse the antique shops in Pittsfield.

Tower Hall Bed & Breakfast

2 Bentley Avenue
Poultney, VT 05764
800-894-4004 • 802-287-4004
E-mail: towerhal@sover.net

Type of Lodging: Bed & Breakfast

Room Rates: $69–$89, including Continental breakfast.

Pet Charges and Deposits: $5 per day per pet. $60 refundable deposit.

Pet Policy: Dogs only, sorry, no cats. Manager's prior approval required.

Amenities: 2 stories (no elevator), interior corridors.

Rated: 2 Paws — 3 rooms.

Enjoy the ambience of a century-old Victorian charmer with stained glass, original woodwork and mantles, imposing staircase, and wraparound porch. Three guest rooms with private baths offer the warmth and comfort of antique and period furniture. The common area features a piano and a cozy fireplace, where guests can relax, read, or socialize. Morning begins with a bountiful breakfast served in the sunny dining room. Adjacent to Green Mountain College and near two state parks, the surrounding area offers activities for every season. Tower Hall is located minutes from Lake St. Catherine, which features a nature center and nature trails, as well as overnight camping, picnicking, boating, and water activities.

The Putney Inn

57 Putney Landing Road
Putney, VT 05346
802-387-5517
www.putneyinn.com

Type of Lodging: Motor Inn

Room Rates: $79–$165, including full breakfast. AAA and AARP discounts.

Pet Charges and Deposits: $10 per day per pet.

Pet Policy: All pets welcome.

Amenities: Restaurant, radios, coffee makers, data port/modem telephones, some VCR's, 2 stories, exterior corridors.

Rated: 3 Paws — 25 rooms.

The Putney Inn is a country-style place, set well back from the highway, yet with easy access. The large front porch, which runs the entire length of the front façade, has wooden rockers, so you can sit and watch the beautiful world go by. It's a place where you'll find memorable food, memorable company, and exceptional lodging. Putney just up the road from Brattleboro. Always a bastion of conservatism, it was shocked in 1838 when John Humphrey Noyes set up his experimental community based on "perfectionism." What was so shocking was that one of the major tenets of "perfectionism" was "complex marriage," translation: free love. It was not long before the perfectionists got booted out of the community. More than 100 years later, in the early 1960's, Putney made its next rocket-like move into the future: it allowed summer residents to wear shorts.

Best Western Inn and Suites

Route 4 East
Rutland, VT 05701
802-773-3200

Type of Lodging: Motor Inn
Room Rates: $99–$199, including Continental breakfast. AAA and AARP discounts.
Pet Charges and Deposits: $25 fee, $5 per day per pet.
Pet Policy: All pets welcome.
Amenities: Winter plug-ins, extended cable TV, hairdryers, some irons, heated pool, two tennis courts, exercise room, coin laundry, meeting rooms, free local telephone calls,, restaurant adjacent, radios, data port/modem telephones, some VCR's (fee), some coffee makers, some refrigerators, some microwaves, 2 stories, exterior corridors.
Rated: 3 Paws — 112 units.

In addition to its standard, clean, comfortable motel rooms, Best Western—Rutland affords one- and two-bedroom housekeeping apartments with private balconies. You'll also find a heated pool, 2 tennis courts, and an exercise room. Rutland is the closest city to the recreational communities of Killington and Mendon. It's headquarters for Green Mountain National Forest. The state's oldest continuously published newspaper, the Rutland Herald, was founded in 1794. The Norman Rockwell Museum on U.S. Highway 4, contains a large collection of Rockwell's work. The more than 2,500 reproductions displayed include illustrations for children's books from 1912, advertisements, and magazine covers. Rockwell evokes the memory of simpler, happier times for all of us.

Econo Lodge

238 S. Main Street
Rutland, VT 05701
802-773-2784

Type of Lodging: Motel
Room Rates: $44–$134. AAA and AARP discounts.
Pet Charges and Deposits: None.
Pet Policy: All pets welcome.
Amenities: Winter plug-ins, extended cable TV, restaurant adjacent, coffee makers, data port/modem telephones, 2 stories, exterior corridors.
Rated: 2 Paws — 54 rooms.

Econo Lodge is clean, simple, comfortable, and affordable—and remarkably placed at the western entrance to the Green Mountain National Forest. Rutland is known as the "Marble City" because of its quarrying activities. This industrial town cannot escape the magnificent beauty of its surroundings—15 miles from the Mendon-Killington resort areas, Rutland is surrounded by the Taconic Mountains to the west, and Killington, Pico, and Shrewsbury mountains to the east. The Chaffee Center for the Visual Arts, containing ten galleries devoted to the work of Vermont artists, is housed in an elegant Victorian mansion. Lake Bomoseen to the West offers all manner of water recreation. Lake Bomoseen State Park, on the west side of the lake, is near the New York border.

Greenmont Motel

138 North Main Street
Rutland, VT 05701
802-775-2575

Type of Lodging: Motel

Room Rates: $44–$129. AAA and AARP discounts.

Pet Charges and Deposits: None.

Pet Policy: All pets welcome.

Amenities: Winter plug-ins, extended cable TV, movies, outdoor pool, free local telephone calls, data port/modem telephones, some VCR's, some refrigerators, 2 stories, exterior corridors.

Rated: 2 Paws — 29 rooms.

Well-priced, affordable Greenmont Motel is convenient to Rutland Fairgrounds, as well as to the downtown area. You get fine views from anywhere in town, surrounded as it is by mountains and forest. In addition to being so close to the Mendon and Killington resort areas, you'll find a number of exciting restaurants in Rutland. A dependable venue throughout New England is the Weathervane Seafood Restaurant, and the Rutland unit is certainly no exception. This reasonably priced restaurant features excellent seafood with a delicious fish or clam chowder, lobster roll, and blue points. The Countryman's Pleasure Restaurant, a charming 19th century farmhouse-style restaurant, invites you to savor fine Austrian-German cuisine, including venison, duck, veal medallions, and sauerbraten. The chef-owner makes sure there's an ample supply of Austrian and German beers and wines.

Holiday Inn

476 U.S. 7 South
Rutland, VT 05701
800-462-4810 • 802-775-1911
Email: reservations@holidayinn.com

Type of Lodging: Motor Inn

Room Rates: $139–$299. AAA and AARP discounts.

Pet Charges and Deposits: $10 per day per pet.

Pet Policy: All pets welcome.

Amenities: Winter plug-ins, extended cable TV, movies (fee), voice mail, irons, hairdryers, heated pool, whirlpools, sauna, area transportation, valet laundry, conference facilities, P.C., fax, kids eat and sleep free with parents, restaurant, radios, coffee makers, data port/modem telephones, some refrigerators (fee), some microwaves (fee), 2 stories, interior corridors.

Rated: 3 Paws — 150 rooms.

The Centre of Vermont Holiday Inn in Rutland offers outstanding facilities, excellent service, and a convenient, central location. The well-appointed guest rooms are warm and comfortably furnished. Start your day with one of many hearty Vermont breakfasts, featuring fresh, home-baked goods served with Vermont maple syrup. After the sun goes down, Centre Stage comes alive with dancing, entertainment, and fabulous refreshments. Centre Sport is a 6,500 square foot sports and leisure area with heated lap pool, two whirlpool spas, sauna, exercise facilities, and activities. Located in the heart of central Vermont's renowned four-season resort area, the Centre offers year-round activities. Nearby activities include the Vermont Marble Exhibit, Wilson Castle, New England Maple Museum, Norman Rockwell Museum, and the Calvin Coolidge Homestead.

Howard Johnson

401 State Route 7
Rutland, VT 05701
802-775-4303

Type of Lodging: Motel

Room Rates: $64–$154. AAA and AARP discounts.

Pet Charges and Deposits: None.

Pet Policy: All pets welcome.

Amenities: Winter plug-ins, extended cable TV, movies, heated pool, sauna, game room, coin laundry, restaurant and health club adjacent, radios, coffee makers, data port/modem telephones, microwaves (fee), some refrigerators (fee), 2 stories, interior corridors.

Rated: 2 Paws — 99 rooms.

HoJo gives you cozy-to-larger rooms, each with a balcony or patio, at a reasonable price for the Rutland-Killington area. There are actually three Rutlands—West Rutland, Center Rutland, and Rutland, which is located at the western terminus of the most beautiful portion of U.S. Highway 4. Pittsford, about ten miles north of Rutland, is proud of its four covered bridges. The first patent in the United States was granted to Rutland resident Samuel Hopkins for devising a way to create potash and pearl ash out of wood ash, for making soap. The New England Maple Museum offers self-guided tours describing the maple sugaring process since Native American times. Dioramas, antiques, and a slide show tell the history of "sweet water."

Ramada Limited of Rutland

253 S. Main Street
Rutland, VT 05701
802-773-3361

Type of Lodging: Motel

Room Rates: $64–$164, including Continental breakfast. AAA and AARP discounts.

Pet Charges and Deposits: None.

Pet Policy: All pets welcome.

Amenities: Extended cable TV, movies, voice mail, irons, hairdryers, heated pool, valet laundry, meeting rooms, free local telephone calls, radios, data port/modem telephones, some coffee makers, some refrigerators and some microwaves, 2 stories, interior corridors.

Rated: 2 Paws — 60 rooms.

Ramada Limited is a clean, comfortable, attractive place to stay if you want to be close to the Mendon-Killington resort area, yet enjoy the amenities of a larger city. With so much to do within such a close area, travelers generally don't wander much farther than a half-hour radius from Rutland. That's fine, because there are enough fine restaurants that you can eat out every night of your holiday. Cottage-style dining, complete with flowers, candles, wood pedestal tables, and a private dining room await you at Royal's 121 Hearthside Restaurant. A specialty here is sole with caper sauce, complemented by golden au gratin potatoes and a fresh medley of zucchini, tomatoes and mushrooms. Sirloin Saloon has a salad bar with organic vegetables, steaks, of course, and a fun, turn-of-the century atmosphere.

Royal Motel

115 Woodstock Avenue
Rutland, VT 05701
802-773-9176

Type of Lodging: Motel

Room Rates: $41–$115. AAA and AARP discounts.

Pet Charges and Deposits: $10 per day per pet.

Pet Policy: All pets welcome.

Amenities: Winter plug-ins, extended cable TV, movies, some rooms with steam bath, coin laundry, free local telephone calls, restaurant adjacent, outdoor pool, data port/modem telephones, some refrigerators, some microwaves, 1-2 stories, interior/exterior corridors.

Rated: 2 Paws — 31 rooms.

Some of the rooms in the Royal Motel have steam baths. Some have whirlpool baths. All are clean, attractive, and comfortable. At Rutland's South Station, a modern, stylish restaurant, you can indulge yourself in a salad bar with 35 offerings and a potato salad that's well-worth breaking your diet for. It's in the Trolley Barn center, and reservations are strongly recommended. The Bistro Café offers an Old World dining experience with classics like chicken piccata, poached salmon, roasted duck breast, and fresh nightly seafood specials. There are few cities in the northeast as scenic as Rutland, surrounded, as it is, by glorious green mountains on every side.

Econo Lodge

287 S. Main Street
St. Albans, VT 05478
802-524-5956

Type of Lodging: Motel

Room Rates: $54–$99, including Continental breakfast. AAA and AARP discounts.

Pet Charges and Deposits: $25 deposit, $10 per day per pet.

Pet Policy: All pets welcome.

Amenities: Winter plug-ins, extended cable TV, movies, hairdryers, free local telephone calls, refrigerators, data port/modem telephones, some radios, some coffee makers, 1-2 stories, interior/exterior corridors.

Rated: 2 Paws — 29 rooms.

Econo Lodge affords simply furnished, clean, affordable rooms, guaranteed to give you a good night's rest. St. Albans, 20 miles south of the Canadian border, was a notorious smuggling center in the early 1800's, an important stop on the Underground Railroad in the 1840's and 1850's, and the headquarters of the New England Central Railway today. Its industries include dairy products, maple syrup, sugar-making equipment, ice cream, and batteries. Farther north, Swanton was an even better known smuggling center. During the War of 1812, enterprising Vermonters drove cattle across the border into Canada and sold them to the British. During the days of Prohibition of the twentieth century, there was a reversal of direction: liquor was run into the states from Canada by automobile.

Fairbanks Inn

401 Western Avenue
St. Johnsbury, VT 05819
802-748-5666

Type of Lodging: Motel

Room Rates: $64–$129. some suites: $180–$230, some whirlpool units: $105–$155, including morning refreshments. AAA and AARP discounts.

Pet Charges and Deposits: $5 per day per pet.

Pet Policy: All pets welcome.

Amenities: Extended cable TV, movies, heated pool, valet laundry, meeting rooms, health club adjacent, radios, data port/modem telephones, some VCR's, some coffee makers, some refrigerators, some microwaves, 3 stories (no elevator), exterior corridors.

Rated: 3 Paws — 46 units.

The Fairbanks Inn is situated in a pleasant setting with spacious grounds extending to Sleeper's Brook. Units are quite spacious, and some have private balconies. St. Johnsbury's location is defined by differing elevations. The Moose River Valley, Sleeper's River Valley, and Passumpsic River Valley all converge here. Thaddeus Fairbanks invented the platform scale in 1830. Then George Cary came up with the idea of flavoring plug tobacco with maple sugar. The town prospered with the success of both these ideas. St. Johnsbury is the industrial, retail, and cultural center of Vermont's Northeast Kingdom. The St. Johnsbury Athenaeum Art Gallery contains paintings by 19th century artists, emphasizing the Hudson River School. A highlight of the Gallery is Albert Bierstadt's monumental painting, "The Domes of the Yosemite."

Holiday Motel

222 Hastings Street
St. Johnsbury, VT 05819
802-748-8192

Type of Lodging: Motel

Room Rates: $41–$99, some suites.

Pet Charges and Deposits: $10 per day per pet.

Pet Policy: Small dogs only, sorry, no cats. Designated units only.

Amenities: Extended cable TV, voice mail, heated pool, valet laundry, restaurant adjacent, health club adjacent, data port/modem telephones, 1 story, exterior corridors.

Rated: 2 Paws — 68 rooms.

You'll find nicely furnished, comfortable units at the Holiday Motel. Its highway location is convenient, and the grounds are well maintained and in the midst of a wooded area. St. Johnsbury's Maple Grove Maple Museum has maple exhibits and a film showing the sugaring process. The Old Sugar House demonstrates the process of boiling down maple sap. The Fairbanks Museum and Planetarium includes more than 4,500 mounted birds and mammals, art and antiques, and crafts tools. The 1892 building was designed by noted architect Lambert Packard to house the collection of the Fairbanks family, whose progenitor, Thaddeus Fairbanks, invented the platform scale. There are planetarium shows daily at 11:00 a.m. and 1:30 p.m.

Yankee Doodle Motel

3972 Shelburne Road
Shelburne, VT 05482
802-985-8004

Type of Lodging: Motel
Room Rates: $39–$129
Pet Charges and Deposits: None.
Pet Policy: All pets welcome.
Amenities: Cable TV, outdoor pool, data port/modem telephones, some refrigerators, some radios, some microwaves, 1 story, exterior corridors.
Rated: 2 Paws — 15 rooms.

The Yankee Doodle Motel is housed in a Colonial style building. The place exhibits a home-like atmosphere, with rooms in a variety of sizes and styles. Shelburne is perfectly located, with the Adirondack Mountains to the west and the Green Mountains to the east. It was settled in 1768 by two German lumbermen and later named for an English earl. The Shelburne Museum is a standout attraction in the Green Mountain state. 36 historic structures have been moved from all over New England to a 45-acre site on U.S. 7. When you enter the living museum, you enter the 18th and 19th centuries. The Vermont Teddy Bear Company offers a glimpse of the step-by-step process used in making the jointed Teddy bears. Shelburne Farms is a 1,400-acre working farm, national historical site, and environmental center.

Anchorage Inn

108 Dorset Street
South Burlington, VT 05403
802-863-7000
www.vtanchorageinn.com

Type of Lodging: Motel
Room Rates: $59–$109, including Continental breakfast. AAA and AARP discounts.
Pet Charges and Deposits: $50, deposit.
Pet Policy: Dogs only, sorry, no cats.
Amenities: Winter plug-ins, extended cable TV, movies, some hair dryers, heated pool, whirlpool, sauna, barbeque grill, free local telephone calls, restaurant adjacent, radios, data port/modem telephones, some coffee makers, some refrigerators (fee), some microwaves (fee), 3 stories (no elevator), interior corridors.
Rated: 2 Paws — 89 rooms.

Anchorage Inn is conveniently located across from a shopping mall. One of Burlington's best lodging values, it affords attractive, well-furnished rooms, an indoor pool, sauna, and whirlpool, free continental breakfast, and discounted ski packages with all northern Vermont resorts. Burlington, Vermont's largest city, is built on terraced slopes above Lake Champlain. It's a principal port of entry on the United States-Canada border. Battery Park was the 1812 scene of an engagement between U.S. land batteries and British vessels on Lake Champlain. Cactus Pete's Steak House & Saloon has a festive, lively Western-saloon atmosphere. The menu has a great variety of finger foods, burgers, steak, ribs—you get the picture—as well as a good selection of domestic and imported beer.

Best Western Windjammer Inn

1076 Williston Road
South Burlington, VT 05403
802-863-1125

Type of Lodging: Motor Inn

Room Rates: $79–$199, some suites $145–$199, including Continental breakfast; AAA and AARP discounts.

Pet Charges and Deposits: $5 per day per pet.

Pet Policy: All pets welcome.

Amenities: Winter plug-ins, extended cable TV, movies (fee), video games, hair dryers, irons, two pools, one heated, one indoor, whirlpool, sauna, nature trails, exercise room, airport transportation, valet and coin laundry, conference facilities, free local telephone calls, restaurant, radios, data port/modem telephones, some VCR's (fee), some coffee makers, some refrigerators (fee), some microwaves (fee), 2 stories, interior corridors.

Rated: 3 Paws — 173 units, including rooms and suites.

Best Western Windjammer Inn features clean, well-maintained units, set back from the main road, so you'll enjoy a quiet, restful sleep. The Ethan Allen Homestead contains a timber frame house and several acres of land traversed by hiking trails. Ethan Allen Park includes part of the farm once owned by Ethan Allen. A tower on the property offers fine views of Lake Champlain and the Adirondack Mountains. Pauline's used to be a truck stop. Now it's an upscale nouvelle cuisine restaurant, highlighting the freshest local produce. Burlington is a convenient southern terminus for a trip to or from the Grand Isles in Lake Champlain. Believe it or not, it's not that far out of the way to drive up to Montreal, Quebec, Canada.

Clarion Hotel / Conference Center

1117 Williston Road
South Burlington, VT 05403
802-658-0250
www.clarion.com

Type of Lodging: Motor Inn

Room Rates: $65–$199, including Continental breakfast. AAA and AARP discounts.

Pet Charges and Deposits: None.

Pet Policy: All pets welcome.

Amenities: Winter plug-ins, extended cable TV, movies (fee), video games, voice mail, irons, hair dryers, heated pool, exercise room, gift shop, airport transportation, valet laundry, area transportation available (fee), conference facilities, administrative services, PC, fax, restaurant, cocktails, radios, coffee makers, data port/modem telephones, refrigerators, some VCR's, 2 stories, interior corridors.

Rated: 3 Paws — 130 rooms.

The Clarion Hotel & Conference Center affords good-sized rooms with very appealing décor. The furnishings are first class, and your comfort is assured. Lake Champlain varies from a quarter of a mile to 12 miles wide, and runs southward from Canada 120 miles. Legends of Lake Champlain's own version of the Loch Ness Monster have persisted since Samuel de Champlain sighted what he described as a serpent-like creature, 20 feet long, as thick as a barrel, and with a head like a horse. Occasional sightings of the elusive creature, nicknamed "Champ," still "occur" from time to time. Lake Champlain ferries offer scenic links between Vermont and New York via three crossings: Burlington-Port Kent, New York (1 hour), Charlotte to Essex, New York (20 minutes), and Grand Isle to Plattsburgh, New York (12 minutes).

Holiday Inn–Burlington

1068 Williston Road
South Burlington, VT 05403
802-863-6363
www.holiday/inn.com

Type of Lodging: Motor Inn

Room Rates: $89–$149; AAA and AARP discounts.

Pet Charges and Deposits: $10 per day per pet.

Pet Policy: Small pets only.

Amenities: Winter plug-ins, extended cable TV, movies (fee), dual phone lines, voice mail, irons, hair dryers, two heated pools, sauna, exercise room, airport transportation, area transportation, valet and coin laundry, conference facilities, free local telephone calls, free newspapers, restaurant, cocktails, radios, coffee makers, data port/modem telephones, some refrigerators, some microwaves, 4 stories, interior corridors.

Rated: 3 Paws — 173 rooms.

Holiday Inn offers attractive, comfortable, modern rooms, with an array of welcome amenities. Two heated pools, a sauna, and an exercise room keep you in top shape, and wonderfully firm beds give you a great rest. The Lake Champlain Islands and a peninsula in Lake Champlain form Grand Isle County. The islands form a picturesque summer resort area. From the "inland sea," you can see the Adirondack Mountains in the west and the Green Mountains to the east. St. Anne's Shrine in Isle LaMotte, is on the site of the first European settlement in Vermont. Herrmann's Royal Lipizzan Stallions spend the summer in nearby North Hero. The barn is open to the public when performances are not being held. Shows take place four times a week.

Sheraton–Burlington Hotel

870 Williston Road
South Burlington, VT 05403
802-865-6600
Email:
Sheraton_vermont@ittsheraton.com

Type of Lodging: Hotel

Room Rates: $169–$259; AAA and AARP discounts.

Pet Charges and Deposits: None.

Pet Policy: Small pets only.

Amenities: Winter plug-ins, extended cable TV, movies (fee), video games, voice mail, irons, hair dryers, heated pool, whirlpools, roof top sundeck, gift shop, valet laundry, conference facilities, administrative services, PC (fee), fax (fee), restaurant, cocktails, radios, coffee makers, data port/modem telephones, some VCR's (fee), some refrigerators (fee), some microwaves (fee), 2-4 stories, interior corridors.

Rated: 3 Paws — 109 rooms.

The Sheraton has just undergone a multi-million-dollar renovation, which means that its rooms and public areas have a fresh, new face. Luxuriously furnished and wonderfully comfortable, you'll enjoy award winning hospitality, an indoor pool and whirlpool, a fitness center and rooftop deck, and a fine restaurant and English pub. The Hyde Log Cabin, on Grand Isle in Lake Champlain, was built in 1783 and is considered the oldest log cabin in the nation. It is furnished with domestic items depicting rural life. Perry's Fish House at 1080 Shelburne Road in Burlington specializes in fresh seafood and steak. The menu also offers combination platters, pasta dishes, saltwater and freshwater fish, and delicious homemade Key lime pie.

Town & Country Motel

490 Shelburne Road
South Burlington, VT 05401
802-862-5786

Type of Lodging: Motel

Room Rates: $49–$99; AAA and AARP discounts.

Pet Charges and Deposits: $5 per day per pet.

Pet Policy: Dogs only, sorry, no cats.

Amenities: Extended cable TV, free local telephone calls, restaurant adjacent, data port/modem telephones, some refrigerators (fee), 1 story, exterior corridors.

Rated: 2 Paws — 12 rooms.

The Town & Country Motel affords price-conscious, simple, and pleasant guest units. You get everything you need for a good night's sleep in this small, nice little lodging. Shelburne Museum & Heritage Park is a must-see—37 buildings on 45 acres bring you back to the 18th and 19th centuries in a wondrous living history museum, where you'll spend the better part of the day. Burlington affords the best of mountains and an [inland] sea. From its position in Lake Champlain, it's ten miles to the closest ski area, Jonesville. Major downhill ski venues can be found less than an hour from Burlington at Mount Mansfield. It's only a little farther to legendary Stowe.

Holiday Inn Express

818 Charlestown Road
Springfield, VT 05156
802-885-4516

Type of Lodging: Motor Inn

Room Rates: $94–$134, some whirlpool units, $159–$199. AAA and AARP discounts.

Pet Charges and Deposits: None.

Pet Policy: Designated rooms only.

Amenities: Extended cable TV, movies (fee), video games, hair dryers, irons, heated pool, exercise room, valet and coin laundry, conference facilities, restaurant adjacent, radios, data port/modem telephones, some refrigerators, some microwaves, 2 stories, interior corridors.

Rated: 3 Paws — 88 rooms.

Holiday Inn Express offers clean, attractive, well-furnished rooms, including some whirlpool units. Springfield has been an industrial town since water-powered mills started operating in the late 18th and early 19th centuries. Though some mills still exist along the Black River, none of them use water power. Built in 1785, the restored 1785 Eureka Schoolhouse is one of the few remaining 18th century public buildings. It stands next to a 37-foot long covered bridge that was built in 1870. Springfield is in eastern Vermont, only a few miles to the Connecticut River, but it's still convenient to skiing at Okemo Mountain and Mount Ascutney, both less than an hour away. The Hartness House Dining Room is located in a comfortable country inn that's on the National Register of Historic Places. It's a locally popular restaurant that features New England cuisine.

Andersen Lodge—An Austrian Inn

3430 Mountain Road
Stowe, VT 05672
802-253-7336

Type of Lodging: Country Inn
Room Rates: $59–$189, including Continental breakfast. AAA and AARP discounts.
Pet Charges and Deposits: None.
Pet Policy: Small pets only.
Amenities: Winter plug-ins, heated pool, whirlpool, sauna, tennis court, cross country skiing, basketball, restaurant, data port/modem telephones, some VCR's, some refrigerators, 2 stories, interior corridors.
Rated: 2 Paws — 18 rooms.

The Andersen Lodge is an Austrian mountain lodge with large, comfortable public areas, and nicely decorated rooms, some larger than others. There's a wonderful European ambience to the place. When the von Trapp family ("The Sound of Music") emigrated from Austria and started a small ski resort, they could not have conceived that Stowe would one day become one of the premier ski venues in the United States. Located in the Green Mountains, Stowe offers year-round recreational activities. Today, there are 47 trails and slopes—some of the best runs on the east coast—in and around Stowe. The Stowe Recreation Path is a 5-mile scenic pathway that follows a mountain stream north toward Mount Mansfield, past corn fields, woodlands, pastures, and swimming holes.

Commodores Inn

823 Main Street
Stowe, VT 05672
802-253-7131
www.commodoresinn.com

Type of Lodging: Motor Inn
Room Rates: $69–$159, AAA and AARP discounts.
Pet Charges and Deposits: $10 per day per pet.
Pet Policy: All pets welcome.
Amenities: Winter plug-ins, two heated pools, whirlpools, saunas, canoeing, paddle boats, fishing, radio-controlled model sailboat races on pond, ice skating, exercise room, conference facilities, fax, free local telephone calls, restaurant, cocktails, radios, data port/modem telephones, some VCR's (fee), some refrigerators, 3 stories, interior corridors.
Rated: 2 Paws — 72 rooms.

Commodores Inn is located in Stowe, the essence of Vermont, where family-owned farms rub boundaries with world-class ski areas. Enjoy comfortable accommodations, fine food, and a host of activities, and friendly, courteous service in a tranquil and picturesque 30-acre setting. Guest rooms feature comfortable king- and queen-sized beds, cable TV, and heat lamps in your private bath. Relax in the comfortable living room and enjoy the warmth of a crackling fire in the majestic fieldstone fireplace, the wide-screen TV, quiet reading, or board games. Visit New England icons, such as a white-spired community church or the ghost on Emily's Bridge, or witness the transformation of sap to syrup at maple sugaring time. Cheer for your favorite Olympic skier at the annual ski challenge. Enjoy model yacht racing and experience performances by the Vermont Symphony Orchestra in an open meadow at sunset.

Edison Hill Manor

1500 Edison Hill Road
Stowe, VT 05672
802-253-7371

Type of Lodging: Country Inn
Room Rates: $85–$269, AAA discounts.
Pet Charges and Deposits: None.
Pet Policy: Designated units only.
Amenities: Winter plug-ins, outdoor pool, boating, boat dock, pond fishing, cross-country skiing, hiking trails, horseback riding (fee), restaurant, radios, data port/modem telephones, 2 stories, interior/exterior corridors.
Rated: 3 Paws — 25 rooms.

Edison Hill Manor is ensconced on 60 acres of rolling, hilly countryside. It offers various sized rooms in a restored manor and in a separate carriage house. Stowe Launch Zone is a specialized park that offers pipes and ramps for skateboarders, in-line skaters, and mountain bikers. If you're so disposed, you can rent such necessaries as helmets, knee pads, elbow pads, and wrist guards. Stowe Alpine Slide is an intriguing sled experience. The Alpine Chairlift at Spruce Peak travels to the top of the slide, affording views of the countryside. Riders descend the mountain on sleds and control the speed of their descent. Stowe is one of Vermont's—and the United States'—premier ski resorts.

Green Mountain Inn

18 S. Main Street
Stowe, VT 05672
802-253-7301
www.greenmountaininn.com

Type of Lodging: Historic Country Inn
Room Rates: $89–$219. Some suites: $149–$499.
Some whirlpool units: $149–$499. AAA and AARP discounts.
Pet Charges and Deposits: $4 per day per pet.
Pet Policy: Small pets only, in designated rooms only.
Amenities: Winter plug-ins, extended cable TV, movies (fee), some CD players, irons, hair dryers, heated pool, whirlpool, sauna, steam room, game room, lawn games, gift shop, afternoon tea, valet laundry, massage (fee), conference facilities, fax, restaurant, cocktails, radios, data port/modem telephones, some VCR's, some coffee makers, some refrigerators, some microwaves, smoke-free premises, 3 stories (no elevator), interior/exterior corridors.
Rated: 3 Paws — 78 units, including rooms and suites.

The 19th century porches and lights of the Green Mountain Inn present a welcoming sight as you reach the heart of 200-year-old Stowe Village. Nearby, a lofty church spire gracefully presides over the old architecture of specialty shops, galleries, restaurants, and lively night spots. Once inside the Inn, you discover special pleasures of another sort. The warm wood tones and fresh flowers in the lobby give way to country elegance in the living room, where guests often relax and relive the day's activities over a glass of Vermont cider and homemade cookies. Guests and their pets will enjoy the five-mile recreation path that begins at the Inn and winds through meadows and over bridges, offering beautiful views of Mount Mansfield.

Hob Knob Inn

2364 Mountain Road
Stowe, VT 05672
802-253-8549
www.hobknobinn.com

Type of Lodging: Motor Inn

Room Rates: $59–$99, Some suites:
$115–$179; Some whirlpool units:
$115–$179; AAA discounts, including
continental breakfast.

Pet Charges and Deposits: $10 per day
per pet.

Pet Policy: All pets welcome.

Amenities: Winter plug-ins, hair dryers,
free local telephone calls, outdoor pool,
restaurant, cocktails, smoke-free
premises, radios, coffee makers, data
port/modem telephones, some refrigerators, some microwaves, 2 stories, inte-
rior/exterior corridors.

Rated: 2 Paws — 21 units.

Hob Knob Inn is a country motor inn and
restaurant that afford spacious accommodations and efficiencies. Some rooms have
fireplaces. Hob Knob is located on a quiet
hillside with beautiful mountain views. The
Inn serves dinners by the fireside, including
certified Angus steaks and fresh fish. The
Helen Day Art Center, situated in an 1860
Greek Revival building, offers changing exhibitions of the works of well-known local,
national, and international visual artists.
Mount Mansfield, rising to 4,395 feet
northwest of town, is Vermont's highest
peak. From the summit, you can generally
see 50-70 miles in any direction. Stowe is an
all-year outdoor recreation venue—un-
bounded beauty, a delightful Swiss-Austrian
atmosphere, and "to die for" skiing areas.

Honeywood Country Lodge

4527 Mountain Road
Stowe, VT 05672
802-253-4124
www.honeywoodinn.com

Type of Lodging: Motel

Room Rates: $74–$145, some suites:
$159–$199; some whirlpool units:
$120–$149., including Continental breakfast. AAA and AARP discounts.

Pet Charges and Deposits: None.

Pet Policy: Designated units only, manager's prior approval required.

Amenities: Heated pool, extended cable
television, whirlpool, picnic area, stream
fishing, winter plug-ins, smoke-free
premises, cross-country skiing, nature
trails, hiking trails, free local telephone
calls, radios, refrigerators, data
port/modem telephones, some VCR's,
some microwaves, 1 story, exterior corridors.

Rated: 3 Paws — 10 units, including
1 two-bedroom unit.

The Honeywood Country Lodge, a Swiss-
style ski lodge, features attractive, individually decorated rooms. You have your
choice of bed & breakfast or motor inn-
style accommodations. The Stowe Auto
Toll Road is a 4.3 mile gravel road travers-
ing heavily forested slopes to the summit of
Mount Mansfield, the highest point in
Vermont. The winding road has some
sharp, steep curves, and is not recommended for novice drivers. Stowe is a year-round
outdoor recreation center. In summer, you
can engage in hiking, mountain biking,
swimming, fishing, canoeing, and boating.
In fall, you watch as colors turn from green
to a glorious multicolored flame of red, orange, and yellow. Winter is ski season, and
the number of ski venues near Stowe is extraordinarily high—47 trails and slopes—
and affords some of the best skiing in the
Eastern United States.

Innsbruck Inn At Stowe

4361 Mountain Road
Stowe, VT 05672
802-253-8582
www.innsbruckinn.com

Type of Lodging: Motel

Room Rates: $59–$179, some whirlpool units: $99–$189; AAA, AARP, AKC, ABA, and *ask about Pets Welcome*™ discounts.

Pet Charges and Deposits: $10 per day per pet.

Pet Policy: Small pets only.

Amenities: Winter plug-ins, extended cable TV, movies, hair dryers, heated pool, whirlpool, sauna, stream fishing, bicycles (fee), afternoon tea, health club adjacent, radios, coffee makers, data port/modem telephones, refrigerators, some VCR's (fee), some microwaves, 1-2 stories, interior/exterior corridors.

Rated: 3 Paws — 20 rooms and 5 suites.

Nestled beneath majestic Mount Mansfield, Vermont's highest peak, you'll find the beautiful Innsbruck Inn. It's situated on a scenic, streamside property, marked by abundant flower gardens, split-rail fences, a covered bridge, and maple and evergreen trees. An authentic Tyrolean bell tower, with handcrafted copper bell, lends Old World charm. For more than 25 years, the family has blended hospitality and the appeal of a country inn with the amenities of a resort hotel. Accommodations include luxurious rooms with private baths and vanity areas. A charming five-bedroom chalet, with full kitchen, living room with wood burning stove, and Swedish sauna, is also available. Your day begins with a hearty breakfast by the fireplace; afternoon tea with tempting baked treats follows later.

Mountain Road Resort

1007 Mountain Road
Stowe, VT 05672
800-367-6873 • 802-253-4566
www.stowevtusa.com

Type of Lodging: Motel / Resort

Room Rates: $99–$249, some suites: $199–$649, some whirlpool units: $169–$279; AAA and AARP discounts.

Pet Charges and Deposits: $15–$25 per day per pet. Guests must sign pet responsibility/liability form.

Pet Policy: Manager's prior approval req'd.

Amenities: Winter plug-ins, extended cable TV, movies, voice mail, hair dryers, some CD players, irons, two heated pools, whirlpools, sauna, tennis court, bicycles, playground, exercise room, French Petanque court, valet laundry, area transportation (fee), conference facilities, free local telephone calls, free newspaper, radios, data port/modem telephones, coffee makers, refrigerators, some VCR's & microwaves, smoke-free premises, restaurant adjacent, 1-2 stories, exterior corridors.

Rated: 4 Paws — 24 rooms and 6 suites.

On seven beautifully landscaped acres, the Mountain Road Resort offers 30 guest rooms and condo-suites, with amenities such as fireplaces, dining areas, lofts, kitchens, and tiled baths with whirlpools. Concierge and room service are also provided. Feast on a French country breakfast outdoors on the Alpine Terrace, and enjoy daily afternoon refreshments beside the massive stone fireplace in the den. Jog, bicycle, or rollerblade the scenic five-mile Stowe recreation path, then plunge into the Mountain Road Resort's large, heated outdoor swimming pool; or take a break from tennis to relax in the outdoor "MoonSpa," then barbecue or play lawn games. If golf is more your style, the nearby Stowe Country Club offers guests preferred rates.

Stowe Inn at Little River

123 Mountain Road
Stowe, VT 05672
800-227-1108 • 802-253-4836

Type of Lodging: Inn

Room Rates: $65–$350.

Pet Charges and Deposits: $10 per day per pet. 50% refundable deposit.

Pet Policy: Manager's prior approval required.

Amenities: Extended cable TV, heated pool, restaurant, 2 stories, interior corridors.

Rated: 3 Paws — 43 rooms and 4 suites.

The Stowe Inn at Little River is a restored circa 1825 manor located in the heart of Stowe Village. Casual, comfortable elegance describes the Inn's 21 guest rooms, all with private baths. Quilts, coverlets, antiques, and country furnishings add to the charm and décor. Selected guest rooms also feature fireplaces and Jacuzzis. The Carriage House has an additional 22 guest rooms, also with private baths. Kitchenettes are available upon request. Lovely gardens and grounds and an outdoor hot tub and pool add to the Inn's amenities. A superb, window-walled restaurant features eclectic American fare. A picturesque terrace overlooks the river and village. Long appreciated for its spectacular mountain scenery and with activities from world-renowned skiing and art galleries to fresh vegetable stands and antique automobile rallies, Stowe welcomes active participation by its many visitors.

Topnotch At Stowe Resort & Spa

4000 Mountain Road
Stowe, VT 05672
800-451-8886 • 802-253-8585
www.topnotch-resort.com

Type of Lodging: Resort

Room Rates: $ 159–$369, some suites: $319–$869; some whirlpool units: $359–$1,000; AAA discounts.

Pet Charges and Deposits: None.

Pet Policy: Small dogs and cats only.

Amenities: Winter plug-ins, extended cable TV, movies (fee), voice mail, safes, irons, hair dryers, two heated pools, whirlpools, saunas, steam rooms, cross-country skiing, ice skating, sleigh rides, hiking trails, jogging, horseback riding (fee), gift shop, afternoon tea, massage (fee), conference facilities, restaurant, cocktails, health club, radios, coffee makers, data port/modem telephones, refrigerators, some VCR's, some microwaves, 3 stories, interior/exterior corridors.

Rated: 4 Paws — 109 units, including rooms and suites.

Located on 120 acres of Vermont countryside at the foot of Mount Mansfield, Topnotch at Stowe is Stowe's only 4-diamond resort. To complement the meeting and spa facilities, the resort offers diverse accommodations, from unusually spacious guest rooms and suites to luxury two- and three-bedroom luxury townhomes. The racquet club offers fourteen year-round tennis courts. Its tennis program is consistently ranked among the best. Certified spa professionals specialize in a wide variety of personal treatments and services, from revitalizing facials to relaxing massages. Take the trolley to the "Ski Capital of the East" for downhill skiing or stay at the resort to cross-country ski on the 20 miles of touring trails.

Arcady at The Sunderland Motor Lodge

6249 Route 7A
Sunderland, VT 05250
802-362-1176

Type of Lodging: Motel

Room Rates: $69–$129; AAA discounts.

Pet Charges and Deposits: $15 fee.

Pet Policy: All pets welcome.

Amenities: Extended cable TV, movies, honor bars, outdoor hot tub, outdoor pool, nature trails, shuffle board, coffee makers, data port/modem telephones, some radios, 1 story, exterior corridors.

Rated: 3 Paws — 15 rooms.

Arcady at The Sunderland Motor Lodge is located in a serene and lovely country setting, with cozy units and hiking trails nearby. Rooms are comfortably and restfully furnished. Sunderland is in the southwest corner of Vermont, on the western edge of Green Mountain National Forest, between Manchester and Arlington. You're in the midst of mountain and forest country, a year-round recreation wonderland. State Route 7A is a beautifully scenic Vermont road. Mount Equinox is northwest of Sunderland, and Stratton Mountain is directly east. Nearby Arlington was founded in 1763 by Jehiel Hawley, a Loyalist. It was first known as Tory Hollow. Because the Green Mountain Boys were active in the area during the Revolutionary War, the Tory town clerk destroyed all records under his care and fled to Canada. Hundreds of Norman Rockwell's Saturday Evening Post covers can be found in Arlington's Norman Rockwell Exhibit.

Boardman House Bed & Breakfast

Box 112
Townshend, VT 05353
802-365-4086

Type of Lodging: Bed & Breakfast

Room Rates: $79–$89, including full breakfast. AAA and AARP discounts.

Pet Charges and Deposits: None.

Pet Policy: Manager's prior approval required.

Amenities: 2 stories, interior corridors.

Rated: 2 Paws — 5 rooms and 1 suite.

Located on the Village Green of Townshend, a pristine and picturesque village, the Boardman House is a newly renovated country home. Guests are accommodated in one of the five private, comfortable rooms, each with private bath. A two-bedroom suite is available upon request. The house comes equipped with a cozy parlor, library, and large lawn, with lovely gardens for strolling. Experience the magic of Vermont any season, with easy access to skiing at Stratton, Bromley, or Magic Mountain. Enjoy canoeing or kayaking the beautiful West River or the extensive recreation areas of nearby Townshend Dam. No matter when you visit, you are invited to simply enjoy the country life and colorful beauty of the setting.

Millbrook Inn & Restaurant

R.D. Box 62
Waitsfield, VT 05673
800-477-2809 • 802-496-2405
E-mail: millbrkinn@aol.com

Type of Lodging: Inn

Room Rates: $61–$84, including full breakfast and dinner.

Pet Charges and Deposits: None.

Pet Policy: Dogs only, sorry, no cats. Manager's prior approval required.

Amenities: Restaurant, 2 stories, interior corridors.

Rated: 2 Paws — 7 rooms on 4 acres.

Millbrook is a classic Cape-style farmhouse built in the 1850's by Jack Dana, who located the farmhouse close to his lumber and brick mills on nearby Mill Brook. Today, the mills are long gone, but the picturesque setting remains, with the Inn situated midway between the ski slopes and the village of Waitsfield. In the tradition of Vermont innkeeping, guests are treated to personalized service in a friendly, unhurried atmosphere. You enter the Inn through the Warming Room, where the antique parlor stove blazes a warm winter welcome. The seven guest rooms all have private baths and are decorated with hand stenciling, antique bedsteads, and handmade quilts. Neighboring Mad River Valley offers excellent hiking, road and mountain biking, canoeing, golfing, soaring, tennis, horseback riding, and swimming.

Golden Lion Riverside Inn

Route 100, Box 20
Warren, VT 05674
802-496-3084

Type of Lodging: Inn

Room Rates: $65–$149, including seasonal breakfast.

Pet Charges and Deposits: $5 per day per pet.

Pet Policy: Manager's prior approval required.

Amenities: Hot tubs, 1-2 stories, interior/exterior corridors.

Rated: 2 Paws — 12 rooms and 2 suites.

Surrounded by the Green Mountain National Forest, the Golden Lion Riverside Inn is family-owned and operated. Situated on the Mad River, it allows guests to enjoy the seclusion of the Inn's private beach and to explore the winding trails that wander through the wooded setting. Contemporary accommodations are mixed with the warmth and hospitality of a traditional New England country inn. Start your day with a delightful breakfast featuring seasonal favorites before you head off to one of the many sites in the area. Explore the spectacular fall foliage. In warmer weather, play a round on the nearby championship golf course or go soaring, hiking, canoeing, swimming, horseback riding, or antiquing. Winter sports are just two minutes away at the Sugarbush Sports Center and Ski Area.

Powderhound Inn & Condominiums

203 Powderhound Road
Warren, VT 05674
800-548-4022 • 802-496-5100
www.powderhoundinn.com

Type of Lodging: Resort Complex

Room Rates: $89–$149; AAA discounts.

Pet Charges and Deposits: $5 per day per pet plus 1 night's deposit, partially refundable.

Pet Policy: All pets welcome.

Amenities: Outdoor pool, whirlpool, tennis court, restaurant (seasonal), cocktails (seasonal), radios, coffee makers, data port/modem telephones, some refrigerators, 2 stories, exterior corridors.

Rated: 2 Paws — 4 guest rooms and 44 guest suites.

The Powderhound is located in the heart of central Vermont, in the scenic Mad River Valley. The 150-year-old converted farmhouse overlooks a peaceful, rustic setting at the entrance to the Sugarbush resort area. Each of the 44 suites features a living room area with cable TV, kitchenette, separate bedroom, and private bath, offering comfort and privacy for up to four guests. There's a cozy common area for reading or relaxing, and spacious grounds for long walks and lawn games. An old-fashioned front porch is a great place to sit a spell and watch the world go by. The Mad River Valley offers an assortment of year-round activities, from hiking to biking, horseback riding, canoeing, and fishing, as well as lots of sightseeing. Sugarbush and Mad River Glen offer some of the best skiing in the East and provide a challenge for every level.

The Sugar Lodge

2197 Sugarbush Access Road
Warren, VT 05674
802-583-3300
www.sugarlodge.com

Type of Lodging: Motel

Room Rates: $74–$164, including Continental breakfast. AAA and AARP discounts.

Pet Charges and Deposits: $10 per day per pet.

Pet Policy: All pets welcome.

Amenities: Whirlpool, smoke-free premises, area transportation, coin laundry, free local telephone calls, restaurant adjacent, cocktails, outdoor pool, radios, 2 stories, interior corridors.

Rated: 2 Paws — 22 rooms.

The Sugar Lodge offers the privacy and amenities of a hotel, with the hospitality of a Vermont country inn. Adequate-sized rooms are beautifully decorated and comfortably furnished. You'll find sightseeing, galleries, antiques, tennis, biking, golf, fishing, hiking, swimming, and all manner of outdoor activities here. Sugar Lodge is the closest lodge to the Sugarbush Ski Slopes. Warren, one of a trio of Mad River Valley communities, is named for physician and general Joseph Warren, who died in action at Bunker Hill. Granville Gulf State Park, covering 1,200 acres between Warren and Granville, lies along the eastern boundary of Green Mountain National Forest. The Mad River cuts through the park, creating picturesque Moss Glen Falls. The park offers a 6-mile scenic drive and the Puddledock Ski Touring Trail.

Holiday Inn of Waterbury-Stowe

45 Blush Hill Road
Waterbury, VT 05676
802-244-7822

Type of Lodging: Motor Inn
Room Rates: $99–$199; AAA and AARP discounts.
Pet Charges and Deposits: $30 deposit.
Pet Policy: All pets welcome.
Amenities: Winter plug-ins, extended cable TV, movies (fee), irons, hair dryers, heated pool, saunas, whirlpool, tennis court, snowmobiling, snow shoes, snow shoe trails, game room, coin laundry, conference facilities, restaurant, cocktails, health club, radios, coffee makers, data port/modem telephones, some VCR's (fee), some refrigerators (fee), some microwaves (fee), 2 stories, interior corridors.
Rated: 3 Paws — 79 rooms.

Holiday Inn is located on a wooded hillside. Its very spacious guest rooms have been newly renovated, with numerous upscale amenities and luxurious, comfortable furnishings. Quick! What do you think of when you think of Waterbury, Vermont? If you answered "Ben & Jerry's Ice Cream," you're absolutely right. You can tour the Ben & Jerry's Ice Cream Factory one mile north of town on State Route 100. Samples are given after a 30-minute tour, and the Cow Over the Moon Theater features a multimedia show. Waterbury is also the closest major town to Montpelier, Vermont's diminutive (8,200 population) capital. The Supreme Court building and the State Capitol are worth seeing, as are the Morse Farm Sugarworks, the T.W. Wood Gallery and Art Center, and the Vermont Historical Society Museum.

Old Stage Coach Inn

18 N. Main Street
Waterbury, VT 05676
802-244-5056

Type of Lodging: Historic Country Inn
Room Rates: $49–$209; AAA and AARP discounts.
Pet Charges and Deposits: None.
Pet Policy: All pets welcome.
Amenities: Smoke-free premises, free local telephone calls, restaurant, cocktails, data port/modem telephones, some coffee makers, some refrigerators, some microwaves, 2-3 stories (no elevator), interior corridors.
Rated: 3 Paws — 8 rooms and 3 suites, with library bar.

The Old Stagecoach Inn provides warmth and hospitality in abundance, in a setting of uncommon elegance and breathtaking Vermont scenery. The coaches and the horses are long gone, but today's traveler is welcomed with traditional service and exceptional comfort. Upon entering the Inn, you are surrounded by a lifetime collection of antiques from New England farmhouses. Situated in the historic village of Waterbury, the Inn has been meticulously restored to recreate the atmosphere of a bygone era. The Old Stagecoach Inn stands at Vermont's recreational crossroads, alongside a trout stream in the shadow of the Green Mountains' highest peaks, with a four-season menu of places to visit and things to do.

Hunt's Hideaway

R.R.I, Box 570
West Charleston, VT 05872
802-895-4432

Type of Lodging: House-Inn

Room Rates: $40–$50, including full Vermont breakfast.

Pet Charges and Deposits: None.

Pet Policy: All pets welcome.

Amenities: Swimming pool, cable TV, refrigerators, microwaves, pond, kitchen and laundry privileges, 2 stories, interior/exterior corridors.

Rated: 2 Paws — 3 rooms on 100 acres of woods.

Located in the Northeast Kingdom of Vermont, near the Canadian frontier, Hunt's Hideaway sits on 100 acres of woods and fields, complete with a brook and pond. This modern, split-level retreat includes cable TV, refrigerators, and microwaves, with hiking, biking, and skiing at your doorstep. Guests can enjoy a 20' × 40' swimming pool, bird watching, fishing, and year-round recreation at incredibly affordable rates. Seymour Lake and four other lakes are conveniently close. Nearby Newport and Orleans offer 18-hole golf courses. West Charleston, situated on the south shore of Lake Salem, is almost within walking distance of the Canadian frontier.

Snow Goose Inn

259 Route 100
West Dover, VT 05356
802-464-3984

Type of Lodging: Bed and Breakfast

Room Rates: $89–$309, some whirlpool units: $155–$215, including full breakfast; AAA discounts.

Pet Charges and Deposits: $20 per day per pet.

Pet Policy: All pets welcome.

Amenities: Extended cable TV, some CD players, complementary evening beverages, free local telephone calls, VCR's, smoke-free premises, data port/modem telephones, some refrigerators, 4 stories (no elevator), interior corridors.

Rated: 3 Paws — 13 rooms.

At the Snow Goose Inn, guest rooms are individually decorated with personal touches. Several rooms have a whirlpool and/or fireplace. Plan on getting exercise if you're on the upper floors—there are no elevators in the building. West Dover is in southern Vermont, situated on State Route 100, one of the prettiest roads in all New England. You're in the midst of ski country, with Mount Snow, Haystack Mountain, and the southernmost portion of Green Mountain National Forest adjacent to the town. West Dover's First Wok Restaurant features Szechuan, Hunan, and Cantonese cuisine, while nearby Wilmington has two fine restaurants, Le Petit Chef, classic French cuisine served in a restored 1789 farmhouse (candlelit tables), and The White House of Wilmington, an elegant English-style dining room in a country inn, high on a hill.

Willoughvale Inn on Lake Willoughby

793 Route 5A
Westmore, VT 05860
802-525-4123

Type of Lodging: Country Inn
Room Rates: $75–$249, some suites: $119–$249, some whirlpool units: $119–$165; AAA discounts.
Pet Charges and Deposits: $20 per day per pet.
Pet Policy: Small pets only.
Amenities: Hair dryers, swimming, snowmobiling, horse shoes, canoeing (fee), kayaks (fee), snow shoes (fee), bicycles (fee), smoke-free premises, meeting rooms, fax, restaurant, radios, data port/modem telephones, some coffee makers, 1 story, exterior corridors.
Rated: 3 Paws — 12 units.

Willoughvale Inn, a modern country inn, has lovely wraparound verandas with excellent lake views. The attractive, spacious guest rooms have high quality furnishings, affording you comfort and elegance. Of the units, there are 3 two-bedroom units and 4 efficiencies. Westmore is in Vermont's Northeast Kingdom, situated on the northeast shore of Lake Willoughby. One of the nicest things about tiny Westmore is that it isn't near *anywhere* of substantial size. Rather, it's a place of peace and extreme quiet, surrounded by lakes and forests, not far from the border of Connecticut (the Connecticut River) or the Canadian frontier. It's a great place to simply relax and recharge your batteries—and perhaps to go a'roaming with your pet.

Darling Family Inn

815 Route 100
Weston, VT 05161-5404
802-824-3223

Type of Lodging: Country Inn
Room Rates: $89–$109.
Pet Charges and Deposits: None.
Pet Policy: Pets in cottages only. Manager's prior approval required.
Amenities: Swimming pool, cottages have fully equipped kitchens, 1-2 stories, interior/exterior corridors.
Rated: 2 Paws — 5 rooms and 2 cottages.

The Darling family welcomes you to their retreat, a 165-year-old farmhouse restored as a charming inn, nestled in a mountain setting. Guest rooms feature canopy beds, spread with locally-crafted quilts. You'll find American and English country antiques and decorative touches throughout. Details, such as wreaths of dried, sliced apples mixed with eucalyptus, and hand-forged ironworks add grace and charm. The affordably priced cottages are conveniently equipped with all the amenities of home, including kitchens, yet the setting is a secluded mountain retreat. Enjoy exploring the Green Mountains, where the hustle and bustle of daily life passes by at a discreet distance. Activities include hiking, fishing, and cross-country skiing right out the door. The village of Weston offers summer theater, antiques, local crafts, and art exhibits.

Best Western At The Junction

306 N. Harland Road
White River Junction, VT 05001
802-295-3015

Type of Lodging: Motel
Room Rates: $75–$150, including Continental breakfast. AAA and AARP discounts.
Pet Charges and Deposits: $10 per day per pet.
Pet Policy: All pets welcome.
Amenities: Extended cable TV, movies (fee), voice mail, hair dryers, heated pool, wading pool, whirlpool, sauna, playground, exercise room, coin laundry, free newspaper, radios, coffee makers, data port/modem telephones, some refrigerators (fee), some microwaves (fee), 2 stories, interior corridors.
Rated: 2 Paws — 112 rooms.

The Best Western offers you good-sized, comfortably-furnished rooms that are guaranteed to make your stay restful and enjoyable. Ascutney State Park and the Mount Ascutney Ski Area are half an hour's drive south of White River Junction, while the Connecticut River affords many water-related activities. It's less than two hours up the interstate to Burlington, and you go straight through the Green Mountain National Forest on the way there. Montpelier, Vermont's capital, is an hour away, via I-89, and the road is gorgeous all the way. You're much closer than you think to numerous ski areas, and a large number of outdoor recreation venues.

Ramada Inn–White River Junction

259 Holiday Drive
White River Junction, VT 05001
802-295-3000

Type of Lodging: Motel
Room Rates: $84–$149; AAA and AARP discounts.
Pet Charges and Deposits: None.
Pet Policy: All pets welcome.
Amenities: Winter plug-ins, extended cable TV, movies (fee), voice mail, safes (fee), irons, hair dryers, heated pool, sauna, putting green, game room, pool table, coin laundry, conference facilities, free local telephone calls, radios, coffee makers, data port/modem telephones, refrigerators, microwaves, 2 stories, interior corridors.
Rated: 2 Paws — 136 rooms.

Ramada Inn features attractive, moderately spacious rooms, as well as cleanliness and comfort in the White River Junction area. White River Junction is located directly on the Connecticut River, an easy stroll over the border to Lebanon, New Hampshire. You're right at the beginning of U.S. Highway 4, which traverses the state from here to New York. Quechee State Park and Woodstock, both cross-country ski areas, are nearby. AJ's Restaurant, very popular with the locals, has a well-stocked salad bar and features steak and seafood dishes. The rustic décor displays crafts items.

Braeside Motel

Route 4 East
Woodstock, VT 05091
802-457-1366

Type of Lodging: Motel

Room Rates: $72–$112; AAA and AARP discounts.

Pet Charges and Deposits: $10 per day per pet.

Pet Policy: Small pets only, limited units only.

Amenities: Smoke-free premises, extended cable TV, free local telephone calls, outdoor pool, radios, data port/modem telephones, some refrigerators, some VCR's (fee), 1 story, exterior corridors.

Rated: 2 Paws — 12 units.

Braeside Motel is on a hillside location overlooking the valley. This is your typical one-story traditional motel—clean, comfortable, and well-maintained. Woodstock is a resort and residential community, noted for its well-preserved old houses and charming village green. Five local church bells were cast in Boston, either by Paul Revere or by a member of his family. Sugarbush farm produces maple syrup and cheeses. But Woodstock also provides ample food for the soul: Stuart Matlins' Jewish Lights Publishing Company is one of the most thought-provoking publishing houses in the country. It explores the great goodness and spirituality to be found in all of us—and you don't have to be Jewish to appreciate the timeless works coming out of this wonderful publishing concern. Stuart and his wife Antoinette are two of the warmest, most gracious people in the industry.

Kedron Valley Inn

Route 106
Woodstock, VT 05071
800-836-1193 • 802-457-1473
E-mail: Kedroninn@aol.com

Type of Lodging: Inn

Room Rates: $129–$209, including full country breakfast.

Pet Charges and Deposits: None.

Pet Policy: Manager's prior approval required.

Amenities: Cable TV, restaurant, 2 stories (no elevator), interior corridors.

Rated: 4 Paws — 23 rooms and 3 suites.

One of Vermont's oldest inns, operating for over 170 years, the Kedron Valley Inn's rural pace and scenic surroundings offer a relaxing hideaway. Most rooms have canopy beds and fireplaces or wood-burning stoves. Hooked rugs, antique rockers, heirloom quilts, and needlepoint fill the rooms with quality comfort. Breakfast consists of hearty fare: homemade muffins or scones, fragrant and hot from the oven, sumptuous omelets, and wondrous creations. The restaurant serves contemporary American cuisine, centered around the finest local products. The Inn has lush bulb and perennial gardens, and several nearby gardens are open for viewing or strolling. Art galleries, antique stores, and shopping are close at hand in Woodstock, and a Discount Outlet Center is a short drive away in Manchester.

The Winslow House

492 Woodstock Road
Woodstock, VT 05091
802-457-1820

Type of Lodging: Historic Bed and Breakfast

Room Rates: $89–$159, including full breakfast; AAA discounts.

Pet Charges and Deposits: None.

Pet Policy: All pets welcome.

Amenities: Smoke-free premises, extended cable TV, exercise room, free local telephone calls, movies, radios, refrigerators, 2 stories, interior corridors.

Rated: 3 Paws — 5 rooms.

The Winslow House, an 1872 farmhouse, is furnished with antiques. It's a wonderful historic inn, a place where you'll find that each room is individually decorated, and where there are unique personal touches everywhere. Billings Farm & Museum encompasses both a modern working dairy farm and a museum of Vermont farm life in the 1890's. Frederick Billings, a Vermont native, lawyer, railroad president, and philanthropist, established the farm in 1871 and stocked it with Jersey cattle. The Vermont Raptor Center houses 26 species of hawks, owls, and eagles that cannot be released into the wild because of various permanent injuries. You'll find some fine walking trails in this area.

Index

A

Adair Country Inn – Bethlehem, NH 173
Admiral Peary House – Fryeburg, ME 84
Airport Economy Inn – West Lebanon, NH 209
American Motor Lodge—Best Western –
    Sturbridge, MA 162
Amerisuites – Mystic, CT 48
Amerisuites – Shelton, CT 54
Amerisuites – South Portland, ME 107
Ammonoosuc Inn – Lisbon, NH 192
Anchorage Inn – Rochester, NH 204
Anchorage Inn – South Burlington, VT 252
Andersen Lodge—An Austrian Inn –
    Stowe, VT 256
Arcady at The Sunderland Motor Lodge –
    Sunderland, VT 261
Atwood Inn – Franklin, NH 183
Auburn Inn – Auburn, ME 63
Augustus Bove House – Naples, ME 96
Avon Old Farms Hotel – Avon, CT 38

B

Balance Rock Inn 1903 – Bar Harbor, ME 67
Bar Harbor Inn – Bar Harbor, ME 68
Barrows House – Dorset, VT 233
Bartram's Bed & Breakfast –
    Middletown, RI 214
Bay Motor Inn – Buzzards Bay, MA 149
Baymont Inn & Suites Hartford Airport –
    Windsor Locks, CT 44
Bayshore Condominiums –
    Provincetown, MA 152
Beau Rivage Motel –
    Old Orchard Beach, ME 99
Bed & Breakfast at B – Guilford, CT 34
Belfast Bay Meadows Inn – Belfast, ME 70
Belfast Harbor Inn – Belfast, ME 71
Bennington Motor Inn – Bennington, VT 227
Bertram Inn – Brookline, MA 134
Best Budget Inn – Claremont, NH 175
Best Inn – Provincetown, MA 153
Best Western At Historic Concord –
    Concord, MA 137
Best Western At The Junction –
    White River Junction, VT 267

Best Western Black Bear Inn – Orono, ME 102
Best Western Colonial Inn –
    East Windsor, CT 40
Best Western Concord Inn & Suites –
    Concord, NH 176
Best Western Hearthside Motor Inn –
    Exeter, NH 180
Best Western Heritage Motor Inn –
    Millinocket, ME 94
Best Western Inn and Suites –
    Rutland, VT 247
Best Western Inn – Bar Harbor, ME 68
Best Western Jed Prouty Motor Inn –
    Bucksport, ME 75
Best Western Merry Manor Inn –
    South Portland, ME 107
Best Western Senator Inn & Spa –
    Augusta, ME 63
Best Western Silver Fox Inn –
    Waterville Valley, NH 208
Best Western Sovereign Hotel –
    Keene, NH 190
Best Western Sunapee Lake Lodge –
    Mount Sunapee, NH 198
Best Western White House Inn –
    Bangor, ME 65
Best Western Windjammer Inn –
    South Burlington, VT 253
Best Western—Waterville – Waterville, ME 110
Blackberry River Inn – Norfolk, CT 50
Boardman House Bed & Breakfast –
    Townshend, VT 261
Boston Harbor Hotel – Boston, MA 121
Braeside Motel – Woodstock, VT 268
Butternut On The Mountain –
    Killington, VT 236

C

Calais Motor Inn – Calais, ME 76
Camden Harbour Inn – Camden, ME 77
Cape Ann Motor Inn – Gloucester, MA 139
Caribou Inn & Convention Center –
    Caribou, ME 78
Carter Notch Inn – Jackson, NH 188
Cavendish Pointe Hotel – Cavendish, VT 231

Cavendish Pointe Hotel – Ludlow, VT 238
Centennial Inn – Farmington, CT 42
Center of New Hampshire—Holiday Inn –
   Manchester, NH 194
Centerville Corners Motor Lodge –
   Centerville, MA 149
Chesterfield Inn – Chesterfield, NH 175
Clarion Hotel / Conference Center –
   South Burlington, VT 253
Clarion Inn – Groton, CT 33
Colonial House Inn – Yarmouth Port, MA 155
Colonial Motel & Spa – Brattleboro, VT 230
Colonial Travelodge – Ellsworth, ME 81
Colonnade Hotel – Boston, MA 122
Combes Family Inn – Ludlow, VT 238
Comfort Inn & Suites – Sturbridge, MA 163
Comfort Inn – Cromwell, CT 38
Comfort Inn – Hyannis, MA 151
Comfort Inn—Airport – Warwick, RI 218
Comfort Inn—Manchester –
   Manchester, NH 194
Commodores Inn – Stowe, VT 256
Concord Comfort Inn – Concord, NH 177
Corner House Inn – Center Sandwich, NH 174
Cornwall Inn – Cornwall Bridge, CT 30
Cortina Inn & Resort – Mendon, VT 240
Country Inn At The Mall – Bangor, ME 65
Cozy Corner Motel – Williamstown, MA 168
Crocker House Country Inn – Hancock, ME 86
Crowne Plaza Hartford Downtown –
   Hartford, CT 35

D

Dana Place Inn – Jackson, NH 188
Darling Family Inn – Weston, VT 266
Darling Kelly's Motel – Bennington, VT 227
Days Inn Taunton – Raynham, MA 159
Days Inn – Dover, NH 178
Days Inn – Keene, NH 191
Days Inn – Lebanon, NH 191
Days Inn – Sturbridge, MA 163
Days Inn – Torrington, CT 57
Days Inn—Braintree – Braintree, MA 133
Days Inn—Plymouth / Middleboro –
   Middleboro, MA 158
Deer Run Motor Inn – Jeffersonville, VT 235
Dexter's Inn – Sunapee, NH 206
Dockside Guest Quarters – York, ME 113
Down-East Village Motel – Yarmouth, ME 113

E

East Gate Motor Inn – Littleton, NH 193
Econo Lodge – Albans, VT 250
Econo Lodge – Manchester, NH 195
Econo Lodge – Rutland, VT 247
Econo Lodge – Waterville, ME 110
Econo Lodge—Killington Area –
   Mendon, VT 241
Edelweiss Motel & Chalets – Mendon, VT 240
Edison Hill Manor – Stowe, VT 257
Eliot Suite Hotel – Boston, MA 122
Ellis River House – Jackson, NH 189

Embassy Suites—Boston Marlborough –
   Marlborough, MA 141
Enchanted Nights Bed & Breakfast –
   Kittery, ME 90

F

Fairbanks Inn – Johnsbury, VT 251
Fairfield Inn—New Haven – New Haven, CT 49
Fairfield Inn—Stamford – Stamford, CT 56
Fairmont Copley Plaza—Boston –
   Boston, MA 123
Farmington Inn – Farmington, CT 42
Fieldstone Country Inn –
   Twin Mountain, NH 208
Fife 'n Drum Motel – Bennington, VT 228
Firefly Ranch – Bristol, VT 230
Fireside Inn & Suites – West Lebanon, NH 209
Five Bridge Inn Bed & Breakfast –
   Rehoboth, MA 159
Four Columns Inn – Newfane, VT 243
Four Seasons Hotel Boston – Boston, MA 124
Franconia Village Hotel & Conference Center –
   Franconia, NH 181
Freeport Inn & Café – Freeport, ME 83

G

Gale River Motel – Franconia, NH 181
Gateway Inn – Medway, ME 93
Golden Lion Riverside Inn – Warren, VT 262
Goodwin Hotel – Hartford, CT 35
Green Acres Motel – Sturbridge, MA 164
Green Mountain Inn – Stowe, VT 257
Greenhurst Inn – Bethel, VT 229
Greenmont Motel – Rutland, VT 248
Greenwood Motel – Greenville, ME 85

H

Hampton Falls Inn – Hampton Falls, NH 186
Hampton Inn Boston—North Andover –
   Lawrence, MA 140
Hampton Inn Boston—Woburn –
   Woburn, MA 147
Hampton Inn Hotel/Conference Center –
   Colchester, VT 231
Happy Trails Motel – Ludlow, VT 239
Harbor Village – Hyannis Port, MA 151
Harbour Inne & Cottage – Mystic, CT 48
Hawthorn Suites, Ltd. – Franklin, MA 139
Hawthorn Suites, Ltd. –
   North Chelmsford, MA 142
Hawthorn Suites—Andover – Andover, MA 131
Hawthorne Hotel – Salem, MA 144
Herbert Inn – Kingfield, ME 90
Hickory Pond Inn & Golf Course –
   Durham, NH 179
High Acres – North Stonington, CT 51
Hill Farm Inn – Arlington, VT 226
Hillside Acres Cabins & Motel –
   Boothbay, ME 73
Hilton Boston Back Bay – Boston, MA 125
Hilton Dedham Place – Dedham, MA 138
Hilton Hartford – Hartford, CT 36
Hilton Southbury – Southbury, CT 56

Hilton—Boston Logan Airport – Boston, MA 129
Hob Knob Inn – Stowe, VT 258
Holiday Inn Bath / Brunswick – Bath, ME 70
Holiday Inn Express – Dayville, CT 32
Holiday Inn Express – Rockland, MA 160
Holiday Inn Express – Springfield, VT 255
Holiday Inn of Waterbury-Stowe – Waterbury, VT 264
Holiday Inn Select – Stamford, CT 57
Holiday Inn – Bridgeport, CT 29
Holiday Inn – Danbury, CT 31
Holiday Inn – East Hartford, CT 39
Holiday Inn – Ellsworth, ME 82
Holiday Inn – North Haven, CT 51
Holiday Inn – Rutland, VT 248
Holiday Inn – Springfield, MA 162
Holiday Inn – Waterville, ME 111
Holiday Inn—Bangor – Bangor, ME 66
Holiday Inn—Burlington – South Burlington, VT 254
Holiday Inn—West – Portland, ME 103
Holiday Motel – Johnsbury, VT 251
Homestead Guest Studios – Norwalk, CT 52
Homestead Guest Studios – Shelton, CT 54
Homestead Village Guest Studios – Marlborough, MA 141
Homestead Village Guest Studios – Waltham, MA 146
Homestead Village Guest Studios—Boston/Burlington – Burlington, MA 134
Homewood Suites By Hilton – Billerica, MA 133
Homewood Suites by Hilton – Windsor Locks, CT 44
Honeywood Country Lodge – Stowe, VT 258
Horse and Hound Inn – Franconia, NH 182
Hotel LeMeridien – Boston, MA 125
House on the Hill – Waterbury, CT 58
Howard Johnson Hotel – Portland, ME 103
Howard Johnson Hotel – Revere, MA 143
Howard Johnson Hotel – South Portland, ME 108
Howard Johnson Inn—Newport – Middletown, RI 214
Howard Johnson Lodge Fenway – Boston, MA 126
Howard Johnson – Hadley, MA 156
Howard Johnson – Rutland, VT 249
Hunt's Hideaway – West Charleston, VT 265

I

Inn at HighView – Andover, VT 225
Inn at Chester – Chester, CT 30
Inn At Harmon Park – York Harbor, ME 114
Inn at Iron Masters – Lakeville, CT 45
Inn At The Hill – Newport, VT 244
Inn by the Sea – Cape Elizabeth, ME 77
Innsbruck Inn At Stowe – Stowe, VT 259
Interlaken Inn Resort & Conference Center – Lakeville, CT 46
International Motel – Calais, ME 76

Isaac E. Merrill House Inn – North Conway, NH 201
Isaac Randall House – Freeport, ME 83
Island Inn – Monhegan Island, ME 95
Ivanhoe Country House – Sheffield, MA 160

J

Jasper's Motel – Ellsworth, ME 82
Jenkins Inn – Barre, MA 120
Jericho Valley Inn – Hancock, MA 157
Jericho Valley Inn – Williamstown, MA 168
Johnny Seesaw's – Peru, VT 245

K

Kawanhee Inn Lakeside Lodge & Cabins – Weld, ME 111
Kedron Valley Inn – Woodstock, VT 268
Kenniston Hill Inn – Boothbay, ME 73
Kineo View Motor Lodge – Greenville, ME 85
Knotty Pine Motel – Bennington, VT 228

L

L'Auberge Country Inn – Bethel, ME 72
Lakeview Motor Lodge – Newbury, NH 200
Larchwood Inn – Wakefield, RI 217
Leen's Lodge – Grand Lake Stream, ME 84
Linnell Motor & Rest Inn Conference Center – Rumford, ME 105
Loafer Inn At The 1792 Whitcomb House – Swanzey, NH 206
Lodge at Turbat's Creek – Kennebunkport, ME 89
Lovejoy Farm Bed & Breakfast – Loudon, NH 193
Lovett's Inn – Franconia, NH 182
Lovley's Motel – Newport, ME 97

M

Machias Motor Inn – Machias, ME 93
Mainstay Suites, Warwick – Warwick, RI 218
Maples Motel – Westbrook, CT 59
Mariner Motel – Falmouth, MA 150
Master Hosts Inn – Warwick, RI 219
Matterhorn Motor Inn – Moultonborough, NH 197
Mendon Mountainview Resort Lodge – Mendon, VT 241
Midway Motel – Cornish, ME 79
Milford Motel – Milford, ME 94
Millbrook Inn & Restaurant – Waitsfield, VT 262
Millennium Bostonian Hotel – Boston, MA 126
Morgan Inn & Suites – Groton, CT 33
Motel 6 – Augusta, ME 64
Motel 6 – Branford, CT 28
Motel 6 – Colchester, VT 232
Motel 6 – Lewiston, ME 91
Motel 6 – Newport, RI 215
Motel 6 – South Yarmouth, MA 154
Mount Madison Motel – Gorham, NH 184
Mountain Road Resort – Stowe, VT 259

Murray House Bed & Breakfast –
Newport, RI 215

N
Nashua Marriott – Nashua, NH 199
Ne'r Beach Motel – Wells, ME 112
Nootka Lodge – Woodsville, NH 211
North Conway Mountain Inn –
North Conway, NH 201
Notchland Inn – Harts Location, NH 186

O
Old Colonial Motel –
Old Orchard Beach, ME 100
Old Lyme Inn – Old Lyme, CT 52
Old Riverton Inn – Riverton, CT 53
Old Stage Coach Inn – Waterbury, VT 264
Olde Orchard Inn – Moultonborough, NH 198
Overlook Motel – Eagle Lake, ME 79

P
Parker's Motel – Lincoln, NH 192
Payne's Hill Bed & Breakfast – Dover, NH 178
Peep-Willow Farm – Marlborough, NH 195
Pentagoet Inn – Castine, ME 78
Penwood Bed & Breakfast – Bloomfield, CT 28
Pine Grove Cottages – Lincolnville, ME 91
Pittsfield Inn – Pittsfield, VT 245
Pleasant Valley Motel –
West Stockbridge, MA 167
Portland Marriott Hotel –
South Portland, ME 108
Powderhound Inn & Condominiums –
Warren, VT 263
Primrose Inn – Bar Harbor, ME 69
Publick House Historic Inn –
Sturbridge, MA 164

Q
Quality Inn – Falmouth, MA 150

R
Rabbit Hill Inn – Lower Waterford, VT 237
Race Brook Lodge – Sheffield, MA 161
Radisson Eastland Hotel – Portland, ME 104
Radisson Hotel & Conference Center –
Merrimack, NH 196
Radisson Hotel—Cambridge –
Cambridge, MA 136
Ram in the Thicket – Milford, NH 197
Ramada Inn – Bangor, ME 66
Ramada Inn – Danbury, CT 31
Ramada Inn – Woburn, MA 148
Ramada Inn—Boston – Boston, MA 130
Ramada Inn—White River Junction –
White River Junction, VT 267
Ramada Limited of Rutland – Rutland, VT 249
Ramada Plaza Hotel – Shelton, CT 55
Red Clover Inn – Mendon, VT 242
Red Roof Inn – Enfield, CT 41
Red Roof Inn – Framingham, MA 138
Red Roof Inn – Hartford, CT 36
Red Roof Inn – Mansfield, MA 158

Red Roof Inn – Nashua, NH 199
Red Roof Inn – New London, CT 50
Red Roof Inn – Salem, NH 204
Red Roof Inn – Southborough, MA 161
Red Roof Inn – West Springfield, MA 167
Renaissance Bedford Hotel – Bedford, MA 132
Residence Inn by Marriott / Downtown –
Hartford, CT 37
Residence Inn by Marriott – Danbury, CT 32
Residence Inn by Marriott – Meriden, CT 47
Residence Inn By Marriott –
Merrimack, NH 196
Residence Inn by Marriott –
New Haven, CT 49
Residence Inn By Marriott –
Portsmouth, NH 203
Residence Inn by Marriott – Shelton, CT 55
Residence Inn By Marriott –
Tewksbury, MA 145
Residence Inn By Marriott – Warwick, RI 219
Residence Inn by Marriott – Windsor, CT 43
Residence Inn Manchester –
Manchester, CT 43
Rodeway Inn – Sturbridge, MA 165
Royal Motel – Rutland, VT 250
Royalty Inn – Gorham, NH 184

S
Sandy Bay Motor Inn – Rockport, MA 143
Sanford-Covell Villa Marina – Newport, RI 216
Scottish Inns – Houlton, ME 86
Seagull Inn – Marblehead, MA 140
Seaport Hotel – Boston, MA 130
Seaview Motel – Old Orchard Beach, ME 100
Seven Hills Country Inn & Restaurant –
Lenox, MA 157
Seymour Lake Lodge – Morgan, VT 243
Sheepscot River Inn – Edgecomb, ME 81
Sheraton Hotel—Airport –
Windsor Locks, CT 45
Sheraton Newton Hotel – Newton, MA 142
Sheraton Providence Airport Hotel –
Warwick, RI 220
Sheraton Waterbury Hotel – Waterbury, CT 58
Sheraton-Boston Hotel – Boston, MA 128
Sheraton—Burlington Hotel –
South Burlington, VT 254
Shore Acres Inn – North Hero, VT 244
Sign of the Owl – Northport, ME 97
Silver Maple Lodge & Cottages –
Fairlee, VT 234
Silver Street Inn – Dover, NH 179
Skaket Beach Motel – Orleans, MA 152
Sky Lodge Motel & Cabins – Jackman, ME 87
Sleep Inn – Willington, CT 59
Small Point Bed & Breakfast –
Sebasco Estates, ME 106
Smuggler's Cove Motor Inn –
East Boothbay, ME 80
Snow Goose Inn – West Dover, VT 265
Snowvillage Inn – Snowville, NH 205
South Gate Motel – Bennington, VT 229
Southern Comfort Motel – Colebrook, NH 176

Spalding Inn & Country Cottages –
  Whitefield, NH 210
Staybridge Suites—Boston/Burlington –
  Burlington, MA 135
Stepping Stones Bed & Breakfast –
  Wilton Center, NH 210
Stonehurst Manor – North Conway, NH 202
Stowe Inn at Little River – Stowe, VT 260
Studio East Motor Inn – Ogunquit, ME 98
Sturbridge Host Hotel / Conference Center –
  Sturbridge, MA 165
Summerfield Suites By Wyndham –
  Burlington, MA 135
Summerfield Suites Hotel – Waltham, MA 146
Super 8 Motel – Campton, NH 174
Super 8 Motel – Cromwell, CT 39
Super 8 Motel – Enfield, CT 41
Super 8 Motel – Hartford, CT 37
Sweet Water Inn – Orient, ME 101
Swissotel Boston – Boston, MA 128

T

Temperance Tavern – Gilmanton, NH 183
The Bluebird Motel – Machias, ME 92
The Brandt House – Greenfield, MA 156
The Briar Lea Inn & Restaurant –
  Bethel, ME 71
The Captain Thomas Resort Motel –
  Ogunquit, ME 98
The Cascades Lodge & Restaurant –
  Killington, VT 236
The Charles Hotel In Harvard Square –
  Cambridge, MA 136
The Colony Hotel – Kennebunkport, ME 88
The Craignair Inn At Clark Island –
  Spruce Head, ME 109
The Earl of Sandwich Motel –
  Sandwich, MA 154
The Eastland Motel – Lubec, ME 92
The Farm By The River B&B –
  North Conway, NH 200
The Glen – Pittsburg, NH 202
The Hilltop Inn – Sugar Hill, NH 205
The Hollow Inn & Motel – Barre, VT 226
The Inn At Buck Hollow Farm – Fairfax, VT 234
The Inn at Goose Rocks –
  Kennebunkport, ME 88
The Inn At Long Lake – Naples, ME 96
The Inn at Rostay – Bethel, ME 72
The Inn on the Common –
  Craftsbury Common, VT 232
The Katahdin Inn – Millinocket, ME 95
The Kings' Rose Bed & Breakfast Inn –
  South Kingstown, RI 217
The Lake Motel – Wolfeboro, NH 211
The Lawnmeer Inn – Southport, ME 106
The Ledgelawn Inn – Bar Harbor, ME 69
The Lodge at Kennebunk –
  Kennebunk, ME 87
The Madison Motor Inn – Rumford, ME 105
The Manor on Golden Pond –
  Holderness, NH 187

The Mare's Inn Bed & Breakfast –
  Ledyard, CT 46
The Meeting House Inn – Henniker, NH 187
The Middlebury Inn – Middlebury, VT 242
The Pines Motel – Boothbay Harbor, ME 74
The Putney Inn – Putney, VT 246
The Ransom Bay Inn – Alburg, VT 225
The Regency Suites – Worcester, MA 169
The Ritz-Carlton—Boston – Boston, MA 127
The Salem Inn – Salem, MA 144
The Sugar Lodge – Warren, VT 263
The Tamworth Inn – Tamworth, NH 207
The Unique Yankee B&B Lodge –
  Fitzwilliam, NH 180
The Villa – Westerly, RI 220
The Villager Motel – Bartlett, NH 173
The Villager Motel – Williamstown, MA 169
The Westin Hotel, Waltham –
  Waltham, MA 147
The Westin Hotel—Copley Place Boston –
  Boston, MA 129
The Westin Providence – Providence, RI 216
The Wilson Inn – Essex Junction, VT 233
The Winslow House – Woodstock, VT 269
The Yachtsman Lodge & Marina –
  Kennebunkport, ME 89
Three Mountain Inn – Jamaica, VT 235
Tilton Manor – Tilton, NH 207
Timber Inn Motel – Ludlow, VT 239
Todd House Bed & Breakfast –
  Eastport, ME 80
Tollgate Hill Inn – Litchfield, CT 47
Top Notch Motor Inn – Gorham, NH 185
Topnotch At Stowe Resort & Spa –
  Stowe, VT 260
Tower Hall Bed & Breakfast – Poultney, VT 246
Town & Country Motel –
  South Burlington, VT 255
Town & Country Motor Inn – Gorham, NH 185
Towneplace Suites By Marriott –
  Danvers, MA 137
Townplace Suites By Marriott –
  Tewksbury, MA 145
Tradewinds Motor Inn – Rockland, ME 104
Travelodge Hotel – Augusta, ME 64
Twin Tree Inn – Brookfield, CT 29

U

University Lodge – Amherst, MA 120
University Motor Inn – Orono, ME 102

V

Val Roc Motel – Killington, VT 237
Viking Motor Inn – Brunswick, ME 75
Village House – Jackson, NH 189

W

Wachusett Village Inn – Westminster, MA 166
Wainright Inn – Great Barrington, MA 155
Waterford Inne – Waterford, ME 109
Waves Oceanfront Resort –
  Old Orchard Beach, ME 101
Wellesley Inn & Suites – East Hartford, CT 40

Whispering Pines Motel – Wilton, ME 112
White Anchor Motel – Boothbay, ME 74
White Deer Motel – Conway, NH 177
White Hart – Salisbury, CT 53
White Rose Inn – Ogunquit, ME 99
White Wind Inn – Provincetown, MA 153
Whitneys' Inn—Jackson – Jackson, NH 190
Willoughvale Inn on Lake Willoughby –
    Westmore, VT 266
Woodbound Inn – Rindge, NH 203
Wyndham Andover – Andover, MA 132
Wyndham Westborough Hotel –
    Westborough, MA 166

Yankee Doodle Motel – Shelburne, VT 252
York Commons Inn – York, ME 114

About the People
Who Put This Book Together

Hugo N. Gerstl is a nationally famous trial lawyer and author *(How To Cut Your Legal Bills In Half; How To Survive & Profit from Your Son's Bar Mitzvah)* whose passion is world travel. He has traveled to 47 states; virtually all of Europe except the Scandinavian and Baltic countries; the Middle East, and South Africa, and has lived in Turkey for two years. Although he is still recovering from the loss of Harry, his 15-year-old *Old* English Sheepdog, he is somewhat consoled by a pesky and frisky cat, Her Royal Highness, the Princess Victoria ("that darned cat," for short), who still manages his home. He counts as his greatest blessing his marriage to Lorraine. Between them, they have raised five adult children. He is co-author of *Pets Welcome™: National Second Edition,* and author of *Pets Welcome™: Great Lakes Edition.*

Colleen M. Flores co-authored *California Wine Country Cooking Secrets.* She was born and raised on California's fabled Monterey Peninsula and has enjoyed successful careers in banking, the legal field (she is a qualified paralegal), and book publishing, where she has served in virtually every capacity. She resides in Monterey. She served as final concept/language editor for *Pets Welcome™: National Second Edition.*

Herb Chelner, a true rocket scientist, was an instrumental part of the team that developed the landing system for the Boeing 747 aircraft as well as the lunar landing module. In 1981, he rescued a struggling company, and has turned it into a substantial and highly respected force in government and commercial measurement instrumentation. He is currently working on the development of a new generation rocket shuttle system. Herb still mourns the passing of his beloved "best friend," Elliott. However, Sharon, his wife of many, many years, and his two adult children serve to somewhat soften the blow.

Tracy Corchine and her son, Jake, reside in the foothills of the Sierras, near Yosemite National Park. In addition to contributing to this book, Tracy works full time as an account executive at a pension management firm, as a full time student at University of Phoenix, where she is securing her accounting degree, and as a full-time mommy to Jake, her wonderful 7½-year-old son.

Jeff Gerstl is married to a professional chef and lives in Santee, outside of San Diego, California. Widely traveled, he holds a Bachelor's Degree in Geography from San

Diego State University, is a manager at Costa Travel, a major national travel agency, and is a computer fanatic. Prior to his employment at the travel agency, he was an on-air radio personality ("Jeff Powers") in the Salinas, Monterey Peninsula, and San Diego areas.

Lorraine Gerstl, author of the popular *Jewish Cooking Secrets From Here & Far* and co-author of *California Wine Country Cooking Secrets,* grew up in Johannesburg, South Africa. After graduating from the University of South Africa, she taught deaf children in all grades before starting her own family. For the past thirteen years, she has taught third grade full time at Santa Catalina School in Monterey, developed national curriculum for the Monterey Bay Aquarium, and served as adjunct editor-reviewer for Allyn & Bacon Educational Publishers. She and her husband, Hugo, reside in Carmel, California. They have five grown children.

Nadine Guarrera, 27, has led many lives. Born in Sicily of Sicilian-Romanian parentage, this beautiful sprite has visited over 100 countries, speaks five languages fluently, and has served as editor and editorial assistant for many books in the popular *Cooking Secrets* series, including *Cooking With The Masters Of Food & Wine,* and *California Wine Country Cooking Secrets,* as well as *Pets Welcome™: National First Edition, Pets Welcome™: California Second Edition, and Pets Welcome™: Mid-Atlantic & Chesapeake Edition.* She has just completed her bachelor's degree at California State University, Monterey Bay, and has lived on California's Monterey Peninsula since she immigrated from Sicily at the age of 13.

River Gurtin moved from his native New Jersey to California in 1970, where he attended Monterey Peninsula College and studied business and theater. In 1976, he opened the first bagel bakery on California's central coast. Under his guidance, the business grew and developed into a seven-store regional chain. Meanwhile, he became a nationwide consultant in opening and establishing bagel bakeries. River retired from The Bagel Bakery in 2000. After 9/11, he volunteered for Red Cross Emergency Relief work and was sent to New York and Texas. He currently spends his time providing small business consulting, developing his practice of professional digital photography, and hiking with his wife, Diana, a practicing psychologist.

Eric Jepson: Say "Duck!" whenever you see Eric. Part-time wildlife conservationist and outdoors kinda' guy, he placed 12th out of 320 designs submitted for the 2001 Federal Duck Stamp Competition. A graduate of Oregon State University (with a stint at Italy's University of Siena), Eric's colorful experience ranges from graphic artist at Nike to children's book illustrator to beer and vodka package/label designer (for grown-ups). Raised on the central coast of California, Eric, his wife Molly and their two daughters reside in Salinas.

Elaine Eakin MacDonald was born in China Lake, California and grew up, among other places, in the San Francisco Bay area. She graduated from Santa Clara University School of Law, then served four years as a Judge Advocate in the United States Navy. Elaine is licensed to practice in both California and Florida. While serving as a Public Defender in Florida that she met her husband, Erle. Now claiming she is "retired" from law (at an age when most lawyers are just starting to hit their stride), this extraordinarily talented interior decorator spends the lion's share of her waking hours as mommy to two beautiful daughters.

Erle T. MacDonald was born in Fairfax, Virginia and grew up in Jacksonville, Florida. On his nineteenth birthday, he joined the Police Force of a suburb of Jacksonville, Florida. A few years later, he walked into a used computer store and presented the owner with a bold proposal: "Teach me all you know about computers and I'll work for free." The rest is a true Horatio Alger story: bought the computer owner out, turned the business into gold, sold it, started another computer business, turned *it* into gold, etc. An entrepreneur of worldwide proportions, Erle, who now owns several businesses, resides in Carmel, California with his wife Elaine and their two daughters.

Greg Migdale graduated with a degree in philosophy and comparative religion from University of California, Santa Barbara. Then he flew to Israel, where he worked for five weeks, toured Israel, then flew to India where he spent the next month. During the following year, he flew to Pakistan, hiked over the Karakoram Highway into China, and made it across China by every means imaginable. He backpacked through Vietnam and ended up teaching English in Phnom Penh, Cambodia. From there, he went to Turkey, and ultimately returned to India for a year. Today he is a successful artist, working in three dimensional copper and metal media.

Karen Migdale got her first overseas job as an *au pair* in Switzerland when she was 17. Afterward, she was supposed to travel through Europe, but turned left instead of right and ended up hiking through Morocco's Middle Atlas mountains. On her return to the U.S., she joined a carnival, then returned to U.C.L.A., where she took a psychology degree *magna cum laude*. She is currently an elementary school teacher and tutor, which she does as a "day job," while waiting to make millions with her first novel, now in progress.

Roslyn Migdale first traveled abroad at age 10, when she went to the Soviet Union on a student exchange. At 16, she joined the *March of the Living*, traveling to Poland to view the Concentration and Death Camps, following that up with a visit to Israel and, subsequently, Egypt. She is currently an instructor and massage therapist at world renowned Esalen Institute in Big Sur, California.

Kristi Padley, a Texan, born and bred, now resides with her husband David (a career Coast Guardsman) and her son, Cameron, in Nashua, New Hampshire. Kristi is a proud graduate of Texas A&M University (Communications, Business). She served as National Sales Director for Four Paws Press' predecessor before moving to the East Coast, where she served in Regional Sales for FOS Sales of New York. She is presently National Sales Director for Four Paws Press.

Reader's Response Card

Please return to:
Four Paws Press
2600 Garden Road, Suite 224 • Monterey, CA 93940
hugo@fourpawspress.com • Fax 831-649-8007

Please assist us in updating our next edition. If you've discovered an interesting or charming lodging that allows pets, please let us hear from you and include the following information. For each suggestion that results in a new entry, we will send the contributor a free copy of a *Pets Welcome*™ book and give the contributor name credit for the find.

Type of Lodging:
☐ Hotel   ☐ Motel   ☐ Suites   ☐ Resort   ☐ B&B   ☐ Condo or Apartment
☐ Motor Inn/Motor Lodge   ☐ Cottage or Cabin   ☐ Guest Ranch   ☐ RV Park

Lodging Name:_____

Lodging Address: _____

City: _____ **State:** _____ **ZIP:** _____

Phone: _____

Website: _____

Comments: _____

_____

_____

Park Name:_____

Address or Cross Streets: _____

_____

🐾 🐾 🐾 🐾 🐾

Your Name:_____

Address (optional): _____

City: _____ **State:** _____ **ZIP:** _____

Telephone (optional): _____ **Fax:** _____

E-mail: _____

Thank you so much. We appreciate your assistance!

Order Form

Four Paws Press, LLC
2600 Garden Road, Suite 224
Monterey, CA 93940
831-375 PAWS (7297)
831-649-8007 FAX
www.fourpawspress.com

Send _____ copies of *Pets Welcome™: National Edition* at $19.95 each.

Send _____ copies of *Pets Welcome™: Great Lakes Edition* at $16.95 each.

Send _____ copies of *Pets Welcome™: New England Second Edition* at $16.95 each.

Send _____ copies of *Pets Welcome™: New York Second Edition* at $16.95 each.

Send _____ copies of *Pets Welcome™: America's South Second Edition* at $16.95 each.

Add $4.50 postage and handling for the first book ordered and $1.50 for each additional book. Please add 7.25% sales tax per book for those books shipped to a California address.

Please charge my ☐ VISA ☐ MasterCard

Card number: _____

Expiration date: _____ Signature: _____

Enclosed is my check for $ _____

Name: _____

Address: _____

City: _____ State: _____ ZIP: _____

☐ This is a gift. Please send books directly to:

Name: _____

Address: _____

City: _____ State: _____ ZIP: _____

☐ Please have this book autographed by the author

To: _____